Revolutionizing Business Practices Through Artificial Intelligence and Data-Rich Environments

Manisha Gupta
Sharda University, India

Deergha Sharma
The NorthCap University, India

Himani Gupta
Jagannath International Management School, India

A volume in the Advances in
Business Information Systems and
Analytics (ABISA) Book Series

Published in the United States of America by
IGI Global
Business Science Reference (an imprint of IGI Global)
701 E. Chocolate Avenue
Hershey PA, USA 17033
Tel: 717-533-8845
Fax: 717-533-8661
E-mail: cust@igi-global.com
Web site: http://www.igi-global.com

Library of Congress Cataloging-in-Publication Data

Names: Gupta, Manisha, 1978- editor. | Sharma, Deergha, 1984- editor. | Gupta, Himani, 1976- editor.
Title: Revolutionizing business practices through artificial intelligence and data-rich environments / Manisha Gupta, Deergha Sharma, and Himani Gupta, editors.
Description: Hershey, PA : Business Science Reference, [2022] | Includes bibliographical references and index. | Summary: "Through various contributed chapters, this book attempts to highlight the importance and benefits of artificial intelligence and data science from four different perspectives: market, organization, people, and technology"-- Provided by publisher.
Identifiers: LCCN 2022016700 (print) | LCCN 2022016701 (ebook) | ISBN 9781668449509 (hardcover) | ISBN 9781668449516 (paperback) | ISBN 9781668449523 (ebook)
Subjects: LCSH: Business--Technological innovations. | Artificial intelligence--Economic aspects. | Information technology--Social aspects.
Classification: LCC HD45 .R44 2022 (print) | LCC HD45 (ebook) | DDC 658.4/063--dc23/eng/20220414
LC record available at https://lccn.loc.gov/2022016700
LC ebook record available at https://lccn.loc.gov/2022016701

This book is published in the IGI Global book series Advances in Business Information Systems and Analytics (ABISA) (ISSN: 2327-3275; eISSN: 2327-3283)

British Cataloguing in Publication Data
A Cataloguing in Publication record for this book is available from the British Library.

All work contributed to this book is new, previously-unpublished material.
The views expressed in this book are those of the authors, but not necessarily of the publisher.

For electronic access to this publication, please contact: eresources@igi-global.com.

Advances in Business Information Systems and Analytics (ABISA) Book Series

ISSN:2327-3275
EISSN:2327-3283

Editor-in-Chief: Madjid Tavana La Salle University, USA

MISSION

The successful development and management of information systems and business analytics is crucial to the success of an organization. New technological developments and methods for data analysis have allowed organizations to not only improve their processes and allow for greater productivity, but have also provided businesses with a venue through which to cut costs, plan for the future, and maintain competitive advantage in the information age.

The **Advances in Business Information Systems and Analytics (ABISA) Book Series** aims to present diverse and timely research in the development, deployment, and management of business information systems and business analytics for continued organizational development and improved business value.

COVERAGE

- Management Information Systems
- Big Data
- Decision Support Systems
- Legal information systems
- Data Management
- Performance Metrics
- Business Decision Making
- Algorithms
- Data Analytics
- Geo-BIS

IGI Global is currently accepting manuscripts for publication within this series. To submit a proposal for a volume in this series, please contact our Acquisition Editors at Acquisitions@igi-global.com or visit: http://www.igi-global.com/publish/.

Titles in this Series

For a list of additional titles in this series, please visit:
http://www.igi-global.com/book-series/advances-business-information-systems-analytics/37155

AI-Driven Intelligent Models for Business Excellence
Samala Nagaraj (Woxsen University, India) and Korupalli V Rajesh Kumar (Woxsen University, India)
Business Science Reference • © 2023 • 300pp • H/C (ISBN: 9781668442463) • US $250.00

Handbook of Research on Foundations and Applications of Intelligent Business Analytics
Zhaohao Sun (Papua New Guinea University of Technology, Papua New Guinea) and Zhiyou Wu (Chongqing Normal University, China)
Business Science Reference • © 2022 • 425pp • H/C (ISBN: 9781799890164) • US $325.00

Utilizing Blockchain Technologies in Manufacturing and Logistics Management
S. B. Goyal (City University, Malaysia) Nijalingappa Pradeep (Bapuji Institute of Engineering and Technology, India) Piyush Kumar Shukla (University Institute of Technology RGPV, India) Mangesh M. Ghonge (Sandip Institute of Technology and Research Centre, India) and Renjith V. Ravi (MEA Engineering College, India)
Business Science Reference • © 2022 • 290pp • H/C (ISBN: 9781799886976) • US $250.00

Business Applications in Social Media Analytics
Himani Bansal (Jaypee University, Solan, India) and Gulshan Shrivastava (National Institute of Technology, Patna, India)
Business Science Reference • © 2022 • 330pp • H/C (ISBN: 9781799850465) • US $195.00

Achieving Organizational Agility, Intelligence, and Resilience Through Information Systems
Hakikur Rahman (Ansted University Sustainability Research Institute, Malaysia)
Business Science Reference • © 2022 • 350pp • H/C (ISBN: 9781799847991) • US $215.00

Handbook of Research on Applied Data Science and Artificial Intelligence in Business and Industry
Valentina Chkoniya (University of Aveiro, Portugal)
Engineering Science Reference • © 2021 • 653pp • H/C (ISBN: 9781799869856) • US $470.00

701 East Chocolate Avenue, Hershey, PA 17033, USA
Tel: 717-533-8845 x100 • Fax: 717-533-8661
E-Mail: cust@igi-global.com • www.igi-global.com

Table of Contents

Detailed Table of Contents

Richa Choudhary, University of Petroleum and Energy Studies, India
Alka Kaushik, University of Petroleum and Energy Studies, India
Kingsley Theophilus Igulu, Kenule Beeson Saro-Wiwa Polytechnic,
Nigeria

Artificial intelligence (AI) is the intelligence of computers in a way that simulates human intellect by learning continually as more data is ingested. Many cutting-edge technological concepts, particularly those aimed at enhancing the general welfare of humanity, use AI. Due to its expanding importance in the general enhancement of human quality of life, the healthcare business has recently drawn a lot of attention from technology leaders. The enhancement of health through disease prevention, diagnosis, treatment, or cure is known as healthcare. AI in healthcare uses advanced analytics to identify solutions to problems by projecting results from medical and scientific experiments. AI can improve healthcare by making predictions, deciding what to do, and acting on those decisions. This chapter discusses the most recent advances in AI and how they are being used in the healthcare sector. It also explores the potential effects of AI on patients and healthcare professionals. The authors discuss the problems and difficulties with AI in healthcare as well as the current state of AI in healthcare.

Chapter 2

The emerging focus of artificial intelligence (AI) in managing the healthcare systems in India has gained new momentum with the COVID-19 pandemic. The benefit of AI lies in the prediction of potential threats like determining COVID-19 hotspots. However, considerable studies have suggested that the greatest challenge in application of artificial intelligence in the healthcare system lies in the lack of exhaustive data to meet the objective of NITI Aayog's National Strategy for Artificial Intelligence in the healthcare sector. Under such a scenario, the current study aims at determining the current condition of AI in hospital management in the Indian subcontinent and also tries to find out the usefulness of AI in healthcare management. The research also aims at conducting a study on the existing literature to determine the potential and existing impact of artificial intelligence in the Indian health industry. The chapter highlights the future challenges that could be faced in implementing AI in the healthcare scenario of India.

Like other domains of life, the food processing industry is also not untouched by the use of artificial intelligence. Though this industry has not been amenable to technology in the past, AI will play the role of catalyst in this industry going forward. Many working people who live alone in far-away cities and students living in PG have resorted to either consuming ready-to-eat food or ordering take-aways from restaurants. Moreover, people opting for tiffin service are usually bound to a single vendor for an indefinite period, giving them fewer options for customization and portion size. This chapter presents a case study for creating an AI-based platform where users can decide which supplier they want their meals from. The system will present the user with nearest tiffin suppliers who can provide home-cooked meals on weekly or monthly subscription bases. The user will also be able to customize the meal quantity and frequency. It will also empower homemakers to start their small businesses and have financial independence from the comfort of their homes.

Chapter 4

    Amit Singh, School of Computer Science, University of Petroleum and
        Energy Studies, Dehradun, India

A combination of social constructivism and critical pedagogy is what is referred to as transformative pedagogy. One industry where pedagogy reform is strongly desired is education. In addition, the COVID-19 curse forced society to choose such options above the demand in order to shore up the aspirants' future. Researchers and industry professionals are looking for automated solution methods to make it more interactive and simple for children and young people to grasp. Artificial intelligence is a technology solution that can be used to equip and improve human relationships and bonding with learning. Along with the beneficial inclusion, there are a few drawbacks that could cause a catastrophe, much like anything in the current educational system. This chapter, therefore, covers both parts of artificial intelligence-based solutions and futuristics with the challenges. The research being done in this area and the solutions that have already been produced are also highlighted. Discussion of the findings and potential future applications in the context of security and privacy follows.

Chapter 5

    Anita Singh, Sharda University, India
    Richa Sharma, Sharda University, India
    Risha Thakur, Sharda University, India

With the continuing development in the e-learning platforms, a great shift can be seen from traditional modes of education to AI-based education to provide lifelong learning prospects to the students. The implementation of e-learning technology has resulted in certain complications on academic professionals. The emphasis of this chapter is to highlight the challenges and factors that influence the usage of AI-enabled e-learning system during the COVID-19 pandemic; though the e-learning systems were introduced in many universities a few years back, the pace for its adaptability was enhanced during COVID-19, without any proper guidance and support to the teaching staff. This study seeks to investigate the challenges and identify the factors that impact the usage of e-learning systems during the COVID-19 pandemic by the teachers. This study will explore the teachers' perceptions towards e-learning and will provide contextual information on usage pattern and the nature of e-learning.

    Ashneet Kaur, Jagannath International Management School, India
    Seema Wadhawan, Jagannath International Management School, India
    Himani Gupta, Jagannath International Management School, India

The current pandemic has brought vital transformation in the education sector. The shift from traditional smart class systems to the online virtual mode is a significant change in the education sector all over the world. Introduction of LMS in the higher educational institutes has not only spanned the gap created due to lack of physical presence but has also brought revolutionary change in the dedicated students approach towards the learning system. The chapter focuses on the growth trajectory of the LMS and aims to discuss the desire of students to use LMS over traditional methods. Perceived ease of use and perceived usefulness combined with perceived enjoyment influence students' intentions to use the learning management system (LMS), which lastly affects the academic performance of students.

    Bikram Pratim Bhuyan, University of Petroleum and Energy Studies,
      India
    T. P. Singh, University of Petroleum and Energy Studies, India

In finance, a portfolio is a person's or company's total financial holdings. Portfolio risk and expected return are managed via portfolio optimization. Portfolio optimization is a kind of diversification that decreases portfolio risk by combining assets with varying risk profiles. Since the global financial crisis of 2008, asset management practices have undergone a sea change. This study examines a wide range of artificial intelligence (AI)-based asset management systems, focusing on the most urgent concerns and highlighting the benefits in the analysis of fundamentals and producing new investment strategies. Trading is another area where AI is making a big impact. One of the most intriguing aspects of AI is its ability to analyze vast amounts of data and generate trading tips. Using AI in asset management comes with certain disadvantages as well. AI models are difficult for managers to keep track of since they are often complex and opaque. This research provides a throughout overview of the avenues where AI is used in financial portfolio management.

Chapter 8

*Neha Garg, Bharati Vidyapeeth Institute of Management and Research,
India*
Mamta Gupta, IP University, India
*Neetu Jain, Bharati Vidyapeeth Institute of Management and Research,
India*

Presently, banks are fronting with many challenges such as deteriorating loan asset quality leading to increasing provisioning requirements, dissatisfied customers, falling profitability, and weakening capital adequacy position. Innovative cutting-edge technologies has made enough space for new, non-traditional players to enter the financial industry, making the banking sector more competitive than ever before. Traditional banks are facing stiff competition from new financial players and foreign banks who are accelerating their business volumes with the help of rising digitisation and AI technology in today's digital era. The focus of the chapter is on understanding how banking is changing in India with the advent of AI applications. The practical use cases of AI in the banking industry shall become inevitable for the entire financial industry in the near future. At last, this chapter analyses various opportunities and threats while adopting AI applications.

Chapter 9

Derya Üçoğlu, Istanbul Bilgi University, Turkey

Artificial intelligence (AI) technology has impacted businesses and industries as well as audit companies. With the emergence of AI-enhanced systems, many tasks performed by auditors can now be completed more efficiently by these technologies. Such systems are used in different audit tasks, such as risk assessment, audit planning, fraud detection, audit inquiry, transaction testing, inventory count, and document testing. AI platforms designed for auditing provide time-saving, higher efficiency and accuracy, minimized risks and biases, and improved audit quality. This chapter provides examples of AI platforms and tools developed by Big 4 audit firms and discusses the benefits and risks of implementing AI technology in auditing regarding the extant literature.

Chapter 10

Madhu Rani, Sharda University, India
Shagun, Sharda University, India
Manisha Gupta, Sharda University, India

Artificial intelligence (AI) is a field of study that focuses on the development and theory of computer systems that are capable of doing tasks that would normally need the intelligence of humans. Language translation, decision-making, and speech recognition are only a few of the tasks that, in general, need the use of a human brain to be performed properly. In the context of content delivery, an OTT platform (also known as over the top) is a platform that does not provide video via traditional cable or receivers. Video and audio distribution via the internet without the involvement of a multiple system operator (MSO) is referred to as online video and audio distribution. When it comes to the administration and transmission of information, there are several options. Viewers are able to access it from any place at any time and save it for later viewing convenience.

Chapter 11

Artificial intelligence, which is one of the most advanced and growing technologies in today's era, has helped a lot in improving the HR activities like recruitment, staffing, training and development, career planning, and so on. With the changing digitalized scenario, there are many technological advancements that take place in the area of human resources, which helps HR professionals to perform their tasks in a better way within a minimum timeframe. In this chapter, the author focuses on the revolution of AI in the field of human resources. The importance of AI in HR is also an area of concern in this chapter. With the fast-moving scenario, the author also focuses in the developmental areas of AI technology-based programs and applications in the organizations. Ethics in AI also needs to be followed by the organizations, which is also an area which is taken into consideration by the author. Among the applications, AI can shortlist the best possible fits in just the wink of eye and hence reduce human effort.

Chapter 12

Disruptive technology is now a tool adopted by the organizations to cater to the HRM practices. Intelligent automation can not only complete manual tasks but also make intelligent decisions, much like a human. Its capabilities could allow machines to comprehend procedures and anomalies. With the escalating demand of artificial intelligence (AI), this chapter offers the fundamentals of AI in job-fit analysis and also shows how AI can enable HR teams to extract insights from data and give appropriate recommendations for real-time job-fit processes. AI is looked upon to change the role of a recruiter and improve their relationships with hiring managers by using data to measure KPIs such as quality of hire. It also emphasizes the significance of artificial intelligence in various aspects of job-fit analysis. The conclusions drawn from the literature are discussed and presented. In the conclusion, some challenges and potential solutions and future research are also presented.

Chapter 13

Business value creation rests in the hands of organizational resources, and no doubt, human resources are one of the prime contributors. HR practices have a high impact, and organizations should leverage human resource competencies. In today's situation, where technology forms the pillar of improving people, structures, and cultures, reviewing the technological impact on HR practices becomes imperative. One such technological intervention can and is seen through artificial intelligence. The chapter thus provides a journey to comprehend the traditional recruitment process which defines the employee life cycle and the limitations faced. A section describes the framework to deploy AI usage in the recruitment process to improve the recruitment metrics for the organization. The laborious task of reducing anchoring bias, confirmatory bias, and similarity bias amongst the recruiters using AI technology is explored. The chapter concludes with analytics power backed by AI to help the stakeholders of the recruitment process to revitalize strategies and improve decision making.

Foreword

At no other point of time in the history of human civilization has technology made such deep inroads into our personal and professional lives as now. Technology has structured not just business processes but also the decision-making processes associated with them. While the industrial age technologies impacted production processes, the information and communication technologies have redefined not only the production processes but also the information processes vital for decision making and distribution logistics. Artificial Intelligence (AI) and Machine Learning have gone step further by liberating man from engaging with not just the iterative processes but also new and unpredictable developments. AI is playing a significant role these days in the ways in which we are running our businesses.

It is, therefore, a welcome development that a book on this significant area is being brought out by Dr. Manisha Gupta, Dr. Deergha Sharma and Dr. Himani Gupta. The researchers have been passionately pursuing research in their respective areas of specialization. It is thoughtful of them to have planned this book as a collaborative venture. All knowledge acquisition activities are best carried out the collaborative mould. This ensures the best of ideas to be generated and compiled on one platform as the contributors look at the issue in hand from their respective loci of specializations.

Appropriately enough, the book looks at the subject from a number of perspectives. It addresses the issue from a variety of theoretical and applied perspectives. The book focusses on AI and Human Resource management, AI based manufacturing, AI and business automation and the role of AI as an enabling technology in the each of the various sectors of business and industry, be it hospitality, healthcare, e-learning, business aggregators, or e-commerce. It also includes articles on business process restructuring, particularly in finance and e-commerce.

I am sure the book will be immense value to researchers in the areas of business strategy, business process re-engineering and business automation. Both undergraduate and post-graduate students can access this book as a window on this exciting area as it has been written in a very lucid and comprehensive style.

Ravi K. Dhar
Jagannath International Management School, India

Preface

Artificial intelligence (AI) is having a transformative effect on enterprises, commercial interfaces, economic activities, and society as a whole all over the globe. Over the past few years, academic research on artificial intelligence has arisen from many empirical and practical fields of knowledge. Even though more and more study is being published to offer light on the challenges posed by AI, there is still a great deal to be gained by bringing innovative, theory-driven research methods to bear on this essential subject. Because of the newly developing nature of this study avenue in various management spheres can be highlighted. The book *Revolutionizing Business Practices Through Artificial Intelligence and Data-Rich Environments* edited by Dr. Manisha Gupta, Dr Deergha Sharma, and Dr. Himani Gupta presents chapters which captures the cases and process which have adopted Artificial intelligence to transform their business in the field of healthcare, banking, education, finance, human resources, and entertainment. Hence this book provides more thorough knowledge of incorporation of Artificial Intelligence in the different industries. The thirteen chapters of this book clearly contribute to enhance knowledge consisting of the various organizational structures, platforms, procedures, and mechanisms that underpin different types of business experiences of many stakeholders with reality-enhancing technology and the management implications of applying these technologies in novel ways.

The first two chapters of this book elaborates the contribution and usage of AI in healthcare management and hospital administration. Further the chapter three, four and five are focusing on how the intervention of AI has transformed the education sectors specifically its impact on higher education institutions. The other chapters in the books illustrate the intervention of AI in the field of banking, finance, Human resource management and entertainment industry.

We have high hopes that the book volume will act as a comprehensive resource for both the business world and the academic community, as well as a road that will lead business organisations in the right direction. The knowledge gained from reading the chapters will inspire innovative new company concepts that can help assist existing companies in an unpredictable and technology-driven economy.

Manisha Gupta
Sharda University, India

Deergha Sharma
The NorthCap University, India

Himani Gupta
Jagannath International Management School, India

Acknowledgment

Bringing out an edited book necessitates the sincere and timely efforts of a number of intellectuals, and we feel honoured to acknowledge this support. First of all, we are thankful to IGI Global for providing us this wonderful opportunity to come-up with this collection and invite the scholars to contribute to this volume.

Our sincere thanks to Prof. Siba Ram Khara (Vice Chancellor, Sharda University) and Dr. Ravi K Dhar (Director JIMS vasant Kunj) for their continued guidance and support towards the completion of this project. We are indebted to Prof. Jayanthi Ranjan (Dean, Sharda School of Business Studies, Sharda University), who has always been kind to support our endeavours. We would like to acknowledge the support of our colleagues and friends: Dr Sudhir Rana (Gulf Medical University, UAE), Dr. Prashant Gupta (Indian Institute of Management Trichy), Dr. Mridul Dharwal and Dr Raj K Kovid (Sharda University) among others from academia who cooperated to their full in order to complete this project in many ways.

We thank all authors who contributed by submitting their scholarly work and worked to respond to the review comments following the tight deadlines. We express our gratitude to all reviewers who volunteered to devout time to review the submissions and suggested improvements. We are also thankful to all members of the Editorial Advisory Board for their valuable inputs and critical observations on various dimensions of this book project.

Without support of administrative and editorial staff from IGI -Global, it was not possible to bring this project to completion and launch stage.

Last but not least, we cannot afford to ignore silent and unabated support of family members who were source of our continuous motivation to work with full spirits.

Acknowledgment

Editorial Advisory Board

Chapter 1
Artificial Intelligence in Healthcare

Richa Choudhary
University of Petroleum and Energy Studies, India

Alka Kaushik
University of Petroleum and Energy Studies, India

Kingsley Theophilus Igulu
Kenule Beeson Saro-Wiwa Polytechnic, Nigeria

ABSTRACT

Artificial intelligence (AI) is the intelligence of computers in a way that simulates human intellect by learning continually as more data is ingested. Many cutting-edge technological concepts, particularly those aimed at enhancing the general welfare of humanity, use AI. Due to its expanding importance in the general enhancement of human quality of life, the healthcare business has recently drawn a lot of attention from technology leaders. The enhancement of health through disease prevention, diagnosis, treatment, or cure is known as healthcare. AI in healthcare uses advanced analytics to identify solutions to problems by projecting results from medical and scientific experiments. AI can improve healthcare by making predictions, deciding what to do, and acting on those decisions. This chapter discusses the most recent advances in AI and how they are being used in the healthcare sector. It also explores the potential effects of AI on patients and healthcare professionals. The authors discuss the problems and difficulties with AI in healthcare as well as the current state of AI in healthcare.

DOI: 10.4018/978-1-6684-4950-9.ch001

Figure 1. Types of AI

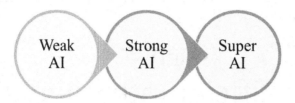

INTRODUCTION

Health systems around the world are confronted with a number of issues, including rising disease load, multimorbidity, and disability brought on by aging and demographic transition, expanding demand for health services, rising societal expectations, and rising health expenditures (Jiang et al., 2017). Inefficiency and low productivity present another difficulty (Artificial Intelligence: Definition, Types, Examples, Technologies, 2022). Fiscal conservatism and misguided economic austerity measures that limit investment in healthcare are the backdrop to these difficulties facing the health sector. To overcome these obstacles and attain universal health coverage (UHC) by 2030, health systems must undergo fundamental restructuring. Machine learning, the most concrete use of artificial intelligence (AI), provides the potential of doing more with less and may serve as the impetus for such a change (What Is Super Artificial Intelligence (AI), 2022). It is also the newest development sector in digital technology. But neither the nature nor the scope of this promise have been systematically evaluated. The effect of digital technology on healthcare systems has been ambiguous so far (McCoy et al., 2022). Is AI the ingredient for such a transformation, or will it face the same fate as earlier attempts at introducing digital technology.

Artificial Intelligence

Artificial intelligence is the ability for machines to think cognitively and reason like humans do, allowing them to learn from their past experiences (Jiang et al., 2017). Machines have the ability to retain past knowledge or information, or what is known as a "state" in technical parlance. Machines gain knowledge from these earlier stages and progressively enhance their capacity for learning in a given subject. In the end, this aids in more accurate forecasting, better decision-making, and the capacity to resolve challenging issues. Three categories best describe AI (Artificial Intelligence: Definition, Types, Examples, Technologies, 2022).

The three main categories of AI—weak AI, also known as Narrow AI, strong AI, or General AI, and super AI—are depicted in Figure 1. The diagram illustrates the sequential nature of the process; weak AI influenced strong AI, which in turn served as a building block for super AI.

Weak AI: that has only been trained for a single domain or task. The system exhibits qualities that are comparable to the intelligence of the human mind after being educated on predetermined input and settings for a certain task. For instance, the ability of computer games, self-driving automobiles, or image screening to predict an illness. The majority of AI-powered computers in use today are subpar (Artificial Intelligence: Definition, Types, Examples, Technologies, 2022).

Strong AI: Strong artificial intelligence (AI) is an advancement over weak AI in that it can learn from past mistakes rather than being dependent on predefined inputs. It can investigate all viable solutions for a particular issue, regardless of whether or not they were included in the training set. Like humans, it is capable of intelligent self decision making. Researchers and scientists are at work.

Super AI: Currently simply a theoretical idea, it is predicted that Super AI would surpass humans in all areas, including sports, math, and emotional intelligence. According to some literatures, this could be the final invention the human species ever needs (What Is Super Artificial Intelligence (AI), 2022).

The basic technologies that underpin AI are machine learning, deep learning, natural language processing, computer vision, robotics, and a few others. At the moment, the majority of organizations or systems use weak AI. One of the fundamental components of AI is machine learning, which can extract hidden patterns from data [McCoy et al., 2022]. Machine learning algorithms come in two fundamental forms.

1. Supervised Learning: Algorithms are taught using a labelled data set in this kind of machine learning. The tagged classes are already present in this dataset. It forecasts the label of a new data value using the characteristics of a labelled dataset. Classification or regression techniques can be used to do this (Ferdous et al., 2020).

2. Unsupervised Learning: Unlike supervised learning, this sort of machine learning does not have access to a labelled dataset for training. This kind of learning uses associations, similarities, etc. to find features. Since unsupervised learning cannot be directly used to classification and regression, these techniques reveal hidden patterns (Ferdous et al., 2020).

Deep learning is a unique subset of machine learning that can process enormous amounts of data and discover hidden patterns in great depth. Natural Language Processing, which converts speech to text and text to speech, is widely used in all fields of artificial intelligence (Jiang et al., 2017). Every facet of human life is experiencing a very rapid evolution of AI. There are applications for it in practically every business field. Many firms are attempting to leverage the power of AI for efficient results as a result of the recent development in sophisticated algorithms. Figure 2 below illustrates the numerous areas of application where AI is enhancing its efficiency in offering better answers to problems. Every industry, including agriculture, transportation, marketing, gaming, healthcare, and pharmaceuticals, has undergone digitization recently (Kovalenko, 2022). These industries collectively produce data at an exponential rate. This enormous amount of data offers the chance to examine the trends and insights to find the solutions. One industry that has been greatly impacted by digitalization and is producing enormous amounts of data is the healthcare sector (Alanazi, 2022). AI approaches can be utilized to investigate the insights in healthcare data.

Healthcare

Healthcare describes procedures carried out, particularly by trained and certified professionals, to maintain or restore a person's physical, mental, or emotional well-being. Healthcare is the most significant work, and the word is generally hyphenated when used attributively (Jiang et al., 2017).

People are becoming more ill due to a stressful lifestyle, an increase in population, and a busy schedule, making it essential to watch how they live and take care of themselves because it is the best form of care. The current situation states that "unless they are both gone, we do not appreciate and respect time and health as valuable resources." Health care is a crucial human right since it affects our daily goals, eases our pain, reduces the number of early deaths, and aids in better life planning. No of their income, gender, or racial status, society has vowed to ensure that all of its members have access to sufficient healthcare (Defining Basic Health Care, 2022; Ngiam & Khor, 2019). Whether it's Article 21 of the Indian Constitution, Section 27 of the South African Constitution, or any other country's law, the necessity of healthcare is recognized all over the world. They all claim that everyone's right to health should be protected as a fundamental freedom.

Health care guarantees a higher standard of living and prevents sickness (Health Care - Healthy People 2030 | health.gov. 2022). People are exposed to numerous bacteria, viruses, and contaminations on a regular basis, and without healthcare, they are in grave danger. Even seemingly little illnesses can progress and be fatal, such as how rapidly a regular cold can turn into pneumonia. By sustaining a higher standard of living and longer life expectancies, healthcare not only benefits the people's health but also the economies of the countries (How Healthcare Industry Helps in Contributing to the Economy, 2022). The healthcare sector must develop and advance in order to guarantee everyone in the country their fundamental right

Figure 2. Major application areas of AI

to health in the current era of rising loads, concerns, and risk of stress-related disorders. And by integrating AI into healthcare, all of this may be accomplished (Kumari, 2022). This might considerably improve the healthcare sector's bottom line and speed up the procedure.

As a result of AI's improved ability to comprehend the daily routines and demands of the people it is designed to care for, healthcare professionals will be better equipped to provide feedback, direction, and support for preserving health.

Artificial intelligence-enhanced computer systems are widely used in the medical sciences. Only a few examples of typical uses include patient diagnosis, comprehensive pharmaceutical discovery and development, improved patient-physician communication, transcription of prescriptions in medical records, and remote patient treatment (Basu et al., 2020).

AI IN HEALTHCARE

The advancement of healthcare will be made possible by artificial intelligence. Artificial intelligence is growing quickly in the medical industry. Basically, the availability of data makes it much simpler to create artificial intelligence. Since deep learning and machine learning are based on data-intensive technologies, artificial intelligence may have a greater impact on the healthcare industry now that there is a greater availability of data. The first is that there is an abundance of medical data available to us right now in the form of patient medical histories (Ferdous et al., 2020).

An important component in the development of AI in healthcare is the implementation of complex algorithms. AI may greatly advance the goals of improved customized, predictive, preventative, and interactive healthcare. Based on a review of the achievements, we forecast that AI will keep its momentum to develop and mature as a powerful tool for biomedicine (Rong et al., 2020).

Examining the Potential of AI in healthcare

- reducing medical errors
- Medical mistakes lead to misdiagnosis. For instance, many women may put off getting breast cancer treatment due to false-negative mammography results. AI is frequently utilized to uncover any such anomalies that human eyes cannot detect.
- making healthcare more humane
- This may be AI's biggest contribution to medical science. It is possible to prevent unnecessary data entry work. The clinician can alternatively compassionately care for the patient without entering any data.
- imaging techniques for diagnosis
- In the future, a diagnosis might be obtained only from a selfie, or "medical selfie." (Michael, 2022).

Healthcare Data and Use of AI Over that Data

In the form of clinical research trials, medical claims, and reports on medical diagnoses, the healthcare industry has access to enormous amounts of data. The most expensive item in today's technologically advanced world is data. Each piece of data is necessary to complete a certain activity and they all differ greatly from one another.

Healthcare Big Data is the term used to describe data in the healthcare sector (Kumari, 2022). The healthcare industry is intricate and always subject to patient requirements (Sarvamangala & Kulkarni, 2022; 21 Examples of Big Data In Healthcare With Powerful Analytics, 2022). The Healthcare Industry has experienced a tremendous increase in data generation as a result of technology innovation and the digitalization of everything. To address the needs of patients for improved medical care and potent medications, healthcare data is necessary and increasingly in demand. The healthcare industry makes extensive use of this enormous amount of data (Kumari, 2022). Electronic health records, which include each patient's digital health record, medical history, results of numerous tests, list of allergies, etc., are one example of this (Davenport & Kalakota, 2019). This includes information in a variety of formats, such as test results that could be in text or image format. Text is also used to describe the patient's past medical issues, allergies, and other ailments. AI can process a range of healthcare data types (structured and unstructured).

Artificial intelligence and machine learning have enormous potential benefits for the crucial healthcare sector. The first category includes machine learning (ML) techniques that analyse structured data, such as genetic, imaging, and EP data. The ML methods applied in healthcare applications aim to categorize patient traits or forecast the possibility that a disease would reveal itself. The second group includes natural language processing (NLP) strategies that use information from unstructured sources, such as clinical notes and medical journals, to supplement and enhance structured medical data.

NLP techniques strive to produce structured machine-readable data from texts that can be used by ML techniques for analysis (Singh et al., 2020). These types of datasets are processed by machine learning algorithms for many purposes, such as disease diagnosis, prescription recommendation, and individualized therapy recommendations (Sarvamangala & Kulkarni, 2022). In order to anticipate diseases like diabetes, liver disease, and many more, machine learning employs these datasets to develop its numerous models, such as Decision trees, Nave Bayes, etc. (Ngiam & Khor, 2019).

The stages of many serious diseases, including cancer and tuberculosis, are classified using a variety of classification techniques, including CNN models (Ngiam & Khor, 2019). To learn how the brain reacts to different stimuli and makes the necessary decisions, data from the MRI are frequently employed (Basu et al., 2020). The management of medical records and the conduct of analysis within the healthcare sector have been dramatically altered by datasets. Healthcare analytics is a very potent instrument that is being utilized to lower treatment costs, anticipate disease breakouts and take necessary precautions, and generally enhance the quality of life

Figure 3. Different types of data in healthcare sector

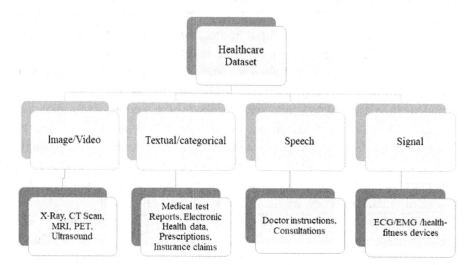

for citizens (21 Examples of Big Data In Healthcare With Powerful Analytics, 2022). The goal of healthcare big data is to use data gathered from all around the world to build models that will one day save lives and make extremely accurate diagnoses of diseases. Figure 3 displays the many data types used in the healthcare sector.

The various sorts of data can be supplied into the AI model in various manners for data processing. Images or videos can be used to represent medical reports such as X-rays, CT scans, and Positron Emission Tomography (PET) results. After preprocessing, the image can be input to the model. Textual data, such as medical reports, electronic health records (EHR), doctor's prescriptions, and information on medical insurance, are another sort of data that is accessible in the medical field. Fitness bands, sensor-based health gadgets, and ECG/EMG machines all undergo processing after being converted into signals (Jiang et al., 2017; Artificial Intelligence: Definition, Types, Examples, Technologies, 2022).

This data can be analyzed by AI to uncover patterns and insights that manual human skill sets usually overlook (K, 2022).

Benefits of AI in Healthcare

1. Lesion identification is widely used to define AI imaging investigations while neglecting the nature and biological aggressiveness of a lesion, which could result in an erroneous assessment of AI's efficacy. Lesion identification facilitates the study of medical imaging. Additionally, the addition of non-patient-focused radiographic and pathological endpoints may boost estimated sensitivity at the

expense of increased false positives and probable overdiagnosis by detecting subtle changes that could be symptomatic of preclinical or indolent disease (Oren et al., 2020).

2. decreased cost of developing drugs Currently, 30% of healthcare costs are attributed to administrative costs. When AI is utilized to automate basic tasks like pre-approving insurance, finding unpaid invoices, and maintaining records, healthcare personnel may be able to concentrate on more complex tasks while simultaneously saving money (From enhancing patient care to driving down costs, AI has enormous potential, 2022).

3. AI enables a sophisticated and integrated drug discovery platform: Small-molecule drug development can benefit from artificial intelligence (AI) in four different ways: by opening up access to new biology, better or distinctive chemistry, greater success rates, and speedier and less expensive discovery methods. The approach can deal with a range of problems and limitations in traditional research and development. Each application gives drug research teams access to new information, and in certain situations, it completely modifies tried-and-true methods. It is critical to know and differentiate between use cases because these technologies can be utilized to detect a number of biological targets and discovery scenarios (Adopting AI in Drug Discovery, 2022).

4. To enable more accurate phenotypic and outcome prediction, AI can help advance kidney disease precision medicine. Renal disease is predictable by AI. By using machine learning to create a model for immunoglobulin risk prediction by identifying a nephropathy, Chen et al. recently made headway toward precision nephrology (IgAN). In contrast to past prediction models for IgAN that used conventional modeling with a limited number of preset components, Chen et al. apply supervised machine-learning algorithms to effectively extract the relevant information from huge data (Xie et al., 2019).

5. AI is a helpful tool for first responders: By engaging with patients and directing them to the ideal setting, virtual nursing assistants could revolutionize the way patients receive treatment. Virtual nurses can swiftly reply to questions, monitor patients, and provide information because they are available 24/7. Applications with AI capabilities, such as Virtual Nursing Assistant, help to cut down on unnecessary hospital visits and have enhanced communication between patients and healthcare workers (Marr, 2022).

6. AI has the potential to improve radiation therapy for cancer patients by increasing staff productivity, raising the bar of care, and providing more clinical data and treatment response forecasts to support and enhance clinical decision-making (Huynh et al., 2020). AI also helps in the study of and treatment of cancer, particularly in radiation therapy.

7. AI can improve hospital management by assisting in the comprehension of regular healthcare patterns. It can analyze the data gathered and aid healthcare professionals in comprehending the needs and issues of the patients. Taking these into account, experts can enhance the support and direction they provide to patients (Marr, 2022).

8. Stethoscope with AI: Unlike conventional stethoscopes, the ability to take readings despite background noise is a significant feature that permits a more precise diagnosis. Anyone can access the records from the digital device and telefax them to the doctor because using it doesn't require any special training. Additionally, this lowers their risk of contracting COVID-19 and makes it easier to provide patients with chronic illnesses in inhospitable regions with better medical care. Computers can now recognize patterns and anomalies in clinical data related to disease through the use of machine learning and artificial intelligence (AI). The same reasoning applies because blood flowing around a blood clot in a blood vessel is different from blood flowing through healthy arteries (Xie et al., 2019).

AI Applications in Healthcare

Although artificial intelligence is being used in many different fields, its influence in healthcare industry is relatively high. AI is pursuing a wide range of applications in the healthcare industry, from handling patient data for common chronic diseases to exploiting patient wellness data related to environmental elements including pollution exposure and weather conditions (Mohammed et al., 2016).

Other potential AI breakthroughs in healthcare, according to Mohammed et al. (2016) include investigating how to use the technology for telemedicine. To help with increased productivity and the work process, many AI businesses are concentrating on the capability to coordinate, supply specialists with patient data during a telemedicine conference, as well as capture data during the virtual visit. The various influences of AI in healthcare is depicted in figure 4.

Various Applications of Machine Learning being incorporated in the Healthcare sector:

AI in Medical Diagnosis and Prediction

Blood, urine, and other body fluid abnormalities can all be precisely identified by AI. The prediction of many severe diseases, including cancer, etc., makes extensive use of AI. By doing inference on medical scans, artificial intelligence (AI) is used in medical image analysis to help medical workers, particularly radiologists, discover, identify, classify, and segment the presence of disease. In most cases, CNN models

Figure 4. AI applications in healthcare

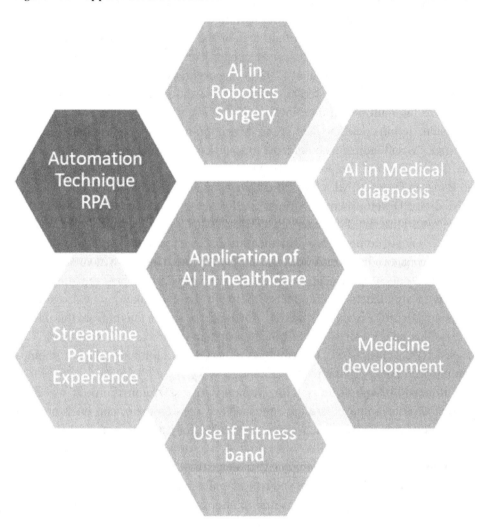

are utilized to find scan-related anomalies. For medical image analysis, organ localization is a crucial pre-processing step (Sarvamangala & Kulkarni, 2022). To conduct a more accurate study of the organ, ML models can recognize areas of interest and separate them from the rest of the data. Additionally, DL models are utilized to find characteristics particular to diseases, allowing them to categorize and propose the potential condition. Medical image analysis has a specific platform thanks to initiatives like MONAI. for determining a diagnosis and determining the best course of treatment. With the help of brain magnetic resonance imaging, doctors can analyze Alzheimer's disease or other types of dementia or predict the progression of moderate cognitive impairment (MCI) to dementia using Machine Learning-based diagnostic (Machine Learning in Healthcare: 12 Real-World Use Cases – NIX United, 2022). On the basis of the patient's records, classification algorithms like Naive Bayes, KNN, and Decision Tree have been extensively utilized to forecast diseases (Ferdous et al., 2020). The accuracy and predictability of these forecasts have increased as study continues. Conventional programming is unable to analyze the multimodal data included in a patient's medical record, including test results, reports, and medical scans, which are necessary for the identification of symptoms and indicators connected to a particular disease (Ferdous et al., 2020; Toh, 2021). For this, Support Vector Machine (SVM), Naive Bayesian classifier, and Random Forest of ML algorithms have been used in AI models.

Medicine Development: Artificial intelligence-enhanced computer systems are widely used in the medical sciences. Only a few examples of typical uses include patient diagnosis, comprehensive medication discovery and development, improved patient-physician communication, transcription of prescriptions in medical records, and remote patient treatment (Alanazi, 2022). Since AI enables the running of millions of simulations and collects data from these simulations, it is a crucial component in drug discovery research. The machine is then taught from this data to increase therapeutic efficacy (Machine Learning in Healthcare: 12 Real-World Use Cases – NIX United, 2022; Bunyamin et al., 2021). Additionally, AI is combined with nanotechnology to improve medicine delivery.

Automation Technique is RPA (Robotic Process Automation): If we use a hospital as an example, there are thousands of records there, and each one has information on the patient, such as age, medical history, and the state of their health at the time. Since these details are so crucial, we simply cannot tolerate data loss. We employ the automation technique to manage these data. The automated process handles transaction management and record maintenance for seamless patient care.

AI in Robotic Surgery: From minor surgery to open-heart surgery, surgical robots have a significant impact on medical procedures. It is applied with a surgeon's supervision. It enables precise and adaptable surgery. Robotic surgeons can precisely control the trajectory, depth, and speed of their actions. Because they can function without becoming tired, they are especially well-suited for treatments that call for the same, repetitive movements. Robots can also move to places where traditional tools cannot and can stand perfectly still for as long as is required. In the Operating Room(OR), experience is invaluable. However, surgical operations can be physically taxing. The longer physicians can continue doing surgery, the better. A lack of motor abilities might hinder the skills and information that surgeons accumulate throughout the course of their careers. Hand tremors can be lessened and unintentional or accidental motions can be avoided with the aid of collaborative robots.

Streamline Patient Experience: Check-ins and appointments are simple. By confirming the doctors' availability in advance, AI simplifies and speeds up notifying patients of their arrival at kiosks, welcome desks, or while arranging an appointment. It keeps the patient from experiencing any annoyances at check-in (Ghodasara, 2022). Managing their EHR is another component of the patient experience. Updating patient records on a daily basis is a laborious undertaking. However, it is still a very important work because AI models may use this information to anticipate diseases, recommend individualized treatments, etc. AI has thus been introduced into record administration, where it has several uses. One of the goals of AI is to use optical character recognition (OCR) technology to quickly and consistently translate the handwriting of doctors (16 Machine Learning in Healthcare Examples, 2022). Other AI tools can then look at this data in order to develop independent guidance and patient consideration. Processing patient records correctly is essential for streamlining the patient experience. Natural language processing enables us to extract data from medical records—the most frequent form of communication in hospitals—that is necessary for treating a patient. This addresses the problem of inconsistent clinical descriptions among hospitals (Mohammed et al., 2016). Models like Bio Discharge Summary BERT, which is presented in the Clinical BERT paper, classify symptoms using supervised learning and then send those labels onto a classifier to help a doctor make a diagnosis. Due to acronyms, different descriptions, and the use of medical words that aren't available in most databases, this field faces a number of difficulties.

Use of Fitness Bands: Because the band contains an embedded sensor and is useful for some predictions, which are achieved by artificial intelligence, we may monitor or track our physical activities and health issues like heart rate, pulse rate, stress level, and many more through the usage of fitness bands. Real-time monitoring can be performed utilizing health data from equipment like ECG monitors, heart, beat, and respiratory monitors in addition to fitness bands. Data collected by IoT sensors can be processed on a server and is continuously checked for anomalies and abnormalities. DL and transfer learning are used to monitor the sensor values and produce reports as necessary. When compared to conventional systems, which are prone to delays and latency problems, these monitoring devices have demonstrated tremendous effectiveness in both meeting the needs of the severely ill and acting as general health monitoring apparatus (Toh & Brody, 2021; Bunyamin et al., 2021).

There are numerous other uses for AI in healthcare in addition to these notable ones. AI can be used to control the spread of contagious diseases, among other things. Tools are available that can be used to identify an infectious outbreak's early warning symptoms. All the information from satellites, web-based entertainment trends, news websites, and video transfers might be processed by machine learning (Mohammed et al., 2016). The data may then be processed using neural networks, ML tools, and applications to create precise predictions, which could then be used to deliver effective preventive actions from one side of the earth to the other. Epidemics could be prevented before they ever had a chance to inflict substantial damage.

ISSUES AND CHALLENGES OF AI IN HEALTHCARE

Here we present some of the issues and challenges of the applications of Artificial Intelligence in healthcare

- In the healthcare sector, trust in AI applications is in its infancy (Davenport & Kalakota, 2019). This is because the computer creates a forecast for the doctors or patients, and it is untrustworthy to rely on that prediction without understanding what factors might have affected the outcome. The application of AI is currently implementable and operates as a "black box," with only the output known and the inner workings unknown (Singh et al., 2020). The problem of what to do is currently solved by AI, but it doesn't explain how it did it, which makes us distrust it.
- AI is attempting to replace doctors, nurses, and many other professionals working in the healthcare sector by fully automating the sector (K, 2022). However, AI should be utilized in conjunction with physicians and nurses to determine the best workflow and should support physicians in making judgments that could save lives.
- Current AI models are somewhat procedurally flawed and prejudiced. Machine learning has achieved considerable success in imaging computing, but it has not yet been demonstrated in other diverse features and applications (Davenport & Kalakota, 2019). Several studies have revealed a higher risk of bias in several healthcare industry areas.
- Ethics is a persistent problem when it comes to machine learning and artificial intelligence, affecting not only the healthcare sector but also many other applications and sectors (Davenport & Kalakota, 2019). What if the AI program made a judgment that had a causal impact on someone's life and it turned out to be incorrect? Who is to be held accountable for that, then? The greatest unresolved issue is this one. It creates a barrier and lessens transparency among the patients or doctors when the model's operation is unknown.
- Disparity in the statistics. AI relies on data, namely more organized, well-structured, and high-quality data (Oren et al., 2020). Furthermore, in the healthcare sector, decisions that could save lives must be made, so data must be completely formatted and updated on a regular basis. However, the lack of resources on the internet plus the fact that those that are there are too

fragmented, duplicated, and available in different formats (Oren et al., 2020) make it difficult to collect data for implementing high accuracy AI Models.

- The enormous strain on healthcare technology and infrastructure: With the current way of life and rising demands on people, health is at risk. The majority of individuals are experiencing health problems, which puts additional burden on the infrastructure.

- Data in this area is expanding quickly thanks to the abundance of healthcare mobile applications, devices that monitor a user's daily vitals, sensor-based devices, and EHR. It's challenging to analyze such a large and varied set of data. As AI continues to advance, it is looking for ways to organize medical data.

- Right before making a decision, producing perfect insights: The process of analyzing data and drawing conclusions from it in order to anticipate illness or provide therapy is developing, and in the future may result in considerably faster and quicker responses.

- Legal concerns: A patient's medical information is private. There are numerous legal and privacy concerns. Government regulations and policies governing the handling of medical data need to be stricter.

CURRENT SCENARIO OF AI IN HEALTHCARE IN INDIA

Healthcare has become one of the largest industries in India in terms of market size and employment potential. By the end of 2022, the Indian healthcare market could reach $8.6 trillion, according to a report (What Is Super Artificial Intelligence (AI)? Definition, Threats, and Trends, 2022). The healthcare industry is expanding quickly. The Indian healthcare system is being strengthened by recent government initiatives (From enhancing patient care to driving down costs, AI has enormous potential, 2022). Public and private hospitals, medical supplies, telemedicine, and health insurance are all part of the healthcare industry. The delivery of healthcare services is the primary problem facing the Indian healthcare sector. Major healthcare facilities are located in Tier I or Tier II cities or in metro areas (Adopting AI in Drug Discovery, 2022). Aside from primary health centers, advanced medical treatments are not available in rural areas. ICT has the ability to close the gap in the provision of healthcare services. The strength of computational technology can aid in expanding the geographic scope of medical services, such as telemedicine (Xie et al., 2019). Healthcare refers to giving someone medical attention. The objective is to offer high-quality, affordable, and individualized healthcare. To accomplish this goal, India faces numerous obstacles, including the following (Marr, 2022; Huynh et al., 2020):

- Inadequate Infrastructure
- Preventive care is at back foot
- Low Medical research
- Cost Effective Treatment

AI can produce high-quality data analysis when combined with powerful computing. The large volume of data helps AI systems since it makes their results more accurate (Xie et al., 2019). Exact models must be created in accordance with the Indian healthcare industry in order to obtain the high accuracy. Addressing the difficulties is necessary in order to acquire the precise model. The standardization of data in the healthcare industry, which can support the maintenance of EHR, is one of the primary challenges (Huynh et al., 2020). The Indian government, medical experts, and pharmaceutical corporations must collaborate closely to address the additional issues described above. Rural India can now receive specialized medical care thanks to telemedicine, one of the promising areas of healthcare improvement (Huynh et al., 2020). The promise of AI must be fully realized despite its broad range of applications.

According to the research, the main challenges facing the healthcare system are the low doctor-to-patient ratio, a shortage of qualified staff leading to diagnostic errors, and a lack of a stable price and policy environment. In addition, the COVID-19 epidemic has strained the infrastructure and exacerbated existing issues. AI can help with early disease outbreak detection, remote diagnosis and treatment, and resource management in the medical field. It's noteworthy that the study makes a number of suggestions for the administration, service providers, and healthcare institutions (Health Care - Healthy People 2030, 2022).

FUTURE SCOPE AND CONCLUSION

With the development of technology, human interaction is gradually disappearing from all spheres of existence. The healthcare industry is likewise evolving quickly. Technologies like cloud storage and processing, maintaining security and privacy, and big data processing have changed the medical industry coupled with promising advancements in artificial intelligence and machine learning. These days, diseases are predicted based on the patient's past medical information. Because of how quickly technology is evolving, robots can now do surgery. With the current changes in healthcare, patients can receive care more effectively and efficiently. It has already sparked significant advancements in the development of novel medications and patient-specific treatments. However, there are difficulties in harnessing the potential of this new machine learning technology in healthcare. It will take the cooperation of the whole medical community, the public, and the government to overcome these obstacles. Infrastructure, money, and time are all necessary to deliver individualized care that is timely, cost-effective, and efficient. Additionally, it necessitates that people have faith in disease predictions and therapies that are based on technology. Another difficulty in maintaining or automating the storage of health records is security and privacy. AI has the potential to transform Indian healthcare if we can overcome these obstacles. The use of data and AI in healthcare is expected to boost India's GDP by $25 to $30 billion by 2025.

The pandemic has taught us the value of anticipating outbreaks and being well-prepared to handle any type of medical emergencies, so this work is helpful in giving a clear and comprehensive view of the potential use of AI to transform the healthcare sector as well as how the adoption of AI can be increased and prioritized in the sector. The COVID-19 epidemic has created a critical necessity for the deployment of cutting-edge technologies.

REFERENCES

16 Machine Learning in Healthcare Examples. (2022). Retrieved 16 July 2022, from https://builtin.com/artificial-intelligence/machine-learning-healthcare

21 Examples of Big Data In Healthcare With Powerful Analytics. (2022). Retrieved 16 July 2022, from https://www.datapine.com/blog/big-data-examples-in-healthcare/

Adopting A. I. in Drug Discovery. (2022). Retrieved 16 July 2022, from https://www.bcg.com/publications/2022/adopting-ai-in-pharmaceutical-discovery

Alanazi, A. (2022). Using machine learning for healthcare challenges and opportunities. *Informatics In Medicine Unlocked*, *30*, 100924. doi:10.1016/j.imu.2022.100924

Artificial Intelligence: Definition, Types, Examples, Technologies. (2022). Retrieved 16 July 2022, from https://chethankumargn.medium.com/artificial-intelligence-definition-types-examples-technologies-962ea75c7b9b

Basu, K., Sinha, R., Ong, A., & Basu, T. (2020). Artificial Intelligence: How is It Changing Medical Sciences and Its Future? *Indian Journal of Dermatology*, *65*(5), 365–370. doi:10.4103/ijd.IJD_421_20 PMID:33165420

Davenport, T., & Kalakota, R. (2019, June). The potential for artificial intelligence in healthcare. *Future Healthcare Journal*, *6*(2), 94–98. doi:10.7861/futurehosp.6-2-94 PMID:31363513

Defining Basic Health Care. (2022). Retrieved 16 July 2022, from https://www.ama-assn.org/delivering-care/ethics/defining-basic-health-care

Ferdous, M., Debnath, J., & Chakraborty, N. R. (2020). Machine Learning Algorithms in Healthcare: A Literature Survey. *2020 11th International Conference on Computing, Communication and Networking Technologies (ICCCNT)*, 1-6, 10.1109/ICCCNT49239.2020.9225642

From enhancing patient care to driving down costs, AI has enormous potential. (2022). Retrieved 16 July 2022, from https://stefanini.com/en/trends/news/7-ways-healthcare-benefits-from-artificial-intelligence

Ghodasara, R. (2022). *Smart Healthcare Solutions To Streamline Patient Experience*. Retrieved 16 July 2022, from https://www.zealousweb.com/smart-healthcare-solutions-to-streamline-patient-experience/#:~:text=Ease%20of%20appointments%20and%20check,the%20time%20of%20check%2Din

Health Care - Healthy People 2030. (2022). Retrieved 16 July 2022, from https://health.gov/healthypeople/objectives-and-data/browse-objectives/health-care

How Healthcare Industry Helps in Contributing to the Economy. (2022). Retrieved 16 July 2022, from https://www.trivitron.com/blog/how-healthcare-industry-helps-in-contributing-to-the-economy/

Huynh, E., Hosny, A., Guthier, C., Bitterman, D. S., Petit, S. F., Haas-Kogan, D. A., Kann, B., Aerts, H. J. W. L., & Mak, R. H. (2020). Artificial intelligence in radiation oncology. *Nature Reviews. Clinical Oncology*, *17*(12), 771–781. doi:10.103841571-020-0417-8 PMID:32843739

Jiang, F., Jiang, Y., Zhi, H., Dong, Y., Li, H., Ma, S., Wang, Y., Dong, Q., Shen, H., & Wang, Y. (2017). Artificial intelligence in healthcare: Past, present and future. *Stroke and Vascular Neurology*, *2*(4), 230–243. doi:10.1136vn-2017-000101 PMID:29507784

Kovalenko, O. (2022). *12 Real-World Applications of Machine Learning in Healthcare - SPD Group Blog*. Retrieved 16 July 2022, from https://spd.group/machine-learning/machine-learning-in-healthcare

Kumari, R. (2022). *What is the Role of Big Data in the Healthcare Industry?* Analytics Steps. Retrieved 16 July 2022, from https://www.analyticssteps.com/blogs/what-role-big-data-healthcare-industry

Liz, K. (2022). *Top 10 Use Cases for AI in Healthcare*. Retrieved 16 July 2022, from https://www.mobihealthnews.com/news/contributed-top-10-use-cases-ai-healthcare

Machine Learning in Healthcare. (2022). *12 Real-World Use Cases – NIX United.* Retrieved 16 July 2022, from https://nix-united.com/blog/machine-learning-in-healthcare-12-real-world-use-cases-to-know/

Marr, B. (2022). *How Is AI Used In Healthcare - 5 Powerful Real-World Examples That Show The Latest Advances.* Retrieved 16 July 2022, from https://www.forbes.com/sites/bernardmarr/2018/07/27/how-is-ai-used-in-healthcare-5-powerful-real-world-examples-that-show-the-latest-advances/?sh=6c5c0e985dfb

McCoy, L., Brenna, C., Chen, S., Vold, K., & Das, S. (2022). Believing in black boxes: Machine learning for healthcare does not need explainability to be evidence-based. *Journal of Clinical Epidemiology, 142,* 252–257. doi:10.1016/j.jclinepi.2021.11.001 PMID:34748907

Michael, G. (2022). Retrieved 16 July 2022, from https://imaginovation.net/blog/5-real-world-applications-ai-in-medicine-examples/

Mohammed, M., Khan, M., & Bashier, E. (2016). *Machine Learning: Algorithms and Applications.* . doi:10.1201/9781315371658

Ngiam, K., & Khor, I. (2019). Big data and machine learning algorithms for health-care delivery. *The Lancet. Oncology, 20*(5), e262–e273. doi:10.1016/S1470-2045(19)30149-4 PMID:31044724

Oren, O., Gersh, B., & Bhatt, D. (2020). Artificial intelligence in medical imaging: Switching from radiographic pathological data to clinically meaningful endpoints. *The Lancet. Digital Health, 2*(9), e486–e488. doi:10.1016/S2589-7500(20)30160-6 PMID:33328116

Ozaydin, B., Berner, E. S., & Cimino, J. J. (2021). Appropriate use of machine learning in healthcare. *Intelligence-Based Medicine, 5.* doi:10.1016/j.ibmed.2021.100041

Rong, G., Mendez, A., Bou Assi, E., Zhao, B., & Sawan, M. (2020). Artificial Intelligence in Healthcare: Review and Prediction Case Studies. *Engineering, 6*(3), 291–301. doi:10.1016/j.eng.2019.08.015

Sarvamangala, D. R., & Kulkarni, R. V. (2022). Convolutional neural networks in medical image understanding: A survey. *Evolutionary Intelligence, 15*(1), 1–22. doi:10.100712065-020-00540-3 PMID:33425040

Singh, R.P., Hom, G.L., Abramoff, M.D., Campbell, J.P., & Chiang, M.F. (2020). AAO Task Force on Artificial Intelligence. Current Challenges and Barriers to Real-World Artificial Intelligence Adoption for the Healthcare System, Provider, and the Patient. *Transl Vis Sci Technol., 9*(2), 45. doi:10.1167/tvst.9.2.45

Super, W. I. (2022). *Artificial Intelligence (AI)? Definition, Threats, and Trends.* Retrieved 16 July 2022, from https://www.spiceworks.com/tech/artificial-intelligence/articles/super-artificial-intelligence/

Toh, C., & Brody, J. (2021). *Applications of Machine Learning in Healthcare.* . doi:10.5772/intechopen.92297

Xie, G., Chen, T., Li, Y., Chen, T., Li, X., & Liu, Z. (2019). Artificial Intelligence in Nephrology: How Can Artificial Intelligence Augment Nephrologists' Intelligence? *Kidney Diseases*, 6(1), 1–6. doi:10.1159/000504600 PMID:32021868

Chapter 2

An Overview of the Application of Artificial Intelligence in Hospital Management in India:
Impact, Challenges, and Future Potential

Madhu Agarwal Agnihotri
St. Xavier's College (Autonomous), Kolkata, India

Arkajyoti Pandit
St. Xavier's College (Autonomous), Kolkata, India

ABSTRACT

The emerging focus of artificial intelligence (AI) in managing the healthcare systems in India has gained new momentum with the COVID-19 pandemic. The benefit of AI lies in the prediction of potential threats like determining COVID-19 hotspots. However, considerable studies have suggested that the greatest challenge in application of artificial intelligence in the healthcare system lies in the lack of exhaustive data to meet the objective of NITI Aayog's National Strategy for Artificial Intelligence in the healthcare sector. Under such a scenario, the current study aims at determining the current condition of AI in hospital management in the Indian subcontinent and also tries to find out the usefulness of AI in healthcare management. The research also aims at conducting a study on the existing literature to determine the potential and existing impact of artificial intelligence in the Indian health industry. The chapter highlights the future challenges that could be faced in implementing AI in the healthcare scenario of India.

DOI: 10.4018/978-1-6684-4950-9.ch002

INTRODUCTION

Artificial Intelligence (AI) refers to the use of Information and computational technologies which are supported by Human intelligence to execute a certain job or to achieve a predetermined goal. It is mainly related to the processes that use computational technologies to automate certain work that are influenced by human intelligence. The scope of AI has reached such an extent that even human interpretation and decision making are now being made using Artificial intelligence. The uses of Artificial Intelligence are hugely interdisciplinary and hence have a wide scope. The onset of AI in Medical Field can be traced back to 1950s when computers were used to enhance their diagnosis. In the Indian subcontinent where lack of doctors and medical staff is becoming a burning issue it is without any doubt that the scenario calls for certain automation of medical systems to promote better Hospital Management (Nirupam Bajpai, 2020). With all over the world AI technology surging at a rapid pace it is highly the need of the hour to determine what is the current scenario of AI in hospital Management in India.

The flooding of patients in the healthcare institutions with their diversified symptoms during the pandemic called for personalized care for them and conclusively demanded medical assistance in the form of Artificial intelligence. (Md. Mohaimemul Islam, 2021). The overburden on the hospitals, lack of skilled doctors for this one of a kind disease can be really complemented by the use of Artificial Intelligence.

In this scenario the current study uses the methods of Structured Literature review to determine the Current scenario of the application of Artificial Intelligence (AI) in Hospital Management. The paper collects information form 60 Research Papers related to the study to find out the current applications of AI in Hospital Management in the Indian subcontinent. It also tries to assess the future challenges in the application of the same technology in Hospital Management.

LITERATURE REVIEW

Substantial amount of research has been carried out all over the world pertaining to the use of AI in organization management, but none of them present a compiled and comprehensive study on the use of AI in the hospital management exclusively in India. Of the researches in the field, mention can be made of the research carried out by Dr Agarwal regarding the varied use of Artificial Intelligence (Agarwal, 2019). The current research paper follows a structured literature review procedure which was motivated from the study of J.E.Andrews (Andrews, 2003). Worthwhile research in predicting the future of AI can be found in the works of G.S. Collins (Collins, 2019). The use of AI in rural areas was vividly highlighted in the works of Dr. Guo (Guo, 2018). The research carried on by Hamid in determining the opportunities of AI in healthcare management is very meticulous (Hamid, 2017). The efficiency of AI in healthcare management is shown to a great extent in the works of Dr.Kallis (Kallis, 2018). The other mention can be made of the phenomenal work by khan in determining the scope of AI in the Indian scenario (Khan, 2019). Prof Mehta has shown with great details how Big data Management can foster more efficient healthcare management (N Mehta, 2019). The work of Dr K.C. Santosh proves the use of AI in tackling the Covid 19 pandemic (Santosh, 2020). The studies conducted by Nirupama Bajpai gives a scenario of the existing literature regarding use of AI for Hospital Management available in India (Nirupam Bajpai, 2020). The importance of the use of text mining mechanism to extract undisclosed information is profoundly visible in the research work of Dr.Hao (Hao T, 2018). The works of dos Santos focuses on the use of data mining to identify health problems (dos Santos BS, 2019). The steady growth of medical big data researches around the world is found in the studies conducted by A. Choudhury (A Choudhury, 2020). Statistics regarding the gradual increase in robotic surgeries could be found in the research paper of Dr. Connelly (Connelly TM, 2020). The publications on the use of AI in health care are found in the works of Y. Guo (Guo Y, 2020). Phenomenal works in the field of using Artificial Intelligence in public safety is found in the research of O Asan (Asan O, 2020). A vivid picture of the challenges faced in application of AI in healthcare can be found in the works of Verda Nizam (Nizam Verda, 2021). The evolution of research of AI in healthcare management is found in the study of BX Tran (Tran BX, 2019). A significant research on the use of AI in treating orthopedic problems is found the studies conducted by Prof. Tagliaferri (Tagliaferri SD, 2020).

RESEARCH OBJECTIVES

The study aims at addressing the following objectives:

1. To investigate the Current scenario of the application of Artificial Intelligence (AI) in Hospital Management using Structured Literature Review.
2. To understand the utility of AI in Healthcare Management in India
3. To determine the probable Challenges that can occur in the future while implementing AI in the Hospital Management in the Indian Sub- Continent.

RESEARCH METHODOLOGY

The research proceeds with Secondary data pertaining to the use of Artificial Intelligence in Hospital Management in the Indian subcontinent. It uses the method of **Structured Literature Review (SLR)** to find out the scientific validity of the existing literature on the application of Artificial Intelligence in Hospital Management in India. As suggested by Dumay, 'the SLR method initiates with **defining the research Question**, followed by **defining the research sample to be analyzed** then **developing codes for analysis** and finally **critically analyzing, discussing and identifying the future research agenda'** (J Dumay, 2016). In the same spirit, the steps taken for research are as follows:

I.   **Framing the Research Questions:**

The existing Research Gap of a lack of a comprehensive and compiled study on application of AI exclusively for hospital Management has fostered the very first Research Question **(Q1): 'Which are the most noteworthy authors, research keywords and citations available in the literature Review of application of AI in hospital Management?'**
A substantial amount of Research all over the world (as evidenced from the literature review) has proved that Artificial Intelligence has been changing the medical field drastically (F Mas Dal, 2020). This very scenario calls for the Second Research Question **(Q2): 'How the existing literature validates the relation of Artificial intelligence in Healthcare in India?'**The Research Question seeks to understand the available state of applications of AI in Hospital Management Scenario of India. Finally the objective of probable challenges in application of AI technology in Hospital Management as well as the future ideas in the same field initiates third Research Question **(Q3): What are the future applications and challenges of Artificial Intelligence for hospital management in India?**

II.   **Defining the Research Sample to be analyzed:**

The research is based on secondary data retrieved from articles as well as reviews published over the last 6 years (2017-2022) in the Scopus database. The studies written only in English were considered and the analysis was done on March 2022. Following this research procedure, 60 viable research studies were selected from a population of 75 researches.

III. **Developing codes for analysis:**

The third step in the research methodology deals with defining the framework that will initiate the analysis of the variables. In the current research study the following are identified:

a) Explanatory information of the research Area
b) **Analysis of the Source** (S Secinaro, 2020)
c) Analysis of Author and Citation
d) Keyword and network Analysis.

IV. **Critically analyzing, discussing and identifying the future research agenda:**

In this final phase of research the paper analyses the results obtained in the previous phases and discusses the current implications and the future prospects of implication of Artificial Intelligence in the Hospital Management.

ANALYSIS

The analysis of the available literature using the Structured Literature Review Method (SLR) starts with answering the first Research Question (Q1), **Which are the most noteworthy authors, research keywords and citations available in the literature Review of application of AI in hospital Management** and the Second Research Question (Q2) **How the existing literature validates the relation of Artificial intelligence in Healthcare in India?** For the very purpose thorough analysis was made in tune with the desired findings as elaborated in Point III of Research Methodology. In order to understand the **explanatory information of the research area and to analyze the source of the documents** the study found out the type of document selected for analysis, the scientific sources of the documents, and the growth of sources. To make the **analysis of author and citation**, the number of articles published by the authors, the dominance ranking of the Author, the author's H-index, G-index, the author's productivity were taken into account. For Keyword and Network Analysis, a tabular representation of the documents with relatively higher contributions as evidenced from article citations was prepared.

The research proceeds with a sample of 75 research Papers identified from the Scopus database. Out of this sample only 60 research papers were selected after thorough screening to assure that the research objectives of these selected papers are in line with the research question of the current study. The total numbers of keywords identified are 321. The period of analysis covers the entire 6 years starting from 2017 April to 2022 March. The study shows that there has been an annual growth in the number of relevant publications in the field to the extent of 5.52% with the most significant increase in published articles occurring in the during the years of 2021 and 2022 during the Corona outbreak. The data has been portrayed graphically in Fig 1.

Figure 1. Trend in number of relevant research documents published per year from 2017-2022

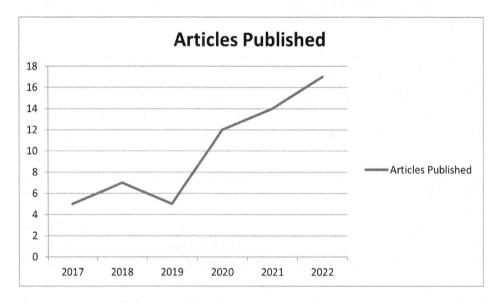

To have finer results, analysis was made to find the number of authors writing a research article on an average. It was found out using Author's Collaboration Index which was calculated using the following formula (Kallis, 2018):

Collaboration Index (CI) =
$$\frac{\text{Total Number of Authors of Multi} - \text{Authored Articles}}{\text{Total Number of Multi} - \text{Authored Articles}}$$

It was found out that the Author's Collaboration Index was **3.32** which symbolizes that on an average 3 authors have written an Article.

All the elements that are analyzed to identify the explanatory information of the research Area are tabulated in Table 1:

Table 1. Explanatory information of the research area

Information	Explanation	Number
Research Studies	Number of scientific papers and review articles	60
Sources	The frequency distribution of sources as Journals	21
Keywords	Total Number of relevant Keywords identified	321
Period	Years of Publication	2017-2022
Authors	Total Number of Authors	199
Authors of single Authored research papers	The number of Single Authors per articles	8
Collaboration Index (CI)	The average number of authors in each document	3.32

An analysis was also done to find out the top 5 Sources related to the study and the discipline they deal in. The same is shown in Table 2. Studies by Dr. Andrews have shown that 'structured literature review is incomplete without identifying the most cited paper' (Andrews, 2003). The very aspect encouraged identifying the most number of cited articles in the study to understand the articles which have a relatively higher contribution. The same is shown using Table 3.

In table 4 the top 5 most number of cited authors has been shown to understand the prominence of the authors in the current field of the study. However Literature suggests that a fraction of the authors have published their articles alone while majority of the authors has acted as Co-Authors. These encouraged the research to find out the dominance of the Top 5 cited Authors. This is found out by using the following formula (Kallis, 2018):

$$\text{Author's Dominance Factor} = \frac{\text{Number of Author's Multi Authored papers as the first Author}}{\text{Total Number of Multi Authored Papers}}$$

The values of dominance factor are shown in Table 5. To add up to the author's prominence, Author's impact in terms of H index and g –index are shown in Table 6[1]. One of the most important analyses goes on with establishing the relationship between two key words **'artificial Intelligence'** and **'Hospital management'**. The analysis is of utter significance in order to identify the gaps in application of AI in hospital management and the future scope of study. Table 7 shows the total number of keywords per author in the top 5 positions. The scientific area of reference is confirmed by this keyword analysis. All the tables are shown below.

Table 2. Top 5 Sources of published research papers pertaining to the current study

Rank	Sources	Discipline	No of Articles
1	Journal of Medical Systems	Medical Informatics	16
2	Decision Support System	Information Technology	11
3	International Journal of Scientific and Technology research	Medical Research	11
4	Journal of Digital Imaging	Technology	8
5	NPJ Digital Medicine	Medicine	7

Table 3. Top 5 most cited papers

Rank	Research Papers	No of Citations
1	Santosh, K. (2020). AI driven tools for Corona Virus outbreak: need of active learning and cross population. *Journal of Medical Systems* .	14
2	MM Baig, H. G. (2017). A systemetic review of wearable patient monitoring system. *Journal of medical Systems* .	11
3	Guo, J. (2018). the application of medical Artificial Intelligence technology in rural areas of developing countries. *Health Equity*, 174-181.	9
4	N Mehta, A. P. (2019). Transforming Healthcare with Big data analytics and artificial intelligence: a systematic mappin (N Mehta, 2019) study. *Decision Suppoert System* .	8
5	Collins, G. (2019). Reporting of Artificial Intelligence Predictions Models. *Lancet* .	6

Table 4. Top 5 cited authors

Rank	Name of Authors	No of Citations
1	K Santosh	16
2	N Mehta	13
3	MM Baig	12
4	G Collins	10
5	J Guo	9

Table 5. Top 5 author's dominance factor

Rank	Author	Dominance factor	Total Articles	Multi Authored	First Authored
1	K Santosh	1	2	2	2
1	MM Baig	1	2	2	2
1	N Mehta	1	2	2	2
2	G Collins	0.50	2	2	1
2	J Guo	0.50	2	2	1

Table 6. Top 5 author's impact

Author	H –INDEX	G- INDEX
K Santosh	1	2
MM Baig	2	3
N Mehta	1	1
G Collins	2	2
J Guo	1	2

Table 7. Author's keywords in articles on artificial intelligence in hospital management

Keywords	No. of occurrences
Artificial intelligence	28
Machine learning	21
Hospital Management	19
Decision Support System	11
Covid 19	9
Medical Informatics	6

RESULTS AND DISCUSSION

The bibliometric analysis of the data as identified in the Analysis section very well provides a vivid image of the application of AI in Hospital Management through the Structured Literature Review mechanism. The Increasing Trend of the number of research papers published in the last five years (2017 – 2022) as visible from Fig1 proves beyond doubt that the role of Artificial intelligence in Hospital management is slowly gaining momentum as the primary data pertaining to the same has been increasing. The huge spike in the number of research papers published in the last

3 years (2020-2022) comes at a juncture when COVID has its onset in India as well as it continued (Hussain, 2020). These prove to a great extent that the use of Artificial Intelligence in the Hospital Management has seen a rapid increase in the COVID-19 era in India.

The second inference that can be drawn after analyzing the sources of the published research papers is that the area of study is not only restricted to one discipline but prevails across various disciplines as evidenced from Table 2. This once again proves that Artificial intelligence is gradually becoming a need across various disciplines of life. The high dominance factor and a fair amount of cited papers prove beyond any doubt that Artificial intelligence in healthcare Management. The presence of impact factor both in the H-index and G-index shows that the researchers involved in the study has been doing so for a considerable amount of time. Finally the keyword analysis proves that in case we applied AI in Hospital Management it would be possible to achieve technological ways for supporting the Medical Field. This very scenario provides the impetus to relate the two Key words 'Artificial Intelligence' and 'Clinical decision Support System'. The relation will without any doubt will help medical fraternity in craving out relevant data from a large pool of clinical data (Agarwal, 2019). However in order to have a clear scenario of the application of Artificial Intelligence in Healthcare Management in India and its usefulness the research divides the findings into four segments as follows:

I.   Management of Health Services
II.   Using AI for disease and Diagnosis prediction
III. Use of AI in Clinical decision Making
IV.   Utility of AI in patient data management

This very analysis aims to address the third research Question '**Q3): What are the future applications and challenges of Artificial Intelligence for hospital management in India?**

I.   **Management of health services:**

Substantial amount of literature on the study have proved that Artificial Intelligence can provide faster and reliable medical Information rather than human based system (Kallis, 2018). The COVID 19 scenario has introduced the concept of app based AI to detect health risk and at the same time get alerts regarding the same (Santosh, 2020). The uses of AI become more pertinent in patient safety and hence provide better nursing (Kallis, 2018). The interesting way in which AI has been developing the health services drastically is how AI is used to keep the patient also engaged and informed with his or her medical team during hospital stays (N Mehta, 2019)

II. Using AI for disease and diagnosis prediction:

When it comes to the utility of Artificial intelligence for disease prediction the most widely used technique found is the use of AI in 'realizing drugs and equipment in a just-in-time supply system totally based on predictive algorithms (Silvana Secinaro, 2021). Researchers have proved that AI can be used by medical practitioners to help in proactive management of disease onset (Hamid, 2017). As it is possible for AI to find out meaningful structured relationships from raw data, it can be used to automate the process of developing new medicines and monitor patient conditions and help provide doctors with concise information to foster faster decision making (MM Baig, 2017)

III. Use of AI in clinical decision making:

The keyword analysis of the current Research paper has shown adequate evidence of using AI to support medical staff in clinical decision making. The use of AI can actually remove human judgment in Health care Specific functional areas (Nirupam Bajpai, 2020). Researchers have also proved that AI can be used to 'help doctors with virtual assistance to understand the semantics of language and learning' (Collins, 2019).

IV. Utility of AI in patient data management:

The study have found out through the SLR method that multiple research studies have proved that AI in can crave out relevant data from a vast pool of data and use it for the purpose of diagnostic efficiency. Technology like 3d Mapping of a person's body have proved the same without any doubt (Guo, 2018)

If the result and discussion section can be properly studied we will find the challenges and future **avenues of Research** in the field of AI in Hospital Management. The studies have proved one another drawback of the Indian Scenario of AI in Hospital Management. It has shown that even though there has been an increase in the application of AI but Government funding in promoting AI in Hospital Management is relatively less (Hamid, 2017). This poses as a challenge in improving the AI sector. When it comes to the future avenues of our research use of primary data in the conducting the same study can always be an option.

CONCLUSION

The study has proved without any doubt that use of AI in the Hospital Management scenario in India is an emerging issue. With the onset of COVID 19 the use of AI in hospital management has indeed gained momentum in from 2020. The increased number of researches has proved that AI in the Indian Hospital Management scenario addresses issue like efficient management of Health care services through disease and Diagnosis prediction. In validating the very first objective of the research paper, it can be said that in the Indian Health care management scenario AI is now mostly used to identify health risks (Hussain, 2020). The Cowin Application in particular provides then and then response to Health hazards pertaining to COVID-19 in no time. Artificial intelligence is also used to monitor the health of elderly citizens in particular. Certain AI based computer software are used to give reminder to elderly people regarding medical check up and taking medicines on time (MM Baig, 2017). Researchers have suggested that though Robotic Surgeries are still not in practice in India but Robot assisted surgeries have taken place in a host of Indian Nursing Homes (Connelly TM, 2020). A substantial amount of Research have proved that AI can be used by medical practitioners to help in proactive management of disease onset (Hamid, 2017). As it is possible for AI to find out meaningful structured relationships from raw data, it can be used to automate the process of developing new medicines and monitor patient conditions and help provide doctors with concise information to foster faster decision making (MM Baig, 2017)

The utility of AI in Hospital Management in India is that AI helps in pooling out concise relevant data from a large set in case of Hospital management and fosters better clinical decision making. It automates certain processes in hospital management which makes the Hospital Management time savvy and cost effective.

However due to lack of poor government funding the use of AI in hospital management is not gaining the adequate momentum which is the need of the hour. The another challenge lies in the fact that even if AI is applied in Hospitals it is found that majority of the patients are reluctant to use it as they are not tech savvy. More importantly patients feel trust issues while relying on machines that on human (Nizam Verda, 2021). Artificial intelligence without any doubt requires a huge collection of data. The research has found out that in majority of the cited papers pertaining to challenges of AI in Hospital management, a major problem pointed out is the fear of personal data being leaked. A substantial amount of studies have suggested that there is no legal framework regarding the extent to which health related data of patients can be made available for use in AI (F Mas Dal, 2020). Added to the issue is the lack of infrastructural development for making an environment worthy of applying AI in Hospital management. It's inevitable that initial cost of applying AI in hospital management is fairly on the higher side, however the benefits is bound to reduce cost in the future. This very aspect of the Indian Health Care scenario is yet to be addressed by the policy makers of the country.

REFERENCES

Agarwal, A. (2019). Exploring the Impact of Artificial Intelligence: Prediction vs Judgement. *Information Economics and Policy, 47*, 1–6. doi:10.1016/j.infoecopol.2019.05.001

Andrews, J. E. (2003). An Author Co-Citation: A literature measure of the intellectual Structure. *Journal of the Medical Library Association: JMLA.*

Asan O, C. A. (2020). Role of Artificial Intelligence in Patient Safety Outcomes: systematic literature review. *JMIR Medical Information, 8*(7).

Baig, H. G. (2017). A systemetic review of wearable patient monitoring system. *Journal of Medical Systems.* Advance online publication. doi:10.100710916-017-0760-1

Choudhury, A. E. R. (2020). Use of machine learning in geriatric clinic care. JAMIA Open, 459-71.

Collins, G., & Moons, K. G. M. (2019). Reporting of Artificial Intelligence Predictions Models. *Lancet, 393*(10181), 1577–1579. doi:10.1016/S0140-6736(19)30037-6 PMID:31007185

Connelly, T. M., Malik, Z., Sehgal, R., Byrnes, G., Coffey, J. C., & Peirce, C. (2020). The 100 most influential robotic surgery: A bibliometric analysis. *Journal of Robotic Surgery, 14*(1), 155–165. doi:10.100711701-019-00956-9 PMID:30949890

dos Santos, S. M. (2019). data Mininig and machine learning techniquesapplied to public health problems: a bibliometric analysis from 2009 to 2018. *Comput Ind Eng.*

Dumay, M. M. (2016). On the shoulders of giants: Undertaking a Structured literarture Review in Accounting. *Account Auditing Account*, 767-801.

Guo, J., & Li, B. (2018). the application of medical Artificial Intelligence technology in rural areas of developing countries. *Health Equity, 2*(1), 174–181. doi:10.1089/heq.2018.0037 PMID:30283865

Guo, Y. H. Z., Hao, Z., Zhao, S., Gong, J., & Yang, F. (2020). Artificial Intelligence in Health Care: A Bibliometric Analysis. *Journal of Medical Internet Research, 22*(7), e18228. doi:10.2196/18228 PMID:32723713

Hamid, S. (2017). *The opportunities and risks of artificial Intelligence in medicine and Healthcare.* Retrieved from www.cuspe.org

Hao, T. C. X. (2018). A bibilometric analysis of text mining in medical research. *Soft Computing*, 22.

Hussain, A. (2020). *AI techbiques for COVID 19.* IEEE Acess.

Kallis, B. (2018). Promising AI applications in Healthcare. *Journal of Medical Systems.*

Khan, G. (2019). Information technology management Domain: Emerging Themes and keyword analysis. *Scientometrics.*

Mas, F., & Dal, A. P.-G. (2020). Knowledge Translation in the Healthcare Sector. *Electronic Journal of Knowledge Management.*

Mehta, A. P. (2019). Transforming Healthcare with Big data analytics and artificial intelligence: a systematic mapping study. *Decision Support System.*

Mohaimemul Islam, Md., T. N. (2021). Application of Artificial Intelligence in COVID-19 pandemic: Bibliometric Analysis. *Health Care.* PMID:33918686

Nirupam Bajpai, M. W. (2020). *Artificial Intelligence and Healthcare in India.* Center for Sustainable Development, Earth Institute, Columbia University.

Nizam Verda, A. A. (2021). Challenges of Applying Health care in India. *Journal of Pharmaceutical Research International.*

Santosh, K. (2020). AI driven tools for Corona Virus outbreak: Need of active learning and cross population. *Journal of Medical Systems.* Advance online publication. doi:10.1007 10916-020-01562-1

Secinaro, S., & Calandra, D. (2020). Halal Food: Structured Literature review and Research Agenda. *British Food Journal, 123*(1), 225–243. doi:10.1108/BFJ-03-2020-0234

Silvana Secinaro, D. C. (2021). *The role of Artificial intelligence in helathcare: a structured literature Review.* BMC Medical Informatics and Decission Making.

Tagliaferri, A. M. (2020). Artificial Intelligence to improve back pain outcomes and lessons learnt from clinical classificatio approaches: three systematic reviews. *NPJ Digi Med, 3*(1), 1-16.

Tran, B. X., Vu, G., Ha, G., Vuong, Q.-H., Ho, M.-T., Vuong, T.-T., La, V.-P., Ho, M.-T., Nghiem, K.-C., Nguyen, H., Latkin, C., Tam, W., Cheung, N.-M., Nguyen, H.-K., Ho, C., & Ho, R. (2019). Global evolution of Research in Artificial Intelligence in Health and medicine: A bibliometric study. *Journal of Clinical Medicine*, *8*(3), 360. doi:10.3390/jcm8030360 PMID:30875745

ENDNOTE

[1]   Source: Google Scholar site.

Chapter 3
A Case Study on the Development of an AI-Enabled Food Delivery System From Home to Home:
Annapurna App

Srishti Rawat
Manav Rachna International Institute and Research and Studies, India

Shreshtha Rana
Manav Rachna International Institute and Research and Studies, India

Gunika Lamba
Manav Rachna International Institute and Research and Studies, India

Shweta Mongia
Manav Rachna International Institute and Research and Studies, India

Thipendra P. Singh
University of Petroleum and Energy Studies, India

ABSTRACT

Like other domains of life, the food processing industry is also not untouched by the use of artificial intelligence. Though this industry has not been amenable to technology in the past, AI will play the role of catalyst in this industry going forward. Many working people who live alone in far-away cities and students living in PG have resorted to either consuming ready-to-eat food or ordering take-aways from restaurants. Moreover, people opting for tiffin service are usually bound to a single

DOI: 10.4018/978-1-6684-4950-9.ch003

vendor for an indefinite period, giving them fewer options for customization and portion size. This chapter presents a case study for creating an AI-based platform where users can decide which supplier they want their meals from. The system will present the user with nearest tiffin suppliers who can provide home-cooked meals on weekly or monthly subscription bases. The user will also be able to customize the meal quantity and frequency. It will also empower homemakers to start their small businesses and have financial independence from the comfort of their homes.

INTRODUCTION

Food has always been a successful sector, not just for producers and suppliers, but also for users and distributors. Because of recent changes in the sector and the growing usage of the internet, an online meal delivery system is in high demand. Bachelors also travel for work and are in high demand. Multi-Vendor Homemade Cloud Kitchen (Beniwal, 2021) is a must-have for the working class, as it will solve numerous food-related issues. This technique would provide a forum for women homemakers, sellers, and vendors to display their delicacies and generate income from the comfort of their own homes.

In today's world, online food delivery is a booming business. The existing systems for this, such as zomato and Swiggy, have some flaws that our proposed model will address. There are no facilities for homemade food service, such as mess and tiffin service, in the current system (Muangmee, 2021). There is a need for a system that can fulfil consumers' needs by delivering freshly prepared food at their doorstep. People who live far away from their homes can use the proposed model. It will also be beneficial for the students studying in distant cities.

Customers can have additional options because multiple food providers register on this system, giving them a wider range of tastes and meals to choose from. Additionally, using the present framework, tiffin service providers suggest to potential clients based on user reviews, and ratings (Thamaraiselvan, 2019). Orders are analysed and forwarded to the suitable vendor on a monthly and weekly basis. In order to eliminate the daily hassle of placing orders, customers can even place orders for the entire week or month, if necessary. Moreover, the Tiffin provider can supply today's special and make changes to previously posted delicacies. Tiffin will be delivered to their doorstep.

The proposed system helps the small-scale female entrepreneurs to establish a source of income and become financially self-sufficient. Also, it brings all small-scale tiffin services together on a single, user-friendly platform. The user can select from a variety of tiffin services by utilising this system (Balakrishnan, 2008). There is no limit on the number of orders a customer can place in the recommended system.

The proposed system is intended to improve the interaction between consumer-tiffin service owner, resulting in the most efficient and effective system possible.

The paper is organized into the following sections. Section I conferred with the prefatory phase.

Section II explores the related research work done on the prediction of educationist performance based on different parameters. Section III enumerates the tools and techniques used. Section IV reveals the methodology used. In Section V, a demonstration of the designated work has been given. Section VI highlights the results and discussions of the stated work. Section VII concludes with the work and show the paper is organized into the following sections. Section I conferred with the prefatory phase.

Section II explores the related research work done on the prediction of educationist performance based on different parameters. Section III enumerates the tools and techniques used. Section IV reveals the methodology used. In Section V, a demonstration of the designated work has been given. Section VI highlights the results and discussions of the stated work. Section VII concludes with the work and shows the future preview

This chapter is organized into the following sections. Section I conferred with the prefatory phase. Section II explores the related research work done on the various food delivery systems. Section III presents the summary of the various existing systems for providing daily meal services. Section IV reveals the proposed system and Section V concludes with the work and shows the future preview.

LITERATURE REVIEW

This section describes a comprehensive discussion around the approaches used for food delivery systems. A detailed and extensive literature review by different researchers are given as follows.

(Adithya, 2017) proposed a food ordering system using wireless communication system which delivers food from restaurants as well as mess services. The same application is also being used to provide recommendations from hotels and food menus. In their proposed system there is no limitation on the amount of order the customer wants. The input dataset includes the name, address, mobile number and the output dataset includes the order, bill, feedback and payment options. For each user a separate ID and password is also provided for secure ordering.

(Maurya, 2021) discussed how cloud kitchens were able to carry on their activities and was one of the businesses that thrived despite the crisis. It also throws light on some of the strategies that were adopted by businesses and chefs who lost their jobs due to pandemic, by turning towards cloud kitchen and partnering with food aggregators. It concluded with stating that innovation is what will help businesses in surviving crisis like this.

(Balakrishnan, 2008) discussed the Dabbawallah System which has been operational in Mumbai for over 100 years. It explained the well-coordinated and meticulously-timed system that delivers tiffin according to the zones. It also explained the timeline of the operations and how the distribution of tiffin happens according to the wide area zones and within a team. The paper also discussed the various challenges that this service is facing due to closure of businesses nearby and how it is slowly evolving according to the changing conditions.

(Patil, 2022) have proposed a system that will act as a platform for homemade food service. The system considers tiffin service as well as mess facility for the customers. The most important objective of this system is to evaluate the security, user-friendliness, accuracy and reliability of the system. The proposed system is designed in such a way that physically challenged can also use their application.

(Shah, 2021) have created an application for small businesses that includes hawkers, grocery stores & tiffin services to connect them to local customers even during crisis like COVID. The application lets businesses create their profile and menu along with pictures of their food items. The services will only be displayed for businesses within a radius of 2km of the customer. This is done so as to empower the local market. The vendor has the flexibility to either accept or reject the order based on the availability of items at the moment.

(Das, 2018) authors have attempted to examine how customers perceive online food ordering and delivery services in Pune. The purpose of this analysis is to determine the influencing factors, customer perceptions, needs and the overall satisfaction with the food delivery service. In addition to this, the study will aim to identify the factors hindering consumers from using online food delivery services. Through perceptual mapping various food delivery brands were analyzed with respect to different factors and it was concluded that Zomato is the best in terms of providing on time delivery and good in terms of customer service.

(Rao, 2018) authors have analyzed the challenges and opportunities of the future in the online food market and even provided insight into the future trends in the online food market. Their study also explores the various drivers for online food service providers and the obstacles/barriers towards their growth. It concluded with highlighting the popularity of online food delivering which is gaining more and more customers every year.

(Gupta, 2019) have aimed to understand the impact of online food delivery start-ups like Zomato and Swiggy on restaurant business and their strategies behind the delivery applications. It has also stated the vision, strategies, and funding of such applications. It has elaborated on the various positive and negative effects of food delivery apps on restaurants. It concluded with saying that the expanding population in the urban communities with longer hours of travel and work can act as drivers for these less expensive alternatives of food.

The main objective of the (Saxena, 2019) was to identify the pros and cons of the online food delivery apps from the point of view of restaurants and customers. A survey was conducted for consumers who order online through apps and those who don't use any food ordering applications. The study indicated the online food delivery business model to be highly demandable, full of potential with high profit margins. Of all the respondents, one-third believed in the bright future of online food delivery.

(Thamaraiselvan, 2019) have examined the growth and relevance of digital apps in the food delivery systems operated by Indian food service providers, especially fast-food companies, and recommending a few strategies they could adopt for sustained business in the future. The analysis was based on secondary data that was collected, for example, sale reports and published documents. It concluded with saying that the rapid urbanization and exposure to western lifestyle is aiding to the growth of online food delivery. Technology and innovation has the potential to take this sector to new heights.

(Muangmee, 2021) aimed to determine factors affecting behavior when considering using food delivery apps during the COVID-19 pandemic. According to the findings, performance expectation, social influence, timeliness, and task technology fit significantly impacted the behavioral intention to use food delivery apps during the COVID-19 pandemic. The study provided managers and owners of food delivery businesses' online with concerns to consider and areas to improve upon when transitioning from in-person food delivery to online distribution.

(Andrew, 2021) have analyzed the historical background and current scenario as well as possible future development in order to help online food delivery services develop better products and strategies to increase sales and customer loyalty. The research was based on secondary data like magazines, journals and internet portals and stated out the main reasons that results into shutting down of new online food delivery startups. It concluded with stating that on-demand delivery and cloud kitchen has the potential to grow and online delivery apps will keep innovating as the demand and competition rises.

(Purohit, 2010) authors have attempted to explain the supply chain management of Mumbai Dabbawallah & their uninterrupted services. It elaborates the organizational and structure and working style of the organizations. It analysis the economic growth of this system and the functioning of the coding system used to identify the starting point and destination of a tiffin. Various strengths, weaknesses, opportunities and threats of this system have also been discussed.

In (NDTV, 2022) authors have talked about four of the most trending apps for home-cooked that are available in different parts of India. It cites some of the office tiffin services that are promising home-cooked meals at an affordable price along with good prices. It concludes by saying that tiffin service apps will remain a staple of the workplace and will continue to satisfy people's appetites.

(See-Kwong, 2017) have analyzed the data collected to determine factors such as, trends, risks, and advantages, that influence business owners' decisions to outsource to online meal delivery. Based on the findings, business owners should pay close attention to the changes in consumer preferences and consider them as part of their strategic planning. According to the study, increasing revenue, exposure, and convenience were the most significant factors influencing the decision to outsource.

(Kanteti, 2018) have studied the different strategies followed food delivery startups in India. They have suggested areas in which innovations are possible such as delivering food through drones. It concludes by saying that the toughest model is the home-cooked food model that has great potential to flourish. For a company to become profitable, it is important to build scalable revenue streams and technologies that evolve at an extremely fast pace with long-term goals.

(Yeo, 2017) have examined the relationship between convenience motivation, post-usage usefulness, consumer attitude and behavioral intention towards OFD services. According to the authors, a person's perception of the usefulness of OFD services and their attitude toward them will improve once their perception of post-usage usefulness improves. By doing so, OFD service usage will increase significantly.

An integrated model of UTAUT, ECM, and TTF, as well as the trust factor is proposed in (Bhandge, 2015) to analyze the intention of Chinese residents to use FDAs during the period of the COVID-19 pandemic. Researchers explained how the continued use of information technology by FDAs during the COVID-19 pandemic leads to its continued adoption. A conclusion of the study was that perceived task-technology fit, trust, expected performance, and social influence all contribute to customers' continuous use of FDAs.

(Bhargave, 2013) have implemented a system that increases the quality of service along with personalized service experience. A key component of their approach is replacing paper-based menus with electronic formats and transferring kitchen orders electronically. Additionally, features such as tablets on the table, a customizable menu, and offering customers offers will help atomize the workings of the restaurant.

Study objectives of (Amis, 2021) include examining consumer perceptions of online food distribution startups, as well as consumer buying habits across various demographics. Their study aimed to identify food preferences of consumers from different demographics and to analyze factors affecting consumer attitudes. It also found out that Swiggy and Zomato are the leading food aggregators and players in the industry due to their discounts offered and wide range of restaurants covered by them.

EXISTING SYSTEMS

The following table states various app initiatives taken for providing daily meal services.

PROPOSED SYSTEM

Annapurna is an Online Food Ordering System is to provides excellent catering services to young students and an active generation of workers and the surrounding community to their homes through an android application. The goals and objectives of the proposed system includes: Offering a healthy, affordable, ethnically diverse daily meal option, Providing diverse menu options to choose from, Providing excellent customer service that strengthens customer-provider relationships by responding to their needs and desires, Development of catering services that acquires the skill development of catering staff, Providing women with career advancement opportunities for ownerships, Providing opportunity to start lunchbox delivering service at home.

The system is proposed for these small-scale entrepreneurs since there is a need to make individual small enterprises self-sufficient in terms of the business opportunities provided to them. The main entities included in the design process of the system includes: the service consumer, the tiffin service owner, and the delivery partner. When a person relocates to a new city, he or she must find a source of hygienic, freshly and high-quality home cooked meals, therefore they will look for home-based food services that fit their needs. The proposed system essentially provide the customer with an integrated platform from which they can choose from a variety of tiffin services on a single platform. The application's operation is depicted in Figure 1.

The working of the proposed system is described as follows:

1. **Customer login/Signup:** Customers will be able to register based on the available options, which include a variety of tiffin services in the area. Entrepreneurs will be able to fill out their profiles with information. Once logged in, the business owners could add the dishes to the available menu and photos of the meal.
2. **Select the tiffin Service:** Customers must select a tiffin service based on their preferences and suitability. A single tiffin service can only be selected by the customer at one time.

Table 1. Existing systems: providing daily meal services

S.no	Existing System/ App name	Description	Advantages	Disadvantages
1	Masala Box (Bangalore)	• It has a network of over 300 home chefs who use fresh garden ingredients to prepare food • A wide rage of menu starting from north Indian to protein-fueled meals and slads.	• Excellent customer support • Menu changes from time to time. • Subscription plans are economical	• Website and app functions are different. Website is easier to understand. • App bug in miscalculation of number of meals • Food items do not match the menu somedays • Subscription plans with no trials • Fails to recognize address on map. • No prior call or notification for tiffin delivery. • Limited to Bangalore only • Customers keep getting ads everywhere
2	Corporate Dhaba (Delhi NCR)	• Provides lunch and dinner in Delhi NCR and has a good menu lined up for the week.	• Good feedback regarding food packaging • Food is affordable • Wide range of customizable options for lunch and dinner • Can order in bulk as well for corporate lunches and dinner (ex. 75) • Has an option for skipping meals for said number of days • Food delivery always on time • Good customer support and management	• Serves lunch and dinner only • No app available. Can order through website only
3	Sprink (Bangalore)	• Entrusted vendors bring quality ingredients hence there is no compromise in quality. • They have a flexible meal plan and offer options for changing preferences.	• Has a wide range of customizable options even for cuisine types, portion size and choice of veg/non-veg • Generated a meal plan according to your preferences • Subscription plan of variable size (ex. 3 days, 7 days, 30 days) • all meal prices are inclusive of the delivery fee, packaging charges, and govt. Taxes. • Has app walled named Sprink wallet • No expiry on the wallet amount	• limited to Bangalore only • No COD available. All payments are done prepaid, cashless or through Sprink wallet • One time order not available • Frequently shows that the delivery boy is inactive/does not exist on the app UI.
4	Spice Box (Mumbai)	• Chefs prepare meals chefs using very little oil and masalas. • They have a cancellation policy, and credits go back to the users' wallets.	• Ordering through the website takes less than 2 minutes • Trials as short as 1 week • No dish is repeated all month • Cancellation is easy with credit provided to your wallet • Has an alternate meal plan for those who don't want to have only either Veg or Non-Veg	• The delivery fee is added to the cost of meals • No app available, can order through website only
5	Dabba Garam (Thane)	• Provides healthy meals that on a subscription basis	• Zero-waste policy • Delivery is done as per chosen time slot • App layout is simple and effective • Affordable prices • Good customer support • Good portion size	• Order can't be canceled once the preparation has started • No meal subscription option • no option to change the payment method • refund takes 5 to 7 days • difficult to change the mode of delivery or pickup
6	Yummy Tiffins (Mumbai)	• It provides customized healthy and nutritious food • Dr Neha Chandna designs diet meals for consumers based on their health requirements.	• Provides nutritious food. • Food can be customized as per the customer's requirement • They serve food in single-use containers.	• Food ordering times are not flexible. They only serve food at certain times of the day. • They collaborate with Mumbai's dabbawalas. • As a result, they lack their own delivery services. • They don't serve breakfast.
7	Kitchen On my Plate (Mumbai)	• This tiffin service in Mumbai prioritizes its customer's health and taste. • They serve Homecooked, balanced and nutritious food	• They serve food at a very affordable price. • Provides homecooked fresh and healthy meals delivered to customer's doorstep	• The interface for ordering food is difficult to use. • Only serves lunch at specific times. • Responds to user inquiries via Whatsapp, which is inefficient for handling customer inquiries. • Food cannot be customized because they serve a set menu. • Ineffective payment system

Figure 1. Flowchart describing the working of the proposed system

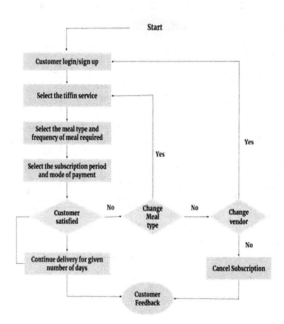

3. **Select the meal type:** Customers can select a meal from a menu of available options. Customers can also choose between vegetarian and non-vegetarian food based on their preferences. They can also select meals from vendors who specialize in a specific domain (vegetarian/non-vegetarian).
4. **Select the subscription period:** Customers must choose a subscription plan as well as a payment method. Customers can pay using the Annapurna wallet. Customers may also choose to pay in cash.
5. **Customers Satisfied**: If the Customer is satisfied he/she can continue the service for a subscribed period of time.
6. **Customers Dissatisfied**: If the customer dislikes the cuisine, he or she will be able to change vendors or terminate the subscription plan.
7. **Customer Feedback:** Consumers can also look for things based on their ratings. The list of services is displayed based on their ratings.

Searching can be accomplished by accepting the distance from the user in which the user wishes to search and displaying service providers within that distance. With the help of the message box, the user can contact the service provider and, if necessary, receive notifications from the provider's end. The service provider, on the other hand, has the ability to accept or deny requests from those who wish to use the service.

CONCLUSION

Author presented various online food ordering system for daily meal services with their pros and cons. This chapter presents a case study for creating an AI based platform from where user can decide which supplier, they want their meals from. The proposed system 'Annapurna' successfully addresses the issues with traditional food delivery systems by incorporating additional elements that provide high-quality service to the user. Also, the system resolves various concerns relating to mess or tiffin service by implementing an online food ordering system that can provide a full-fledged system. In the proposed system, tiffin service menus can be built up online and customers can easily place orders. Annapurna will provide online food menus, tracking of orders and features of customers feedback and wireless communication. The system assist mess/tiffin services in receiving orders and updating menus as per their convenience. The proposed system is beneficial for many people who are shifting from their homes get wholesome, affordable, and ethnically diverse daily meal options.

REFERENCES

Agrawal, B. (2021). Use of Social media by small women entrepreneurs of India for growing their business. *SMS Journal of Entrepreneurship & Innovation*, 8(1), 72–79.

Amist, D. A. D., Tulpule, D. D., & Chawla, D. M. (2021). A Comparative Study of Online Food Delivery Start-ups in the Food Industry. *International Journal of Current Research, 13*(5), 17540-17549.

Babu, J., Xavier, J. D., & Sophia, J. (2020). *Consumer perception towards online food ordering and delivery services with special reference to zomato, swiggy and uber eats.* Academic Press.

Balakrishnan, N., & Teo, C. P. (2008). Mumbai Tiffin (Dabba) Express. In *Supply Chain Analysis* (pp. 271–278). Springer. doi:10.1007/978-0-387-75240-2_12

Beniwal, T., & Mathur, D. (2021). Multi-Brand Cloud Kitchens: The Efficient Route. *IARJSET, 8*. Advance online publication. doi:10.17148/IARJSET.2021.8892

Bhandge, K., Shinde, T., Ingale, D., Solanki, N., & Totare, R. (2015). A proposed system for touchpad based food ordering system using android application. *International Journal of Advanced Research in Computer*.

Bhargave, A., Jadhav, N., Joshi, A., Oke, P., & Lahane, S. R. (2013). Digital ordering system for restaurant using Android. *International Journal of Scientific and Research Publications*, *3*(4), 1–7.

Chakraborty, D. (2019). Customer satisfaction towards food service apps in Indian metro cities. *FIIB Business Review*, *8*(3), 245–255. doi:10.1177/2319714519844651

Das, J. (2018). Consumer perception towards "online food ordering and delivery services": An empirical study. *Journal of Management*, *5*(5), 155–163.

Deepa, T., & Selvamani, P. (2018). Online Food Ordering System. *International Journal of Emerging Technologies and Innovative Research*.

Dirsehan, T., & Cankat, E. (2021). Role of mobile food-ordering applications in developing restaurants' brand satisfaction and loyalty in the pandemic period. *Journal of Retailing and Consumer Services*, *62*, 102608. doi:10.1016/j.jretconser.2021.102608

Ganapathy, V., Mahadevan, P., & Ravikeerthi, J. V. (2016). An Empirical Study of the Feasibility of Introducing the Mumbai Dabbawala Food Delivery System in Bangalore. *SAMVAD*, *12*, 9–22.

Gupta, M. (2019). A Study on Impact of Online Food delivery app on Restaurant Business special reference to zomato and swiggy. *International Journal of Research and Analytical Reviews*, *6*(1), 889–893.

Izzati, B. M. (2020). Analysis of customer behavior in mobile food ordering application using UTAUT model (case study: GoFood application). *International Journal of Innovation in Enterprise System*, *4*(01), 23–34. doi:10.25124/ijies.v4i01.45

Jain, V., Ambika, A., & Sheth, J. N. (2022). Customer-Centric Service Ecosystem for Emerging Markets. In The Palgrave Handbook of Service Management (pp. 393-410). Palgrave Macmillan. doi:10.1007/978-3-030-91828-6_21

Joshi, S. (2021). Impact of Covid 19 Induced Conditions on the Consumer Behavior on A Short, Mid and Long Term, for Consumption of Services. *Turkish Journal of Computer and Mathematics Education*, *12*(2), 1906–1923.

Kanteti, V. (2018). Innovative strategies of startup firms in India-A study on online food delivery companies in India. *International Research Journal of Management Science & Technology*, *9*(3), 17–23.

Kapale, G., Naikwadi, R., Devkar, R., Pardeshi, O., & Gorde, S. (n.d.). *Online tiffin service*. Academic Press.

Kozelka, E. E., Jenkins, J. H., & Carpenter-Song, E. (2021). Advancing Health Equity in Digital Mental Health: Lessons From Medical Anthropology for Global Mental Health. *JMIR Mental Health, 8*(8), e28555. doi:10.2196/28555 PMID:34398788

Leung, X. Y., & Cai, R. (2021). How pandemic severity moderates digital food ordering risks during COVID-19: An application of prospect theory and risk perception framework. *Journal of Hospitality and Tourism Management, 47*, 497–505. doi:10.1016/j.jhtm.2021.05.002

Lingle, J. C., Tiffin, L. O., & Brown, J. C. (1963). Iron uptake-transport of soybeans as influenced by other cations. *Plant Physiology, 38*(1), 71–76 doi:10.1104/pp.38.1.71 PMID:16655756

Mahajan, K., & Deore, A. (2020). On-line Food Ordering Tiffin Service using Reusable Containers. *IJETT, 3*(3).

Malik, P. (2020). *Expat Life Under Quarantine: Reflections of a Reluctant Cook*. Academic Press.

Mathur, M., Mehta, R., & Swami, S. (2020). Developing a marketing framework for the bottom of the pyramid consumers. *Journal of Advances in Management Research, 17*(3), 455–471. doi:10.1108/JAMR-01-2020-0015

Maurya, A., Subramaniam, G., & Dixit, S. (2021, January). Laying the table from the cloud during Lockdown: Impact of Covid crisis on Cloud Kitchens in India. In *2021 2nd International Conference on Computation, Automation and Knowledge Management (ICCAKM)* (pp. 299-302). IEEE.

Mehta, M., & Sinha, R. (2022). Women Entrepreneurs and Information Communication Technology: The Journey from Intention to Usage. *Journal of Entrepreneurship and Innovation in Emerging Economies*.

Mishra, S., & Anand, S. (2020). Migration and Dietary Diversity Changes among the Students: Case Study of the University of Delhi in India. *Space and Culture, India, 8*(3), 58–70. doi:10.20896aci.vi0.906

Mohamad, A. H., Hamzah, A. A., Ramli, R., & Fathullah, M. (2020, May). E-commerce beyond the pandemic coronavirus: Click and collect food ordering. *IOP Conference Series. Materials Science and Engineering, 864*(1), 012049. doi:10.1088/1757-899X/864/1/012049

Mohan, D., Bashingwa, J. J. H., Dane, P., Chamberlain, S., Tiffin, N., & Lefevre, A. (2019). Use of big data and machine learning methods in the monitoring and evaluation of digital health programs in India: An exploratory protocol. *JMIR Research Protocols*, *8*(5), e11456. doi:10.2196/11456 PMID:31127716

Muangmee, C., Kot, S., Meekaewkunchorn, N., Kassakorn, N., & Khalid, B. (2021). Factors determining the behavioral intention of using food delivery apps during COVID-19 pandemics. *Journal of Theoretical and Applied Electronic Commerce Research*, *16*(5), 1297–1310. doi:10.3390/jtaer16050073

NDTV Food. (2022). *4 Tiffin Service Apps For Ghar Ka Khana Delivered To Your Office*. NDTV Food. Available at: https://food.ndtv.com/food-drinks/4-best-tiffin-service-apps-for-home-cooked-meals-delivered-to-your-office-2833488

Ricky, M. Y. (2014). Mobile food ordering application using android os platform. In *EPJ Web of Conferences* (*Vol. 68*, p. 00041). EDP Sciences. 10.1051/epjconf/20146800041

Samsudin, N. A., Khalid, S. K. A., Kohar, M. F. A. M., Senin, Z., & Ihkasan, M. N. (2011, September). A customizable wireless food ordering system with realtime customer feedback. In *2011 IEEE Symposium on Wireless Technology and Applications (ISWTA)* (pp. 186-191). IEEE. 10.1109/ISWTA.2011.6089405

Saxena, A. (2019). An analysis of online food ordering applications in India: Zomato and Swiggy. *International Journal of Research in Engineering, IT and Social Sciences*, *9*, 13–21.

SC, B., S. A. S., & Andrew, S. A. (2021). *Emerging Trends Towards Online Food Delivery Apps in India*. Available at *SSRN* 3837117.

See-Kwong, G., Soo-Ryue, N. G., Shiun-Yi, W., & Lily, C. (2017). Outsourcing to online food delivery services: Perspective of F&B business owners. *Journal of Internet Banking and Commerce*, *22*(2), 1–18.

ShahN.ShahH.ShethS.ChauhanR.DesaiC. (2021). *Local Food Delivery System*. Available at SSRN 3867478.

Struszczyk, S., Galdas, P. M., & Tiffin, P. A. (2019). Men and suicide prevention: A scoping review. *Journal of Mental Health*, *28*(1), 80–88. doi:10.1080/09638237.2017.1370638 PMID:28871841

Syamala Rao, G., & Nagaraj, K. V. (2018). A conceptual study on opportunities and challenges of online food services market in India. International Journal of Business. *Management and Allied Sciences*, *5*, 48–50.

Tanpure, S. S., Shidankar, P. R., & Joshi, M. M. (2013). Automated food ordering system with real-time customer feedback. *International Journal of Advanced Research in Computer Science and Software Engineering*, *3*(2).

Thamaraiselvan, N., Jayadevan, G. R., & Chandrasekar, K. S. (2019). Digital food delivery apps revolutionizing food products marketing in India. *International Journal of Recent Technology and Engineering*, *8*(2), 662–665.

Trupthi, B., Rakshitha Raj, R., Akshaya, J. B., & Srilaxmi, C. P. (2019). Online food ordering system. *International Journal of Recent Technology and Engineering*, *8*(2), 834–836.

Wadhwa, O. (2022). Social Media: An Upswing For The Marketing Business. *DME Journal of Management*, *2*(01), 72 80.

Wasnik, P. B., Bhandarkar, A. S., Memon, N. A., Urkude, L. R., & Awathare, P. (2018). *Android Application for LUNCHEON Services. Academic Press*.

Yang, F. (2014). *Mobile food ordering application*. Academic Press.

Yeo, V. C. S., Goh, S. K., & Rezaei, S. (2017). Consumer experiences, attitude and behavioral intention toward online food delivery (OFD) services. *Journal of Retailing and Consumer Services*, *35*, 150–162. doi:10.1016/j.jretconser.2016.12.013

Chapter 4

Pedagogical Shift in Education:
Artificial Intelligence–based Practices

Amit Singh

School of Computer Science, University of Petroleum and Energy Studies, Dehradun, India

ABSTRACT

A combination of social constructivism and critical pedagogy is what is referred to as transformative pedagogy. One industry where pedagogy reform is strongly desired is education. In addition, the COVID-19 curse forced society to choose such options above the demand in order to shore up the aspirants' future. Researchers and industry professionals are looking for automated solution methods to make it more interactive and simple for children and young people to grasp. Artificial intelligence is a technology solution that can be used to equip and improve human relationships and bonding with learning. Along with the beneficial inclusion, there are a few drawbacks that could cause a catastrophe, much like anything in the current educational system. This chapter, therefore, covers both parts of artificial intelligence-based solutions and futuristics with the challenges. The research being done in this area and the solutions that have already been produced are also highlighted. Discussion of the findings and potential future applications in the context of security and privacy follows.

INTRODUCTION

The creation and dissemination of information to an audience constitute education. Learning and education are not dissimilar from one another. However, in contrast to learning, which is the process of repeating understanding, education instills

DOI: 10.4018/978-1-6684-4950-9.ch004

Figure 1. Growth of the educational system

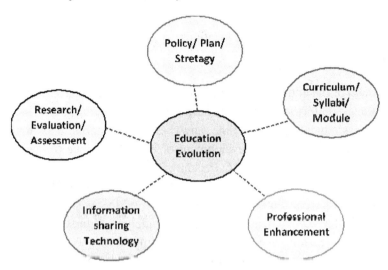

sense i.e. civic sense, and intelligence. The goal of the educational system (Dewey, 1986) is to provide society with knowledge that will enable it to understand itself and discriminate between humans and other living things. Education gives people an understanding of their civic obligations, rights, and responsibilities. Moreover, social behavior is influenced by the local educational system. People have been learning from their forebears and passing on their knowledge and talents to their offspring since the beginning of time.

Any system is temporary and can become tainted by unethical behavior and practices. The information being spread is not reliable and consistent given the era's natural dynamic nature. Hence, it needs to be changed in order to improve and keep up in line with the development of technology and, by extension, the educational system.

EDUCATION TRANSFORMATION

The way that knowledge is transmitted to society is rapidly evolving. These changes can occur as a result of the demand or compulsiveness of the moment, or they can occur for the betterment of the diffusion of knowledge. As can be shown in Fig. 1, success in any educational transformation (Ball, 2021; Price, 2015) primarily depends on several factors:

To develop a learning ecosystem, the following four components are fundamentally necessary (Rogers, 2016):

1.   Education for learning pedagogy
2.   Learning acknowledgment
3.   Diversifying populations and locations
4.   Exploiting technology

The growth of the educational system has seen several changes, from gurukuls, madrasas, etc. educatory systems to online teaching and learning processes. Students can now access education at any time, anywhere using mobile apps for iOS and Android. Table 1 presents the development of education since the beginning of human history (Ornstein et al., 2016; Packard, 2013):

The information in Table 1 is based on learning methods that were used in the past before computers were invented. Every area of human life saw significant alteration when the computer was innovated and became widely used in society. As a result, the new teaching-learning age had a significant impact on the education industry as well. Afterward, the Internet development and free international voice and text communication became a reality for many people. As a result, there is no longer a border for education at the beginning of the twenty-first century.

ARTIFICIAL INTELLIGENCE

Artificial Intelligence (AI) is the imitation of human cognitive functions by computers, particularly computer systems (Charniak, 1985; Winston, 1992). AI further categories into several computing systems and is somehow inspired by human intelligence systems, evolution theory, or natural insects and creatures. John McCarthy, the inventor of artificial intelligence, claims that "The science and engineering of making intelligent machines, especially intelligent computer programs". Moreover, AI is a technique for teaching a computer, a robot that is controlled by a computer, or a piece of software to think critically, much like an intelligent person might (Andresen, 2002).

When the term "artificial intelligence" first appeared in the early days of computers, it was unfathomable that a machine could learn and behave like a human. The goal behind the development of AI was to imbue robots with intellect that is comparable to and valued highly by humans.

The primary objective of AI is:

Expert Systems Development

Instilling human behavior and intelligence in a machine that can learn from experience and further provide guidance to users is the process of creating an expert system.

Table 1. Education system evolution

Years → Particulars ↓	7000 BCE -5000 BCE	3000 BCE -1900 BCE	1600 BCE - 600 CE	700 CE - 1600 CE	1700 CE – 1900 CE
Education goal	• Survival Knowledge • Team identity	Rule and govern the empire/ state	• Civic senses and responsibilities, philosophy, and law • prepare leaders/ soldiers for the armed forces	Expertise in mathematics, since, and medicine, Christian and Muslim beliefs, and practices	Expertise in science, art, mathematics research-based learning, philosophy, journalism, mass communication
Targeted people	Children in team	Gentry/ upper class/ high society	Male youngsters	Upper-class male and female kids/ youngsters	All male and female kids and youngsters
Approach	Informal guidelines	Delivery of authoritative texts/ memorization	Lectures, discussions and dialogs, drills, memorization	Lectures, discussions and dialogs, drills, memorization	Lectures, discussion, classroom-based learning/ discussions/ memorization
Curriculum	Survival skills	Believer/ truster/ Confucian texts	Reading, writing, poetry, drills, patriotic songs, etc.	Reading, writing, mathematics, religious discussions, scientific lectures, and textual analysis.	Reading, writing, research, analysis, religious books
Service provider	Parents, Tribal elders, and Priests	Ruler/ Emporer/ government personnel	Parents, religious ministers, private schools, teachers	Mosques, court schools,	Conversational schools, traditional schools for upper class

Human Intelligence to be Incorporated into Machines

Constructing systems that comprehend, reflect, adapt, and act like people is possible only through AI. It can interact with human beings and surroundings and keep on learning to enhance its capability.

AI encompasses more than just computer science; it also draws on biology, psychology, arithmetic, linguistics, and other engineering specialties as depicted in Fig. 2. Together, they create an intelligent system that performs complicated thinking, solves real-world issues, and is connected to computer functionality.

AI dominantly serves the measure area domains of the recent era (Abduljabbar, 2019; Dilek et al., 2015; Haleem et al., 2019; Li et al., 2017). Image processing, computer vision, robotics, cybercrime, natural language processing, health sector, expert systems, speech recognition, and handwriting recognition are among the major research domains that AI mostly supports. The Symbolic and Connectionist approaches to AI are used to provide answers for the aforementioned domains. The

Figure 2. Components of artificial intelligent systems

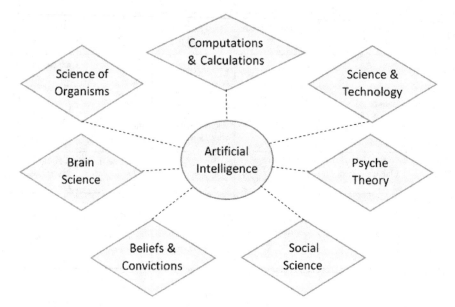

first one uses symbols to analyze the process in a top-down approach and without simulating the human brain. The second, on the other hand, involves a bottom-up simulation of the basic makeup of the human brain system.

To improve educational outcomes at every learning level, AI can be combined with education. AI can be used in education to help students achieve their goals by giving them individualized feedback on their assignments, tests, and other assignments based on AI algorithms. The next parts are devoted to AI solutions within the framework of the educational system and throughout current transformations.

EDUCATION WITH ARTIFICIAL INTELLIGENCE

In the beginning, artificial intelligence (AI) was represented by computers and computer-related technologies. It then evolved into web-based and online intelligent education systems, and finally, with the use of embedded computer systems and other technologies, humanoid robots and web-based chatbots were used to perform the responsibilities and functions of instructors either alone or in collaboration with instructors (Chen et al., 2020). These AI-enabled platforms have helped teachers to improve the quality of their instructional activities and carry out other administrative tasks, such as discussion, reviewing, and grading students' assignments and quizzes, more transparently, quickly, and effectively.

Robots in the Classroom

For instance, AI, computers, and other supporting technology can be integrated into robots to enable the development of robots that enhance student learning, starting with the most fundamental kind of education, early childhood education. Children are being taught basic skills like spelling and pronunciation using robots i.e. popularly known as cobots that adapt to the children's and students' abilities. (Fang et al., 2019; Snyder, 2019; Timms, 2016).

To investigate the usage of robots in early childhood and lower-level education, a meta-analysis and review were conducted (Toh et al., 2016). The authors take into account four key factors to evaluate the impact and i.e. sort of study conducted, robotics' impact on children's behavior and mental and physical growth, stakeholders' opinions about educational robots, and children's opinions about the looks or layout of robots. The authors consider the children, parents, and educators as the stakeholders. The authors complemented the deep research investigation presented in the literature. However, some quantitative results are also expected along with the survey and theoretical exploration.

LEGO robotics program is deployed in elementary education in Science, Technology, Engineering, and Mathematics (STEM) and the efficacy is evaluated (Varney et al., 2011). The following Table 2 shows the categories of student participants in the experimentation from the year 2005 to 2008:

According to the data in the table above, middle-aged and high school students participate less than elementary school kids do. An average of 8% of participants attended more than one session in a year. Study shows the influence of LEGO robotics in elementary schooling is higher. Additionally, robotics was considered a useful technique for cultivating students' team skills and constructivism.

Another study (Reich-Stiebert and Eyssel 2016) demonstrated the benefits of integrating robots with human experts in the classroom for STEM courses. However, the authors also touched on the concerns of teachers over the decline in student interpersonal interactions.

Another technological test is conducted through POWERTECH (Hong, 2011). The POWERTECH competition is created as a way of group learning for project creation. The authors support the improvement of collaborative learning in primary school children using these technologically-propelled devices.

According to other findings (Lin et al., 2012), the majority of parents would view educational robots as advantageous for their kids in the context of the teaching and learning process. Parents, on the other hand, were less at ease utilizing robots to play with and instruct their kids simultaneously.

In the Ber research (Bers, 2010), teachers used the TangibleK application to help young children acquire computational thinking and the engineering design process.

Table 2. LEGO robotics program for Technological-assisted STEM: analysis and outcome

year ↓	Number of participants	Elementary Education (%)	Middle Schooling (%)	High School (%)	returning students from the previous year (%)	More than one session (%)
2005	110	70.9	26.4	2.7	47.3	7.3
2006	174	79.5	26.4	4.0	57.5	5.7
2007	130	69.2	23.8	6.9	57.7	15.4
2008	101	70.3	27.7	2.0	41.6	7.9

(Varney et al., 2011)

It incorporated additional disciplinary learning in a method that was suitable for young children's developmental stages.

Affective and cognitive outcomes were separated and annotated for the additional papers that were added to the dataset in relation to the stated outcomes (Belpaeme et al., 2018).

In the above Fig. 3m, the authors tried to find out the participation of adults and children age groups.

Value-sensitive parenting support through social robotics is presented to analyze the psychological behavior of kids (Smakman et al., 2020). The authors survey and reviewed existing literature to demonstrate and conclude the impact of the study area. The psychological welfare and happiness along with efficiency and usability are analyzed in this research article. Similar work has been presented to demonstrate the physical and social interaction of educational robots (Alnajjar et al., 2021). The authors investigated the implications of attitudinal changes in kids and youngsters.

The advancement of robots in regular teaching practice is still not evident, despite global government initiatives to introduce engineering and technology to students sooner. The cost of robots, their restricted use in classroom activities, the absence of teacher training, and the inclusion of teachers in the robot's design are a few reasons why robots are not widely accepted in educational settings (Johal et al., 2018). The impact of these robots' use in educational activities demonstrates how difficult it is to create a technology for use in educational settings like schools.

Robotic telepresence systems (Fitter et al., 2018) have the ability to keep absent students socially and physically present in the classroom. In this study, fitter et al. examine how K–12 students' views of the robot, perceptions of themselves, and sensations of self-presence are affected by the customization of telepresence robots. Participants aged 9 to 13 in this study worked remotely with a telepresence robot

Figure 3. Demographic of the participants in the study

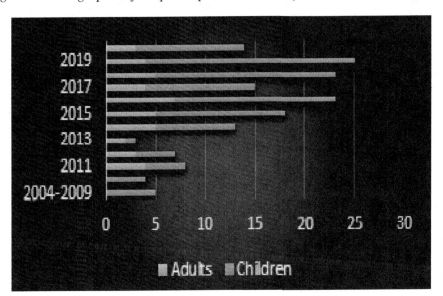

to perform an educational task. A child's social and educational development may suffer from prolonged absences from school during their K–12 education (Large, 2010). For kids with health issues, Mobile Remote Presence (MRP) (Cha, 2016) can make it possible for them to continue attending K–12 schools. The majority of MRP platforms, however, are geared toward adult users in settings like the workplace.

AI-based Robotics and simulators can alter the way kids learn in the classroom, resulting in students who are more informed and socially adept. In addition, robots can be used to enroll students in classes who might not otherwise be able to do so.

Web-Based Education

Another way of learning is accomplished through the web-based education system. The uploading of study contents and materials over the web can be referred by the students using a client-server architecture-based accessing approach. Assignments, tests, and quizzes can be completed at any time by students, and instructors can grade them from any location at any time. Teachers and students can have varied experiences thanks to adaptive and interactive web-based educational solutions (Devedžic, 2004). According to another review (Chassignol et al., 2018), artificial intelligence has been integrated into administration, instruction or teaching, and learning in the field of education.

A Web-based Teaching Support (WTS) is presented in (Cheng et al., 2005) to improve residential teaching and learning that takes place in classrooms. WTS also has features like tailored notifications for students, online attendance tracking, and several tools to help professors prepare lectures and process them afterward. Real-time implementation is demonstrated and data captured are analyzed for various feature validation.

A case study on higher education is adopted for web-based teaching-learning (Samarawickrema and Stacey, 2007). The research targeted a large urban multiple campus-based Australian universities. The technological and legislative issues surrounding the adoption of web-based learning are examined using Roger's theory of Diffusion of Innovation (DOI) (Sahin, 2006) and Actor-Network Theory (ANT) (Murdoch, 1998). Roger's DOI theory first appeared in communication to describe how an idea or product gathers steam and diffuses (or spreads) within a particular population or social system over time. However, A theoretical and methodological approach to the social theory called ANT holds that everything in the social and natural worlds is composed of dynamic networks of relationships. With several assumptions taken into account, the authors came to the conclusion that this was the optimal method of teaching and learning.

When putting the web-based learning model into practice, it is examined the organizational and educational hurdles and problems from the changes required in comparison with traditional learning in Turkey (Akbulut et al., 2007). The authors made an effort to determine whether teaching staff members were prepared for the changes and what skill sets they would need.

Web-based education overcomes the distance and time barrier in the education system (Cook, 2007). However, at the same time, a lot of cons, such as social isolation, infrastructural cost, technical skill sets, and connectivity issues are the most important to be considered while switching the education methodology. Parents must simultaneously keep a watch on their children and students to monitor their access to the content in order to avoid any potential problems due to the availability of different category contents.

Online Class Teaching-Learning

While online learning is a synchronous mode where students must attend classes at a set time, web-based learning is an asynchronous learning tool that allows students to access the study material whenever it is convenient for them. Online learning is comparable to face-to-face instruction in a traditional classroom.

The COVID'19 epidemic has caused a major collapse in the whole educational system, which has been repaired using internet resources. Different software sectors have created a variety of online portals and application programs to help students and the teaching community at different levels. The new transformation was used by a number of universities and colleges for regular classes and subsequent assessment and evaluation procedures. Mishra et al. investigate a comprehensive view of such an online form of teaching-learning process within the framework of the Indian educational system (Mishra et al., 2020; van et al., 2020). Junior schools frequently use online teaching and learning to keep pupils interested during the global lockdown. However, prior to COVID'19, which focused on the higher education system, a similar body of material spanning 2009 to 2018 is given in (Martin et al., 2020). The authors came to the conclusion that the vast majority of the software was quantitative in nature.

By merging adaptive and intelligent methodologies used in hypermedia models, the issues facing future generation educational systems can be resolved. AI-based chatbots offer individualized online education and convert teacher-to-student chat sessions (Kahraman et al., 2010; Peredo et al., 2011). In this research, the Authoring Tool, the Assessment System, and the more Interactive Voice System make up the online learning environment. Moreover, the virtual laboratory engagement framework additionally makes the complete package for the aspirants.

Every year, there is more and more interest in using AI algorithms and systems in education. Researchers are attempting to use cutting-edge AI approaches, such as deep and robust learning and data analysis and mining, to cope with difficult problems and tailor teaching-learning approaches for each unique student as schooling progresses.

There are various educational aspects, such as administration, instruction, learning, assessing, and grading to know the level of understanding. It is noted that AI is the result of decades of study and creation that have united product designers, information analysts and scientists, system designers, statisticians, linguists, cognitive analysts and scientists, psychologists, educationalists, teachers, and many others to develop educational systems with some level of intelligence and the ability to perform different functions, including to assist teachers (Pokrivcakova, 2019).

Gaining knowledge and skills through the use of electronic devices like computers, smartphones, laptops, etc. while connected to the internet is known as online education. The list below includes a few of the most popular online learning resources used following the pandemic:

Educomp: Evolution of Education in the 21st Century

In 1994, a private limited firm called "Educomp" with an Indian base paved the way for online teaching and learning in the twenty-first century (Anju and Sharma, 2016; Balihara and Venkatesh, 2011). The business also increased the reach of its educational digital products and solutions in countries including Singapore, the United States, and others. To transition physical tutoring to a technology-enabled virtual tutoring system, the Educomp business has introduced "Online Tutoring" for a few particular disciplines. To pique students' interest, it has translated the traditional curriculum into 2D-3D digital information.

Blackboard: A Leading Global Educational Technology

For homework, tests, quizzes, and online synchronous and asynchronous classrooms, teachers, and students can utilize the learning management system known as Blackboard (Alturki and Aldraiweesh, 2016). Participants who are unfamiliar with the system may experience certain difficulties and unease as a result of the design framework. However, the blackboard's capabilities and support make it worthwhile as a learning model.

In addition to the aforementioned, grading students, monitoring content access, and online activity submission offer a comprehensive digital platform for monitoring, instructing, evaluating, and assessing students. To determine the effectiveness of Blackboard across various user categories, a study/survey was done and sentinel analysis was employed (Al-Omar, 2018). The authors analyzed that while the instructor was appreciative, there was a problem on the part of the students.

MOODLE: An Open-Source Learning Platform (Modular Object-Oriented Dynamic Learning Environment)

A free program called MOODLE was created to enable digital teaching using conventional pedagogy (Cole and Foster, 2007). It is open-source software covered by the guidelines of the GNU General Public License. It allows for flexibility for those who freely use, alter, and share others but leaves the core GNU license intact.

A sophisticated and user-friendly course management system, MOODLE has several limitations when it comes to EFL writing, which is highlighted in the literature (Wu and Hua, 2007).

MOOCs: Massive Open Online Courses

There is a tonne of study material available through the open-access, open-source MOOCs available online (Waks, 2016). The most popular open-access platforms, such as Edx (Kolowich, 2013), Coursera (Bates, 2019; Kumar et al., 2015; Young, 2012), and Alison (Rehman et al., 2019), take advantage of online services and recruit students with the help of world-class lecturers. Similar to this, the Indian government launched an open-courseware program called NPTEL (Sheeja, 2018) for engineering students all around the world.

Regarding their economic model and suitability for students and professors, all MOOCs have their advantages and disadvantages (Busteed, 2019; Oktavia et al.,

2018). It must be better nurtured because it may contribute to society more efficiently and significantly to the digital transformation of the education sector.

In addition to the aforementioned, there are some apps for Android, iOS, and macOS that offer online learning, meetings, and conversation. Examples include Udacity, Udmey, Skillshare, Canva, Padlet, G Suite, Adobe Spark, Book Creator, MasterClass, and Anchor. Among the vast array of similies, online evaluation software programs like Google Forms, Kami, Quizzes, Kahoot, EdPuzzle, and Gimkit are particularly popular. The efficiency of these platforms for online teaching-learning to gain new skills during the COVID-19 pandemic depends on several factors, like technical knowledge of users, internet bandwidth, size of the conversation or discussion forum, etc.

AI-Based Voice Assistance

Everyone who is connected to the internet via various tools or interfaces can get information on particular subjects and interests whenever they want, wherever they are. Nowadays, almost every child owns a mobile device or at the very least has access to one that is online (Daley and Pennington, 2020; Schoegler et al., 2020).

A new age of widely used virtual or cognitive assistants was introduced by Apple's Siri, Amazon Echo, and later Google's home mini (Şerban and Todericiu, 2020). Millions of Virtual Assistance gadgets have penetrated homes and classrooms over the past few decades, although earlier virtual assistants were often problematic. The goal is to create a prototype Alexa skill that will train first-graders 1x1 arithmetic skills in a pleasant and engaging manner (Kepuska and Bohouta, 2018). Since children are already completely drawn to Alexa's speech assistant, the 1x1 calculating skill's feedback was better than anticipated, which encouraged us to improve the base functions. In order to create a suitable virtual environment platform for both students and teachers, Serban and Todericiu (Terzopoulos and Satratzemi, 2019) suggest a software application component employing the Alexa smart speaker that integrates several services, such as Amazon Web Services, Microsoft Services, etc. The use of AI-based tools addresses the key issues with the current educational system and offers a clever solution.

Recommender System in Education

An enormous amount of educational data is being generated with the introduction of web-based e-learning systems. Big data emerged in the educational sector as a result of this enormous data (Kulkarni et al., 2020). It has always been difficult for university administration to assign courses and research students based on faculty topic specialization and area of interest.

According to students' grade points on other topics, employ collaborative filtering-based recommendation approaches to suggest elective courses to them (Dwivedi and Roshni, 2017). To create a set of suggestions, the authors investigated the item-based Mahout machine learning library on top of Hadoop.

To help students find their way in higher education, a machine learning-improved ontology-based recommender system is being developed (Obeid et al., 2018). The recommender system proposed in this work serves as a tool for evaluating students' interests, skills, and areas of vocational strength and weakness.

In order to make recommendations for course teaching, research supervision, and industry-academia collaboration, the suggested system, dubbed ScholarLite, uses machine learning to mine faculty members' resumes for research interests and to extract research themes from their past publications (Samin and Azim, 2019). The higher education landscape of Pakistan is shown in this case study.

Automation is Good for the Economy: Robots in Education from a Business Perspective

How the company may expand while upholding the moral principles of the robotics sector and other stakeholder groups, including parents and students. Such a case study is conducted for small group sessions in the Netherland with the representatives of 13 robotics companies (Goudzwaard et al., 2019). Results suggest that only six of the 26 corporate values were primarily significant for robot tutors and shown below in Fig. 4:

When it comes to educational robots, following ethical guidelines is crucial because failing to do so could risk the students' lives. Building trust between children and young people and these mechanical devices is difficult from the perspective of their parents and guardians. The business model values and their effects are described as follows, as seen in the following figure:

Business Profit in Education

Everyone acknowledges that the robot industry is still expanding, which also applies to education. Discoveries in science and technology, however, won't translate into products that benefit society unless significant risks are taken. It requires more than just good technology to succeed in the education profession.

Figure 4. 6-Business values relevant to robot-tutors

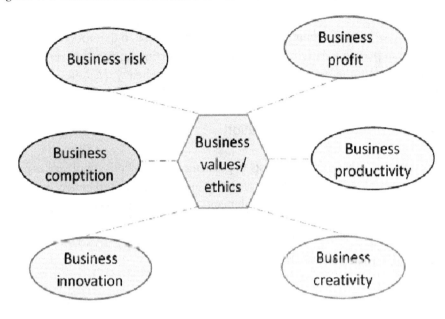

Business Productivity in Education

The adoption of robots has usually increased production and efficiency, but the results have varied by industry and over time. The education industry is also not untouched and defers respect to various related parameters.

Business Creativity in Education

Unique concept combinations are a key component of creativity. Amazing creativity emerges from the unique blending of brainstorming sessions from several stakeholders during the evolution of robots for education. The authors (Gubenko et al., 2021) analyze the beneficial impact of developing and programming robots on students' creative output using a confluence model of creativity. Within the framework of current models of creative cognition, the authors concentrate on the cognitive aspects of the process of building and programming robots. Further, a discussion about how meta-reasoning and emergent strategies fit into the creative process is presented. In addition, how the idea of creativity relates to robots specifically in terms of the creative processes that can be embodied in these artificial agents.

Business Innovation in Education

Recent advancements in robotics have already demonstrated that robots can play a crucial role in people's daily lives. Robots are supporting humans in every type of business, from automating complex processes to lifting heavy machines, leading to higher-quality products with less downtime.

Business Competition in Education

The competition among industrialists is growing as the robotics industry expands into all spheres of daily life. In terms of robots and artificial intelligence, education becomes the industry with the highest demand. In order to compete and win market share in the education sector, numerous businesses are investing in it.

Business Productivity in Education

While the use of robotics and artificial intelligence in education is expanding, there are also numerous hazards. When people engage with robots and machines, there are seven potential hazard factors: human errors, control faults, illegal access, equipment issues, environmental sources, power, and backup connection, and inappropriate installation.

Despite the fact that research has advanced significantly since the COVID'19 pandemic. But a lot more needs to be spoken in order for it to become a reality everywhere in the world. All parties involved must work together to create a reliable society that allows for the development of mechanical and technical robots. Despite the scientific data, there is still considerable resistance to the employment of robots in the workplace and the sectors of education and human care. However, students' caring must be on top of any other parameter (Smakman et al., 2021). The Unified Theory of Acceptance and Employ of Technology (UTAUT) model is used to assess the practical applicability, education, and care of students (Conti et al., 2017). This model may have an impact on the choice to use a robot as an instrument in practice.

CONCLUSION AND FUTURE SCOPE

For youngsters in schools or at home, for the elderly to retain cognitive and physical capacities, and for students with disabilities to adapt the curriculum to their capabilities, robots are beginning to show significant promise as learning or teaching partners (Popenici and Kerr, 2017). Robots have the ability to enhance individual adaptation through user-based learning. The impact of artificial intelligence on education can be summaries as follows:

1. Study design to present relevant and statistically significant findings, effects of robots on children's behavior and development, the importance of stakeholders' perceptions of employing robots in and outside of the classroom, and users' (particularly kids') responses to the robot's design.
2. In order to record the different activities and attendance, artificial intelligence-based camera setups are used in educational institutions. Additionally, warn and alarm the students for any inappropriate behavior.
3. Course recommender system is another benefit of AI that can guide the users for the next related courses and topics wish to cover. Similarly, assistance-enabled devices, such as AI-based Alexa, google home mini, eco dot, etc are also helpful for the students to learn through internet sources with voice commands.

A significant quantity of multidisciplinary knowledge dissemination is needed as a future direction. Following are a few of the domain areas in this direction:

1. If a robot records everything—audio, visual, spoken words, voice, and face recognition—some parties or organizations must monitor the data acquired for misuse. Consequently, it is necessary to protect the data and everyone from illegal access.
2. The study of human-robot interaction may be advanced via social educational robotics. To use robots to construct and assess novel learning paradigms, stronger collaboration with educators and learning science researchers can be made. Contributions from different disciplines that are published in learning environments with increased technology could accomplish this.
3. No one is safe from unethical hacking or unauthorized access to personal information once connected to the internet. Therefore, there is more work to be done on the security and privacy of data that is available on the Internet. In some instances, Bluetooth-enabled virtual assistance devices have been used to cause Denial of Services (DoS) (Yüksel et al., 2022).

REFERENCES

Abduljabbar, R., Dia, H., Liyanage, S., & Bagloee, S. A. (2019). Applications of artificial intelligence in transport: An overview. *Sustainability*, *11*(1), 189. doi:10.3390u11010189

Akbulut, Y., Kuzu, A., Latchem, C., & Odabaşi, F. (2007). Change readiness among teaching staff at Anadolu University, Turkey. *Distance Education*, *28*(3), 335–350. doi:10.1080/01587910701611351

Alnajjar, F., Bartneck, C., Baxter, P., Belpaeme, T., Cappuccio, M. L., Di Dio, C., & Reich-Stiebert, N. (2021). *Robots in Education: An Introduction to High-tech Social Agents, Intelligent Tutors, and Curricular Tools*. Routledge. doi:10.4324/9781003142706

Andresen, S. L. (2002). John McCarthy: Father of AI. *IEEE Intelligent Systems*, *17*(5), 84–85. doi:10.1109/MIS.2002.1039837

Anju, P., & Sharma, H. L. (2016). Effectiveness of EDUCOMP smart classroom teaching on achievement in mathematics at elementary level. *IJAR*, *2*(6), 683–687.

Alturki, U. T., Aldraiweesh, A., & Kinshuck, D. (2016). Evaluating the usability and accessibility of LMS "Blackboard" at King Saud University. *Contemporary Issues in Education Research*, *9*(1), 33–44. doi:10.19030/cier.v9i1.9548

Al-Omar, K. (2018, February). Evaluating the Usability and Learnability of the" Blackboard" LMS Using SUS and Data Mining. In *2018 Second International Conference on Computing Methodologies and Communication (ICCMC)* (pp. 386-390). IEEE. 10.1109/ICCMC.2018.8488038

Balihara, A., & Venkatesh, G. (2011). *A study on rapid growth of educomp solutions limited*. Academic Press.

Ball, S. J. (2021). *The education debate*. Policy Press. doi:10.2307/j.ctv201xhz5

Bates, T. (2019). *What's right and what's wrong about Coursera-style MOOCs*. EdTech in the Wild.

Belpaeme, T., Kennedy, J., Ramachandran, A., Scassellati, B., & Tanaka, F. (2018). Social robots for education: A review. *Science Robotics*, *3*(21), eaat5954. doi:10.1126cirobotics.aat5954 PMID:33141719

Bers, M. U. (2010). The TangibleK robotics program: Applied computational thinking for young children. *Early Childhood Research & Practice*, *12*(2), n2.

Busteed, B. (2019). Why Goodwill (Not Udacity, EdX Or Coursera) May Be The World's Biggest MOOC. *Forbes*, *26*, 2019.

Cha, E., Sajid, Q., & Mataric, M. (2016, March). Enabling access to K-12 education with mobile remote presence. *2016 AAAI Spring Symposium Series*.

Charniak, E. (1985). *Introduction to artificial intelligence*. Pearson Education India.

Chassignol, M., Khoroshavin, A., Klimova, A., & Bilyatdinova, A. (2018). Artificial Intelligence trends in education: A narrative overview. *Procedia Computer Science*, *136*, 16–24. doi:10.1016/j.procs.2018.08.233

Cheng, K., Xiang, L., Hirota, T., & Kazuo, U. (2005, July). A web-based classroom environment for enhanced residential college education. In *International Conference on Web-Based Learning* (pp. 56-65). Springer. 10.1007/11528043_6

Chen, L., Chen, P., & Lin, Z. (2020). Artificial intelligence in education: A review. *IEEE Access: Practical Innovations, Open Solutions*, *8*, 75264–75278. doi:10.1109/ACCESS.2020.2988510

Cole, J., & Foster, H. (2007). *Using Moodle: Teaching with the popular open source course management system*. O'Reilly Media, Inc.

Conti, D., Di Nuovo, S., Buono, S., & Di Nuovo, A. (2017). Robots in education and care of children with developmental disabilities: A study on acceptance by experienced and future professionals. *International Journal of Social Robotics*, *9*(1), 51–62. doi:10.100712369-016-0359-6

Cook, D. A. (2007). Web-based learning: Pros, cons and controversies. *Clinical Medicine*, *7*(1), 37–42. doi:10.7861/clinmedicine.7-1-37 PMID:17348573

Daley, S., & Pennington, J. (2020). Alexa the Teacher's Pet? A Review of Research on Virtual Assistants in Education. *EdMedia+ Innovate Learning*, 138-146.

Devedžić, V. (2004). Web intelligence and artificial intelligence in education. *Journal of Educational Technology & Society*, *7*(4), 29–39.

Dewey, J. (1986). September. Experience and education. In *iñe. The Educational Forum*, *50*(3), 241–252. doi:10.1080/00131728609335764

Dilek, S., Çakır, H., & Aydın, M. (2015). *Applications of artificial intelligence techniques to combating cyber crimes: A review*. arXiv preprint arXiv:1502.03552.

Dwivedi, S., & Roshni, V. K. (2017, August). Recommender system for big data in education. In *2017 5th National Conference on E-Learning & E-Learning Technologies (ELELTECH)* (pp. 1-4). IEEE. 10.1109/ELELTECH.2017.8074993

Fang, Y., Chen, P., Cai, G., Lau, F. C., Liew, S. C., & Han, G. (2019). Outage-limit-approaching channel coding for future wireless communications: Root-protograph low-density parity-check codes. *IEEE Vehicular Technology Magazine*, *14*(2), 85–93. doi:10.1109/MVT.2019.2903343

Fitter, N. T., Chowdhury, Y., Cha, E., Takayama, L., & Matarić, M. J. (2018, March). Evaluating the effects of personalized appearance on telepresence robots for education. In Companion of the 2018 ACM/IEEE international conference on human-robot interaction (pp. 109-110). doi:10.1145/3173386.3177030

Goudzwaard, M., Smakman, M., & Konijn, E. A. (2019, August). Robots are good for profit: A business perspective on robots in education. In *2019 Joint IEEE 9th International Conference on Development and Learning and Epigenetic Robotics (ICDL-EpiRob)* (pp. 54-60). IEEE. 10.1109/DEVLRN.2019.8850726

Gubenko, A., Kirsch, C., Smilek, J. N., Lubart, T., & Houssemand, C. (2021). Educational Robotics and Robot Creativity: An Interdisciplinary Dialogue. *Frontiers in Robotics and AI*, *8*, 178. doi:10.3389/frobt.2021.662030 PMID:34222352

Haleem, A., Javaid, M., & Khan, I. H. (2019). Current status and applications of artificial intelligence (AI) in medical field: An overview. *Current Medicine Research and Practice*, *9*(6), 231–237. doi:10.1016/j.cmrp.2019.11.005

Hong, J. C., Yu, K. C., & Chen, M. Y. (2011). Collaborative learning in technological project design. *International Journal of Technology and Design Education*, *21*(3), 335–347. doi:10.100710798-010-9123-7

Johal, W., Castellano, G., Tanaka, F., & Okita, S. (2018). Robots for learning. *International Journal of Social Robotics*, *10*(3), 293–294. doi:10.100712369-018-0481-8

Kahraman, H. T., Sagiroglu, S., & Colak, I. (2010, October). Development of adaptive and intelligent web-based educational systems. In *2010 4th international conference on application of information and communication technologies* (pp. 1-5). IEEE. 10.1109/ICAICT.2010.5612054

Kepuska, V., & Bohouta, G. (2018, January). Next-generation of virtual personal assistants (microsoft cortana, apple siri, amazon alexa and google home). In *2018 IEEE 8th annual computing and communication workshop and conference (CCWC)* (pp. 99-103). IEEE.

Kolowich, S. (2013). How EdX plans to earn, and share, revenue from its free online courses. *The Chronicle of Higher Education*, *21*, 1–5.

Kumar, A., Agrawal, A., & Agrawal, P. (2015). *Massive open online courses: EdX. org, Coursera. com and NPTEL, a comparative study based on usage statistics and features with special reference to India.* Academic Press.

Kulkarni, P. V., Rai, S., & Kale, R. (2020). Recommender system in elearning: a survey. In *Proceeding of International Conference on Computational Science and Applications* (pp. 119-126). Springer. 10.1007/978-981-15-0790-8_13

Large, A. (2010). *Mobile technology for children: Designing for Interaction and Learning.* Academic Press.

Li, B. H., Hou, B. C., Yu, W. T., Lu, X. B., & Yang, C. W. (2017). Applications of artificial intelligence in intelligent manufacturing: A review. *Frontiers of Information Technology & Electronic Engineering, 18*(1), 86–96. doi:10.1631/FITEE.1601885

Lin, C. H., Liu, E. Z. F., & Huang, Y. Y. (2012). Exploring parents' perceptions towards educational robots: Gender and socio-economic differences. *British Journal of Educational Technology, 43*(1), E31–E34. doi:10.1111/j.1467-8535.2011.01258.x

Martin, F., Sun, T., & Westine, C. D. (2020). A systematic review of research on online teaching and learning from 2009 to 2018. *Computers & Education, 159,* 104009. doi:10.1016/j.compedu.2020.104009 PMID:32921895

Mishra, L., Gupta, T., & Shree, A. (2020). Online teaching-learning in higher education during lockdown period of COVID-19 pandemic. *International Journal of Educational Research Open, 1,* 100012. doi:10.1016/j.ijedro.2020.100012 PMID:35059663

Murdoch, J. (1998). The spaces of actor network theory. *Geoforum, 29*(4), 357–374. doi:10.1016/S0016-7185(98)00011-6

Obeid, C., Lahoud, I., El Khoury, H., & Champin, P. A. (2018, April). Ontology-based recommender system in higher education. In *Companion Proceedings of the The Web Conference 2018* (pp. 1031-1034). 10.1145/3184558.3191533

Oktavia, T., Prabowo, H., & Supangkat, S. H. (2018, September). The comparison of MOOC (massive open online course) platforms of edx and coursera (study case: Student of programming courses). In *2018 International Conference on Information Management and Technology (ICIMTech)* (pp. 339-344). IEEE. 10.1109/ICIMTech.2018.8528178

Ornstein, A. C., Levine, D. U., Gutek, G., & Vocke, D. E. (2016). *Foundations of education.* Cengage Learning.

Packard, R. (2013). *Education transformation: How K-12 online learning is bringing the greatest change to education in 100 years.* Beyond Words Publishing.

Peredo, R., Canales, A., Menchaca, A., & Peredo, I. (2011). Intelligent Web-based education system for adaptive learning. *Expert Systems with Applications, 38*(12), 14690–14702. doi:10.1016/j.eswa.2011.05.013

Pokrivčáková, S. (2019). Preparing teachers for the application of AI-powered technologies in foreign language education. *Journal of Language and Cultural Education.*

Popenici, S. A., & Kerr, S. (2017). Exploring the impact of artificial intelligence on teaching and learning in higher education. *Research and Practice in Technology Enhanced Learning, 12*(1), 1–13. doi:10.118641039-017-0062-8 PMID:30595727

Price, J. K. (2015). Transforming learning for the smart learning environment: Lessons learned from the Intel education initiatives. *Smart Learning Environments, 2*(1), 1–16. doi:10.118640561-015-0022-y

Winston, P. H. (1992). *Artificial intelligence.* Addison-Wesley Longman Publishing Co., Inc.

Reich-Stiebert, N., & Eyssel, F. (2016, November). Robots in the classroom: What teachers think about teaching and learning with education robots. In *International conference on social robotics* (pp. 671-680). Springer. 10.1007/978-3-319-47437-3_66

Rogers, D. L. (2016). *The digital transformation playbook: Rethink your business for the digital age.* Columbia University Press. doi:10.7312/roge17544

Snyder, H. (2019). Literature review as a research methodology: An overview and guidelines. *Journal of Business Research, 104,* 333–339. doi:10.1016/j.jbusres.2019.07.039

Samin, H., & Azim, T. (2019). Knowledge based recommender system for academia using machine learning: A case study on higher education landscape of Pakistan. *IEEE Access: Practical Innovations, Open Solutions, 7,* 67081–67093. doi:10.1109/ACCESS.2019.2912012

Sahin, I. (2006). Detailed review of Rogers' diffusion of innovations theory and educational technology-related studies based on Rogers' theory. *Turkish Online Journal of Educational Technology-TOJET, 5*(2), 14–23.

Samarawickrema, G., & Stacey, E. (2007). Adopting Web-Based Learning and Teaching: A case study in higher education. *Distance Education, 28*(3), 313–333. doi:10.1080/01587910701611344

Schoegler, P., Ebner, M., & Ebner, M. (2020, June). The Use of Alexa for Mass Education. In EdMedia+ Innovate Learning (pp. 721-730). Association for the Advancement of Computing in Education (AACE).

Şerban, C., & Todericiu, I. A. (2020). Alexa, What classes do I have today? The use of Artificial Intelligence via Smart Speakers in Education. *Procedia Computer Science, 176*, 2849–2857. doi:10.1016/j.procs.2020.09.269 PMID:33042313

Sheeja, N. (2018). Open Educational Resources in India: A Study of NPTEL and its Usage. *Library Herald, 56*(1), 122–129. doi:10.5958/0976-2469.2018.00012.X

Smakman, M,, Jansen, B., Leunen, J., & Konijn, E. A. (2020, March). Acceptable social robots in education: A value sensitive parent perspective. In *Proceedings of the INTED2020 Conference* (pp. 7946-7953). 10.21125/inted.2020.2161

Smakman, M. H., Konijn, E. A., Vogt, P., & Pankowska, P. (2021). Attitudes towards social robots in education: Enthusiast, practical, troubled, sceptic, and mindfully positive. *Robotics, 10*(1), 24. doi:10.3390/robotics10010024

Terzopoulos, G., & Satratzemi, M. (2019, September). Voice assistants and artificial intelligence in education. In *Proceedings of the 9th Balkan Conference on Informatics* (pp. 1-6). 10.1145/3351556.3351588

Timms, M. J. (2016). Letting artificial intelligence in education out of the box: Educational cobots and smart classrooms. *International Journal of Artificial Intelligence in Education, 26*(2), 701–712. doi:10.100740593-016-0095-y

Toh, L. P. E., Causo, A., Tzuo, P. W., Chen, I. M., & Yeo, S. H. (2016). A review on the use of robots in education and young children. *Journal of Educational Technology & Society, 19*(2), 148–163.

ur Rehman, I., Bano, S., & Mehraj, M. (2019). MOOCS: A case study of ALISON platform. *Library Philosophy and Practice*, 1-8.

van Twillert, A., Kreijns, K., Vermeulen, M., & Evers, A. (2020). Teachers' beliefs to integrate Web 2.0 technology in their pedagogy and their influence on attitude, perceived norms, and perceived behavior control. *International Journal of Educational Research Open, 1.*

Varney, M. W., Janoudi, A., Aslam, D. M., & Graham, D. (2011). Building young engineers: TASEM for third graders in Woodcreek Magnet Elementary School. *IEEE Transactions on Education, 55*(1), 78–82.

Waks, L. J. (2016). MOOCs and career qualifications. In *The evolution and evaluation of massive open online courses* (pp. 83–101). Palgrave Pivot.

Wu, W. S., & Hua, C. (2008). The application of Moodle on an EFL collegiate writing environment. *Journal of Education and Foreign Languages and Literature, 7*(1), 45–56.

Young, J. R. (2012). Inside the Coursera contract: How an upstart company might profit from free courses. *The Chronicle of Higher Education, 19*(7).

Yüksel, T., Aydin, Ö., & Dalkiliç, G. (2022). Performing DoS Attacks on Bluetooth Devices Paired with Google Home Mini. *Celal Bayar University Journal of Science, 18*(1), 53–58.

Chapter 5
E-Learning:
A Tool for Sustainability in the Education Industry

Anita Singh
Sharda University, India

Richa Sharma
iD https://orcid.org/0000-0002-5752-4572
Sharda University, India

Risha Thakur
Sharda University, India

ABSTRACT

With the continuing development in the e-learning platforms, a great shift can be seen from traditional modes of education to AI-based education to provide lifelong learning prospects to the students. The implementation of e-learning technology has resulted in certain complications on academic professionals. The emphasis of this chapter is to highlight the challenges and factors that influence the usage of AI-enabled e-learning system during the COVID-19 pandemic; though the e-learning systems were introduced in many universities a few years back, the pace for its adaptability was enhanced during COVID-19, without any proper guidance and support to the teaching staff. This study seeks to investigate the challenges and identify the factors that impact the usage of e-learning systems during the COVID-19 pandemic by the teachers. This study will explore the teachers' perceptions towards e-learning and will provide contextual information on usage pattern and the nature of e-learning.

DOI: 10.4018/978-1-6684-4950-9.ch005

INTRODUCTION

Change is an inescapable and ongoing element of existence; it is an unavoidable occurrence. Today's entities are increasingly confronted with a dynamic and fluctuating environment. "Change or die," is a common rallying cry in today's scenario. Such a dynamic event necessitates enhanced operating methodologies and complementary approaches. Changes result in the acceptance of new inventions and the development of contemporary techniques of operation. Survival in today's all-inclusive economy necessitates firms and individuals being adaptable and quick to respond to the ever-changing marketplace. Change has become the new normal. Such kind of change took place in the year of 2020, when covid-19 pandemic forced the world into lockdown. Every company, institutes, departments, households and economies closed down in a matter of few months, this method was implemented to curb the infection from spreading. Every industry and sector came to stand still. One of those sectors was educational sector. Student couldn't go to their universities, professors and general public were bound to stay at home because of the implementation of nationwide lockdown imposed by the government. The virus's virulence has been devastating; one of the consequences of the COVID-19 epidemic was the closure of colleges and schools. Using technology in education for instructional reasons during the epidemic is also unavoidable; several recent publications have emphasized this issue (Mashamba-Thompson, T. P., & Crayton, E. D, 2020).

Because of the sudden shutdown of educational establishments as a consequence of COVID-19's appearance, administrators suggested using alternatives to traditional learning techniques in crises to guarantee that learners really aren't left without a way to learn and to stop the pandemic from growing. (Lizcano, D., Lara, J. A., White, B., & Aljawarneh, S, 2020). Approximately 250 million kids in India were impacted by school closures as a result of COVID-19-induced lockdown (Ramaswamy, N., et al 2021). The benefit from this sort of education was that e-learning is the best alternative available to ensure that diseases do not spread since it ensures geographical distance. Several challenges which arise due the pandemic was: Curbing dropouts through-post pandemic period, weakening of education and welfare system, incorporation of digital enabled learning infrastructure, educators' issues and compatibility, sustainability of self-aided universities/institutions.

This paper was written to better evaluate the significance that predict subsequent adoption of the e-learning method by Indian educators and academicians using route assessment. Also, the main aim of this study is to recognize problems associated with the usage, rewards, shortcomings and complications of e-learning education system in India higher education system through analyzing the perceptions of Indian educators who opted this method of learning during covid-19 pandemic.

REVIEW OF LITERATURE

- **Sustainable Education Development**

In the current situation, universities, as knowledgeable community leaders, can play a critical role in encouraging long term viable means of education, with a comprehensive responsibility for achieving the Global Goals, and, as the related literature suggests, ITC is playing a critical part in achieving the Sustainable development goals (Wakunuma & Jiya, 2019). Educational sustainability is a complicated problem that is revolves around indefinite and uncertainty. As a result, depicting new behavioural patterns demands a high level of involvement, communication, knowledge and patience. Universities may play an important role as innovators in this setting by leveraging the networking, research-oriented education and technological infrastructure. Through their curricula and operational areas, they may provide in-depth information (Howarth et al., 2019) in the education system that will provide an extensive support to promote sustainability in the education and learning. Education Sustainable Development refers to multidimensional stages of learning surroundings, learning material, and the learning method (UNESCO, 2018).

E-learning platforms, in and of themselves, answer the demand for long-term educational resources, offering multiple benefits and welcoming innovative learning opportunities. Learning accustomed education provides a superior option for employing an e-learning dais, where scholars are well equipped and competent to create self-adaptive surroundings through socializing and inter connecting. E- learning platforms are welcoming students from deprived and isolated places to participate in the knowledge exchange environment. However, in a competitive market, e-learning, like other types of platforms, may be susceptible and fickle, and imitations are hard to regulate (Zarra, 2019).

- **Transformation in Learning in Education for Sustainability**

For sustainability in the education there is a need for transformation in learning methods and this requires the faculty and academics commitment. The change in the content and methods can only be materialized when the faculty are motivated to put their sincere effort, and innovative ideas. It has been observed that there is limited example of complete reform in curriculum and its reorientation towards sustainability (Von Blottnitz et al., 2015).

Due to the global swift advancement of Information, Communication and Technologies (ICT) and the boom in the adoption of Artificial Intelligence (AI), online learning has become cohesive with the traditional educational structure (Corbeil, J. R., & Corbeil, M. E, 2015). Information Communication and Technologies (ICT) rules the educational world, and our industries are based mainly on it. Since the inception of E-Learning throughout the mid-1990s, fundamental transition has been visible in a variety of sectors in postsecondary learning, with far-reaching implications for the spread of sustainable growth. According to (Gaebel, M et al., (2014) 'E-learning' is a tool which is utilized in educational domain through various kinds of ICT and automated gadgets. In industrialized countries, e-learning has changed conventional education into more flexible and efficient learning. The emergence of the E-Learning technique was a game-changing revolution in the education business.

Higher education is being redefined by pedagogical and technical advancements. E-learning has been at the core of this confluence. Sequential excellence and cost-cutting demands are laying the groundwork for higher education reform. The use of pervasive and low-cost technology to access knowledge and connection of learners has substantially transformed higher education thought. It is commonly assumed that new technology will change the way people learn. Many proponents of e-learning believe that everyone should have a basic understanding of technology and be able to use it to achieve educational goals.

The benefits of new, ubiquitous, and strong telecommunication infrastructure, as well as their capacity to form and foster networks of users, have gradually ushered e-learning into postsecondary education's forefront. Through facilitating educator and pupil exchanges, curriculum material delivery, and e-learning evaluations, e-learning technological advances have made it feasible to establish a digital learning environment on the Internet. Digital and communications technology have aided in the transformation of conventional media, like books, charts, figures, and whiteboard text, into online and interaction versions of education. Educators may use the Technology to browse various new domains of educational services and resources from everywhere and during any time. In the process of developing academic technologies, improving student learning effectiveness and educators experience has been the main focus of attention. It provides strong and long-lasting learning experiences by utilizing social networks, such as online communities, where learners discuss, develop, and exchange knowledge/information.

E-learning is a critical component of the current educational system, since it transforms the overall education framework and is already one of the most popular subjects among intellectuals (Abou El-Seoud, M. S., et al, 2014). E-learning has become a popular way for colleges all around the globe to provide educational resources in postsecondary learning. As a result of these developments, there is a growing demand for education that may be delivered in a variety of ways. As stated by (Aljawarneh, S. A., 2020) various methods used for e-learning are internet-based education, communicating education, digital education, computer-enabled education and web-enabled teaching are acknowledged as the mediums of E-learning systems.

Yet, in industrialized countries, research on the implementation of the e-learning approach, particularly on topic areas, is still sparse. The importance of technology in transforming the learning experience, supporting sustainable education, and enabling remote learning instruction for educators and students all over the world has opened up a world of opportunities.

Universities must keep up with the requirements and aspirations in the present higher education (HE) system, which is undergoing ongoing transition. As a result, technological advancement and e-learning technologies are becoming extremely relevant in the execution of university operations, with institutions progressively engaging with online systems and equipment (Alalwan, N., et al, 2019). Throughout the adoption of digital and online education in universities, problems such as providing funding, training, improved working conditions, technological background, skills, copyright security, and professional growth are always essential (Maatuk, A. M , et al, 2021). Plenty of the beliefs that regulate individuals have altered as a result of today's amazing breakthroughs. By far the most influential factor in education transformation is the subject to the growth of ICT infrastructure is this contemporary world.

- **E-Learning**

New advanced developments in technical knowhow have bridged the gap between distance education and traditional face to face education system (McBrien et al., 2009). Online mode of learning, multimedia-based learning, computer-centric learning and combined form of learning are all associated to computer-based learning linked with network across the globe that extends the learners an opportunity to adapt knowledge from any corner of the world without any time restrictions" (Cojocariu et al., 2014). Digital education is viewed somewhat as basis for formulating the classroom instruction experience highly pupil- centric, dynamic, and versatile. Synchronous situations provide opportunities for learning using different types of gadgets like smart phones and laptops with internet connection. In the Internet world students can independently learn and interconnect with mentors and peers (Singh & Thurman, 2019). Students attend live classes in the coeval learning environment. There are healthy real time conversations between the professors and students. Asynchronous learning environments are not designed with the modern, updated and structured features. In asynchronous learning environment, the teaching and learning material is not accessible online; it is made accessible to the students in the alternate modes of learning forums.

- **Covid 19 Pandemic and E- Learning.**

A vast chunk of the planet is under quarantine due to the exponential spread of this global pandemic. As a result of Covid-19, many cities have become deserted and its repercussions can be seen in all educational institutions. A vast chunk of the planet is under quarantine due to the alarming spread of this global pandemic. Academic institutions have been asked to adapt an online mode of education as a result of the Corona Virus. As a result of the crisis, universities that were previously inflexible will be compelled to acknowledge innovative technologies. The economic potential of e-learning will be asserted by the disaster. Using online teaching possibilities, we can profess to a significant number of people at any time and from across the world. Many academic higher education institutions have completely databased their processes, recognizing the importance of doing so.

During the spread of this fatal disease, these digital services are required in which video and audio communication can be made possible with students. The online platforms should equip students with multimedia technologies to make their classes live and interactive. The online classes should also be facilitated with recordings option of previous lectures, so the student can access the lecture later during internet connectivity problems. (Basilaia et al., 2020). In the middle of the pandemonium, digital learning is blossoming as a victorious standard bearer. There is a demand for a speedy transition to web - based learning pattern; thus, e- learning tools can be extremely valuable in such scenarios. Trello, Google Drive, Momentum, Mural, Just Press Record, Tomato Timer, Camtasia, Elucidat, Articulate Storyline, Google Forms, Google Jam board, Ms Teams, Google Classroom, Google Docs, Wistia, Canva, Grammarly, Zoom, Pexels. These mechanisms are often utilized as a viable substitute for traditional one to one physical classes. (Basilaia et al., 2020).

E-learning is receiving greater significant role in today's classroom context, since it is transforming the overall education structure and is among the most major themes among higher education (Samir et al. 2014). It is described as the application of various types of ICT and smart gadgets in the classroom (Gaebel et al. (2014).

E-Learning, is primarily strives to employ information and communications technology to assist and accelerate all forms of educating and learning situations (ICT). This is made up of a variety of innovations, techniques, and applications. Web - based learning, collaborative learning, online tutorials, and blogs and social networking platforms are some of the learning and teaching environments for E-Learning. Instructional videos, virtual world tour, online interactive sessions are examples of digital software and tools that can be used to create online learning.

The wide definition of E-Learning also demonstrates that online teaching and learning not necessarily have to precede the web and Internet, as a diversity of knowledge contexts and delivery methods may be applied beyond the use of internet. The majority of the learners around the world are unable to access online mode of education because they are residing in extremely rural areas which have restricted internet connectivity and therefore cannot access to online learning. Due to high benefits of maximum participants wants to join the e-learning programme and wants to get enrolled in universities and colleges to save their travelling time and expenses. (Ms & Toro, 2013).

Most subscribers of e-learning portals believe digital learning makes it easier to manage e-learning and allows learners to easily retrieve instructional resources (Gautam, 2020; Mukhtar et al. 2020). The expenditures associated with conventional learning are also reduced to a great extent with the concept of e-learning as there is no travelling cost involved. Organizational burden of maintaining attendance registers, students' entry exit burden, preparation of class notes and other physical hurdles were all greatly reduced by e-learning.

- **E-Learning and Role of Instructors**

According to the study of (Yengin et al. 2011), online instructors play a very important function in the web-based learning. As a consequence, it is essential to review the problems that affect instructors' efficiency. Satisfaction is one of the factors that influences the project's functionality and speakers' performances. The findings revealed that the features associated with teachers' satisfaction in e-learning systems were examined in order to create a simple program named the "E-learning Achievement Model for Educators' Overall satisfaction," which is related to social, logical, and scientific communications of coaches in the complete online learning system. In distance learning, the key role is of faculty coordinators who are working hard to deliver quality content to the students who are residing at remote locations. As a result, instructors' opinions of virtual learning must be investigated and recognized in order to bring awareness for the growth and enhancement of learning process quality.

The Arab Open University in Jordan has been used as a research study for academic staff perspectives of virtual learning programs by (Saleh and Mrayan (2016). The researcher concluded that faculty's perceptions of the efficiency of distance learning, the relationship between the instructor and the student, the institute's offered technology, the instructional approaches employed, and student achievement. Despite preferring traditional education and hybrid courses in teacher training programs, researchers observed that faculty members are typically happy with online education.

- **Educators Perspectives**

Gürer et al. (2016) investigated the perspectives of educators who have taught online in order to enhance the distant education system. They spoke with 12 teachers in order to come up with some recommendations for improving web - based learning. From the viewpoints of the surveyed teachers, the study illustrates the good and bad aspects of online learning.

Shreaves (2019) designed a survey at Pacific Lutheran University on lecturers' perspectives of e-learning in order to identify the elements that support and impede virtual learning implementation. The study's major purpose is to support and stimulate Pacific Lutheran University's use of digital training. The theory of planned behaviour (TPB) is used to give an institutional theory through which to study the effect of mindsets, behavioural control, and behavioural intention, and half of those surveyed identified 17 elements that determine about whether or not to learn digitally.

Boliger and Wasilik divide the satisfaction of educators into three categories: teacher-related, pupil-related, and organization. Faculty judgments about the overall advantages of e-learning platforms have an impact on student happiness, according to their study. Academic staff, for example, prefer to instruct digitally since they believe it allows them to reach a more varied number of students and that the communication methods are more involved with students in an online learning environment.

Faculty views of digital learning as an academic exercise and a desire in employing technology were considered as strong instructor satisfaction criteria by Boliger and Wasilik. But at the other extreme, researchers suggest that academicians desire trustworthy and consistent techniques to complete their jobs, and that they'll be disappointed if they are unable to do such duties because they are unable to utilize them.

According to Rockwell et al., the majority of instructors are apprehensive regarding teaching course load in online and blended educational programs. Teachers feel that electronic learning takes substantially longer than one to one offline instruction. To make e-learning methods more effective Moore identifies web-based learning performance parameters using the Sloan Consortium's five-pillar approach. Instructional efficacy, economic viability, accessibility, teacher sense of accomplishment, and student performance are all elements in this paradigm. A set of variables for e-learning are presented to promote instructor satisfaction is presented in their model. As a result, teachers must make a significant contribution to and gain advantage from e-learning; teachers should be acknowledged for educating students and undertaking research to enhance teaching online; and faculty should be encouraged to share their knowledge, strategies, and insight regarding online learning.

Samuel (2016) investigated the "physical appearance" of an educational process, or the fact that shows some misleading appearance of anyone present in a physical classroom.

The purpose of the research was to learn more about how faculty consider the application of using online courses and understand involvement of the students. For example, (Frazer et al. (2017) did research on instructor impressions of virtual professional nursing education. Their objective was to identify and convey instructional efficiency and attributes in an internet context where instructors and students do not have to be available online at the same time. To accomplish this, eleven professors were questioned. The investigation arrived at the conclusion by recommending some helpful methods for digital learning.

Wingo et al. (2017) performed a literature review from 1995 to 2015 to assess instructor perspectives of online instruction. To do this, they looked at 67 research. The analysis uncovered challenges that teachers face while educating online, including academic achievement, requisite technical assistance, job duty cycle, and more. McKenzie (2019) did a participant observation that looked into educator/pupil contact in distance learning and examined several forms of exchanges as well as certain connection impediments. This research offers teachers and program directors with relevant and extensive explanations of cutting-edge instructor/student online engagement approaches.

- **E-Learning Benefits & Drawbacks**

The research detailed in (GOYAL & S., 2012) aimed to highlight the relevance of digital-learning in current education and to demonstrate its benefits and drawbacks. The possibility of using E-learning instead of traditional classroom instruction was also examined, as was the contrast with Instructor Led Training (ILT). Furthermore, the studies revealed the fundamental disadvantages of ILT in organizations and how Digital-learning might help overcome these issues.

When it comes to time, place, and medical issues, digital-learning is a great option. It improves expertise and efficacy by allowing entry to a large quantity of data, improves cooperation, and develops instructional connections. Despite the fact that digital-learning can improve educational standards, there is a debate regarding having digital-learning resources open, that result in improved academic achievement just for particular forms of collective assessments. Virtual -learning, on the other hand, would lead to excessive usage of specific sites. Furthermore, it is unable to handle sectors that necessitate research work. The biggest disadvantage of adopting e-learning is the lack of important close relations, not only between professors and students, but also among peers (Somayeh et al. 2016). In comparison to wealthy nations, emerging economies confront a number of problems when it comes to implementing digital-learning, including inadequate web access, a lack of expertise about how to utilize smart technologies, and poor content production (Aung & Khaing, 2015). Many instructors, particularly at the higher education level in developing nations, are yet unfamiliar with the supply of content such as audio-video and technological applications (Aljawarneh, 2020; Lara et al. 2020; Lizcano et al. 2020).

By interpreting the viewpoints of learners and lecturers that utilize this method of learning in protracted uncommon situations, this study attempts to uncover concerns connected to the utilization, advantages, disadvantages, and difficulties of digital-learning programs in a public institution. The study's participants were students and university staff from the University of Benghazi's Faculty of Information Technology. Students and teachers have been given two sorts of surveys. To accomplish the desired outcomes, four factors are characterized: the degree about which digital-learning is employed, as well as the advantages, disadvantages, and impediments to the Faculty of IT's deployment of E-learning. In the statistical analysis of the results, the explanatory approach is applied. By analyzing the data, they were able to come up with some encouraging outcomes that show some of the issues, challenges, and benefits of implementing the E-learning approach in higher education.

- **Barriers in Virtual Teaching and Research**

Though there are number of techniques which are easily accessible for online teaching, and occasionally there is possibility, lot of problems may occur. Users of the techniques may not be interested in reading the instructions. Learners seldom find opportunity to perform web - based learning as more time and flexibility is required. One of the significant problem of E- learning is personal involvement. Learners aspires for two-way communication, which is a great challenge for the instructors.

The process of learning achieves maximum potential when students apply whatever they've acquired over the years. Online information can be explanatory at times, making it difficult for learners to perform and understand successfully. Core curriculum that isn't up to par is likewise a huge concern. Learners believe that the main impediments to online learning are a scarcity of network, technology factors, and issues in comprehending educational objectives (Song et al., 2004).

Learners are more likely to be underprepared towards a variety of virtual-learning and intellectual abilities. Their preparation to use E- learning is very poor (Parkes et al., 2014).

- **Remedies for Making Online Learning More Efficient and Effective**

Although there are various drawbacks in E-learning, but its advantages cannot be denied in critical situations. One could always just come up with answers to these problems. In advance making the video tapes of lectures, verifying the material in advance, and keeping a Back Up Plan on hand may all help to ensure that perhaps the education process is not disrupted. It is very pertinent to understand that E-learning should be engaging, collaborative, and innovative. To make the E- learning effective instructors need to provide deadlines to the learners.

It is necessary to take feasible, steps to personalize the process of learning. Learners should be given individualized attention so that they may readily adjust to this new virtual classroom context. To connect with learners, teachers can make use of social media and numerous national and international platforms. Virtual courses should be intended to be innovative, engaging, meaningful, pupil-focused, and cluster based (Partlow & Gibbs, 2003). Instructors should focus more in developing effective web training and learning methodologies. Efficient web tutorials encourage the students to provide comments, make suggestions, and deepen their understanding of the course material (Keeton, 2004). Through online guidance, universities should concentrate on methodological concerns and stress student involvement, experiential understanding, and research-based learning (Kim & Bonk, 2006).

The problem for educational establishments isn't discovering innovative innovation and implementing it, but also reinventing education in order to assist learners and university employees desiring online learning assistance.

MAIN FOCUS AND RATINALE OF THE CHAPTER

In the 21st century the educational institutions around the world are working to provide quality education in all the countries. With the continuing development in the e-learning platforms a great shift can be seen from traditional modes of education to AI based Education to provide lifelong learning prospects to the students. E- learning offers to reduce the geographical and societal borders to propose remote education, this is moving towards amalgamations of academic values and opinions. The implementation of e-learning technology has also resulted in certain complications on academic professionals. In the timeline of COVID 19 Pandemic big number of Schools, Universities and Institutions have appreciated the vitality of E-learning as crucial element of their education scheme. Many Universities have arranged the Information and communication technologies (ICTs) training sessions to propose exclusive instructive and training prospects as they expand the teaching opportunities. Consequently, additional research needs to be carried out to have a more detailed understanding about the complications, compensations, and challenges of e-learning in higher education. One of the reasons of difficulty in e- learning is the excess use of AI based technology. It is generating an undesirable stress on the employees, which are leading to strict monitoring on e-learning system, to check the efficacy of e-learning system. The effective usage of e-learning structure heavily depends on cognizance of acceptance factors of the system. The implementation is challenged by the various difficulties level in the system as it is a new area to explore. The discrepancy in the standardised agreement stating about the serious aspects and issues that help in for the successful implementation of e-learning structure during COVID-19 pandemic. The reported problems have the serious impact that can affect the Academician quality in the class interactive sessions. Lack of Personal interactive sessions with the students are the foremost disadvantage of e-learning application. Another disadvantage of e-learning is that most of the information is shared theoretically. The practical portion teaching is likely another challenge faced by the academicians during the pandemic period. Students have learned theoretically without practical applications. The face-to-face interaction is missed during e-learning, which is the major portion of pedagogy to analyse learners learning level. Some additional difficulties related to e-learning faced by the academicians is in the online assessments criteria. Issues associated to the safety and security of online education programs and user trustworthiness are among the challenges of e- learning. Technological misuse is also one of the biggest threats in online teaching.

Limited study in Indian context created the scope for this study. The emphasis of this chapter is to highlight the challenges and factors that influence the usage of AI enabled e-learning system during COVID-19 pandemic; though the e-learning systems were introduced in many universities few years back but the pace for its adaptability was enhanced during the COVI 19, without any proper guidance and support to the teaching staff. This study seeks to investigate and identify the factors that impacts the usage of e-learning system during COVID-19 pandemic by the teachers. This study will explore the teachers' perceptions towards e- learning and its' s impact on their teaching and the learning of the learners, it will provide contextual information on usage pattern and nature of e- learning.

METHODOLGY

For the purpose of this study, a combination of exploratory research and descriptive analytical method was used. An online survey was conducted. For data collection Questionnaire were used as data collection tool to collect the primary data from lecturer's, working in education sector. A pre tested questionnaire containing 25 statements on 5- point Likert scale was used to collect the primary data. These statements were included to measure the perceptions of respondents towards the factors influencing e-learning The data was collected from the respondents of above 25 years of age and was analysed using statistical techniques to examine the impact and relationship between the datasets. An exploratory factor analysis was carried out to identify the different factors of e- learning that influences the usage and nature of E-learning.

ANALYSIS AND DISCUSSION

The set of questionnaire were tested for reliability using SPSS 22. The value of Cronbach's alpha was identified to be 0.959. The Cronbach's alpha is above 0.7 that is considered to be good (Nunnaly & Bernstein, 1994). It was observed that mean score of 25 set of questions was found to be 92.4865 and standard deviation was recorded as 19.92861(refer tables 1 & 2)

Table 1. Reliability statistics

Cronbach's Alpha	Cronbach's Alpha Based on Standardized Items	N of Items
.959	.957	25

Table 2. Scale statistics

Mean	Variance	Std. Deviation	N of Items
92.4865	397.149	19.92861	25

Source: Authors compilation

An Exploratory Factor analysis was conducted to ascertain the factors influencing perceptions of the Instructors towards the use of e-learning contributing to usage. An online survey was conducted on 148 respondents on 5-point Likert scale. To examine the correlations, the Bartlett test of Sphericity was used to investigate the variables to examine the overall significance of correlation matrix. The value of KMO (Kaiser-Mayer-Olkin) was found as 0.794 which seems to be good (refer table 3).

Table 3. KMO and Bartlett's Test

Kaiser-Meyer-Olkin Measure of Sampling Adequacy.		.794
Bartlett's Test of Sphericity	Approx. Chi-Square	4375.638
	df	300
	Sig.	.000

Source: Authors compilation

For factor analysis, principal component analysis was used to extract possible factors out of 25 statements. Varimax orthogonal rotation was used and factors with more than 1 Eigen values were considered significant (refer Table 3).

Factor 1: Efficient and Differentiated

The first most prominent factor Efficient & Differentiated with cumulative variance of 51.881% indicates that online teaching provides effective teaching to the diverse classroom community of learners. It helps the learners to understand the subject and meet their needs with different learning styles (Carol Ann Tomlinson, 2004). It helps the teachers to assist in giving one-to-one attention to learners (UNESCO, 2018). It helps in saving lecturers' times. Online classes put emphasis on research topics and research based discussions and acts as a catalyst to solve the queries of learners more effectively in achieving individual learners' needs. Lecturers are of the opinion that online learning helps the learners to work collaboratively with peers in the classroom and equips them more effectively for future employment. Online instructors play a very important function in the on line learning (Yengin et al. 2011).

Factor 2: Effective Communication and Accessibility

The second factor with cumulative variance of 8.350% suggests that online classes improves the communication among learners and students and help them in presenting written work/data more effectively. It helps the teachers to enable the students to work in collaboration with their peers. Effective in depth information in the online class through the curricula and operational areas (Howarth et al., 2019), promotes sustainability in the education and learning and helps the learner to access missed lectures and they can retrieve instructional resources easily (Gautam, 2020; Mukhtar et al. 2020) and organise their work more effectively when the online classes are recorded (Basilaia et al., 2020)

Table 4. Factor matrix

S. No	Items	Factor Loadings	% Variance Explained	Factor	Alpha
1.	online classes help to develop learners' understanding of the subject	787			
2.	online classes help to meet the needs of learners with different learning styles	.826			
3	online classes help to track learners' progress	.729			
4.	online classes help to deliver differentiated lessons	.777			
5.	online classes are efficient	.823			
6	In online teaching individual target setting for learners are manageable	.750			
7.	online classes help to assist in giving one-to-one attention to learners in the	.672	51.881	Efficient & Differentiated	.959
8.	online classes help to save lecturers' time by using online resources	.755			
9.	online classes emphasize on research topics and research based discussions	.803			
10.	helps in achieving individual learners' needs	.722			
11.	online classes help to solve the queries of learners more effectively	.746			
12.	it is easy to work collaboratively with peers in the classroom	.740			
13.	help to equip learners more effectively for future employment	.748			
14	online classes help to improve how staff communicate with learners	.662			
15	online classes help to present written work/data more effectively by the students	.570	8.350	Effective communication & Accessibility	.885
16	help to work collaboratively with peers outside of the classroom	.776			
17	help to access missed lectures	.786			
18.	help to organize their work more effectively	.559			
19	I have attempted to apply online teaching technique in my classroom, but I still	.706			
20	online classes have increased my technological literacy	.908	7.819	Technological Efficacy	.755
21	online classes make course materials easily available to learners	686			
22	I have experience with online teaching	.772			
23	online classes help to create visual presentations	.857	5.139	Virtual Competence	.782
24	help the learners to submit their assignments/work on time	.675			
25	I feel comfortable using digital portfolios with my class	.912	4.319	Friendly & easy to use	.675

Source: Authors compilation

Factor 3: Technological Efficacy

The next factor is Technological Efficacy with 7.819 value of cumulative variance. This factor indicates the efficacy of the teachers towards the technology of e-learning and AI. Technological efficacy is built up when the teachers are aware how to operate online teaching techniques in the class. Instructors are of the opinion that during COVID 19 lockdown they have attempted to apply online teaching technique in their classroom, and with the continuous usage online classes have increased their technological literacy. It was easier for the teachers to provide the course materials to the learners. Learners prefers e- learning as it is easy to use and helps in getting the job specific skills (Singh Anita, Singh Lata, 2017). But many instructors, particularly at the higher education level, are yet unfamiliar with the supply of content such as audio-video and technological applications (Aljawarneh, 2020; Lara et al. 2020; Lizcano et al. 2020).

Factor 4: Virtual Competence

The fourth important factor is Virtual Competence having cumulative variance 5.139%. Instructors are of the opinion that experience in e-learning and virtual competence positively influence the outcome of e-learnings (Zeying Wan, Yinglei Wang, Nicole Haggerty, 2008). Virtual competence helps in using digital portfolios in the class and helps to create effective visual presentations and also helps the learners to submit their assignments/work on time.

Factor 5: Friendly and Easy to Use

The last factor with cumulative variance of 4.319% depicts that Instructors feel comfortable using digital portfolios in their class.

FUTURE RESEARCH DIRECTIONS

This study is limited to E-Learning, the future research directions related to the sub-fields like artificial intelligence, machine learning, and deep learning needs further analysis. There is a huge scope to conduct future research in this area.

CONCLUSION

From the study conducted above, it can be concluded that E-learning played a very important role during pandemic COVID 19. It has been observed that though the traditional teaching and learning cannot totally overcast the education system and may never completely replace physical or face to face learning but e-learning extends educational resources to individuals who may not have the access otherwise. Further it can be assumed that e-learning will continue to grow as it is sustainable and it has added value to the education system by its high degree of efficiency. Findings of the study indicates that one of the major factor that influence the E–learning is

Efficient & Differentiated that caters the diverse classroom community of learners and the other factors that impacts the E- learning are Effective Communication & Accessibility, Technological Efficacy, Virtual Competence and Friendly & easy to use.

REFERENCES

Abou El-Seoud, M. S., Taj-Eddin, I. A., Seddiek, N., El-Khouly, M. M., & Nosseir, A. (2014). E-learning and students' motivation: A research study on the effect of e-learning on higher education. *International Journal of Emerging Technologies in Learning, 9*(4), 20-26.

Alalwan, N., Al-Rahmi, W. M., Alfarraj, O., Alzahrani, A., Yahaya, N., & Al-Rahmi, A. M. (2019). Integrated three theories to develop a model of factors affecting students' academic performance in higher education. *IEEE Access: Practical Innovations, Open Solutions, 7*, 98725–98742. doi:10.1109/ACCESS.2019.2928142

Aljawarneh, S. A. (2020). Reviewing and exploring innovative ubiquitous learning tools in higher education. *Journal of Computing in Higher Education, 32*(1), 57–73. doi:10.100712528-019-09207-0

Anita, S., & Lata, S. (2017). E-Learning for Employability Skills: Students Perspective. *Procedia Computer Science, 122*, 400-406.

Basilaia, G., Dgebuadze, M., Kantaria, M., & Chokhonelidze, G. (2020). Replacing the classic learning form at universities as an immediate response to the COVID-19 virus infection in Georgia. *International Journal for Research in Applied Science and Engineering Technology, 8*(3), 101–108. doi:10.22214/ijraset.2020.3021

Cojocariu, V. M., Lazar, I., Nedeff, V., & Lazar, G. (2014). SWOT anlysis of e-learning educational services from the perspective of their beneficiaries. *Procedia: Social and Behavioral Sciences, 116*, 1999–2003. doi:10.1016/j.sbspro.2014.01.510

Corbeil, J. R., & Corbeil, M. E. (2015). E-learning: Past, present, and future. In International Handbook of E-Learning Volume 1 (pp. 79-92). Routledge.

Frazer, C., Sullivan, D. H., Weatherspoon, D., & Hussey, L. (2017). Faculty perceptions of online teaching effectiveness and indicators of quality. *Nursing Research and Practice, 2017*, 2017. doi:10.1155/2017/9374189 PMID:28326195

Fredericksen, E., Pickett, A., Shea, P., Pelz, W., & Swan, K. (2000). *Factors influencing faculty satisfaction with asynchronous teaching and learning in the SUNY learning network*. Academic Press.

Gaebel, M., Kupriyanova, V., Morais, R., & Colucci, E. (2014). *E-Learning in European Higher Education Institutions: Results of a Mapping Survey Conducted in October-December 2013*. European University Association.

Gautam, P. (2020). *Advantages and Disadvantages of Online Learning*. https://elearningindustry.com/advantages-and-disadvantages-online-learning

Goyal, S. (2012). E-Learning: Future of education. *Journal of Education and Learning, 6*(2), 239-242.

Gürer, M., Tekinarslan, E., & Yavuzalp, N. (2016). Opinions of instructors who give lectures online about distance education. *Turkish Online Journal of Qualitative Inquiry, 7*(1), 47–78.

Howarth, R., Ndlovu, T., Ndlovu, S., Molthan-Hill, P., & Puntha, H. (2019). Integrating education for sustainable development into a higher education institution: Beginning the journey. *Emerald Open Research, 1*, 9. doi:10.12688/emeraldopenres.13011.1

Jain, S., Lall, M., & Singh, A. (2021). Teachers' voices on the impact of COVID-19 on school education: Are ed-tech companies really the panacea? *Contemporary Education Dialogue, 18*(1), 58–89. doi:10.1177/0973184920976433

Keeton, M. T. (2004). Best online instructional practices: Report of phase I of an ongoing study. *Journal of Asynchronous Learning Networks, 8*(2), 75–100.

Kim, K.-J., & Bonk, C. J. (2006). The future of online teaching and learning in higher education: The survey says. *EDUCAUSE Quarterly, 4*, 22–30.

Lara, J. A., Aljawarneh, S., & Pamplona, S. (2020). Special issue on the current trends in E-learning Assessment. *Journal of Computing in Higher Education, 32*(1), 1–8. doi:10.100712528-019-09235-w

Lizcano, D., Lara, J. A., White, B., & Aljawarneh, S. (2020). Blockchain-based approach to create a model of trust in open and ubiquitous higher education. *Journal of Computing in Higher Education, 32*(1), 109–134. doi:10.100712528-019-09209-y

Maatuk, A. M., Elberkawi, E. K., Aljawarneh, S., Rashaideh, H., & Alharbi, H. (2021). The COVID-19 pandemic and E-learning: Challenges and opportunities from the perspective of students and instructors. *Journal of Computing in Higher Education*, 1–18. PMID:33967563

Mashamba-Thompson, T. P., & Crayton, E. D. (2020). Blockchain and artificial intelligence technology for novel coronavirus disease 2019 self-testing. *Diagnostics (Basel), 10*(4), 198. doi:10.3390/diagnostics10040198 PMID:32244841

McBrien, J. L., Cheng, R., & Jones, P. (2009). Virtual spaces: Employing a synchronous online classroom to facilitate student engagement in online learning. *International Review of Research in Open and Distributed Learning, 10*(3).

Mckenzie, W. (2019). *Experiences of graduate-level Faculty regarding interaction in online courses* (Doctoral dissertation). Sam Houston State University.

Moore, J. C. (2002). *Elements of Quality: The Sloan-C Tm Framework*. Olin College-Sloan-C.

Ms, P., & Toro, U. (2013). A review of literature on knowledge management using ICT. *Higher Education, 4*(1), 62–67.

Parkes, M., Stein, S., & Reading, C. (2015). Student preparedness for university e-learning environments. *The Internet and Higher Education, 25*, 1–10. doi:10.1016/j. iheduc.2014.10.002

Partlow, K. M., & Gibbs, W. J. (2003). Indicators of constructivist principles in internet-based courses. *Journal of Computing in Higher Education, 14*(2), 68–97. doi:10.1007/BF02940939

Rockwell, S. K., Schauer, J., Fritz, S., & Marx, D. B. (1999). Incentives and obstacles influencing higher education faculty and administrators to teach via distance. Faculty Publications: Agricultural Leadership, Education & Communication Department, 53.

Saleh, A., & Mrayan, S. A. (2016). Faculty Perceptions of Online Teacher Education Programs in Jordan: A Case Study. *Asian Journal of Education and e-Learning, 4*(6).

Samuel, A. (2016). *Faculty perceptions and experiences of" presence" in the online learning environment* (Doctoral dissertation). The University of Wisconsin-Milwaukee.

Shreaves, D. (2019). *Faculty Perceptions of Online Teaching at a Mid-Sized Liberal Arts University in the Pacific Northwest: A Mixed Methods Study*. Academic Press.

Singh, V., & Thurman, A. (2019). How many ways can we define online learning? A systematic literature review of definitions of online learning (1988-2018). *American Journal of Distance Education, 33*(4), 289–306. doi:10.1080/08923647.2019.166 3082

Somayeh, M., Dehghani, M., Mozaffari, F., Ghasemnegad, S. M., Hakimi, H., & Samaneh, B. (2016). The effectiveness of E-learning in learning: A review of the literature. *International Journal of Medical Research & Health Sciences, 5*(2), 86-91.

Song, L., Singleton, E. S., Hill, J. R., & Koh, M. H. (2004). Improving online learning: Student perceptions of useful and challenging characteristics. *The Internet and Higher Education, 7*(1), 59–70. doi:10.1016/j.iheduc.2003.11.003

Tomlinson, C. A. (2004). Sharing responsibility for differentiating instruction. *Roeper Review, 26*(4), 188. doi:10.1080/02783190409554268

UNESCO. (2018). *Guidebook on Education for Sustainable Development for Teachers. Effective teaching and learning in teacher education institutions in Africa.* UNESCO.

von Blottnitz, H., Case, J. M., & Fraser, D. M. (2015). Sustainable development at the core of undergraduate engineering curriculum reform: A new introductory course in chemical engineering. *Journal of Cleaner Production, 106*, 300–307. doi:10.1016/j.jclepro.2015.01.063

Wakunuma, K., & Jiya, T. (2019). Stakeholder Engagement and Responsible Research & Innovation in promoting Sustainable Development and Empowerment through ICT. *European Journal of Sustainable Development, 8*(3), 275–275. doi:10.14207/ejsd.2019.v8n3p275

Wan, Z., Wang, Y., & Haggerty, N. (2008). Why people benefit from e-learning differently: The effects of psychological processes on e-learning outcomes. *Information & Management, 45*(8), 513–521. doi:10.1016/j.im.2008.08.003

Wingo, N. P., Ivankova, N. V., & Moss, J. A. (2017). Faculty perceptions about teaching online: Exploring the literature using the technology acceptance model as an organizing framework. *Online Learning, 21*(1), 15–35. doi:10.24059/olj.v21i1.761

Yengin, I., Karahoca, A., & Karahoca, D. (2011). E-learning success model for instructors' satisfactions in perspective of interaction and usability outcomes. *Procedia Computer Science, 3*, 1396–1403. doi:10.1016/j.procs.2011.01.021

Zarra, A., Simonelli, F., Lenaerts, K., Luo, M., Baiocco, S., Shenglin, B., … Kilhoffer, Z. (2019). *Sustainability in the Age of Platforms.* EMSD Challenge Fund-Final Report.

Chapter 6
Transformation and Acceptance of Learning Management Systems in HEI

Ashneet Kaur
Jagannath International Management School, India

Seema Wadhawan
Jagannath International Management School, India

Himani Gupta
Jagannath International Management School, India

ABSTRACT

The current pandemic has brought vital transformation in the education sector. The shift from traditional smart class systems to the online virtual mode is a significant change in the education sector all over the world. Introduction of LMS in the higher educational institutes has not only spanned the gap created due to lack of physical presence but has also brought revolutionary change in the dedicated students approach towards the learning system. The chapter focuses on the growth trajectory of the LMS and aims to discuss the desire of students to use LMS over traditional methods. Perceived ease of use and perceived usefulness combined with perceived enjoyment influence students' intentions to use the learning management system (LMS), which lastly affects the academic performance of students.

DOI: 10.4018/978-1-6684-4950-9.ch006

INTRODUCTION

Coronavirus which started in Wuhan in March 2019 changed the fate of lot of countries. It brought transformation in various sectors; Education was one of them. With disruption in technology, the Education sector saw enormous growth in technology-oriented learning and redesigning the existing frameworks. E-learning initiatives enable quality learning frameworks with enormous benefits to teaching with the use of information communication technology (Yusoff et.al, 2015). With internet technology, the use of new ICT tools in learning has been augmented. New tools of learning in the learning classroom have changed the environment of learning and teaching pedagogy (Abdel- Wahab, 2008; Al-Qaysi, 2021). The amalgamation of LMS with e-learning from smartphones has brought a flux of e-learning and the use of LMS. The primary, secondary, and higher education institutions had to shift from the traditional model of education to introduce Learning Management System (LMS) by linking e-learning with LMS (Kasim and Khalid, 2016). Alias and Zainuddin (2005) described this system, as LMS as a "software program or web-based technology used to organize, carry out, and evaluate a certain educational procedure.". The Learning Management system is a web-based application that is customized to handle the content, activities of students, teaching-learning pedagogy, student interaction, assessment, and reports. LMS is not just registration and records of the student, it is much more. LMS is a system where students can have the choice of online course, submitting assignment and activities, evaluation and assessment. The platform facilitates active interaction between teacher and student (Jurubescu, 2008). This mode of learning (LMS) has seen a sharp positive drift in the higher education sector LMS (Fathema, Shannon, & Ross, 2015). According to studies, the global market for learning management systems is anticipated to increase at a CAGR of 18.7% during the forecast period, from $13.38 billion in 2021 to $44.49 billion in 2028. The unprecedented expansion of online education in India is largely a result of its flexibility with regard to timing, possible cost savings associated with attendance, and geographic scope. (Appana. S, 2008). Furthermore, the growth of LMS is directly inclined to the features it offers to its instructor and the student. According to instructor, LMS is a comprehensive application which builds and maintains course website as a teaching learning strategy (Naveh et. al., 2010). According to (Lin & Wang, 2012) LMS is an applicant which help student gather knowledge. There are different types of LMS platform: Open and Commercial. Open source LMS implies that the person or individual can build the LMS such as Moodle. However, it may or may not be free of cost. On the other hand Commercial System which is chargeable may be customised as per the requirement of HEI.A customised LMS system also provides better knowledge management leading to better performance (Thomas A et. al. 2022)

This technology driven system has an edge over traditional learning with respect to faster communication, academic collaboration and learning material (Rahmi et. Al. 2019) and has increased the use of it. Other factors which contribute to the swift growth of the LMS system are its interoperability, automation and custom-made learning. Interoperability is the inclination of the system to integrate and interpret the student data. (Brown, Dehoney, & Millichap, 2015). Thus, posing a major challenge in E learning system (Naim, A. & Alahmari, F., 2020). Also the successful implementation of E learning will finally resort to full automation and technology up-gradation (Govindasamy, T. 2001). LMS system needs to provide a personalised pace of learning based to on the students need. (Abbott et al., 2014).

REVIEW OF LITERATURE

Plethora of theories has explained the phases through which Technology has made its way to acceptance among the consumers. Briefly deliberating these phases to understand the acceptance of technology, the diffusion of Innovation theory propounded by Roger (1995) focused on the idea that innovation and acceptance are likely acceptable after going through specific stages, such as comprehension, persuasion, decision, implementation, and confirmation. As illustrated in the graph below, he created an S-shaped curve of innovators, early adopters, early majority, late majority, and laggards.

Figure 1. Innovation adoption curve
(Roger, 1995)

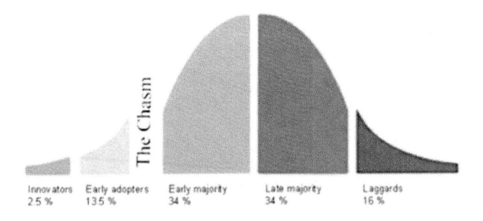

Supplementing Rogers theory, Parsuraman and Colby, 2001 categorised customers' technological readiness into five groups: explorers, pioneers, sceptics, paranoids, and laggards. According to Goodhue et. al., (1995) Task technology Fit highlights that a good fit between technology and its individual impact on usage, majorly used to get the feedback of the novel technology introduced.

One of the most significant theories which contributed in understanding the behavioral intention of the person toward a particular subject was Theory of Reasonable Action (Fishbein and Ajzen, 1975). Defining "attitude" as a person's assessment of a thing, "belief" as a connection between a thing and a characteristic, and "behaviour" as an outcome or a goal. He maintained that attitudes are affective and founded on widely held notions about the behavior's target. The other reason for a set of behaviour is the community or peer approach. Ajzen (1991) along with the two previously discussed factors i.e. Attitude and Subjective Norms introduced the third variable, Perceived Behavioural Control in his theory of planned behaviour. He advocated that it is this variable which motivates the consumers to limit their behaviour. Literature (Bertea, 2009) shows that the usefulness of technology, access of technology, perception towards using the technology, age and gender are some of the factors that lead to generation of attitude towards it

Figure 2. Theory of planned behavior

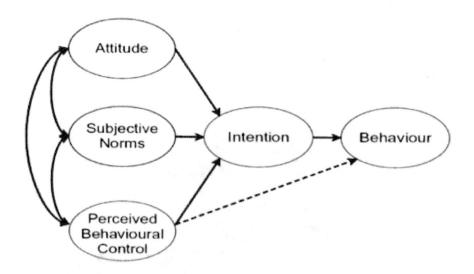

An adaptation of Theory of Reasonable Action (1980), Technology Acceptance Model was familiarized by Fred Davis (1986). TAM caters to the acceptance of technology or information systems by its users. This theory primarily focuses on adoption of information communication technology in line with theory of reasoned action (Taylor & Todd, 1995). He used it to explain the behavior of the computer users across a broad range of computing technologies.

He believed Perceived Usefulness and Perceived Ease of Use have direct influence on the intention of the end user. TAM Model has also been modified and the final version of TAM Model was presented by Venkatesh and Davis (1996). According to this model, external variables affect Perceived Usefulness and Perceived Ease of Use which directly affect the Behavior intention of the user and eliminating the variable of attitude and accept the technology, as shown in Figure 4.

Figure 3. Technological acceptance model
(Davis, 1986)

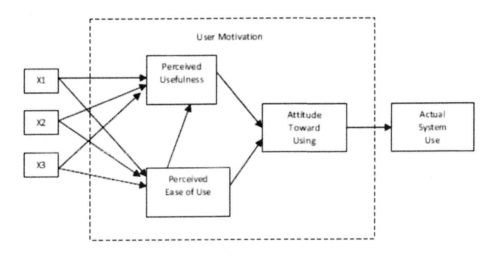

Figure 4. Technological acceptance model
(Venkatesh and Davis, 1996)

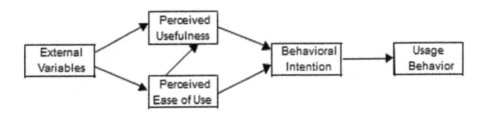

Perceived Ease of Use

The degree to which the learning user views the learning management system as straightforward and easy is the subject of the construct known as perceived ease of use (Davis, 1989). According to earlier studies, students' intentions to use technology for online learning were indirectly affected by perceived ease of use through perceptions of its usefulness and enjoyment. Including Lee (2005) Improving student performance and outcomes is the goal of using the LMS in education. It is crucial to understand how the LMS functions, how to use it, and how easily the students find it to use. E-learning that is web-assisted, online, and software-based is thought to be devoid of the cognitive effort that causes PEU. (Park 2009)

Perceived Usefulness

Previous studies have demonstrated that extrinsic motivation is an ideology that applies whenever an action is taken to achieve a distinct consequence (Ryan and Deci, 2000). Consequently, perceived utility is an extrinsic motive (Davis, Bagozzi, & Warshaw, 1992). Use of Information technology enables the users to improve their performance (Edelman, 1981). This led to the development of customized LMS as it provides the student's flexibility to learn at their own pace and convenience, thus it is likely to make this system more useful. However, the performance of students is based on the willingness to accept the use of the system. Thus, Perceived usefulness is the degree to which users/ students believe that this particular system will enable them to enhance their performance in HEI (Davis, 1989).

Perceived Enjoyment

Pleasure and fulfilment are attained from a certain set of behaviours due to intrinsic motivation (Doll & Ajzen:1992). If someone is driven by their own intrinsic motivation, they are motivated by challenges or enjoyment rather than peer pressure and rewards. (Ryan and Deci:2000) Intrinsic motivation, which is defined by a student's delight, ecstasy, pleasure, and positive holistic experience, is a key factor in determining user acceptance and usage behavior of web-based learning, according to previous research (Saadé et al., 2008). (2009) Wang et al. According to the theory put forth by Venkatesh, Speier, and Morris in 2002, people who are intrinsically driven use technology because they love it and frequently underrate how difficult it is to use. The learners of HEI will use the Learning management systems when they view the program for fun, accompanied with learning. The person who experiences pleasure and feel amused in using the application are likely to form an intention to use the system (Davis et. al., 1992). Application based learning when associated with fun indulges user engagement and gives enjoyment. Along with fun the gaming education activity must meet the purpose of learning (Tripathy, 2020). Studies show that emotion of joy and the star rating instill the action to use the learning application (Singh & Suri, 2022). Thus, when the students of HEI perceive the LMS provided as enjoyable, will often use this system.

Intension to Use

This refers to the desire of the user to use the technology in future (Ajzen 1991; Turner et al. 2010) since it is the predictor of actual technology usage. With learning management system being implemented in the HEI and schools, students have created zeal to use it.

Student Academic Performance

Implementation of LMS in the HEI is with the objective to improve the performance of the student. LMS is a tool which enables to plan and conduct student assessment easily. Student assessment is dependent upon the scores they achieve. The perception of student towards LMS used in the HEI for their performance can increase its use and also the performance. Positive learning, performance expectation will create an urge among the students to use the system and e-learning mode. Students and teachers will develop the attitude towards it only if they recognize the application will improve the learning (Rahamat et al., 2012)

Proposed Model

There has been a significant amount of research on technology acceptance with regard to online learning and learning management systems. However, there is a scarcity of research on the relationship between student academic achievement and the constructs of the technology acceptance model, such as perceived ease of use, perceived usefulness, and reported enjoyment. The TAM model, created by Davis (1989), demonstrates the use and acceptance of cutting-edge technology.

Today, gamut of information is available for different users. LMS is an integrated management system which is being used by schools and HEI to plan, implement and evaluate the learning of students. In the digital era it has become imperative to study the rationale behind the application of TAM for Learning Management systems. This system provides credibility and authenticity for learning. Students take up the LMS, not only for the useful content, easy availability but also due to the enjoyment they get while studying online from this system. Thus, in the current chapter, to the above variables of perceived usefulness and perceived ease of use we propose to study perceived enjoyment as a factor that influences the intention of user toward learning management systems and student performance.

Figure 5. Proposed model

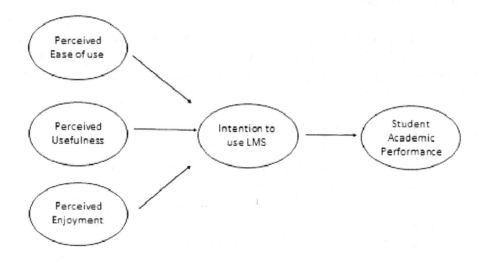

Proposition of Relationship

Figure 5 gives the conceptual framework of how perceived ease of use, perceived usefulness, perceived enjoyment influence the intention to use and in turn effecting student academic performance.

Proposition 1: Perceived Ease of Use, Perceived Usefulness, and Perceived Enjoyment influence the Intention to Use LMS.

Proposition 2: Intention to use LMS leads to effect on Student Academic performance.

RESEARCH METHODOLOGY

To prove the above prepositions a preliminary study was conducted on 100 people. A self-structured questionnaire was made to find out the factors which might affect the intention to use LMS. The demographic profile of the sample is discussed below

Table 1. Demographic profile

Gender	Frequency	Percentage
Male	43	43%
Female	57	57%
	100	
Age	**Frequency**	**Percentage**
12-20	27	27%
20-25	64	64%
25-30	8	6%
Total	**100**	

Table 1 describes the demographic profile of the respondents. Out of 100 respondents 57 were female and 43 were males. More than 60% of the respondents belonged to age bracket of 20-25 years. So most students who were at Undergraduate and Postgraduate levels were taken as samples.

The reliability of the questionnaire was checked using Cronbach Alpha in SPSS containing all 38 statements.

Table 2. Reliability statistic

Cronbach's Alpha	No of Items	N of Items
0.876	38	38

The Cronbach's a score for all the variables are .876 which is higher than i.e.0.60 which reflects a good score. Thus, we can say that our questionnaire is reliable and consistent.

KMO and Bartlett's Test

Before conducting the factor analysis, Kaiser–Meyer–Olkin (KMO) and Bartlett 's test of sphericity tests are confirmed as these two tests are the prerequisites and indicate the suitability of the data for factor analysis. The Kaiser–Meyer–Olkin (KMO) measure of sampling adequacy indicates whether the sample size is large enough to extract reliable factors (Field, 2009) and Bartlett 's test of sphericity indicates the relation of the variables pursued to test the fitness of the data.

Table 3. KMO and Bartlett's

Kaiser-Meyer- Olkin Measure of Sampling Adequacy.	.732
Bartlett's Test of Sphericity Approx. Chi-Square	1622.300
Df	703
Sig	.000

Exploratory factor analysis was used to identify all of the variables, yielding three factors. KMO Bartlett's test for sample adequacy was used to determine sample suitability. KMO = 0.732, which is significant at 0.00 and less than p = 0.01, as shown in the above table.

Factor Analysis: Extraction Method

It is a method for breaking down a huge number of variables into smaller groups of factors. This method creates a common score by combining all variables' highest common variance. Three major factors were obtained by the Principal Component Analysis with Varimax solution. Perceived enjoyment is one of them. Only variables with coefficients greater than 0.5 were used.

Factor Loading

From the various reliability test derived, we have received 3 effective factors from the factor analysis

Table 4. Factor loading

FACTOR NAME	Cronbach Alpha
Perceived Ease of Use	0.75
Perceived Usefulness	0.81
Perceived Enjoyment	0.76

The 38 variables were condensed into 3 factor groups using factor analysis. The factor's labelling was assigned using the items with the highest loadings. The first three factors were chosen based on the findings of the factor analysis since they explained a significant amount of the original variance and had Eigenvalues larger than 1.

CONCLUSION AND RECOMMENDATION

Research has been conducted on how e-learning and different platforms are influencing the student intention to use this technology. The present study makes an attempt to understand the how the constructs of technology acceptance model influence the intention to use the new LMS Learning management system. Secondly, it analyzes the effectiveness of student academic performance. Thereby helping the higher education institution to understand where to they need to make amendments in the system to suit the requirement of the students. Technology is the key element to transform the education system. Use of LMS is not only the responsibility of technology department but of top management. The believe management and faculty in LMS in as a student learning tool will capture the attention of students as well. Analysis of data shows that like any other technological system, LMS cater to students by being user friendly, easy to use. Usability is the degree with which student can use system effectively and efficiently. Moreover, the learning system that provides good user experience and requires less learning curve is suggested to apply. This is possible only when the user are trained and motivated to regularly use it. However, motivation and regularity cannot increase the usage of the application, pleasure, interest; enjoyment perception of the system will enhance its usage. Thus by using the learning application system the students can enhance their academic performance. Above all, the new method of teaching by adoption of LMS is beneficial over conventional classroom learning system. This technology assisted paradigm shift has made learning possible anytime and anywhere. Thus, supporting universities to make substantial improvement in learning through LMS system. By doing this the goal of e-learning will be achieved.

REFERENCES

Abbott, J., Basham, J., Nordmark, S., Schneiderman, M., Umpstead, B., Walter, K., & Wolf, M. A. (2014). *Technology-enabled personalized learning: Findings & recommendations to accelerate implementation.* Friday Institute for Educational Innovation. https://www. fi. ncsu. edu/resources/technology-enabled-personalized-learning-findings-recommendations-to-accelerate-implementation

Abdel-Wahab, A. G. (2008). Modeling Students' Intention to Adopt E-learning: A Case from Egypt. *The Electronic Journal on Information Systems in Developing Countries, 34*(1), 1–1. doi:10.1002/j.1681-4835.2008.tb00232.x

Ajzen, I. (1991). The Theory of Planned Behavior. In Organization Behavior and Human Decision Processes. Academic Press, Inc. doi:10.1016/0749-5978(91)90020-T

Al-Nuaimi, M. N., & Al-Emran, M. (2021). Learning management systems and technology acceptance models: A systematic review. *Education and Information Technologies*, 26(5), 5499–5533. doi:10.100710639-021-10513-3

Al-Qaysi, N., Mohamad-Nordin, N., & Al-Emran, M. (2021). Factors affecting the adoption of social media in higher education: a systematic review of the technology acceptance model. *Recent advances in intelligent systems and smart applications*, 571-584.

Al-Rahmi, W.M., Yahaya, N., Aldraiweesh, A.A., Alamri, M.M., Aljarboa, N.A., Alturki, U., & Aljeraiwi, A.A. (2019). Integrating technology acceptance model with innovation diffusion theory: An empirical investigation on students' intention to use E-learning systems. *IEEE Access, 7*, 26797–26809.

Appana, S. (2008). A review of benefits and limitations of online learning in the context of the student, the instructor and the tenured faculty. *International Journal on E-Learning*, 7(1), 5–22.

Bertea, P. (2009). Measuring students' attitude towards e-learning: A case study. *Proceedings of 5th Inter-national Scientific Conference on e-Learning and Software for Education*.

Coogle, C., Floyd, K., Cole, A. W., Timmerman, C. E., Holbeck, R., Greenberger, S., ... Becker-Lindenthal, H. (2015). Synchronous and asynchronous learning environments of rural graduate early childhood special educators utilizing Wimba© and Ecampus. *Journal of Online Learning and Teaching, 11*(2).

Davis, F. D. (1986). *A technology acceptance model for empirically testing new end-user information systems: Theory and results*. Sloan School of Management, Massachusetts Institute of Technology.

Davis, F. D. (1989). Perceived usefulness, perceived ease of use, and user acceptance of information technology. *Management Information Systems Quarterly, 13*(3), 319–340. doi:10.2307/249008

Davis, F. D., Bagozzi, R. P., & Warshaw, P. R. (1992). Extrinsic and intrinsic motivation to use computers in the workplace 1. *Journal of Applied Social Psychology, 22*(14), 1111–1132. doi:10.1111/j.1559-1816.1992.tb00945.x

Davis, F. D., & Venkatesh, V. (1996). A critical assessment of potential measurement biases in the technology acceptance model: Three experiments Internet. *J. Human-Comput. Stud., 45*, 19–45.

Doll, J., & Ajzen, I. (1992). Accessibility and stability of predictors in the theory of planned behavior. *Journal of Personality and Social Psychology*, *63*(5), 754–765. doi:10.1037/0022-3514.63.5.754

Edelman, F. (1981). Managers, computer systems, and productivity. *Management Information Systems Quarterly*, *5*(3), 1–19. doi:10.2307/249287

Fishbein, M., & Ajzen, I. (1975). *Belief, attitude, intention, and behavior: An introduction to theory and research*. Addison-Wesley Pub. Co.

Friedel, J. M., Cortina, K. S., Turner, J. C., & Midgley, C. (2010). Changes in efficacy beliefs in mathematics across the transition to middle school: Examining the effects of perceived teacher and parent goal emphases. *Journal of Educational Psychology*, *102*(1), 102–114. doi:10.1037/a0017590

Goodhue, D. L., & Thompson, R. L. (1995) Task technology fit and individual performance. *Management Information Systems Quarterly*, *19*(2), 213 236 doi:10.2307/249689

Govindasamy, T. (2001). Successful implementation of e-learning: Pedagogical considerations. *The Internet and Higher Education*, *4*(3-4), 287–299. doi:10.1016/S1096-7516(01)00071-9

Jurubescu, T. (2008). Learning content management system. *Revista Informatica Economica*, *4*(48), 91–94.

Jurubescu, T. (2008). Learning Content Management Systems. *Informações Econômicas*, *12*(4), 91 94.

Kasim, N. N. M., & Khalid, F. (2016). Choosing the right learning management system (LMS) for the higher education institution context: A systematic review. *International Journal of Emerging Technologies in Learning*, *11*(6).

Lee, M. K., Cheung, C. M., & Chen, Z. (2005). Acceptance of Internet-based learning medium: The role of extrinsic and intrinsic motivation. *Information & Management*, *42*(8), 1095–1104. doi:10.1016/j.im.2003.10.007

Lin, W. S., & Wang, C. H. (2012). Antecedences to continued intentions of adopting e-learning system in blended learning instruction: A contingency framework based on models of information system success and task technology fit. *Computers and Education*, *58*(1), 88–99. doi:.compe du. 2011.07.008 doi:10.1016/j

Naim, A., & Alahmari, F. (2020). Reference Model of E-learning and Quality to Establish Interoperability in Higher Education Systems. *International Journal of Emerging Technologies in Learning (iJET), 15*(2), 15-28. https://www.learntechlib.org/p/217170/

Naveh, G., Tubin, D., & Pliskin, N. (2010). Student LMS use and satisfaction in academic institutions:The organizational perspective. *The Internet and Higher Education, 13*(3), 127–133. doi:10.1016/j.iheduc.2010.02.004

Parasuraman, A., & Colby, L. C. (2001). *Techno-Ready Marketing*. The Free Press.

Park, S. Y. (2009). An Analysis of the Technology Acceptance Model in Understanding University Students' Behavioral Intention to Use e-Learning. *Journal of Educational Technology & Society, 12*(3), 150–162.

Rahamat, R., Shah, P. M., Din, R., Puteh, S. N., Aziz, J. A., Norman, H., & Embi, M. A. (2012). Measuring learners' perceived satisfaction towards e-learning material and environment. *WSEAS Transactions on Advances in Engineering Education, 3*(9), 72–83.

Rogers Everett, M. (1995). *Diffusion of innovations*.

Ryan, R. M., & Deci, E. L. (2000). Intrinsic and extrinsic motivations: Classic definitions and new directions. *Contemporary Educational Psychology, 25*(1), 54–67. doi:10.1006/ceps.1999.1020 PMID:10620381

Saadé, R. G., Tan, W., & Nebebe, F. (2008). Impact of motivation on intentions in online learning: Canada vs China. *Issues in Informing Science & Information Technology, 5*, 137–147. doi:10.28945/1001

Singh, Y., & Suri, P. K. (2022). An empirical analysis of mobile learning app usage experience. *Technology in Society, 68*, 101929. doi:10.1016/j.techsoc.2022.101929

Taylor, S., & Todd, P. A. (1995). Understanding information technology usage: A test of competing models. *Information Systems Research, 2*(6), 144–178. doi:10.1287/isre.6.2.144

Thomas, A., Prajapati, R. T., & Kaur, A. (2022). Technology-Powered Education Post Pandemic: Importance of Knowledge Management in Education. In S. Iyer, A. Jain, & J. Wang (Eds.), *Handbook of Research on Lifestyle Sustainability and Management Solutions Using AI, Big Data Analytics, and Visualization* (pp. 185-196). IGI Global. . doi:10.4018/978-1-7998-8786-7.ch011

Tripathy, S., & Devarapalli, S. (2021). Emerging trend set by a start-ups on Indian online education system: A case of Byju's. *Journal of Public Affairs, 21*(1), e2128. doi:10.1002/pa.2128

Venkatesh, V., Speier, C., & Morris, M. G. (2002). User acceptance enablers in individual decision-making about technology: Toward an integrated model. *Decision Sciences, 33*(2), 297–316. doi:10.1111/j.1540-5915.2002.tb01646.x

Wang, Y. S., Lin, H. H., & Liao, Y. W. (2010). Investigating the individual difference antecedents of perceived enjoyment in the acceptance of blogging. *World Academy of Science, Engineering and Technology, 67*.

Yusoff, M., McLeay, F., & Woodruffe-Burton, H. (2015). Dimensions driving business student satisfaction in higher education. *Quality Assurance in Education, 23*(1), 86–104. doi:10.1108/QAE-08-2013-0035

Yusoff, R. M. M. (2015). Tahap Kesediaan Pelajar Dalam Penggunaan Teknologi, Pedagogi, Dan Kandungan (TPACK) Dalam Pembelajaran Kurikulum Di IPT. *Proceeding of the 3rd International Conference on Artifical Intelligence and Computer Science (AICS2015)*, 307–315.

Chapter 7
Artificial Intelligence in Financial Portfolio Management

Bikram Pratim Bhuyan
University of Petroleum and Energy Studies, India

T. P. Singh
University of Petroleum and Energy Studies, India

ABSTRACT

In finance, a portfolio is a person's or company's total financial holdings. Portfolio risk and expected return are managed via portfolio optimization. Portfolio optimization is a kind of diversification that decreases portfolio risk by combining assets with varying risk profiles. Since the global financial crisis of 2008, asset management practices have undergone a sea change. This study examines a wide range of artificial intelligence (AI)-based asset management systems, focusing on the most urgent concerns and highlighting the benefits in the analysis of fundamentals and producing new investment strategies. Trading is another area where AI is making a big impact. One of the most intriguing aspects of AI is its ability to analyze vast amounts of data and generate trading tips. Using AI in asset management comes with certain disadvantages as well. AI models are difficult for managers to keep track of since they are often complex and opaque. This research provides a throughout overview of the avenues where AI is used in financial portfolio management.

DOI: 10.4018/978-1-6684-4950-9.ch007

INTRODUCTION

The term 'portfolio' in finance can be defined as an individual's or a company's whole financial assets (Paulson, 1991). There are a wide variety of investments that may be made in the stock market and other financial markets. The term 'portfolio' refers to all of the investments, which may or may not be held in one account. We can think of portfolio management as a method of putting money to work in accordance with the objectives, timetable, and level of risk tolerance. Portfolio management is the process of selecting and monitoring assets including stocks, bonds, and mutual funds (Graves & Sunstein, 1992; Long, 1990). Portfolio risk and projected return are measured and controlled via the process of portfolio optimization. Basically, portfolio optimization is a kind of diversification that reduces the risk of a portfolio by mixing assets with different risk profiles. However, optimization also takes into account the correlations between assets—the degree to which their values tend to move in tandem. Combining stocks from various groups with complementary price movements allows an optimizer to design a portfolio that gives the best return for each level of risk (Brinson et al., 1986; Kalayci et al., 2019).

In the context of artificial intelligence (AI), the phrase covers any technology that allows computers to do tasks formerly only performed by humans (Bullock et al., 2020; Zhao et al., 2020). As an example, Apple's Siri uses NLP algorithms to comprehend English, whereas Amazon's Alexa uses machine learning algorithms to beat a world champion in 'Go'. AI is a popular issue right now since it has disrupted so many businesses in the last few years, including financial services. There has been a shift in some of the industry's most fundamental procedures as a result of fintech, which places a focus on artificial intelligence. Asset allocation, trading, risk management, and other portfolio management functions might be substantially changed by artificial intelligence. In reality, many robo-advisors currently employ these technologies to provide clients with portfolios that perform better out-of-sample while also automatically rebalancing and managing risks with little transaction costs. Asset management firms are increasingly running trading and investing platforms with the use of artificial intelligence and statistical models. AI's usage in asset management is requiring a more systematic analysis of the many approaches and applications involved, as well as the potential and difficulties they offer to the industry ().

This research gives an in-depth look at a broad variety of AI-based asset management applications, emphasizing the most pressing issues. Asset allocation choices are made to design a portfolio with certain risk and return characteristics as part of portfolio management. In this way, artificial intelligence may assist in the examination of fundamentals and generate new investing methods. Additionally, AI may overcome the flaws of conventional portfolio development methods. Artificial

Intelligence has the ability to provide superior asset return and risk estimations and solve portfolio optimization issues with complicated constraints, resulting in portfolios with improved out-of-sample performance ().

AI applications are also widely used in the field of trading (). Artificial intelligence approaches are becoming more important in trading because of the increasing speed and complexity of deals. AI's capacity to analyze massive volumes of data and produce trading signals is one of its most appealing features. A new sector called algorithmic (or algo) trading has emerged as a result of these signals, which can be taught to automatically execute transactions. Furthermore, by automatically assessing the market and then determining the ideal timing, size, and location for trading, AI approaches may push down transaction costs even further.

AI's impact on portfolio risk management is enormous. There has been a dramatic shift in asset management strategies since the financial crisis of 2008. Traditional risk models may no longer be adequate for risk assessments in light of the rising complexity of financial assets and global markets. In addition, AI systems that learn and adapt from data might give additional monitoring tools. The use of artificial intelligence helps risk managers validate and evaluate risk models. Additionally, AI technologies can extract information more effectively from multiple sources of structured or unstructured data, and create more accurate predictions of bankruptcy and credit risk, market volatility, macroeconomic trends, financial crises, and so on than conventional methodologies can. Furthermore, the public's interest in robo-advice has grown significantly in recent years (Belanche et al., 2019). Robotic financial advisers (or robo-advisors) are automated computer systems that provide investors personalized financial advice based on mathematical principles or algorithms. One reason robo-advisors are so popular is that they've been so successful at democratizing financial advice services by making them more affordable and accessible to the average investor. Generation Y investors (millennials), for example, find robo-advisors especially appealing. Typical robo-advising algorithms depend significantly on AI application across all aspects of asset management, with AI serving as the backbone.

The use of artificial intelligence in asset management has its drawbacks, as well. Managers have a hard time keeping track of and scrutinizing AI models since they are typically opaque and sophisticated. Because of the models' dependence on and sensitivity to data, there is a significant potential for error. Poor-quality or inadequate data might lead to incorrectly trained AI models. By failing to properly supervise humans, a lack of knowledge of investing techniques and performance attribution by investors might result, which could lead to systemic disasters. The advantages of AI's research and deployment have yet to be shown, which raises the question of whether such costs can be justified (Winston, 1984).

BACKGROUND

Artificial Intelligence

The field of artificial intelligence is poised to revolutionize the world in the next decade, if not the decade before that. What it is, how it works, why it is essential, and what we can do to address the challenges it presents in the review of this report are all straightforward concepts ().

Artificial intelligence has always been defined in part by its ability to seem intelligent, and this has been true from the beginning of the field's development. People have difficulty distinguishing between robotic and human behaviour, which is why various "Turing tests" have claimed that robots are intelligent. Nowadays, it is typical to include additional requirements in current formulations, such as autonomy and the restriction of intellect to certain domains.

'Artificial Intelligence' is made up of two words. 'Artificial' and 'Intelligent.' These two terms are combined to form the phrase "Artificial Intelligence". In the context of artificial intelligence and non-natural intelligence, the phrases "artificial" and "intelligent" refer to anything made by humans or non-natural entities, respectively. Despite the fact that artificial intelligence is not a system, it is incorporated within it ().

The term artificial intelligence may be defined in a variety of ways, the most common of which is "the study of how to teach computers to accomplish activities that presently human beings can do better." As a result, it is a kind of intelligence that aspires to merge all of the talents that individuals possess into computerised systems. Artificial intelligence may be divided into two categories: based on the ability (Type 1) and functionality or capability (Type 2). The Figure 1 shows the distinction (Dick, 2019; Holzinger et al., 2019).

Figure 1. Artificial intelligence and its sub-types

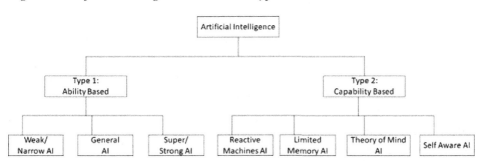

Type 1 AI: It is subdivided into three types.

1. **Artificial Narrow Intelligence**

Weak AI, often known as ANI, is a stage of artificial intelligence in which robots can only do a restricted number of specific tasks. At this time, the machine is merely capable of executing a given set of instructions and does not possess the ability to think for itself (Singh, 2019).

This category contains all of the existing applications of artificial intelligence that we are acquainted with, as well as any future applications. The Artificial Intelligence systems that are part of the ANI platform are listed. These robots are unable to do a previously unthinkable task for which they were not particularly created as a consequence of this limitation. According to the categories listed above, this system is a combination of all reactive and limited memory artificial intelligence. Today's most sophisticated Prediction Modelling is accomplished with the use of artificial intelligence algorithms that fall under this category. Week AI, also known as Artificial Narrow Intelligence, is one of the most prevalent types of artificial intelligence. This is possible because of technological advancements. Today, we see and use artificial intelligence devices that are a part of this discipline, which operates under strict guidelines. For example, the dataset used to train voice recognition AI may be used to predict the voices of individuals in the future. Apple Siri's is a fantastic example of Narrow AI since it only has a limited range of pre-defined capabilities. For example, the "Limited Memory" kind of deep learning model may be used to illustrate what a "Reactive Machine" is. Playing chess, providing buy suggestions on an e-commerce website, self-driving autos, speech recognition, and image identification are all instances of limited artificial intelligence applications.

2. **Artificial General Intelligence**

Machines will one day be able to think and make decisions like people do, and this is known as Artificial General Intelligence (AGI) (Pennachin & Goertzel, 2007).

Even though we haven't yet seen any examples of Strong AI, it's believed that we'll be able to build robots that are just as clever as humans are in the near future. In the same way that a typical human person would be able to train, learn, comprehend, and do tasks, AGI is capable of accomplishing the same things. These systems will be capable of doing tasks across a broad variety of disciplines. When presented with new and unexpected scenarios, these systems will be able to adapt and improvise much like individuals. No real-world instances of this form of AI exist, but it has made major breakthroughs in recent years.

3.   Artificial Super Intelligence

The degree of Artificial Intelligence known as Artificial Super Intelligence (ASI) is reached when computers' capabilities surpass those of human beings, and it is currently under development (Gill, 2016). When we consider that robots have taken over the world, we can only fathom what it would be like to live in a world controlled by artificial intelligence. The development of Artificial Super Intelligence will mark the peak of artificial intelligence. When it comes to artificial superintelligence, it will be the most powerful kind of intelligence that has ever existed on Earth. In addition to having stronger data processing, memory, and decision-making capabilities, it will be able to do all operations more efficiently than humans. As a result of ASI, some experts believe a "Technological Singularity" will occur. This will be the culmination of all technological advances. In this hypothetical scenario, technology advancement spirals out of control, triggering a major change in human civilisation that no one could have anticipated.

After the development of a more sophisticated kind of artificial intelligence, it will be hard to forecast what our future will look like. However, it is evident that we are still a long way from reaching that position in the development of advanced artificial intelligence, given that we are still in the very early phases of the process. For AI proponents, we may just be scratching the surface of what is possible, and for AI sceptics, it is still too early to be concerned about the Technological Singularity. One of the most significant characteristics of a competent artificial intelligence is its ability to think, solve issues, make choices, plan, learn, and communicate on its own without human assistance.

Type 2 AI: It is subdivided into four types. When it comes to quality, they are not all created equal: Some persons are substantially more evolved than others in terms of intellectual development. In other circumstances, this kind of artificial intelligence is not even technologically conceivable at this moment. According to the current way of categorization, the four fundamental classes of artificial intelligence are reactive, limited memory, theory of mind, and self-aware (Marr, 1977).

1.   Reactive Machines AI

Reactive artificial intelligence is the most fundamental kind of artificial intelligence, and it is meant to provide predictable results in response to the input it receives. Despite being presented with the same set of conditions time and over again, reactive robots are incapable of learning from their errors or envisioning the past or the future. Computers that respond only on current input and take just the present situation into account are included in this kind of artificial intelligence. Reactive artificial intelligence robots are unable of making predictions about their future behaviour based on the information they have at their disposal. They are restricted to a certain set of responsibilities.

When it comes to artificial intelligence systems, reactive machines are the most basic and fundamental. Computers, in contrast to humans, do not need the storage of information or the use of previously acquired knowledge. As a consequence, these artificial intelligence systems are unable to learn from their previous actions. According to these gadgets, the best course of action is dictated only by the current scenario. This is shown by the Deep Blue system developed by IBM and the AlphaGo system developed by Google. The IBM Chess programme that beat the world champion, Garry Kasparov, is an example of Reactive Artificial Intelligence. Filters that prevent unwanted email, such as spam and phishing attempts, from accessing our inboxes are becoming more popular.

2.   Limited Memory AI

Because it is referred to as "Limited Memory AI," this kind of artificial intelligence is able to draw on its earlier experience in order to make better decisions in the present. This results in it having a limited amount of long-term memory from which it may draw in order to form conclusions about its own behaviour. As with Reactive Machines, this AI includes memory capabilities, allowing it to draw on earlier knowledge and experience in order to make better decisions in the future. There are a number of well-known applications that fall within this category. These artificial intelligence systems may learn by using a large quantity of training data stored in a reference model. Artificial intelligence with limited recall can only learn from prior experiences since it has a limited quantity of stored information in memory. This kind of artificial intelligence takes use of historical, observational data in conjunction with pre-programmed information in order to generate predictions and complete complex classification tasks, among other things. Today, it is the most widely used kind of artificial intelligence, accounting for over half of all applications.

For example, self-driving cars use limited memory artificial intelligence to identify the speed and direction of other vehicles on the road, enabling them to "read the road" and adjust their speed and direction appropriately. Their safety on the road is enhanced because of this way for processing and deciphering incoming information.

However, the brain can only hold so much information at a time. Artificial intelligence (AI) is still in its infancy, as implied by the term "artificial." The information processed by an autonomous vehicle is not saved in the vehicle's long-term memory.

3.   Theory of Mind AI

Until recently, the next generation of artificial intelligence, known as "theory of mind," had little to no influence on our daily lives. These types of artificial intelligence are often at the "Work in Progress" stage and are only available in research facilities. These artificial intelligence systems will be able to comprehend human desires, likes, and emotions, as well as their brain processes, in the future. The AI will be able to adapt its own response in light of their understanding of human psychology. The notion of mind machines is just a theory, yet it outlines a high-tech category. An in-depth understanding of both the emotions and behaviours of people and objects in a particular situation is required for this kind of artificial intelligence. This kind of artificial intelligence is a significant technological achievement since it can filter through people's sentiments, ideas, and attitudes. Even though significant progress has been made, artificial intelligence has not yet reached this level of sophistication. With this kind of artificial intelligence, machines will be able to make judgments that are on par with those made by humans. The theory of mind AI will enable computers to recognise and react correctly to the emotions of their human interlocutors while they are engaging with them in the real world.

Psychiatric theory Artificial intelligence is still a long way off, in part because human communication is so prone to changing behaviour in reaction to rapidly shifting emotions, which makes AI a long way off. Increasingly emotionally sophisticated technologies we attempt to design become more difficult to reproduce as their complexity increases.

Scientist Researcher Winston demonstrated a prototype robot that can walk down a small corridor with other robots coming from the opposite direction; the AI can anticipate the movements of other robots and can turn right, left, or any other way in order to avoid a possible collision with the incoming robots, according to the research. According to Wilson, this robot makes predictions about the behaviour of other robots by using "common sense."

4.   Self-aware AI

Artificial intelligence that is self-aware is a prominent topic in science fiction films, particularly in Hollywood. The main AI robot that thinks for itself and kills mankind is one that is motivated by ideology and is created by self-aware AI. People like Elon Musk and Stephen Hawking, both superstars in the field of information technology, have frequently cautioned us that artificial intelligence is on the cusp of becoming self-aware, and we should pay attention. Self-aware artificial intelligence will be the dominant kind of AI in the future. They will be able to articulate their own ideas and emotions as their intelligence grows, and they will become more conscious of their own existence as their intelligence grows. As of right now, this is only a theoretical proposition to consider. Artificial intelligence has finally achieved its pinnacle. Only in science fiction films can we discover proof of its current existence, which is totally fictitious and impossible to verify. Aside from having the ability to evoke human emotions, they are also capable of holding their own feelings and ideas. These kind of artificial intelligence will be decades, if not centuries, away in the future. When an AI recognises that humans is a potential threat, it may go into self-preservation mode, and it may make measures to eradicate humanity either directly or indirectly.

AI and Machine Learning

It is possible for computers to learn on their own via the analysis of historical data, which is achieved through the use of artificial intelligence. If computers are able to learn from data, they will be able to deliver more precise findings. The basic goal of machine learning (ML) is to do this. In machine learning, we utilise data to teach computers on how to do a certain task and provide an accurate result, which is called training (Das et al., 2015).

The purpose of machine learning is to make judgments about huge datasets based on patterns found in the data. Machine learning is the process through which a computer system learns from prior data in order to generate predictions or judgements on its own. A considerable amount of structured and semistructured data must be employed in order for a machine learning model to deliver trustworthy findings or to generate predictions based on the data it receives (Greene et al., 2019).

Self-learning algorithms are used to educate the robot how to use past data. The application of machine learning models is limited to specific domains. For example, if we are developing a machine learning model to recognise dog photographs, the model will only provide results for dog photographs and will become unresponsive if we submit a different dataset, such as a cat image. Machine learning is being used in a variety of applications right now, including online recommendation systems, Google search engines, spam filters in email, and Facebook's auto-friend tagging recommendations, to name a few (Berry et al., 2019).

When constructing expert agents, one of the difficulties we face is that, despite their capacity to learn on their own, these systems never come up with their own questions to ask. The experience of subject matter specialists is instead relied upon to supply them with the information they want.

It was as a result of this that the field of Machine Learning was established, with the goal of enabling computers to learn on their own. However, this sounds a lot easier than it really is, since computer technology has not always been able to perform the more demanding algorithms. Fortunately, the situation has been rectified now.

However, although expert agents are capable of self-learning, they are not capable of generating new questions; these systems get continuous input from subject-matter experts, but they are continually restricted to external knowledge by utilising very simplistic artificial intelligence algorithms. Because of this, a new area called Machine Learning was established, with the ultimate objective of allowing computers to learn on their own. While this seems to be a straightforward technique, the processing capacity of computers has not always been adequate to tackle the more complicated ones. Fortunately, this stumbling block has been overcome (Das et al., 2015).

Because of the complexity and variety of the underlying mathematics that underpins this pattern, we will present just a high-level overview of some of the algorithms that are involved, rather than going into great detail about each of them. The term "Artificial Intelligence algorithms" is frequently used to refer to the algorithms listed below; however, the term "Machine Learning algorithms" is more appropriate because, as we have seen in previous articles (), Artificial Intelligence is a superset of technologies that includes Machine Learning, and it would be impossible to specify all of the algorithms involved in such a field in one article. Algorithms may be divided into three types that are important to understand. The three basic types of machine learning are supervised machine learning, unsupervised machine learning, and reinforcement-based machine learning (Berry et al., 2019).

1. Unsupervised Learning

When compared to supervised learning algorithms, unsupervised learning algorithms change just the parameters of their model in response to the incoming data. To put it another way, the algorithm is self-learning and does not need any outside assistance. Unsupervised learning cannot be applied to a regression or classification problem right away, unlike supervised learning, which can be applied right away provided we have input data and matching output data. Through the use of unsupervised learning, it is possible to organise data into groups based on similarities, and then represent the groups in an efficient and compact manner, which is the major goal of this kind of training.

In a variety of datasets, such as a collection of images of cats and dogs, unsupervised learning techniques may be utilised to make predictions. The algorithm has no previous knowledge of the features of the input dataset since it has never been exposed to it before. The unsupervised learning approach identifies features in photographs on its own, without the assistance of a teacher. This procedure will be carried out using an unsupervised learning algorithm, which will categorise the photographs in the collection into groups based on their similarity to each other in terms of content.

2.   Supervised Learning

Predictive models based on training data serve as the foundation for supervised learning techniques. If the system can provide a certain output given a set of known data, the model may be adjusted (trained) until it produces results that are acceptable to all parties involved. When computers are trained given "labelled" training data and then utilise that data to predict outputs based on the training data, this is considered machine learning. The term "labelled data" merely refers to the fact that a portion of your input has already been given a result.

The computers are trained to properly anticipate their output by utilising the training data that has been provided to them. This is accomplished via the use of supervised learning. It is founded on the same ideas that students learn under the supervision of their teacher over the course of their studies.

The training of a machine learning model may be done with the assistance of a human teacher. The purpose of using supervised learning to construct a mapping function that transforms the input variable (x) into the output variable (y) is to reduce the amount of time spent on the problem (y). Modelling techniques are taught to models via the use of labelled datasets, in which the model is educated about each type of data. The model is evaluated using test data (a subset of the training set) and then the anticipated output is obtained after the conclusion of the training phase.

3.   Reinforcement Learning

When developing software, developers use a method called as reinforcement learning to reward good behaviour while discouraging undesirable behaviour. In this approach for motivating the agent, positive values are allocated to desired actions and negative values are assigned to unwanted behaviours in order to motivate the agent. In order to come up with the optimum solution, the agent is instructed to think about the long term and the entire return.

These long-term objectives prevent the agent from being bogged down in the pursuit of lesser objectives. As time progresses, the agent gains the capacity to concentrate on the positive aspects of the situation rather than the negative. This learning strategy, which has been extensively adopted in artificial intelligence, allows unsupervised machine learning to be directed via the application of incentives and penalties. "Trial and error," as well as "reward," are important concepts in robotics. Robots are capable of executing in record time under defined conditions or provided settings (for example, the laws of the game), all with a particular purpose known as "reward," which is the objective of reinforcement learning (a classic example is winning a game of chess). The past expertise of a machine creates a plethora of data that may be leveraged to develop fresh insights and conclusions from the data. An example of DeepMind's AlphaZero chess AI learning models.

Figure 2. Relationship between Artificial Intelligence, Machine Learning and Deep Learning

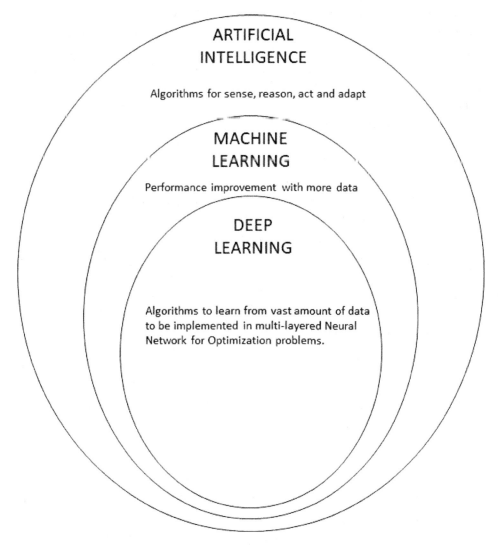

Deep Learning

In machine learning, the ultimate objective is to allow computers to learn on their own, without needing to be explicitly taught in the process. Although they have made significant progress, they are still far from being able to perform certain complex jobs, such as extracting data from video or image files.

Deep learning models, which are closely related to the human brain in terms of structure and function, represent a major advancement in the field of machine learning. Because of the building of sophisticated, multi-layered "deep neural networks," data may be conveyed between nodes (such as neurons) in a highly connected manner. At the conclusion of the process, the data goes through a non-linear transformation and becomes more abstract (Kamilaris & Prenafeta-Boldu´, 2018).

This kind of system needs large quantities of data to "feed and develop," but once the algorithms are in place, it may begin providing results almost immediately and with little or no human intervention. If you're interested in understanding the foundations of artificial intelligence, you can break down many AI breakthroughs into two concepts: machine learning and deep learning. Machine learning is a kind of artificial intelligence that can learn from data.

Examples of deep learning and machine learning may be found in a variety of contexts in daily life. In the case of self-driving cars and Facebook's facial recognition tool, machine learning is the driving force behind both of these innovations in technology.

Despite the fact that these two names are sometimes used interchangeably, there are substantial differences between them. Understanding the difference between machine learning and deep learning starts with an acknowledgement that deep learning is a subset of machine learning, and that machine learning is a subset of deep learning. The figure 2 shows the relationship between all three of them.

Deep learning is a recent advancement in machine learning, specifically in deep reinforcement learning. A customised neural network is used in this instance, and it enables robots to make right decisions without the need for human intervention or oversight.

A deep learning model employs a logical framework that is similar to that of human thinking in order to continually review data and draw conclusions. When it comes to deep learning applications, an artificial neural network (ANN) is employed to do this kind of analysis. The fact that an artificial neural network is based on the biological network of neurons in the human brain means that it is capable of learning substantially more than a conventional machine learning model can now.

Deep learning models, like other types of artificial intelligence, need extensive training to ensure that they do not draw incorrect conclusions. As with other types of artificial intelligence, perfecting the learning processes takes a long time. When it works as intended, functional deep learning, on the other hand, is often regarded as the cornerstone of true artificial intelligence.

AlphaGo, developed by Google, is an excellent example of deep learning in action. Google, the world's largest search engine, developed computer software that used its own neural network to learn to play the abstract board game Go. While competing against elite Go players in real-world games, AlphaGo's deep learning model developed abilities that had never before been obtained by an artificial intelligence (as a standard machine learning model would require).

Many world-renowned "masters" of the game were taken aback when AlphaGo defeated them, not only because a machine was able to comprehend the game's complex strategy and abstract elements, but also because it was quickly becoming one of the top players. Ultimately, when the choice was between human and machine intelligence, it was the latter that triumphed.

Using an image recognition tool to identify a flower or bird species based on a photograph may be handy in a variety of situations in one's daily life. A massive neural network was used in order to achieve this level of photo classification accuracy. Deep learning is also employed in speech recognition and translation, as well as in self-driving autos, among other applications.

Financial Portfolio Management

Stocks, shares, mutual funds, bonds, and cash are all examples of investment products that might be included in a portfolio depending on an individual's financial status and investing horizon, among other factors. In order to stabilise the nonperformance risk of diverse investment pools, it is structured in such a way that they are all equal in size.

It is the art and science of making decisions about investment mix and policy, aligning investments to objectives, allocating assets to individuals or organisations, and managing risk and performance while maintaining a high level of transparency.

To put it another way, the fund manager has been entrusted with someone else's hard-earned money, and the responsibility is to come up with strategies to assist them build their investment portfolio. The risk-to-return ratio should be maintained appropriately by considering gains and holding periods while making this decision (Spronk & Hallerbach, 1997).

When it comes to portfolio management, the term refers to the process of managing an individual's bonds, stocks, cash, and mutual funds in order for him or her to earn the maximum money feasible within the time period indicated. Portfolio management is the ability to manage an individual's money with the assistance of a portfolio manager or a team of portfolio managers.

When determining the best investment option to take, whether it's in the form of a loan or equity investment in either the domestic or international markets, it's important to consider the strengths, weaknesses, opportunities, and threats of the venture. We now in a state to venture upon the usage of Artificial Intelligence in the Financial Portfolio Management domain.

ARTIFICIAL INTELLIGENCE IN FINANCIAL PORTFOLIO MANAGEMENT

The asset management business has seen a considerable increase in the use of artificial intelligence. It has improved the efficiency and accuracy of portfolio management, trading, and risk management operations, allowing them to be more efficient, accurate, and in compliance with regulatory requirements. Artificial Intelligence has the potential to be used to construct portfolios that have more exact risk and return estimates, as well as more intricate limits. In order to produce fresh trading signals and lower transaction costs, trading algorithms make use of artificial intelligence. Another advantage of artificial intelligence is that it allows for more accurate risk modelling and forecasting. Finally, artificial intelligence techniques may be credited with the success of robo-advisors. New threats and challenges may occur as a result of the use of artificial intelligence, including model obscurity, complexity, and the need for data integrity (Spronk & Hallerbach, 1997).

Even as well-documented challenges in the company grow more severe, investment management organisations throughout the world are finding themselves in an operating environment that is constantly changing. Organic growth has been weak, capital market returns have been volatile, and margins have been squeezed, all of which have contributed to a more challenging environment. In this new paradigm of change, technology continues to be a key enabler of rapid organisational transformation, as well as opportunities for increased efficiency, innovation, and value creation. To far, the use of intelligent robots in the workplace has mostly been focused on boosting operational efficiency in front, middle, and back office functions. A number of these use cases and applications have been developed with an eye toward identifying common patterns that can be applied to a variety of sales and distribution activities such as product pricing, market share allocations (including trade), portfolio construction, risk assessment, and customer onboarding, to name a few (including account set-up).

Investment management is becoming increasingly commoditized, and artificial intelligence is providing new alternatives that go beyond cost reduction and operational efficiency to provide new possibilities. There has been a lot of interest, and many investment management organisations are vigorously testing the waters, incorporating cognitive technologies and artificial intelligence into diverse business processes along the value chain of the industry.

Advanced fundamental analysis employing artificial intelligence methodologies, such as text analysis, is also viable, as is asset allocation optimization in financial portfolios (Spronk & Hallerbach, 1997). When it comes to anticipating returns and covariances, Artificial Intelligence technologies may be superior than conventional portfolio optimization approaches in the majority of instances. These estimates may then be used by traditional portfolio optimization techniques to improve their performance. Portfolios that are more closely linked with performance objectives than those developed using traditional procedures may be constructed with the application of artificial intelligence.

AI in Fundamental Analysis

For decades, investors and organisations have been on the lookout for the most effective investment analysis tools. Fundamental, technical, and sentiment analysis

Figure 3. Artificial intelligence in financial portfolio management

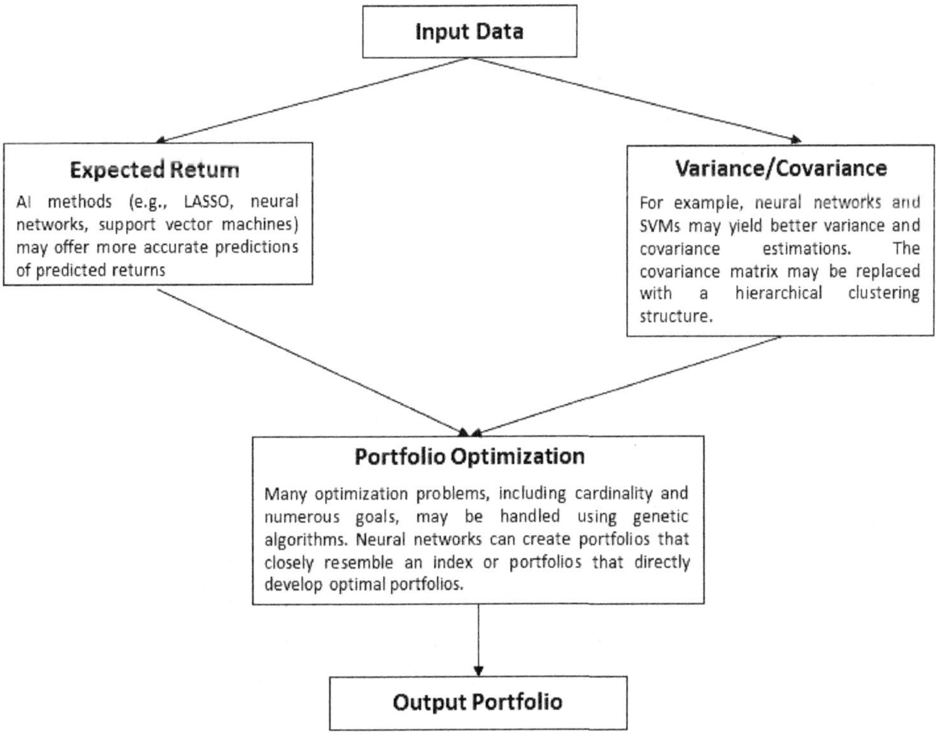

are the three types of asset prediction models that may be used in the financial industry. Figure 3 shows a procedure for portfolio optimization in finance using AI.

Investing in stocks is a method for businesses to raise capital. An initial public offering, often known as an IPO, is the first time a firm makes its stock available to the general public for purchase (Baker & Gompers, 2003). During an initial public offering (IPO), the starting price of a single shares is decided by an investment banking firm. When a corporation already has shares listed on the market, it may decide to offer more shares to the public. It is referred to as "seasoned" shares in these sales. The primary market is where seasoned shares as well as initial public offerings are sold for distribution. Investors and institutes of higher learning may trade existing shares of a firm on secondary markets, which are also known as secondary markets. Shareholders are individuals or entities who own a share of a corporation's equity. Investors are entitled to a portion of earnings when a firm decides to distribute dividends to its shareholders. Various theories on asset price have been put forth. Asset pricing models such as the B&H method, the capital asset pricing model, and Fama-French multi-factor models were found to be the most often used benchmarks in the meta-analysis (Womack & Zhang, 2003).

Definition 1. The Capital Asset Pricing Model (CAPM) (Perold, 2004) is described as:

$$E[A_r] = A_{rf} + \beta_r(E[A_m] - A_{rf}) \tag{1}$$

where $E[A_r]$ is the expected return of the resource specified. β_r is the beta of the resource and $(E[A_m] - A_{rf})$ is the risk premium.

In principle, the return on a government bond is taken into account when calculating the risk-free rate of return since it is believed to be the least dangerous investment option available. The beta of an asset is defined as the asset's sensitivity to changes in the value of the asset relative to the market. The following are the characteristics of this sensitivity: When an asset has a beta of one, it follows the precise fluctuations of the market. The movements of an asset with a beta of -1.0 are diametrically opposed to the movements of the broader market. The market risk premium is the difference between the return on the market and the return on an investment that is not exposed to risk. Despite the fact that the CAPM may provide an accurate estimate, the CAPM has significant drawbacks. For example, it assumes that the only factor influencing an asset's return is the asset's risk in relation to the market risk. Furthermore, Black said that there is no such thing as a risk-free investment. As a consequence of his zero-beta CAPM modification, which is a risk-free rate of return replacement, the empirical findings of the CAPM have been improved significantly. Fama and French, on the other hand, suggested that the CAPM should only be utilised as a theoretical framework for the link between risk and return since empirical difficulties were discovered in the study conducted.

Textual analysis is an essential use of artificial intelligence in basic analysis. Natural language processing (NLP) algorithms are capable of extracting economically important information from a wide range of textual sources, including corporate annual reports, news articles, and Twitter messages. In contrast to traditional textual analysis tools, such as dictionary-based techniques, artificial intelligence systems may analyse context and sentence structure in addition to textual content (Katsikis & Mourtas, 2021).

LASSO regression automatically picks the components of a portfolio that have the greatest predictive power for future returns from a large number of return-predictive indicators that have been published in the literature (Mishra et al., 2021). It is also possible to discover lead–lag relationships between asset categories or markets by using the LASSO technique. Consider the possibility of determining whether domestic industry or market returns are the most significant predictors of returns among all other markets and industries, to name just a few of examples. LASSO regression is supplemented by the "elastic nets" approach, which makes use of a more extended version of LASSO regression to make variable selection more accurate. It is possible for AI models to apply a number of economic and firm-level factors in order to identify stocks that are projected to prosper or underperform. Results of these evaluations may help portfolio managers decide whether to enhance (reduce) the weight of assets with high (low) alpha during the portfolio optimization process. The artificial intelligence may also be educated using genuine experts' stock buy and sell recommendations, which has been demonstrated to be beneficial (Mishra et al., 2021).

Accuracy is the key factor in determining whether ANNs outperform other artificial intelligence techniques for return prediction, such as conventional leastsquares regression, elastic nets, latent-state stochastic optimization regressions, random forests, and gradient-boosted regression trees (Riesener et al., 2019). Interestingly, an ANN with three hidden layers outscored a gradient boosted regression tree, the second best-performing technique among the six, by around 30 percent on the test data set. Always remember that these conclusions may be taskor data-dependent. It is, however, the ability of neural networks to capture intricate nonlinear connections that is responsible for the majority of their success in this scenario. As a result of their adaptability, functional forms, and topologies, neural networks are able to learn from data more effectively than other techniques, which distinguishes them from other models. With the use of confidence intervals and a grading system for the significance of input variables and their interactions, it is now feasible to statistically analyse neural networks (Mishra et al., 2021; Riesener et al., 2019).

Of course, neural networks are one of the most widely used artificial intelligence approaches for projecting stock returns, company fundamentals, and returns on other asset classes such as bonds, among other things. When correctly calibrated, vector machines, on the other hand, have been demonstrated to be more accurate than artificial neural networks (ANNs) in forecasting the first two seconds of an asset's returns. As a result, a widely used strategy is based on getting the average prediction from a number of artificial intelligence systems. When compared to individual artificial intelligence systems, the "ensemble" method has provided more accurate projections. The results of studies show that AI signals generate significant profits in both short and long positions (a monthly abnormal return of 0.78 percent is found in the case of a long, value-weighted portfolio), and that these profits continue to be statistically and economically significant even after the year 2001, during which a global decline in abnormal returns is observed (Zhang & Chen, 2017).

Especially when dealing with derivatives, predicting the value of an asset becomes much more complex. As a result, it is difficult to construct an optimal portfolio that includes derivatives since they have a broad range of prices and payoffs that are dependent on the performance of other assets. In order to price derivatives, the vast majority of conventional procedures rely on theoretical models like as Black–Scholes, which are themselves dependent on assumptions that are themselves limited in scope. Artificial intelligence may also play a role in this field. If nonparametric option pricing frameworks are shown to be more effective than the standard Black–Scholes model (Sharma et al., 2012) when it comes to delta hedging and estimating future option prices, they may be combined with ANNs to price and hedge options using nonparametric option pricing frameworks.

In the end, it is still up in the air whether artificial intelligence implementations in stock selection, factor investing, or asset allocation are superior to more traditional implementations. It is vital to have more evidence that artificial intelligence models, particularly their ability to capture nonlinearities, outweigh the expenses and potential data issues, such as collinear variables. Because many asset managers have just began using artificial intelligence, it is possible that AI-based investment approaches could soon be arbitraged away. As a result, the additional evidence will become much more meaningful. There are more reasons to be cautious as well. Several studies proposing the use of artificial intelligence in portfolio management have only examined a small sample of assets or emerging markets that are deficient in liquidity and efficiency. The process of "feature engineering," in which interesting variables from raw data are identified and then turned into acceptable forms for AI models, is another tough aspect of implementing artificial intelligence. This is an extremely important and timeconsuming step in alpha research (Sharma et al., 2012).

Portfolio Optimization

The selection of a portfolio manager entails the distribution of funds among a number of individuals in order to attain a certain aim (e.g., imitating an existing portfolio). (Increasing the Sharpe ratio to the greatest extent possible) within particular limits which is the average (Fabozzi et al., 2007). In practise, the variance framework developed by Markowitz (Zhang et al., 2018) serves as a theoretical foundation. In practise, however, there are two significant obstacles to overcome. To begin, it is necessary to calculate the optimal asset weights. People's choices are heavily influenced by their expectations of future returns. Because future predicted return estimations are often uncertain, it is possible that the optimization process may produce weights that perform poorly outside of the sample. To put it another way, if return estimates are distorted, the benefits of diversification may be diminished or even eliminated. When it comes to specific cases, for example, an equally weighted portfolio has a higher out-of-sample Sharpe ratio than the ideal Markowitz portfolio. This is true of all the best possible portfolios, including the best possible portfolios. Following the determination of the variance–covariance matrix, which serves as the central component of the study. With a long period of data and the assumption that Markowitz's theory is valid, we can see that there are stable correlations between asset returns over time. In addition, the matrix is changed in some way. When asset correlations increase, which occurs at a time when diversification is most important but also the most difficult to achieve, the market becomes more unstable.

Artificial intelligence addresses these difficulties in two ways. As a matter of first and foremost, it can produce more accurate returns and risk predictions than those provided by other methodologies, and it may be included into standard portfolio design frameworks. In addition, AI-based approaches to portfolio construction may be able to produce more accurate portfolio weights and optimise portfolios that perform better out-of-sample than portfolios constructed using traditional linear techniques. Despite the fact that there is a paucity of empirical evidence to support this assertion, academics and practitioners alike seem to be getting increasingly interested. Using artificial neural network systems, it is possible to train them to make asset allocation decisions that are difficult to include into the mean–variance framework. Portfolios may be chosen based on a value-at-risk constraint that optimises returns, as determined by the learning criteria of a neural network's learning algorithm. Artificial neural networks are capable of handling complex multi-objective optimization problems as well. A mean-variance-skewness optimal portfolio may be generated fast and economically using a neural network-based technique, which is described here (Briec et al., 2007). Aside from that, ANNs may use a methodology to include future asset performance into portfolio optimization, resulting in higher out-of-sample Sharpe ratios than those achieved by the market portfolio (Khan et al., 2020).

Another prominent AI strategy in portfolio construction is the use of evolving algorithms (Liang et al., 2018), which are capable of dealing with increasingly complex asset allocation challenges. If you have a portfolio with a restricted number of assets, an evolutionary algorithm may be able to assist you in resolving optimization problems. Using an evolutionary algorithm, for example, may assist you in solving optimization problems if you have a restricted number of assets in your portfolio. Evolutionary algorithms may be modified to accommodate additional objectives. To minimise forecasting inaccuracy, for example, model risk may be included into the optimization problem throughout the optimization process (Liang et al., 2018). Model risk refers to the possibility of failing to offer accurate estimates of asset returns and volatility as a result of model mis-specification.

Nonlinear relationships between assets can be captured by neural networks without the need for prior knowledge of the underlying structure of the data, making synthetic replication—replicating a benchmark portfolio such as an index by holding a fraction of the constituents while matching some risk factors—a useful tool for synthetic replication. This reduces transaction costs associated with portfolio rebalancing while simultaneously lowering administrative and monitoring costs (Beraldi et al., 2021). The out-of-sample performance of this framework is promising, and it is versatile enough to design target portfolios with a variety of characteristics. In order to construct a portfolio that beats a particular index by 1 percent each year, it is necessary to discover the optimal strategy (i.e., the one that involves the least risk or expense).

Algorithmic Trading

It is feasible for algorithmic trading to take place at any stage of the process, including the beginning. Aspects of the trading process include pre-trade analysis, trade execution, and post-transaction analysis among others. Data is used to study the characteristics of financial assets in order to forecast their future performance as well as the risks and costs involved with trading such assets. On the basis of the information gathered from this analysis, trades are entered into. Asset managers may decide to include pre-trade analysis results into their decision-making during the manual stage of the pre-trade analysis process, along with risk assessments and client preferences. Pre-trade analysis in high-frequency trading or entirely automated systems does not need the involvement of a human. Trade execution ensures that transaction expenses are kept to a minimum. In order to maintain track of performance and make adjustments to the trading system, post-trade analysis analyses real trading outcomes. In post-trade analysis, it is common to use human supervision or overlay. As a consequence, pre-trade analysis, as well as trade execution, fall primarily within the purview of algorithms.

Artificial intelligence plays a role in trading through allowing algorithmic trading (Hansen, 2020), which is defined as algorithms that automate one or more steps of the trading process. Three recent developments have had a role in the emergence of algorithmic trading in the realm of financial asset management. As a consequence of technological advancements in computers, data science, and telecommunications, significant structural changes have occurred in the financial markets. The technology available today allows computers to acquire and analyse massive amounts of data in milliseconds, as well as conduct transactions without the need for human intervention. To begin with, developments in quantitative finance and machine learning have provided computers with the tools they need to do intelligent financial analysis more rapidly and efficiently than anybody could have dreamed conceivable in the previous century. While complex artificial intelligence techniques such as neural networks can now be implemented in real time or near real time, keeping up with the markets and making real-time trading decisions has become increasingly difficult for humans, owing to the increasing complexity and speed of financial markets, as well as the breadth of new structural products on the market (Velu et al., 2020).

Techniques such as technical analysis, which evaluates previous stock and market data in order to estimate future asset returns, are often used in algorithmic trading methods. Basic research is possible, but because to the high frequency of algorithmic transactions, it is difficult to analyse lower-frequency data, such as the performance of individual enterprises. Furthermore, evidence reveals that technical indicators trump fundamental indicators when it comes to generating profitable artificial intelligence trading recommendations. As a result, artificial intelligence-based solutions for technical analysis are becoming more popular.

Price and trading volume data from the past serve as the major inputs to traditional types of technical analysis. Strategies based on pricing often replicate patterns, such as momentum or reversal, and cycles, in order to anticipate future returns based on historical data. When using volume-based forecasting methodologies, the recent trading behaviour of investors is utilised to estimate future outcomes. Modern technical analysis makes use of a variety of other sources of information, including money flows, investor transactions, and textual data from news articles or online sources (Velu et al., 2020). These new, unstructured data sources may reap significant benefits from artificial intelligence approaches based on natural language processing (NLP).

Additionally, artificial intelligence may be used to analyse the market effect of transactions in assets that have little (or no) previous trade data, since traditional methods of estimating the market impact costs in this situation are very difficult to apply. This problem may be solved by using a cluster analysis approach, which makes use of historical data to locate linked assets that behave in a similar fashion. For example, cluster analysis may split bonds into groups based on their length, age, or outstanding value, and then analyse the bonds within each group to determine how similar they are to one another. Within a cluster, the knowledge of other ties is used to supplement the knowledge of bonds that do not have enough information on their own. This technique is widely utilised by Bloomberg's liquidity assessment tool (Bartram et al., 2021), which provides liquidity information for a wide range of assets using this approach.

Risk Management

The application of artificial intelligence in risk management may be beneficial, both in terms of market risk and credit risk (Sunchalin et al., 2019). Credit (or counterparty) risk refers to the probability that a counterparty may fail to satisfy its contractual obligations, resulting in a decline in the value of the underlying asset or liability. Market risk refers to the probability of incurring a loss as a result of movements in the stock market. Market risk analysis may be used to predict, analyse, and forecast the risk associated with an investment portfolio's performance. Use of qualitative data for risk modelling, validation and backtesting of risk models, and better forecasts of aggregate financial or economic variables are all examples of how artificial intelligence might make a difference in this area (Sunchalin et al., 2019).

Extracting information from text or image data sources is one area where artificial intelligence may be used in market risk management (Bartram et al., 2020). Financial contracts, central bank minutes and announcements, news reports, and social media posts all include text data that may be valuable in lowering market risk in the future. Satellite images may be used to forecast the number of people who will visit supermarkets. Other quantitative variables often fall short of fully describing the information that may be gained from a variety of different sources. A recent research discovered that artificial intelligence algorithms that leverage textual information, rather than information acquired from other data sources, provide better market collapse and interest rate projections (Zheng et al., 2019). It is possible to create systematic risk profiles for a corporation by combining these approaches with information available via public filings. As a consequence of all of these applications, central banks are now more interested than ever in incorporating artificial intelligence-based text mining techniques into their macroprudential analytical processes and procedures. There aren't many real-world instances of this in action to draw inspiration from.

In addition to artificial neural networks and support vector machines, artificial intelligence techniques can also predict market volatility and financial crises, especially due to their ability to capture nonlinear dynamics. It is possible to predict market volatility using both ANNs and a variant of the GARCH model (Zhang, 2021). A number of studies, on the other hand, have shown that SVMs outperform ANNs in terms of accuracy (Zhang, 2021). In addition to volatility models, artificial neural networks and support vector machines are used to predict financial crises. Early warning systems, which perform this forecasting function, are referred regarded as models in certain circles. A systemic risk monitoring system is in place at the majority of large financial institutions, which is complemented with early warning systems. ANNs and SVMs have been shown to accurately predict currency crises, banking crises, and recessions in general with a reasonable level of accuracy. Therefore, given the lack of a statistically significant number of crises in the sample, one can question the ability of artificial intelligence models to predict future crises with accuracy (Lotfi & El Bouhadi, 2022).

The purpose of credit risk management is to ensure that the portfolio does not suffer a negative impact if a counterparty fails to meet its contractual obligations. It is essential for asset managers to keep a careful eye on the credit risk of the whole portfolio, as well as the credit risk of particular assets and transactions. This is a way for determining the level of risk associated with financial products produced by financial institutions, such as stocks, bonds, swaps, and options. It is possible to represent different aspects of solvency or bankruptcy risk in a number of ways. There is a lot of reliance on traditional methodologies such as multivariate discriminant analysis, logit, and probit models. In addition to SVMs and ANNs, a plethora of other artificial intelligence approaches may be used for credit risk modelling (Bussmann et al., 2021). The use of an ensemble strategy, which utilises a variety of modelling methodologies, each with its own set of advantages and disadvantages in order to get the best results, is preferred in order to achieve the best outcomes.

DISCUSSION AND CHALLENGES

Despite the countless studies showcasing artificial intelligence's advantages and benefits, users of AI should be aware of the actual or imagined hazards and drawbacks that the technology poses when it comes to asset management. In many cases, the main causes of these issues may be traced back to their complexity, opacity, and dependence on data integrity ().

It is almost hard to comprehend or describe in detail the conclusions of the vast majority of artificial intelligence models. As a job or programme becomes more complicated, human monitoring may become less effective as a result of the opacity of the environment. There are three possible ways in which this problem might have an effect on asset managers. Furthermore, it is difficult to forecast how artificial intelligence models will behave to big shocks or "black swan" occurrences in the future (Batrouni et al., 2018; Bhanja & Das, 2022). This is due to a combination of two factors: Systems that use artificial intelligence have the ability to commit the same mistakes over and time again, culminating in a stock market meltdown. Because artificial intelligence tools and algorithms are so expensive to develop, most asset management organisations have used the same ones. Because we've witnessed earlier cascading algorithmic catastrophes, it's possible that AI-driven failures may become more common. The use of fundamental quantitative methodologies, such as value investing, may also result in algorithmic catastrophes. Due to the opacity of artificial intelligence, it may be difficult to assess and mitigate such dangers.

Additionally, AI has the ability to misunderstand patterns in data, which might result in incorrect conclusions (). To provide an example, an ANN trained to choose equities with high expected returns may instead select illiquid or problematic securities. Third, when artificial intelligence algorithms are applied, it is possible that attribution of investment performance may become more complex. A standard risk component analysis method based on linear factor models may be unable to identify nonlinear relationships between features and return. Explaining to investors why and how the fund's investment strategy failed may be challenging, and as a result, investors may lose confidence in the fund or the industry as a whole. Some people create "surrogate models" in order to better understand the prediction behaviour of artificial intelligence models, which are simpler and more interpretable than the original models. Shapley values, which are derived from game theory, may be used to assess how much a prediction is impacted by different feature values.

Another significant source of concern is the quality and sufficiency of the information (Hovorushchenko et al., 2019; Samtani et al., 2020). As with any other empirical model, the dependability and accessibility of data are critical to artificial intelligence models. Trash in, rubbish out is a well-known adage that alludes to the difficulties that might develop when data is of inferior quality. Because AI findings are often taken at face value, the quality and amount of data become more important. By analysing the model's results, one of the most fundamental tasks may be to identify datarelated issues. Furthermore, the learning phase of AI models necessitates the use of a large amount of data, which is usually greater than is available. Because the signal-to-noise ratio is so low for low-frequency financial data, it is possible that an erroneous calibration would result as a result of the large number of missing observations. However, imputation, which is the use of statistical values to substitute missing data, may be beneficial to a certain extent, but it is clearly restricted in its use. According to others, historical data in general may not be able to effectively forecast the future. Because financial data is only available for a limited period of time, it is more probable that AI models may fail during a collapse or crisis, increasing the likelihood of a catastrophic failure. Artificial intelligence is becoming more popular, and its growing presence in the investment industry may raise the cybersecurity risk faced by asset managers as a consequence of this trend (Ghimire et al., 2020).

It is not yet clear if the benefits of artificial intelligence outweigh the costs of investing in the software, hardware, human resources, and data systems that will be required to implement them. Because asset managers have limited resources to test and develop new strategies, each investment in artificial intelligence must be balanced against other research endeavours that may be mutually incompatible. In addition, if the current AI bubble goes away, it is possible that investors may become less interested in investing in AI-driven funds, making investment in AI infrastructure even more challenging. As a result, asset managers must carefully consider the benefits and drawbacks of artificial intelligence in order to avoid having cold feet when the next AI winter arrives.

CONCLUSION

Increasingly, academics and practitioners are interested in AI in asset management. Portfolio management, trading, and risk management are all areas where AI has applications in financial services. This foundation also supports algorithmic trading and robo-advice. But AI will never be able to completely replace humans. Humans control the overwhelming bulk of its asset management tasks. This article focused on ways that automate or facilitate (often minor) aspects of asset management, such as portfolio optimization or fully automated algorithmic trading systems. The ability to manage data without theoretical comprehension or supervision is artificial intelligence's greatest capability. Man believes that artificial intelligence will always provide a result, even when one is not desired. This tendency causes issues when data quality is poor, work is too complex for humans to monitor and understand, and cascading systemic failures occur as a result of several AI systems communicating with each other. As AI's impact expands, asset managers must keep these points in mind.

REFERENCES

Albuquerque, P. H. M., de Moraes Souza, J. G., & Kimura, H. (2021). Artificial intelligence in portfolio formation and forecast: Using different variance-covariance matrices. *Communications in Statistics. Theory and Methods*, 1–18. doi:10.1080/03610926.2021.1987472

Bahrammirzaee, A. (2010). A comparative survey of artificial intelligence applications in finance: Artificial neural networks, expert system and hybrid intelligent systems. *Neural Computing & Applications*, *19*(8), 1165–1195. doi:10.100700521-010-0362-z

Baker, M., & Gompers, P. A. (2003). The determinants of board structure at the initial public offering. *The Journal of Law & Economics*, *46*(2), 569–598. doi:10.1086/380409

Bartram, S. M., Branke, J., De Rossi, G., & Motahari, M. (2021). Machine Learning for Active Portfolio Management. *The Journal of Financial Data Science*, *3*(3), 9–30. doi:10.3905/jfds.2021.1.071

Bartram, S. M., Branke, J., & Motahari, M. (2020). *Artificial intelligence in asset management*. CFA Institute Research Foundation. doi:10.2139srn.3692805

Batrouni, M., Bertaux, A., & Nicolle, C. (2018). Scenario analysis, from BigData to black swan. *Computer Science Review*, *28*, 131–139. doi:10.1016/j.cosrev.2018.02.001

Belanche, D., Casalo, L. V., & Flavi'an, C. (2019). Artificial Intelligence in FinTech: Understanding robo-advisors adoption among customers. *Industrial Management & Data Systems*, *119*(7), 1411–1430. doi:10.1108/IMDS-08-2018-0368

Beraldi, P., Violi, A., Ferrara, M., Ciancio, C., & Pansera, B. A. (2021). Dealing with complex transaction costs in portfolio management. *Annals of Operations Research*, *299*(1), 7–22. doi:10.100710479-019-03210-5

Berry, M. W., Mohamed, A., & Yap, B. W. (Eds.). (2019). *Supervised and unsupervised learning for data science*. Springer Nature.

Bhanja, S., & Das, A. (2022). A Black Swan event-based hybrid model for Indian stock markets' trends prediction. *Innovations in Systems and Software Engineering*, 1–15. doi:10.100711334-021-00428-0 PMID:35018169

Briec, W., Kerstens, K., & Jokung, O. (2007). Mean-variance-skewness portfolio performance gauging: A general shortage function and dual approach. *Management Science*, *53*(1), 135–149. doi:10.1287/mnsc.1060.0596

Brinson, G. P., Hood, L. R., & Beebower, G. L. (1986). Determinants of portfolio performance. *Financial Analysts Journal*, *42*(4), 39–44. doi:10.2469/faj.v42.n4.39

Broussard, M. (2018). *Artificial unintelligence: How computers misunderstand the world*. MIT Press.

Bullock, J., Luccioni, A., Pham, K. H., Lam, C. S. N., & Luengo-Oroz, M. (2020). Mapping the landscape of artificial intelligence applications against COVID-19. *Journal of Artificial Intelligence Research*, *69*, 807–845. doi:10.1613/jair.1.12162

Bunz, M. (2019). The calculation of meaning: On the misunderstanding of new artificial intelligence as culture. *Culture, Theory & Critique*, *60*(3-4), 264–278. doi:10.1080/14735784.2019.1667255

Bussmann, N., Giudici, P., Marinelli, D., & Papenbrock, J. (2021). Explainable machine learning in credit risk management. *Computational Economics*, *57*(1), 203–216. doi:10.100710614-020-10042-0

Das, S., Dey, A., Pal, A., & Roy, N. (2015). Applications of artificial intelligence in machine learning: Review and prospect. International. *Jisuanji Yingyong*, *115*(9),

Dick, S. (2019). *Artificial Intelligence*. Academic Press.

Dunis, C., Middleton, P., Karathanasopolous, A., & Theofilatos, K. (2016). *Artificial intelligence in financial markets*. Palgrave Macmillan. doi:10.1057/978-1-137-48880-0

Fabozzi, F. J., Kolm, P. N., Pachamanova, D. A., & Focardi, S. M. (2007). Robust portfolio optimization. *Journal of Portfolio Management*, *33*(3), 40–48. doi:10.3905/jpm.2007.684751

Ferreira, F. G., Gandomi, A. H., & Cardoso, R. T. (2021). Artificial intelligence applied to stock market trading: A review. *IEEE Access: Practical Innovations, Open Solutions*, *9*, 30898–30917. doi:10.1109/ACCESS.2021.3058133

Ghimire, A., Thapa, S., Jha, A. K., Adhikari, S., & Kumar, A. (2020, October). Accelerating business growth with big data and artificial intelligence. In *2020 Fourth International Conference on I-SMAC (IoT in Social, Mobile, Analytics and Cloud) (I-SMAC)* (pp. 441-448). IEEE. 10.1109/I-SMAC49090.2020.9243318

Gill, K. S. (2016). Artificial super intelligence: Beyond rhetoric. *AI & Society*, *31*(2), 137–143. doi:10.100700146-016-0651-x

Goertzel, B. (2007). *Artificial general intelligence* (C. Pennachin, Ed., Vol. 2). Springer. doi:10.1007/978-3-540-68677-4

Graves, D. H., & Sunstein, B. S. (1992). Portfolio portraits. Heinemann.

Greene, D., Hoffmann, A. L., & Stark, L. (2019). *Better, nicer, clearer, fairer: A critical assessment of the movement for ethical artificial intelligence and machine learning*. Academic Press.

Guo, L., Wu, J., & Li, J. (2019). Complexity at Mesoscales: A common challenge in developing artificial intelligence. *Engineering, 5*(5), 924–929. doi:10.1016/j.eng.2019.08.005

Hansen, K. B. (2020). The virtue of simplicity: On machine learning models in algorithmic trading. *Big Data & Society, 7*(1). doi:10.1177/2053951720926558

Holzinger, A., Langs, G., Denk, H., Zatloukal, K., & Mu¨ller, H. (2019). Causability and explainability of artificial intelligence in medicine. *Wiley Interdisciplinary Reviews. Data Mining and Knowledge Discovery, 9*(4), e1312. doi:10.1002/widm.1312 PMID:32089788

Hovorushchenko, T., Pavlova, O., & Medzatyi, D. (2019, May). Ontology-based intelligent agent for determination of sufficiency of metric information in the software requirements. In *International Scientific Conference "Intellectual Systems of Decision Making and Problem of Computational Intelligence"* (pp. 447-460). Springer.

Kaastra, I., & Boyd, M. S. (1995). Forecasting futures trading volume using neural networks. *The Journal of Futures Markets, 15*(18), 953.

Kalayci, C. B., Ertenlice, O., & Akbay, M. A. (2019). A comprehensive review of deterministic models and applications for mean-variance portfolio optimization. *Expert Systems with Applications, 125*, 345–368. doi:10.1016/j.eswa.2019.02.011

Kamilaris, A., & Prenafeta-Boldu´, F. X. (2018). Deep learning in agriculture: A survey. *Computers and Electronics in Agriculture, 147*, 70–90. doi:10.1016/j.compag.2018.02.016

Katsikis, V. N., & Mourtas, S. D. (2021). Binary beetle antennae search algorithm for tangency portfolio diversification. *Journal of Modeling and Optimization, 13*(1), 44–50. doi:10.32732/jmo.2021.13.1.44

Khan, A. H., Cao, X., Katsikis, V. N., Stanimirovi'c, P., Brajevi'c, I., Li, S., Kadry, S., & Nam, Y. (2020). Optimal portfolio management for engineering problems using nonconvex cardinality constraint: A computing perspective. *IEEE Access: Practical Innovations, Open Solutions, 8*, 57437–57450. doi:10.1109/ACCESS.2020.2982195

Li, L., & Abu-Mostafa, Y. S. (2006). *Data complexity in machine learning.* Academic Press.

Liang, Z., Chen, H., Zhu, J., Jiang, K., & Li, Y. (2018). *Adversarial deep reinforcement learning in portfolio management.* arXiv preprint arXiv:1808.09940.

Lotfi, I., & El Bouhadi, A. (2022). Artificial Intelligence Methods: Toward a New Decision Making Tool. *Applied Artificial Intelligence, 36*(1), 1992141. doi:10.10 80/08839514.2021.1992141

Long, J. B. Jr. (1990). The numeraire portfolio. *Journal of Financial Economics, 26*(1), 29–69. doi:10.1016/0304-405X(90)90012-O

Marr, D. (1977). Artificial intelligence—A personal view. *Artificial Intelligence, 9*(1), 37–48. doi:10.1016/0004-3702(77)90013-3

Mishra, S., Padhy, S., Mishra, S. N., & Misra, S. N. (2021). A novel LASSO–TLBO–SVR hybrid model for an efficient portfolio construction. *The North American Journal of Economics and Finance, 55*, 101350. doi:10.1016/j.najef.2020.101350

Paulson, F. L. (1991). What Makes a Portfolio a Portfolio? *Educational Leadership, 48*(5), 60–63.

Perold, A. F. (2004). The capital asset pricing model. *Journal of Economic Perspectives, 18*(3), 3-24.

PK, F. A. (1984). *What is Artificial Intelligence?* Academic Press.

Rashidi, H. H., Tran, N. K., Betts, E. V., Howell, L. P., & Green, R. (2019). Artificial intelligence and machine learning in pathology: The present landscape of supervised methods. *Academic Pathology, 6*. doi:10.1177/2374289519873088 PMID:31523704

Riesener, M., Doelle, C., Schuh, G., Zhang, W., & Jank, M. H. (2019, August). Implementing Neural Networks within Portfolio Management to Support DecisionMaking Processes. In *2019 Portland International Conference on Management of Engineering and Technology (PICMET)* (pp. 1-7). IEEE. 10.23919/PICMET.2019.8893760

Russell, S. J. (2010). *Artificial intelligence a modern approach.* Pearson Education, Inc.

Samtani, S., Kantarcioglu, M., & Chen, H. (2020). Trailblazing the artificial intelligence for cybersecurity discipline: A multi-disciplinary research roadmap. *ACM Transactions on Management Information Systems, 11*(4), 1–19. doi:10.1145/3430360

Sharma, B., Thulasiram, R. K., & Thulasiraman, P. (2012, July). Portfolio management using particle swarm optimization on GPU. In *2012 IEEE 10th International Symposium on Parallel and Distributed Processing with Applications* (pp. 103-110). IEEE.

Singh, S. P. (2019). *Artificial narrow intelligence adaptive audio processing* [Doctoral dissertation]. Dublin Business School.

Smith, M. R., Martinez, T., & Giraud-Carrier, C. (2014). An instance level analysis of data complexity. *Machine Learning*, *95*(2), 225–256. doi:10.100710994-013-5422-z

Spronk, J., & Hallerbach, W. (1997). Financial modelling: Where to go? With an illustration for portfolio management. *European Journal of Operational Research*, *99*(1), 113-125.

Sunchalin, A. M., Kochkarov, R. A., Levchenko, K. G., Kochkarov, A. A., & Ivanyuk, V. A. (2019). *Methods of risk management in portfolio theory*. Academic Press.

Tan, C. N. (1999). A hybrid financial trading system incorporating chaos theory, statistical and artificial intelligence/soft computing methods. *Queensland Finance Conference*.

VanLehn, K. (1990). *Mind bugs: The origins of procedural misconceptions*. MIT Press.

Vanstone, B., Coast, G., & Tan, C. (2003). A survey of the application of soft computing to investment and financial trading. *Pattern Recognition*, *6*, 7.

Velu, R., Hardy, M., & Nehren, D. (2020). *Algorithmic Trading and Quantitative Strategies*. Chapman and Hall/CRC. doi:10.1201/9780429183942

Winston, P. H. (1984). *Artificial intelligence*. Addison-Wesley Longman Publishing Co., Inc.

Womack K. L. Zhang Y. (2003). *Understanding risk and return, the CAPM, and the Fama-French three-factor model*. Available at SSRN 481881.

Yuan, M., Fang, Y., Lv, J., Zheng, S., & Zhou, Z. (2019, June). Research on power trading platform based on big data and artificial intelligence technology. *IOP Conference Series. Materials Science and Engineering*, *486*(1), 012109. doi:10.1088/1757-899X/486/1/012109

Zawacki-Richter, O., Marín, V. I., Bond, M., & Gouverneur, F. (2019). Systematic review of research on artificial intelligence applications in higher education–where are the educators? *International Journal of Educational Technology in Higher Education*, *16*(1), 1-27.

Zhang, C., & Lu, Y. (2021). Study on artificial intelligence: The state of the art and future prospects. *Journal of Industrial Information Integration*, *23*, 100224. doi:10.1016/j.jii.2021.100224

Zhang, X., & Chen, Y. (2017, September). An artificial intelligence application in portfolio management. In *International Conference on Transformations and Innovations in Management (ICTIM 2017)* (pp. 775-793). Atlantis Press. 10.2991/ictim-17.2017.60

Zhang, Y., Li, X., & Guo, S. (2018). Portfolio selection problems with Markowitz's mean–variance framework: A review of literature. *Fuzzy Optimization and Decision Making*, *17*(2), 125–158. doi:10.100710700-017-9266-z

Zhang, Y. J. (2021). *Forecasting the Artificial Intelligence index returns: a hybrid approach*. Department of Economics, University of Pretoria.

Zhao, S., Blaabjerg, F., & Wang, H. (2020). An overview of artificial intelligence applications for power electronics. *IEEE Transactions on Power Electronics*, *36*(4), 4633–4658. doi:10.1109/TPEL.2020.3024914

Zheng, X. L., Zhu, M. Y., Li, Q. B., Chen, C. C., & Tan, Y. C. (2019) FinBrain: when finance meets AI 2.0. *Frontiers of Information Technology & Electronic Engineering*, *20*(7), 914-924.

Chapter 8
Emerging Need of Artificial Intelligence Applications and their Use cases in the Banking Industry:
Case Study of ICICI Bank

Neha Garg
Bharati Vidyapeeth Institute of Management and Research, India

Mamta Gupta
🆔 https://orcid.org/0000-0002-9870-9100
IP University, India

Neetu Jain
Bharati Vidyapeeth Institute of Management and Research, India

ABSTRACT

Presently, banks are fronting with many challenges such as deteriorating loan asset quality leading to increasing provisioning requirements, dissatisfied customers, falling profitability, and weakening capital adequacy position. Innovative cutting-edge technologies has made enough space for new, non-traditional players to enter the financial industry, making the banking sector more competitive than ever before. Traditional banks are facing stiff competition from new financial players and foreign banks who are accelerating their business volumes with the help of rising digitisation and AI technology in today's digital era. The focus of the chapter is on understanding how banking is changing in India with the advent of AI applications. The practical use cases of AI in the banking industry shall become inevitable for the entire financial industry in the near future. At last, this chapter analyses various opportunities and threats while adopting AI applications.

DOI: 10.4018/978-1-6684-4950-9.ch008

INTRODUCTION

The worldwide coronavirus pandemic hit the India's economy during the phase where it was at a hold, slightly slowing because of dogged financial sector weakness. Banking and other financial organizations faced enormous compression to safeguard business performance according to the standards amid covid outbreak and lockdowns. In that situation, balance between employee's well-being and safety and client's continuous service and expectation was the chief difficulty confronted by Banks during the Covid-19 outbreak. It was the need of the hour for other industries to seamlessly shift from conventional workspaces to virtual workspaces, without hampering their fundamental banking or customer facilities. Pandemic led to a standstill situation for practically all businesses, but continuous banking services has certainly helped commerce and employees in uninterrupted fund transfer, cash withdrawal and safeguarded smooth day to day bank operations like transfer of funds, locker facilities, cheque clearing, facility of gold loans, personal covid loan, moratorium in loan accounts, and to name a few. After the outbreak of Covid-19, financial organizations like banks were experiencing problems like employees contact to public, long queues, loan repayment issues, increasing non-performing assets, rise in internet frauds, customers dissatisfaction, operational time per transaction raised, decline in efficiency, to mention a few. In forthcoming months, there are chances that technological advancement would be initiated by banks that will emphasise on the electronic platforms to increase the use of these facilities. Banking sector is endeavouring to recognize latest trends that will arise after the covid19 pandemic and level up with latest technological advanced products demanded from prevailing and projected customers suggestions and feedback. The pandemic has left a lot of learning behind. It encourages us to recognise the gaps and formulate innovative plan to try and attain them. Banking system should attempt to advertise and hold clients with the help of AI tools and make appropriate benefit of technological advancement in the industry. Post covid the speedily budding digital banking services demand is retorting to shift changes to grow and flourish. This has resulted in integration of numerous digital services with the support of latest innovations in technology in the banking sector. Technological advancement builds the groundwork that supports nearly all innovation, invention and modern concepts with a target to boost business, commerce and administrative processes as enormous volume of information forms the base for efficiency, productivity, scalability and convenience.

With changing times consumers are progressively but gradually getting acquainted with upgraded technology in day- to-day life, it is expected that banks will have petite queues, shorter waiting times, decreased paperwork usage to as little as possible and irregular site visits. Banking sector is boarding a little jarring but lucrative venture in the long run by taking a leap towards digitalisation to emphasize their critical banking services.

OBJECTIVES OF THE STUDY

1. To assess the various artificial intelligence applications transforming the banking Industry
2. To analyse the AI applications used by ICICI Bank along with their opportunities and threats

LITERATURE REVIEW

With Covid19 disrupting jobs and income sources of millions of people, defaults from the retail sector and commercial sector are likely to soar. People are finding it difficult to repay existing loans and make new expenditure (Sengupta, April, 2020). Now with the Banking industry priority shifting from comfort and growth to stability and survival, creating a holistic customer experience and understanding the financial needs of consumers is even more critical. The business model of the banks has been challenged by three developments: low interest rates affecting the profitability of banks, increased regulatory requirements and compliance costs, and massive application of latest technologies (Elena Carletti, 2020).

Since banks play a very important role in the economic development of the entire country, the use of the latest technology to successfully implement strategies will not only create added value for one's own business, but also contribute to the economy and growth of the country. Banks must keep pace with the ever-increasing expectations of today's rapidly changing environment. Banking products have far surpassed traditional banking in India (Kurode, Jan 2018).

Traditional banking continues to evolve and banks have gradually introduced innovative technologies such as AI, block chain and cloud computing. The Indian banking industry is looking for ways to integrate artificial intelligence that can improve customer service and banking in the near future (Jewandah, July 2018).

Currently, Artificial Intelligence technology has huge impact on many industries such as healthcare, oil and gas construction, retail, and manufacturing. The latest technologies have been used to improve efficiency, reduce costs, and offer a wide range of commercial benefits (Dubey, October 2019).

The bank uses AI-based anti-money laundering, anti-fraud, compliant credit underwriting and smart contract technologies in its operations, in order to improve profitability and quality of the decisions made at different management levels (Vedapradha R., 2018)

Employees are reserved for innovation and implementation of the expected strategies that are in line with the original vision and the macroeconomic situation. Currently, the bank's employees perform many repetitive, unproductive tasks, and skilled human resources are limited due to their creative and high-level decision-making role (Kurode, January 2018).

It can be seen from the above paragraphs that researchers have done a lot of work in this area, and due to the current needs and requirements of the banking industry for artificial intelligence, more and more studies are being added to the knowledge base every day.

Artificial intelligence has become mainstream in large number these days. Companies and start-ups are looking for different opportunities. AI adoption in banking industry could increase by around 2035 and India's economy will reach $ 1 trillion. Its adoption is still at infant stage and more needs to be done to achieve its full potential. (B. R., June 2019).

Not only does AI plays a significant role in enhancing customer satisfaction, real time fraud detection also plays an important role in finance and banking, especially due to the Covid-19 pandemic. India's digital banking is largely being adopted by the customers (RBI Director, 2020).

Innovative technologies are being upgraded in each and every second towards the change in customer requirement and characteristics for effective work processes in business. These upgradations in technology ensures ease, safety and security and also proves to be more beneficial for organisations (Jeevan, May 2015).

Author analysed through factor analysis that for mobile banking services - convenience, responsiveness, security, accessibility, assurance, knowing the customer and efficiency are the significant factors responsible for customer satisfaction and service quality regarding the ICICI Bank services (Ayswarya, Sarala, Muralidharan, & Ilankadhir, 2019)

DISCUSSION AND ANALYSIS

Advancement in technology has always led to growth in the economy of the country. Using intelligent machines is an added advantage in every field like healthcare systems, industries, space research, to name a few. Availability of data growing exponentially has helped in precise and accurate analysis through Artificial Intelligence. Utilization of information in the form of humongous amount of data and computerized reasoning which is replication of human insight has led to development of computational framework to handle situations with more precision. Controlling of the sensors and electronic appliances, automation of the processes, development of intelligent networks are few of the technological advancements based on AI across the globe. Comparing the previous times wherein the data entry, filling of the forms, maintain ledgers were done manually. With technological advancements, banking industry has been using various techniques for enhancing the efficiency and to detect suspicious activity. Artificial intelligence technologies in banking have led to drastic change in the current business scenario. Nevertheless, the banking sector has also shown profound improvements in customer interaction, cost savings, back-office operations and customer satisfaction through the advancements in AI. AI has been responsible in creating approachable customer involvement, reducing mistakes by staff, saving customer information accurately, portraying better investment options. Adoption of AI is a technological revolution in banking which has led to transformative impact on every aspect of the services such as investment options evaluation, customer experience. Managing huge amount of data and identifying the fraudulent transactions has been a few of the key objectives of banks. These goals have been judiciously achieved through harnessing technology like chatbots, AI based fraud detection mechanism, digital payment advisors leading to increment in profits. Fintech players have already been using AI based techniques such as Voice recognition, Predictive analytics to improve compliance and AI algorithms to derive insights from large volume of data. Developed nations are using Artificial intelligence since a decade. Banking areas where AI is implemented in United States of America is mentioned below:

Table 1. Percentage of AI adaptation in Banks at different areas

S No.	Area where AI is implemented in Banking	Percentage of adaption %
1	Risk Assessment	49%
2	Financial Research	45%
3	Investment/ Portfolio management	37%
4	Trading algorithm	33%
5	Credit approval process	29%
6	KYC/ Anti money laundering	29%
7	Regulation and compliance	26%
8	Administrative work	17%
9	Sales and marketing strategies	17%

Figure 1.

Source: Nuvento.com https://nuvento.com/blog/artificial-intelligence-in-banking-trends-in-usa/

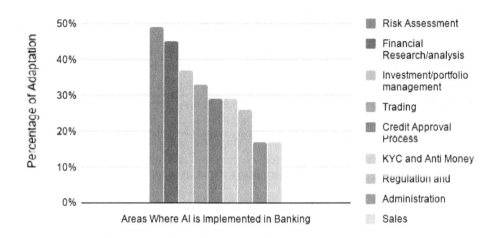

HOW AI IS ADOPTED IN INDIAN BANKING

Technology as we all know is expected to bring major revolution in all the industries. Large giants like Google, Amazon, Facebook, and alike have already started taking advantage of AI and other technologies transforming service industry. Banks are facing tough competition from FinTech and other FIs who are reaping the fruits of AI applications in their field. Unsatisfied customers and mass amount of data that can be analyzed and further converted to satisfied customers and new customers. Generation of increased levels of value and added customised experience to clients, lessen threat and growing chances of becoming contemporary economic and monetary engines are some of the benefits provided by continuous use of AI tools and technologies that helped to modernize the banking industry companies.

REVOLUTION OF TECHNOLOGY: AN APT SOLUTION TO CONQUER BANKING CHALLENGES

Artificial Intelligence (AI) is rapidly evolving and has become a win-win arrangement for global companies to provide personalized experiences to individuals. Artificial Intelligence (AI) is an application that allows the system to automatically learn, adapt, grow, and improve from experience without the need for explicit programming. Artificial intelligence is a technology that allows machines to learn from their actions and history over time and make decisions on behalf of humans without manual intervention. This is the field of science that aims to use humans to solve problems on an equal footing with modern computer systems, such as the diverse abilities of cognition, learning and self-correction (Alzaidi, October 2018).

AI involves both innovation as well as technology leading AI to become a subject of political and economic matter. Countries that have an extensive range policy apprises on AI and are determining the international dialogue. It is the need of the hour for Indian banking industry to upgrade their technology and meet their customer's expectations when compared to foreign banks and Financial Institutions.

Globally AI applications are used all over the world in developed nations and also it is found to be used at low level in developing nations. Global revenues from Enterprise AI applications are expected to grow and the same has been depicted in graph shown below:

Figure 2.
Source: Statista.com / Forbes.com issued in Jan 2018

Enterprise artificial intelligence market revenue worldwide 2016-2025

Revenues from the artificial intelligence for enterprise applications market worldwide, from 2016 to 2025 (in million U.S. dollars)

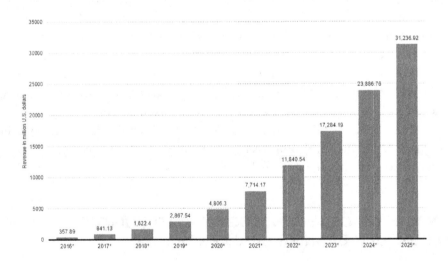

International worldwide revenues from AI use are projected to increase from $1.622 billion to $ 31.236billion in 2025 achieving a CAGR of 52.59% in the forecast period. Better Human resource systems, smart recruitment applications, voice and image recognition, machine learning algorithms to detect fraud, predictive analysis and quick data processing may be some AI applications that may see rise in future.

Banking is a data centric industry now it has become beyond the capacity of the human mind to review, analyze and interpret the huge complex data patterns in copious transactions that are taking place in the banking industry every second. Artificial Intelligence can easily help bankers to identify transaction patterns and understand the trend that helps in making relevant decisions with more speed and accuracy. Artificial Intelligence can help bankers in improving their customer personalization services leading to enhanced customer delight and loyalty. It further helps in completing their routine banking issues in real time. Organizations, financial institutions and businesses moguls all over the world are betting big on AI tool. They are investing billions of dollars in undertaking research and development centres and also run pilot programs for new and innovative start. With the help of AI techniques consisting of Machine learning, Natural language processing, Expert systems, Robotics, Automation, and alike; banks are able to detect fraud, manage high speed data and also obtain valuable feedback. It leads to superior quality of customer service and broader customer base.

Niti Aayog, a government think tank, published a paper entitled "Towards Responsible AI for All People" in June 2020, stating that it is possible to adopt AI on a large scale in various social areas and plans a roadmap. They proposed the establishment of a special group that will play a promotional role in the technical, legal, political and social aspects of artificial intelligence. Niti Aayog further mentioned that India can become 40% of the global artificial intelligence garage and also include a National Artificial Intelligence Centre in support and coordination of Electronics and IT department. The Treasury Department also has approved NITI Aayog's Rs. 7000 crore plans. Bank is facing various challenges and that needs to be overcome on war front basis. Banking Industry has prioritized its various policies with the main aim to focus on enhancing customer experience through digitalization, process automation, reducing its cost of operations, recruit skilled staff and other strategic priorities. Mentioned below is a table which reflects the overview of Top strategic priorities of Financial Institutions:

Figure 3.
Source: The financial brand, Digital banking report @ Feb 2020

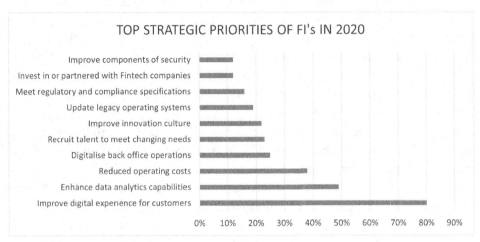

NEED OF AI IN BANKING INDUSTRY

Now, banks are burdened with additional responsibility to accommodate more customers with less expenses on workforce. Customers are exceptionally tech savvy and expect the high-tech services at their platter with comfortable experience from the banking sector. The banks are providing the services such as mobile banking, e banking and real time money transfers to meet the customers' expectations. These technology features have brought comfort to the customers but added costs to the banks. AI has put forward the expectations of the customers and play a vital role in keeping the preferences as a priority. Artificial Intelligence has been responsible for substantial economic growth, many industries have captured this opportunity. National strategy on Artificial Intelligence announced by NITI Aayog provides guiding principles for new era skills, R & D, cyber security, safety, legal and ethical issues focusing on growth across all sectors. Adoption of Artificial Intelligence provides a competitive edge by reducing operational cost and increasing revenue. After digitalization of banks, adopting AI techniques such as voice recognition, Predictive analytics, etc. by banks will make them stand ahead of the competitors. With technological advancement, AI would be a necessity since it not only reduces risks, frauds but also makes the banking process smooth and intelligent for client and employee. To perform operations effectively and efficiently banks will engage AI driven technology and employees would more focus on core operations. Use of cognitive systems, which think like human experts and give optimal solution for the given data would help the banking industry in effective decision making.

TOOLS OF ARTIFICIAL INTELLIGENCE

The banking industry continues to use AI tools and technologies to innovate companies in the banking industry, deliver higher levels of value and a more personal experience to customers, reduce risk and increase the chances of becoming modern economic and financial engines. AI is fast becoming political and economic issue as it is a matter of great modernization in terms of technology. The developed nations like USA, China, Canada, European Union, Japan are following wide range of AI policy guidelines and are shaping the global dialog in this regard. Presently India, despite having so many opportunities, is not a part of mainstreams talks and policy makers meetings and deliberations on AI. AI technologies can help lift revenues through increased personalization of customer services, reduced costs through competences generated by higher automation, reduced errors rates, and improved resource utilization and discover new and unrealized opportunities based on better ability to process and generate valuable insights from large volumes of data sets. Below are some applications where artificial intelligence is playing dominating role in the banking industry.

A. CHATBOT/ VIRTUAL ASSISTANT

Use of chatbots lead to huge savings in cost, leading to most commonly used AI technique in Banking and financial industry. It can efficiently manage routine bank work such as real time account statement, generating mini statements, quick fund transfer, credit card statement, details of last transactions, and alike.

Example 1: Bank of America introduced an AI driven intelligent virtual assistant named ERICA. It uses NLP (Natural Language Processing) to understand customer text messages and speech instructions. The chatbot performs daily routine transactions carried out by human staff and is available 24*7 and wherever whenever customer needs it. It also leverages predictive analysis and cognitive tools to provide customized financial guidance with the aim to achieve their financial goals. It is a self learning device, gets even refined over time while dealing with multiple difficult queries.

Example 2: Capital one also introduced a money managing chatbot on technology-based platform called ENO. This was targeted for more than 1 lakh users which allowed them to manage funds through mobile phones. This chatbot adapts itself to users' personality and automatically learns customer behaviour with passage of time to guide them in a better way. This chatbot accepts instruction in the form of voice and text.

B. EARLY FRAUD DETECTION TECHNIQUES

These techniques provide a platform where application of a customer / existing loan account details get connected with its bank account details. This system powered by Machine Learning technology ensures security of each and every transaction. These high-tech algorithms carry out real time analytics and verify authenticity and nullify the chance of any fraudulent activity.

Example 1: Citibank investment and acquisition division name Citi Ventures invested in Feedzai which is a data science firm that can sense and remove fraud from the systems in real time. It also monitors potential banking related threats at supersonic speed and great accuracy by conducting detailed analysis of customer actions and their history of transactions.

C. RPA (Robotic Process Automation)

Nowadays Banks, Financial Institutions and Fintech companies successfully leverage Robotic Process Automation to increase the transaction speed and improve their backend operations. RPA is now getting more complicated in transforming into cognitive behaviour and understanding the history and pattern of the human transactions. RPA algorithms increase accuracy and operational efficiency, help bankers to avoid mistakes and reduce human errors. It also reduces the cost by automating the time-consuming repetitive task such that the employees are able to focus on more important decisions that require human environment.

Example 1: J P Morgan Chase Bank has leveraged RPA technology by executing massive routine data extraction, timely completing regular government compliances and reviewing document capturing processes. It also helps in ensuring smooth cash management processes.

Example 2: AI is also used by BNY Mellon Bank to drastically reduce the cost and saves time on repetitive massive task. More than 200 bots were deployed by them over the last few years to process the automated different assignments. Most of the banking routine work has been automated such as account opening, account closure, trade entry, fund transfer, responding to data requests from auditors, formatting and correcting the data mistakes answering to customer requests.

D. DATA ANALYTICS

In banking Industry, AI driven Data analytics help to receive better data driven decision and led to improved operational efficiency. Data analytics also help in framing marketing strategies where segmentation can be done for each user group leading to increased sales.

Example 1: Contract intelligence was recently introduced by J P Morgan Chase bank to analyse bulk documents at an incredible speed which saves plenty of human work hours. This platform can also evaluate and review lengthy legal documents and extract relevant points important for the case. Detailed review of Credit agreements which human take weeks to analyse it takes few seconds to complete the task.

E.   WEALTH MANAGEMENT / PORTFOLIO MANAGEMENT

AI wealth advisors provide personalised tips on how to manage funds and make smart investments. It leverages deep learning algorithms and provides valuable insights and share precise predictions on stocks, commodities and currencies. This tool analyses the financial statements of the company and understand the movements in stock price by capturing real time data from financial markets across the world.

Example 1: Well Fargo, large financial player, introduced Greenhouse, a mobile banking app to attract tech savvy individuals who wish to manage their present savings for security of their future. The app assists customers on various aspects such as savings, investments, future prospects, bills, demand in market, and alike. It further provides valuable insights on combining daily spending with long term planning.

Example 2: Swiss Bank UBS launched a new AI system wherein it identifies trading patterns after screening mass amount of real time market data. It predicts trading strategies resulting into higher returns and improved profits for clients.

ADVANTAGES OF BANKING AI APPLICATIONS

The banking industry uses artificial intelligence in a variety of ways to outline the banking world. AI technology is essential as it enables software to become more and more effective, less expensive, to replicate human skills such as understanding, thinking, planning, delegating, and perceiving. Here are just a few of advantages for a detailed discussion:

Regulatory Compliance and Fraud Detection

It is beneficial for the banks to automate compliance, employing Decision Management System (DMS) caters for fraud detection and comprehensive audit documentation. Using the desired software the data will be accurate and the errors will be highlighted automatically. AI can analyze humongous amount of data, which may not be possible manually. With AI enabled fraud detection system, illegal financial activities have been reduced. Any suspicious activity can be easily detected through AI based software.

Improved Investment Evaluation

Apart from interest income banks now also rely on noninterest revenue such as investment income, commissions for which the institution has to explore the options which provide higher returns at minimal risk. The AI software guides the investment options by including more variables and thus provides lucrative investment opportunities. Risk factors and the customer funding proposals can be accurately evaluated with the right investment software. The evaluation process considers the various aspects like industry sector diversification, funds allocation to different asset classes, identifying perfect time to liquidate an investment option or enter a transaction. Evaluating the global investments options manually would be a challenge, rather Investment software can speed the process and assess the global environment more accurately. It caters larger customer base and provides broader investment avenues by taking into consideration the risk tolerance and time horizon. AI analytics assist in collecting, analyzing the data in readable format, making it easier to identify the loopholes and thus providing scope for repurpose the processes. Predictive analytics in AI can foresee the volatile situations such as political turmoil, currency fluctuation, scams and accommodate such external global factors with minimal risk.

Enhanced Customer Experience

Innovation has been constantly backed by the customers' convenience. ATM and smart phones have helped customers avail the services at any location or time. Chatbot, a conversational interface has eliminated repetitive tasks, thus the employees can focus on other complex situations. Chatbot and other virtual assistants have eliminated the long queues of traditional banking, a customer can acquire information at his comfort. An intelligent decision management system reduces the errors in capturing KYC. Financial products or any changes in tariffs can be communicated to the customers on time. Introduction of AI has led to gain trust of clients through smooth and approachable automated systems set up by banks. Customer finds the AI based system user friendly with its increased accessibility and flexibility. Based on the history of client's behaviour, AI assist the banks to customize its services as per the requirement of the customer, and hence build committed relationship with the customers.

Reduced Operational Cost and Risks

To err is human, and the financial errors are at times irreparable. Decision management system captures the required details of the clients before proceeding for any financial transaction. It creates the logical flow of details mandatory for any transaction, thus reducing risk, labour cost and at the same time increase accuracy. The data entry work is minimized which can be replaced by focusing on core innovations in business development tasks. Eventually increasing the efficiency and productivity of the employees. Predictive analytics helps to optimize capital investment decisions and recommend products and services to the clients based on the past data such as work experience, credit scores which leads to reducing risk.

Improved Loan and Credit Valuation

AI based system gathers information about the clients and consider more variables for taking decision for rejection or approval of business proposal. AI plays a key role in credit valuation process by collecting data from internal as well as external data sources such as social networks, central banks, etc. to check client's credit worthiness. Thus, the financial bodies maintain and update the customer details regularly to reduce the regulatory risk involved with KYC non-compliance.

MAJOR CHALLENGES FACED BY BANKS WHILE ADOPTING AI TECHNOLOGY

The bank automates its processes with the help of these technologies to create seamless customer journey. Although artificial intelligence has achieved several improvements and advanced applications for innovations in the banking and finance industries, its introduction in the industry is still at its infancy (Vedapradha R., 2018). Even it is proved that efficiency and speed of AI is unmatchable but human intervention cannot be ignored when it comes to smoothly handle complex customer transactions, specific requests, understanding their deep sentiments, building an emotional trust and visioning with NRI Clients to capture his attention and also to gain branch loyalty and trust. Future demands appropriate blend of functions of AI along with bank staff human touch as per case-to-case basis.

a. **Lack of Expert Operators/ Engineers** –There is huge demand of highly technical skilled people who can make Machine learning algorithms which can create seamless transaction process for companies. For rapid and widespread application of AI tools, existing IT staff should be well versed with current technical tools and applications. There is a huge deficiency of persons with the suitable IT developed knowledge base in India.

Possible mitigation: Skills should be developed in AI Field; this can be done by gathering some magnificent data scientists with expertise in artificial intelligence, to collaborate with Indian universities to nurture competent data scientists, and advance domestic training programs to educate personnel in data science. In house training programmes and tie up with universities can be done to impart AI technical knowledge.

b. **Confidentiality of Data** – Rise in digitalization has led to development of banking facilities related transactions. Accessibility of data and protection of data are the key aspects of AI workbench. These aspects have become more critically important due to the emergence of European regulations like European General Data Protection Regulation (GDPR). Currently GDPR regulations are applicable for European citizens, but citizens of India and other countries have to abide by their own privacy regulations. Compilation with data protection regulations is urgently required by banks to develop AI systems.

Possible mitigation: This problem can be overcome by applying robust data protection regulations and latest guidelines in IT Act. There is an immediate requirement of globally accepted regulatory guidelines for use of new technologies in a safe and ethical way, not harming the interest of probable users.

c. **Mass Unemployment Risk–** Adoption of AI technology at large scale in banking sector shall lead to risk of job loss to existing staff base. It may lead to large scale layoffs.

Possible mitigation: Existing staff needs to upgrade their knowledge as to feel comfortable and compatible while working on AI systems. Human workforce needs to manage queries and upgrade algorithms while utilizing AI systems.

CASE STUDY

ICICI Bank Using AI Applications

ICICI Bank Ltd. is one of the biggest private banks in India. It offers a diverse range of products and services in financial field catering to corporate and retail segment through its wide range of branches and ATMs. It also has subsidiaries outside India in around seventeen nations.

This bank was established in 1994 by ICICI (Industrial Credit and Investment Corporation of India) which is an Indian FI wholly owned subsidiary in Vadodara. ICICI Bank has always been a leader in providing latest technology services to its customers through various digital platforms such as mobile banking and internet banking. Its goal is to preserve its leadership by continuing to invest in technology, developing new ideas and utilizing partnerships.

Bank's app highlighting walk-in-module is a NLP and ML based technology solution for handling large level recruitment drive. It analyses cognitive intelligence, behavior and voice recognition and helps in managerial decision making. For all stakeholders, it is designed for scalability, speed and ease. As a result, the entire recruitment system has been converted to a paperless digital approach. The aim of ICICI business is to increase core operating earnings while staying within risk and regulatory parameters. The Indian economy is becoming more formalized, and technology is being adopted at a rapid pace. Technological skills need to be upgraded along with achievement of organization's financial goals. ICICI STACK, a digital platform which delivers approx. 500 services to ensure smooth banking services. Digital platform allows the customer to manage online account opening, faster loan processing, support in health and term insurance. With the use of What's app banking and i- Pal chatbot, customer service become seamless and easier. As part of 2025 technology strategy of Bank, enterprise architecture structure includes data analytics, cognitive intelligence, cloud computing and other emerging technologies. Retail and SME customers' data analytics-driven onboarding, credit evaluation, and monitoring, as well as the generation of solutions for their supply-chain finance needs, were all improved by the bank. Supply chain financing is an important aspect of SME operations and a target area for expanding our corporate ecosystem coverage. Using Application Program Interfaces (APIs) or host-to-host protocols, our Corp Connect technology allows businesses to combine their Enterprise Resource Planning (ERP) systems. Digital Lite, our plug-and-play digital supply chain finance technology, allows customers to be on boarded easily and rapidly. These two solutions allow businesses to manage their dealers and vendors supply chain financing, payments, collection and reconciliation needs in a convenient and paperless manner.

Analytics is utilized to monitor the existing book and identify early danger signals. As a result, the overall quality of the current corporate portfolio has improved. To make the portfolio more granular, bank also concentrated on lowering concentration risks. ICICI Bank has established an Innovation center and activities like forecasting models, performance monitoring and business analytics are handled by a sophisticated team of professionals.

Following are the AI use cases that are presently being adopted by ICICI.

Table 2. Various AI use cases adopted by ICICI Bank

VIRTUAL FINANCIAL ASSISTANT		
Application description	**ICICI Use case**	**Benefits**
To provide real time support and feedback to customers along with personalized experience banks are looking forward to Virtual Financial Assistants. These services result in enhanced customer engagement and help banks to collect real time feedback, generate accurate leads and ultimately drastically reducing marketing expenses.	ICICI has launched its multi-channel chatbot named ipal that can be accessed through online banking, smartphone, and through other devices as well. Additionally, the intelligent bot provides services through the mobile app and website. Since its inception, the virtual assistant has interacted with more than 3 million customers replying 6 million queries with 90% accuracy rate	24 /7 availability Quick response Accessible anytime anywhere
ROBOTIC PROCESS AUTOMATION		
Application description	**ICICI Use case**	**Benefits**
Routine and regular banking operations executed by Artificial intelligence software RPA (Robotic Process Automation) leads to enhanced results. Diverse banking functions such as withdrawal of amount, statement generation, cash deposit, clearing of cheques, and other regular routine transactions can be smoothly handled by RPA software. Big business houses are betting heavily on Artificial intelligence tools.	Bank has re-engineered more than 200 business processes with the help of Software robotics facility and these software's are processing more than 10 lakhs transactions daily. With the advent of software robots' response time has been declined upto 60% and accuracy has reached almost 100% thereby resulting in improved productivity and efficiency. The bank has also initiated a pilot project wherein fund transfer cross border transaction gets settled in few minutes which was earlier taking a couple of days.	Enhanced productivity cost efficiency operational efficiency better time management focus of staff on valued added services
DATA ANALYTICS		
Application description	**ICICI Use case**	**Benefits**
Banks have enormous amount of data available on daily basis, meaningful insights can be derived from these data sets after analyzing and understanding user behavior pattern. It also helps in offering personalized services and customized targeted solutions to customers.	AI technology collects vital information such as address, age, spending pattern, history of employment, information available on social media platform and other information to make accurate and quick decisions.	Quick and accurate data for decision making Personalized targeted solutions Converting raw data to meaningful insights
EARLY FRAUD DETECTION APPLICATIONS		
Application description	**ICICI Use case**	**Benefits**
With increasing no. of online transactions, hackers and jammers are also increasing their malpractice. It has become even more important to deploy Machine learning algorithms which can successfully prevent, identify and eliminate real time fraud and other type of suspicions entries. Whenever there is a change in pattern or deviation from normal transaction pattern, alert is triggered using AI technologies. AI solutions identify, analyze and control fraudulent transactions and specious payments much before these are processed.	ICICI Bank offers real-time credit evaluation of clients using a new Big Data based algorithm. The algorithm employs an intelligent mix of the customer's financial and digital activity, including credit bureau checks, purchase patterns, and frequency of purchase, to determine the customer's creditworthiness in a matter of seconds. ICICI Bank is developing new machine learning (ML) algorithms that deploys satellite images to determine a farmer's creditworthiness, allowing the bank to provide the necessary timely services. Pay Later is a latest digital credit facility that enables customer to access to credit in very less time and also in paperless manner. It uses bank's Big data based algorithm for analyzing the credit score of customer.	Improved asset quality Quick decision making Understanding the borrower account details for timely necessary action
WEALTH AND PORTFOLIO MANAGEMENT		
Application description	**ICICI Use case**	**Benefits**
This application helps in managing personal finances in a better way. The software identifies trading history, transactions and patterns and after analyzing market trend, then formulate personalized strategies for bank customer leading to higher return. It enables customer to make fast and secure transactions and also promote financial literacy.	Money Coach is the ICICI Bank's sophisticated Robo adviser which is the country's first automated and robotics-based financial advice solution for clients. It is a financial management tool for individuals that assist them in aiding and reaching financial objective. It provides accurate customized future forecast for trading platforms.	Customized and accurate tips as per individual risk-taking ability Increased wealth portfolio Quick settlement of transactions Motivates customer to stay organized with their portfolio details.
ROBO SECURITY ALERTS		
Application description	**ICICI Use case**	**Benefits**
System shall give an alert when unauthorized person tries to login the details of another customer. AI algorithms detect the fraud by integrating biometrics, voice recognition; face recognition technologies with account login module.	The access to locker rooms is secured by debit card and biometric authentication. The advanced robotic technology scans customer request and then allow access. Smart vault uses high level intelligent safety system.	Enhanced security and safety Reduced risk Safe access Improved customer satisfaction

SIGNIFICANCE OF RESEARCH

This study is important from the perspective of entire Indian banking system. The Bank managers can use the implications of this study in customer acquisition and entrustment. Banks can use findings of the research in improving their key performance parameters. This research will also help Banks in understanding the importance of different AI tools and which one can be implemented on immediate basis as per the requirement of present competitive environment. As the study talks in detail about the various challenges faced by Indian banks, they may use the findings to overcome these challenges to the great extent by using AI latest technologies and solutions suggested. This research will provide bankers the authentic perspective of the AI tools and the Bank can change their policies as per the longing, customer requirements and need of the hour.

FUTURE TRENDS

AI is here to stay and in addition to the growth assisted by AI in banks, it will further enhance the precision in credit decisions, fraud detection and management, financial advisory services and personal banking. The impact of AI is visible in all the sectors and it is changing the way customer think by redefining the industries. Thus, in this new era every sector needs to evaluate the options and alternatives to compete in AI technology driven world.

Few of the ways in which AI will shape the banking sector in future:

Risk management (Analyse the data sources and predict the defaulters)

Personalized banking (Track any deviations in behaviour and provides 24 hours banking benefits to the customer with prompt responses)

Process automation (Replace manual work with intelligent systems resulting in better customer experience and scale the operations)

Secure Transactions (Detect fraudulent cases in real time through analysing millions of data)

Better customer experience (study customer spending pattern, provide relevant engagements and offers which builds better relationship and leads to growth of banks)

Predict future and trends (analyse data to reach right customer at right time and provide right offer)

Wealth and portfolio management (assess market trends, spending behaviour and chooses best funds for the portfolio)

Intelligent character recognition system (collects information from the existing documents and contracts, saves it in central database making it accessible to all stakeholders)

Lending (analyse creditworthiness of the customer, market trends, risk in lending, likelihood of the fraud to simplify the complex process of lending)

AI in banking sector will see a wider adoption in future, although it is in the infancy stage. Institutions have learned the fact that AI has to be adopted to compete with tech driven world. Despite the operational and organizational challenges banking sector need to accept the AI based intelligent machines and algorithms to become technologically powered organization.

For future directions, different AI applications or emerging technologies adopted by other Indian banks can also be explored. Quantitative analysis can also be taken under consideration while understanding the impact of AI on financial performance of banks. Further, Foreign banks and Indian banks financial performance after AI adoption can be compared using secondary data.

CONCLUSION

Artificial intelligence influences the future of almost every industry and everyone. Latest technologies like cloud, robotics, big data and the Internet of Things are driven by Artificial intelligence. It will resume acting as the uppermost technological pioneer in the predictable future. In the current scenario, when Covid-19 has brought a negative effect on the lives of people, Artificial Intelligence has appeared as a blessing in countries for both banks and commercial industries as well as for massive consumer base. AI provides customers the benefit of boosted customised facilities at the comfort of our home without being physically present at bank or without physical contact with the banking staff. Portfolio can be maintained cautiously with the help of robot advisor alerts, robotic safety mechanism enables fund transfer, opening of accounts and screening of KYC at the luxury of their homes, providing customers a sense of monetary safety.

Artificial intelligence helps in attaining competitive advantage as chatbots helps to leap forward of their competitors. As on March 2019, it was observed that there were 6 million customers of Bank of America's Erica and 10,000 daily inquiries are handled by SBI's SIA. Initial deception detection, assessment of advanced credit risk, efficiency in operational field and improved risk management are some of reliefs provided by AI. Artificial intelligence not only enhances the overall performance of the bank but also supports the development of a sturdy relationship, by generating confidence and assurance among the clients and the bank.

Lastly, it is seen that AI continues to develop as an incredible pillar to the banking sector. It can attain its highest potential if strengthened by an entirely innovative supported framework.

The banks should be ready to deal with newly improved regulatory conditions and mutual acquiescence as reliance on artificial intelligence is increasing. As it is likely said "With great power comes great responsibility", fast data analysis and projecting models generates great power whereas maintenance of data security and data privacy generates great responsibility.

REFERENCES

Aaron Smith, H. N. (2020). Artificial Intelligence in Banking A Mini Review. SSRN *Electronic Journal*.

Alzaidi, A. A. (2018, October). Impact of Artificial Intelligence on Performance of Banking Industry in Middle East. *International Journal of Computer Science and Network Security, 18*(10), 140–148.

Ambrish Kumar Mishra, A. P. (2021). Impact of Covid19 Outbreak on performance of Indian banking sector. *International Semantic Intelligence conference*.

Ashish Bagewadi, D. D. (2020). Analysis of Banking sector in India: Post Covid 19. *International Journal of Research and Analytical Reviews, 7*(3), 299-308.

Ayswarya, R., Sarala, D., Muralidharan, P., & Ilankadhir, M. (2019). Service Quality of Mobile Banking Services in ICICI Bank Limited. *Journal of Service Science and Management*.

B.R., P. L. (2019, June). Advent of Arificial Intelligence and its impact on Top leading Commecial Banks in India. *International Journal of Trend in Scientifc Research and Development, 3*(4), 614–616.

Christian Catalini, C. F. (2018, August). *Machine Intelligence vs. Human judgement in new venture finance*. Academic Press.

Das, S. R. (2019). Future of Fintech. *Financial Management,* (48), 981-1007.

Dhingra, A. B. (2020). Analysis of Banking sector in India. *International Journal of Research and Analytical Reviews, 7*(3), 299-308.

Director, I. (2020). *AI in Banking*. Reserve Bank of India.

Dr Navleen Kaur, M. S. (2020, June). Banking 4.0: The Influence of Artificial Intelligence on the banking industry and how AI is changing the face of modern day banks. *International Journal of Management, 11*(6), 577–585.

Dubey, V. (2019). Fintech innvovations in Digital Banking. *International Journal of Engineering Research and Technology*, 597-601.

Elena Carletti, S. C. (2020). *The Bank business model in the Post Covid 19 world.* IESE Banking Initiative.

Fintech Innovations in Digital Banking. (2019). *International Journal of Engineering Research and Technology, 8*(10), 597-601.

Inaki Aldasoro, I. F. (2020, May). Effect of Covid 19 on the Banking sector. *BIS Bulletin.*

Jeevan, P. (2015). A Conceptual Study on Customers Adoption of IMobile App Technology In *National conference on Recent trends in Management.* K S School of Engineering and Management.

Jewandah, D. S. (2018, July). How Artificial Intelligence is changing the banking sector. *International Journal of Management. Technology and Engineering, 8*(7), 525–531.

Jonathan Donner, A. T. (2008, December). Mobile banking and economic development:Linking adoption, impact and use. *Asian Journal of Communication, 18*(4).

Keenam, J. M. (2020). Covid, Resilience and the built environment. *Springer. Environment Systems & Decisions, 40*(2), 216–221. doi:10.100710669-020-09773-0 PMID:32412522

Kunwar, M. (2019, Aug). Understanding how Automation and Machine learning is transforming the financial industry. *Artificial Intelligence in Finance*, 36.

Kurode, T. (2018, January). Review of applicability of Artificial Intelligence in various financial services. *Journal of Advance Management Research, 6*(1), 2019–2214.

Marie Paule, O. P. (2020, May). *Banking model after Covid 19: Taking model risk management to the next level.* McKinsley and Company.

Ms Bhavna Aggarwal, D. H. (2019). Application of Artificial Intelligence for successful strategy implementation in India's Banking Sector. *International Journal of Advanced Research, 7*(11), 157–166. doi:10.21474/IJAR01/9988

Namratha, S. J. (2019). *Impact of Artificial Intelligence in chosen Indian Commercial Bank- A Cost Benefit Analysis.* Academic Press.

Phillipe Dintrans, B. H. (2019). *Artificial Intelligence in Financial Services: From nice to must have.* Cognizant.

Rajesh Bansal, A. B. (2020, Sep). *Recovery, Resilience and Adaptation: India from 2020 to 2030.* Carnegie India.

Salunkhe, R. T. (2019, November). Role of Artificial Intelligence in providing customer service with Special reference to SBI and HDFC Bank. *International Journal of Recent Technology and Engineering, 8*(4), 12251–12260. doi:10.35940/ijrte.C6065.118419

Sengupta, S. M. (2020). *Impact of Covid19 on Indian economy.* Mumbai: Indira Gandhi Institute of Development Research.

Vedapradha, H. R. (2018). Application of Artificial Intelligence in Investment Banks. *Review of Economic and Business Studies, 11*(2), 131-136.

Veerla, V. (2021). To study the impact of Artificial Intelligence as Predictive model in banking sector: Novel approach. *International Journal of Innovative Research in Technology, 7*(8), 94-105.

Vijai, D. C. (2019). Artificial Intelligence in Indian Banking Sector. *International Journal of Advanced Research, 7*(5), 1581-1587.

Chapter 9
Artificial Intelligence and Auditing:
Benefits and Risks

Derya Üçoğlu

https://orcid.org/0000-0001-5510-3574

Istanbul Bilgi University, Turkey

ABSTRACT

Artificial intelligence (AI) technology has impacted businesses and industries as well as audit companies. With the emergence of AI-enhanced systems, many tasks performed by auditors can now be completed more efficiently by these technologies. Such systems are used in different audit tasks, such as risk assessment, audit planning, fraud detection, audit inquiry, transaction testing, inventory count, and document testing. AI platforms designed for auditing provide time-saving, higher efficiency and accuracy, minimized risks and biases, and improved audit quality. This chapter provides examples of AI platforms and tools developed by Big 4 audit firms and discusses the benefits and risks of implementing AI technology in auditing regarding the extant literature.

INTRODUCTION

Artificial intelligence (AI) is a multidisciplinary field of psychology, computer science, and philosophy. AI replicates human brain activity and reasoning, advances its capabilities through continuous learning, and applies knowledge to make higher quality decisions (Qureshi et al., 1998).

DOI: 10.4018/978-1-6684-4950-9.ch009

Due to the audit profession becoming more sophisticated and the attention being drawn to the profession as a result of audit scandals, the audit companies began adopting emerging technologies like artificial intelligence. Instead of traditional audit practices, audit companies incorporate AI technology into audit procedures by spending significant resources. In this way, the aim is to achieve improved risk assessments, reduced auditing costs, enhanced audit quality, and more efficient control tests (Alrashidi et al., 2022).

The changing highly technological business environment based on web-based, real-time data also compels audit companies to use AI-based technologies rather than traditional approaches. Although there are numerous arguments for conducting internal and external audits by adapting AI systems, AI is perceived as a faster and more efficient way of audit functioning in times of increased uncertainty and complexity (Eulerich & Kalinichenko, 2018).

This chapter covers the benefits and risks of using AI technology in auditing, the areas and tasks that AI can automate, and how AI will change the auditing profession based on a detailed analysis of current literature.

ARTIFICIAL INTELLIGENCE TECHNOLOGY

More than 60 years ago, John McCarthy defined AI as "the science and engineering of making intelligent machines, especially intelligent computer programs". In the 1950s and 1960s, people expected AI to develop rapidly into robots and computers that can mimic the intelligence of human (Bolander, 2019). Nevertheless, after the 1950s, much attention and scientific obscurity were not paid to AI for over a half-century. Following the developments in computer technology and the increasing rise of big data, AI gained more importance in the business environment and among the public (Haenlein & Kaplan, 2019).

AI supports businesses by automating the business processes, providing insights by analyzing data, and engaging with employees and customers (Hung & Sun, 2020). For this purpose, AI uses various techniques for simulating human cognition. The programs designed for specific purposes allow AI-based applications to drive cars, engage in dialogues, play chess or recognize skin diseases (Bolander, 2019). AI even affects every aspect of daily life through many applications such as personal assistants in mobile phones, cyber protection, and customization of products and services (PwC, 2017).

Although AI has some weaknesses compared to human intelligence, combining human experts and AI systems seems to provide a better solution. For instance, the Corti company in Denmark developed a pattern recognition algorithm that identifies probable cardiac arrest cases by listening to emergency calls. The algorithm had some false positives and negatives. Still, more cardiac arrests were detected, only at the cost of sending a few more ambulances than would have been sent otherwise (Bolander, 2019). Moreover, during the COVID-19 pandemic, AI-based applications helped small and medium-sized enterprises target customers online, make cash flow forecasts and facilitate HR activities for better operational strategies, and have better-informed financial planning through pricing and risk analysis. In this way, AI enabled companies to increase efficiency and reduce business risks by developing defense mechanisms and finding solutions for the challenges posed by the COVID-19 pandemic (Drydakis, 2022).

There are different subsets of AI technology, of which the most common ones are mentioned below.

Expert Systems

The most popular AI system for replacing human specialization in a specific area of decision-making is called an expert system. Expert systems consist of computer programs that simulate the way experts think, considering the level of particular expertise (Chukwudi et al., 2018).

Eining et al. (1997) differentiated expert systems from other traditional decision aids to emphasize knowledge rather than algorithmic solutions and give user access to the knowledge base. Moreover, sophisticated expert systems offer the potential to enhance the dialogue between the system and the user (Omoteso, 2012). The early AI systems which replicated human intelligence through a series of if-then statements led to the lack of progress in the AI field, as expert systems performed poorly in many areas (Haenlein & Kaplan, 2019).

Machine Learning

Machine learning is an AI application that employs mathematical models for solving business problems by extraction of knowledge from data (Alarcon et al., 2019). The analytical models analyze data for identifying patterns and trends, and produce the most accurate predictions (Dickey et al., 2019).

Machine learning is widely used in daily life. For instance, tasks related to the classification of emails as spam and non-spam, image recognition, speech recognition, big data analytics, and automatic translation are conducted by machine learning algorithms by generalizing a problem from a set of labeled sample datasets (Alarcon et al., 2019; Taniguchi et al., 2018). So, people use machine learning technologies every day via smartphones through applications such as Cortana, Siri, Pandora, Amazon Echo, or social networks such as Facebook and LinkedIn (Alarcon et al., 2019).

Machine learning is also employed by accounting and auditing companies. Traditional procedures like inspection of assets or physical inventory count are automated using a drone empowered by machine learning. Moreover, machine learning algorithms can assess the reliability of management estimates related to allowances for bad debt, depreciation, or warranty liabilities to prevent human manipulations and errors (Cho et al., 2020).

Deep Learning

A subset of machine learning and AI is a deep learning which is based on deep neural networks trained with big data. Automated driving and speech translation are typical examples of deep learning applications (Aksoy & Gurol, 2021).

Deep learning is more efficient than traditional data mining approaches because it can identify patterns and trends without the involvement of humans and requires fewer steps for pre-processing data. Deep learning algorithms achieve a higher level of accuracy as the model is improved with more data (Sun & Vasarhelyi, 2017).

APPLICATION OF ARTIFICIAL INTELLIGENCE IN AUDITING

Artificial intelligence, one of the crucial technological developments, has also captured the attention of auditing companies. As auditing involves gathering information, organizing, processing, assessing, and presenting data to prepare a reliable audit report (Omoteso, 2012), it is specifically suitable for AI and data analytics. AI can quickly process and analyze vast amounts of data related to companies, whether structured or unstructured. Moreover, most of the duties performed during audits are repetitive and structured, which can be achieved by automation (Kokina & Davenport, 2017).

Large auditing firms have already made massive investments in artificial intelligence technology. They want to reduce the amount of personnel time spent on data analytics-based processes and complex audits (Nickerson, 2019) and increase the efficiency of tasks. AI bots handle basic tasks such as communicating with clients and employees and identifying unusual transactions or risk areas more proficiently (Raschke et al., 2018). Thus, AI allows auditors to focus on high-value tasks rather than devoting too much time to repetitive and monotonous duties (Shimamoto, 2018).

The utilization of AI technology also provided conducting audit and control processes in a continuous manner (Wang et al., 2020), thereby developing the continuous auditing concept.

Continuous Auditing

The American Institute of Certified Public Accountants (AICPA) and the Canadian Institute of Chartered Accountants (CICA) introduced the term "continuous auditing" in 1999. According to their definition, continuous auditing is considered an approach used for providing written assurance on a subject matter under the responsibility of entity management, using a series of auditor reports published shortly after or virtually simultaneously with the occurrence of events (Bumgarner & Vasarhelyi, 2015). Continuous auditing enables auditing events and transactions within the shortest time after they occur (Eulerich & Kalinichenko, 2018).

According to Brown et al. (2007), rapid advancements in technology made continuous auditing a cost-effective approach. Automation reduces the cost of examining additional transactions, and auditors can base their audit opinion on more reliable and higher-quality evidence due to greater sample sizes (Raschke et al., 2018).

The most repetitive tasks of the traditional audit process are related to business transactions and internal controls. Analyzing the control tests and reviewing the business transactions by substantive procedures can easily be automated. Some steps in continuous auditing that AI can enhance are continuous monitoring and auditor inquiry (Raschke et al., 2018).

Continuous Monitoring

According to Daigle et al. (2008), continuous monitoring is usually an automated process conducted on a repetitive and recurring basis to determine whether activities comply with legal rules and regulations and the company's procedures and policies (Eulerich & Kalinichenko, 2018).

AI-Enhanced Audit Inquiry

According to AICPA (2016), although it does not provide adequate evidence, audit inquiry is considered a crucial part of the auditing process that gives the auditors additional information to identify contradictions with other evidence or verify them. The audit inquiry includes communicating with clients and related parties, such as suppliers and customers. As this communication generally occurs in email form, an AI-based system used for audit inquiry can improve the audit efficiency by automating the initial inquiry (Raschke et al., 2018).

Continuous Audit Report

Audit firms can deliver a continuous audit report by employing AI-enabled auditing techniques. Compared to traditional audit techniques, the audit reports prepared by AI can be continuous and achieve a higher level of assurance. Besides, the true financial position and performance of companies can be precisely confirmed (Hu et al., 2021).

Current Applications of AI in Auditing

AI applications allow auditors to employ real-time continuous audit procedures. Therefore, the traditional audit processes may no longer be considered as effective and efficient as AI-enabled audit processes (Acar et al., 2021).

The audit process generally has seven steps, and AI can help automate these phases, enabling auditors to spend more time evaluating the results rather than collecting, correlating, and summarizing data (Issa et al., 2016; Qayyum et al., 2020).

Due to the opportunity to automate a large part of the audits, the auditing companies have focused on AI applications for devoting auditors' time to more value-added tasks. As the latest trends and innovations are followed by Big Four (EY, Deloitte, PwC, and KPMG) companies, the AI applications introduced by these companies have been reviewed in this chapter (Acar et al., 2021; Ucoglu, 2020; Zemankova, 2019).

The AI-enabled applications of Big Four companies are identified by keyword searches on search engines, also considering the names of applications mentioned in other websites, articles, or book chapters.

Deloitte

Analytics Library: This library provides industry-specific data analytics and visualizations (Deloitte, 2017a).

Argus: Argus is Deloitte's first cognitive audit tool to extract information from electronic documents by employing natural language processing (NLP) and advanced machine learning techniques (Davenport, 2016). Argus that has virtual eyes enable auditors to have higher precision and conduct more comprehensive audit procedures by identifying potential anomalies, risks, and trends from the whole population rather than sampling (Deloitte, 2017b).

Automated Control Testing Tool (ACTT): ACTT assesses system control environments of companies to determine existing control deficiencies and overall internal control quality for employing the appropriate audit strategy (Deloitte, Differentiate with quality, n.d.).

Table 1. Differences between traditional and AI-enabled audit processes

Audit Steps	Traditional Audit Processes	AI-Enabled Audit Processes
Pre-Planning	Auditors examine and collect data	AI collects and analyzes big data
Contracting	Auditors prepare engagement letters considering the estimated risks to their clients	AI calculates the total number of hours and corresponding audit fees based on the estimated risk level (significant impact on pricing - reduced cost of auditing)
	The contract is signed	The contract is signed
Identification of Risk Factors	Auditors aggregate all types of information, such as questionnaires, flowcharts, and narratives, and identify risk factors based on their judgment	AI analyzes data by text mining and image recognition applications
		AI identifies risk factors by employing pattern recognition and visualization
Risk Assessment	Auditors examine the internal control procedures and policies, assess risks, test controls, and document the results	AI verifies the proper implementation of internal control with the help of continuous control monitoring systems
Substantive Tests	Auditors conduct sampling-based tests	AI conducts continuous tests for the entire population
Evidence Evaluation	Auditors assess the clarity, sufficiency, and acceptability of the evidence collected	AI performs continuous pattern/trend recognition, analysis of evidence for unusual transactions or balances, benchmark identification, and visualization of results
	Auditors may gather additional evidence or withdraw from the engagement depending on the evaluation	
Preparation of Audit Report	Auditors aggregate all the information collected for preparing the categorical audit report	AI employs a predictive model for estimating the identified risks, and reporting is continuous

Source: (Fotoh & Lorentzon, 2021; Issa et al., 2016; Qayyum et al., 2020)

Auvenir: Considering the limits of resources and capabilities, Auvenir is a platform that provides automated and intelligent audit services to small to medium-sized accounting firms (Deloitte, Explore audit innovation with Deloitte AI Robot #8, n.d.).

BrainSpace: BrainSpace is a relativity software suite and a categorization and visualization tool that uses machine learning algorithms for evidence gathering from digital data and documents. It searches millions of records instantly and categorizes relevant data with higher precision. It can be used in legal cases of clients for providing evidence to be used in defense and can significantly contribute to contract analysis (Deloitte, 2018a).

Coinia: This platform verifies and analyzes information stored on blockchains and enhances the audit capability of digital information, such as smart contracts (Deloitte, Explore audit innovation with Deloitte AI Robot #8, n.d.).

Cortex: Cortex is a multi-cloud platform used initially for audit and tax clients regarding client engagements. Its application has recently expanded to risk, consulting, and financial advisory services, providing data storage and management, data analytics, and solution development. For instance, it has provided automation and advanced analytics for more than 100,000 loan forgiveness applications processed according to the requirements of Coronavirus Aid, Relief, and Economic Security Act (CARES Act). In this way, anomaly and fraud analyses have been conducted regarding the applications of those unfavorably impacted by the coronavirus pandemic (Deloitte, 2020a).

Deloitte Connect and Deloitte Online: Audit teams can collaborate through these secure online platforms, share information, and track progress (Deloitte, 2017a).

DocQMiner: DocQMiner uses machine learning and NLP technologies to read and analyze contracts. For instance, according to IFRS 16 Leases standard, all lease contracts should be listed on the statement of financial position. For this reason, DocQMiner is used for extracting the relevant information from lease contracts by understanding language and sentence structure and how each word relates to other words. Although DocQMiner was developed for the lease contracts of clients, it is currently used in different situations, such as Brexit repapering or checking purchase contracts per General Data Protection Regulation (Deloitte, 2018a).

Eagle Eye: Eagle Eye uses the web to determine early signals of potential opportunities and threats for different types of events, such as a company being likely to encounter financial distress soon. Financial statements, bank accounts, or credit transfers of companies are examined under conventional monitoring systems. In contrast, the open-source intelligence of Eagle Eye collects and analyzes signals and recognizes specific patterns. This tool may also be used for fraud detection, compliance monitoring, and early identification of potential takeovers (Deloitte, 2018a; Deloitte, 2018b).

Guided Risk Assessment Personal Assistant (GRAPA): It functions as a personal assistant in determining the most appropriate risk management approach while considering the collective experience of Deloitte auditors. So, GRAPA enables auditors to learn what has happened in similar cases, as the associated risks to be considered in choosing risk strategy and appropriate audit method might be similar (Deloitte, 2018a).

I-count: It is a web and mobile-based application that takes photos, scans barcodes, and uses voice-to-text technology for streamlining physical asset inspections and reporting the results in real-time (Deloitte, Welcome to Icount, n.d.).

Jellyfish: Jellyfish is a related party transaction online analytics tool that assists auditors by processing, consolidating, and reporting information regarding related parties and related party transactions (Deloitte, Differentiate with quality, n.d.).

myProcess: myProcess is a digital process mining and design tool that monitors the processes and workflows of businesses in order to detect anomalies and potential risks in internal control processes (Deloitte, Differentiate with quality, n.d.).

Omnia DNAV: Omnia DNAV is a cloud-based AI application, which transforms time-consuming, manual audit procedures using intelligent algorithms to value investments and securities (Deloitte, 2020b).

Optix: Optix is an analytics tool that performs advanced real-time pattern recognition by analyzing large journal entry datasets to improve the quality of audits (Deloitte, 2017b).

ReportWizard: This tool provides an intelligent and highly automated report review process by checking primary statements and their notes to enhance audit delivery quality (Deloitte, Differentiate with quality, n.d.).

Reveal: Reveal is a regression analytics platform that combines statistical theory with the company's audit methodology for determining outliers and potential misstatements. For instance, the account balance relationships between the amounts to be tested and data anticipated to be predictive of the amounts are modeled to assist auditors in identifying areas of audit interest (Deloitte, 2017b; Deloitte, Differentiate with quality, n.d.).

Signal: Signal examines publicly available financial data by employing risk and trend analysis to detect potential risk factors and provide a complete risk assessment (Deloitte, 2017b).

EY

EY employs AI technology to extract and analyze data to gain further audit evidence and identify material misstatement risks with higher efficiency and accuracy (Ucoglu, 2020).

Atlas: Atlas is a global research platform for financial reporting, accounting, and regulatory filings connected with EY Canvas to provide a consistent, integrated, easy-to-use way of finding information and content (EY, EY Atlas, n.d.).

Blockchain Analyzer: Due to the increasing adoption of blockchain, EY'S Blockchain Analyzer is an audit-supporting solution for enhanced transparency of the customers' blockchain transactions (EY, Audit Innovation, n.d.).

Canvas: Clients and audit experts can communicate online through the Canvas tool. With Canvas, auditors can concentrate on risks and the related responses. Offering centralized planning, real-time monitoring, consistent coordination of audits, and audit management regardless of location, size, and complexity, Canvas helps auditors spend less time on audit administration. Auditors can record inventory counts, provide real-time status updates, monitor specific tasks, and evaluate documents using Canvas's mobile applications, such as Canvas Engage, Canvas Inventory, and Canvas Pulse (EY, EY Canvas, n.d.).

Helix: Helix is a global audit analytics tool for handling any data size. Helix has several key analyzers that examine and analyze journal entries, inventories, payables and related expenses, revenues and receivables, and mortgage portfolios of clients. Helix identifies trends, hidden patterns, and significant risks through the data capture and extraction tools (EY, EY Helix, n.d.).

KPMG

Ignite: Ignite is an AI tool that uses machine and deep learning algorithms, natural language processing, optical character recognition (OCR), and document ingestion to extract value from any data type for automating decisions, optimizing costs, and managing risks (KPMG, Artificial intelligence, n.d.).

Clara: Clara is an intelligent and intuitive cloud-based audit application which uses new and emerging technologies to provide greater insights into anomalies and risks (KPMG, KPMG Clara, n.d.).

PwC

Cash.ai: AI audit for cash is an application for analyzing cash balances, bank confirmations, reconciliations, foreign exchange, and financial conditions to conduct cash audits using AI technology (PwC, AI and the Audit, n.d.).

GL.ai: GL.ai is a revolutionary tool that employs AI algorithms for analyzing massive data and detecting anomalies. It examines all of the transactions, accounts, amounts, and users to find fraud or potential errors (PwC, Harnessing the power of AI to transform the detection of fraud and error, n.d.).

Halo: is a server-based analytics platform that directly collects data from clients' systems and analyzes huge volumes of data to conduct a more focused audit analysis by concentrating on risk areas to improve risk assessment (PwC, Audit of General Ledger with Halo, n.d.)

Benefits of AI in Auditing

Based on the review of prior literature, the benefits of employing AI technologies in auditing are summarized.

Big Data Handling and Higher Efficiency

AI can deal with big data efficiently to support audit findings by converting them into usable and comparable formats. Moreover, AI can improve risk assessment, going-concern decisions, analytical review procedures (Bizarro & Dorian, 2017), internal control evaluation, audit planning, specific account analysis, evidence assessment, issuance of reports (Meskovic et al., 2018), and other audit tasks. For instance, instead of sampling from a population, AI is a game-changer in analyzing bigger populations of financial data (Pash, 2016). In this manner, AI will end dependency on manual methods and sampling that cannot meet current expectations (Whitehouse, 2015).

As AI collects and processes vast amounts of data from different internal and external sources, multi-dimensional audit evidence is established and used in auditor judgments. It also ensures a more effective assurance function and provides enhanced auditing quality (Gao & Han, 2021).

AI can work on large data sets containing financial and non-financial data. AI's learning function can clear outliers and exceptions instead of manual clearing by auditors (Shimamoto, 2018). Furthermore, AI provides higher efficiency as it can work 24/7 without downtime, break, or interruption and performs many tasks simultaneously. By AI, the processes are conducted faster, which leads to lower time spent and significant cost reduction (HCL Technologies).

Natural Language Processing

AI applications use machine learning techniques for analyzing and extracting valuable information from documents, invoices, contracts, meeting minutes, or others to learn from human interaction (Whitehouse, 2015). This way, it is possible to focus on textual data from different sources such as social networks and social media, captured imagery, or video recordings rather than only financial information. The auditors may benefit from data collected by AI technology from various sources. Examining source documents and analyzing news, emails, or press releases can also be automated to provide additional supporting evidence for financial analysis regarding irregularity detection (Issa et al., 2016). Moreover, data collection by AI may lead to shortened time for decision-making (Nickerson, 2019).

Anomaly and Fraud Detection

Financial statement fraud has many direct and indirect costs, such as financial losses, unfavorable impact on employees and investors, damage to the reputation of the company and the auditors, and reduced reliability of financial statements leading to inefficient markets and higher transactions costs for companies (Perols, 2011;

Summers & Sweeney, 1998). According to ACFE's "Occupational Fraud 2022" report, financial statement fraud is the least common type of fraud. On the other hand, such frauds are the most costly, with a median loss of $593,000. Against all kinds of fraud, external and internal audits are listed in the top common anti-fraud controls (ACFE, 2022).

Modern AI applications can detect anomalies in the data. Such possible anomalies may be related to future corporate events such as bankruptcy, material misstatements (Ding et al., 2019), or individual errors and fraud. For instance, high expense items filed only by one employee, unexpected increases in sales figures or certain expenses incurred right before the year-end, or unusually favorable contract terms for certain suppliers can be easily spotted, as AI can identify outliers or determine trends and patterns (Kokina & Davenport, 2017).

Therefore, for audit practice, AI can serve as a tool for anomaly detection and be a part of analytical procedures in assessing potential risks (Ding et al., 2019). For instance, the risk of financial statement fraud, money laundering, credit card fraud, or employee fraud can be assessed, or such fraud can be detected by machine learning methods (Song et al., 2014)

Improvement in Accounting Estimates

Machine learning algorithms can enhance accounting estimates for auditors and provide more relevant financial information. The amounts presented for many financial statement items are based on the company management's subjective estimates. Machine learning techniques can be used as an effective predictive tool as they learn from data patterns and reduce errors (Ding et al., 2020). In estimating the allowance for uncollectible accounts, rather than using the rate set by the management, an independent model can be constructed by AI applications for predicting the likelihood of non-performing receivables (Qayyum et al., 2020).

For instance, the study by Ding et al. (2020) has provided evidence of more accurate loss estimations provided by machine learning applications. For enhancing consistency and reliability, auditors can use the accounting estimates offered by machine learning techniques as benchmarks against estimates made by the company management.

Elimination of Errors and Human Bias

Due to preprogrammed logistics, AI systems do not forget transactions, activities, or processes and are consistent and more accurate when providing suggestions or advice. This way, possible human mistakes, and errors are minimized, and audit quality is enhanced (Qureshi et al., 1998).

Applying AI to the audit procedures, such as sample selection and evaluation, may eliminate human error and increase efficiency, resulting in enhanced reliability of financial information (Zemankova, 2019).

Other Benefits

All types of audit risks, control, inherent, and detection risks can be minimized by using AI in auditing. AI may help enhance going concern decisions (whether a company is in financial distress), materiality assessments, bankruptcy predictions, and analytical review procedures (Zemankova, 2019).

In addition, AI-based applications may provide the proper required documentation regarding the audit judgments that form the basis for evaluating risks. Moreover, AI can increase the consistency of decisions and problem-solving approaches due to decreasing behavior variance (O'Leary, 2009).

As AI systems are beneficial in conducting time-consuming tasks and processing data in a shorter time, increased efficiency may result in lower audit fees to be charged to customers (Zemankova, 2019).

Risks of Employing AI in Auditing

Although AI has many advantages, there are also challenges in using artificial intelligence-based systems in auditing.

Legal Issues

One of the main issues related to AI is legal responsibility. There are discussions about who will be held responsible when an AI system makes a decision or conducts an analysis, or financial fraud cannot be detected using AI algorithms (Nickerson, 2019).

The extensive use of AI in auditing necessitates access to enormous volumes of confidential client information. Due to privacy and confidentiality concerns, auditing clients could be reluctant to provide such valuable and sensitive data (Qayyum et al., 2020). Therefore, audit companies should place more emphasis on privacy, security, and data protection regulations (Alarcon et al., 2019).

Ethical Issues

Ryan & Stahl (2021) discussed the guidelines for AI ethics and focused on main ethical principles such as transparency, privacy, responsibility, justice and fairness, trust, freedom and autonomy, sustainability, non-maleficence, and beneficence. But there is still no agreement on high-level, fundamental ethics standards (Mökander & Floridi, 2021).

The ethical implications of using AI technologies in the audit profession can be considered an essential issue. The ethical code of conduct has guiding principles such as objectivity, public interest, due care, responsibility, and integrity. However, when auditors do not know how the algorithms make reasoning, auditors' due professional care may be affected. Furthermore, it is not known whether such emerging technologies can meet the requirements of the ethical code, which does not yet take into account the use of AI systems in the profession (Munoko et al., 2020).

The nature of AI systems and difficulty in interpreting them, the possibility of tests not indicating real-world behavior of AI systems, and auditors not having sufficient information to evaluate AI systems are some of the constraints to ethics-based auditing for managing the AI's ethical risks (Mökander & Floridi, 2021).

Data Risks

Machine learning models need a large and well-balanced dataset representing the actual population to maintain high prediction accuracy, whereas real data is generally biased (Applegate & Koenig, 2019; Taniguchi et al., 2018). Biased data may generate bad results and lead to wrong decisions (Alarcon et al., 2019). AI can be effective if the underlying data is complete and accurate. Any changes to the data field's nature, such as a definition change, or location change on a screen, may affect the reliability and integrity of data used by AI (Qayyum et al., 2020).

Moreover, inappropriately sourced or unauthorized datasets may increase the risk of inaccurate or irrelevant system predictions. Data recycling risk may also occur if the wrong dataset is recycled for a new application, or datasets used for creating or updating a new application are also used for increasing the performance of existing systems. So, there are many risks related to data regarding the training, testing, or production phases of the AI system development (Applegate & Koenig, 2019).

The regulatory, statutory, confidentiality and ethical requirements may prevent auditing companies from accessing vast amounts of high-quality data from data stores, limiting the ability to build training datasets (Dickey et al., 2019).

Auditing AI Systems

As auditing companies use AI systems more frequently, the need to audit such systems will increase. Especially data analysis approaches used by machine learning algorithms, the level of precision regarding the estimates of outcome probabilities, the representation power of data sets concerning the actual population, the relevance and origin of data sets, and authorization for accessing sensitive data should be continuously examined (Applegate & Koenig, 2019). AI sector is highly innovative, but AI auditing expertise is unfortunately not significantly developed yet (Mökander et al., 2021).

Technical Drawbacks

AI has several advantages, but technical drawbacks can unfavorably affect the audit process. For instance, although machine learning is widely used for audit tasks to analyze texts, it can misclassify information which can be misleading (Raschke et al., 2018).

AI tools such as optical character recognition and natural language processing can automatically analyze texts and derive meanings and relationships among concepts, but they have limited use in identifying the content. Therefore, it cannot be used in generating responses to client emails for additional inquiries (Raschke et al., 2018).

Lack of Soft Skills and Technology Acceptance

According to Mlekus et al. (2020), new technologies can only be considered an innovation when widely used and accepted. Also, the way auditors perceive the usefulness and easiness of AI will impact the acceptance of this technology (Albawwat & Frijat, 2021). An essential challenge to the widespread use of AI in auditing is the lack of trust arising from the "black box problem". When the relationships between large volumes of data are to be identified, neural networks can be used for determining the cause-and-effect patterns by employing a series of algorithms. These sophisticated AI tools lack transparency or explainability, as it is hard to document or comprehend how the relationships or patterns were recognized (Qayyum et al., 2020).

Moreover, AI technology will impact the role of auditors. Rather than testing and examining transactions, auditors will test algorithms and monitor their effectiveness (Shimamoto, 2018). In addition to professional knowledge, auditors need to master information technology, data management, and analytics skills (Luo et al., 2018).

Other Challenges

One main drawback of AI is dehumanization and lack of intuition in problem-solving and decision-making (Qureshi et al., 1998). Also, AI does not have human consciousness, and it will take time for AI to process transactions like a human (Aksoy & Gurol, 2021).

The capabilities of AI-based technologies are limited to the developers' abilities (Aksoy & Gurol, 2021). In addition, although it is proposed that AI-based applications will eliminate human error and bias, unidentified human biases and human logic errors might be embedded in AI technology (IIA, 2017). So, the risk of biased human decision-making may not be cured with AI. Sometimes, it can even create more significant problems by deploying human biases on sensitive issues, such as gender, sexual orientation, or race (Manyika et al., 2019). Moreover, a new type of overconfidence bias in auditors might emerge. The auditors may rely too much on the outcomes of AI systems, and they may not investigate whether the input data or weights of the results are appropriate or not (Dickey et al., 2019).

Due to the higher efficiency and work time of AI and automated tasks and processes, a reduction in the number of auditors and thus an increase in unemployment rates might be expected (Pereira et al., 2021). Also, the cost of implementation is an essential factor to be considered when applying AI to audit tasks (Nickerson, 2019).

SOLUTIONS AND RECOMMENDATIONS

As a result of increasing business complexity, highly regulated environment, and higher expectations for financial reporting and disclosure, there is more pressure towards automation not to lose competitive advantage (Bizarro & Dorian, 2017). Therefore, AI has made qualitative changes in the procedures of audits, provided multi-dimensional sources for audit evidence, and helped make more rational judgments (Gao & Han, 2021).

Although some professionals may lose their jobs due to the advancements in AI technology, different jobs with new skills will emerge. Therefore, auditors should be trained to focus on judgment-related skills rather than prediction-related ones (Bizarro & Dorian, 2017). Moreover, skills for making moral and wise decisions regarding AI and other technological advancements and related privacy, data bias, and transparency challenges will be needed (Dolev & Itzkovich, 2020). In this sense, the collaboration between practitioners and academics should be increased to modernize the accounting curriculum by including new technologies. Thus, it will be possible to cope with the market change by enhancing the employability of graduates as auditors who possess technical skills and knowledge (Dickins & Urtel, 2021; Qasim & Kharbat, 2020).

AI technology provides cost savings and efficiency in data processing, but it does not have the abilities of a human. For instance, essential characteristics of an auditor, such as professional skepticism and judgment, thoroughly reasoning, or expressing emotions, are not present in AI systems (Bizarro & Dorian, 2017). Furthermore, the cognitive abilities of humans enable them to generalize new concepts even from small and biased samples (Taniguchi et al., 2018).

AI-based systems are open to biases in different steps of the project. Transparent and explainable models can be employed to avoid representation, aggregation, measurement, evaluation, information availability, or other biases. However, it is argued that the disclosure and transparency of AI algorithms may result in increased vulnerability of the algorithm being hacked or subject to legal action (Cho et al., 2020). Thus, adopting AI technology in auditing may lead to cybersecurity and privacy risks, and the need for auditors to investigate the anomalies and understand the rationale behind the decisions made by AI is required (Munoko et al., 2020).

The proposed European Artificial Intelligence Act (AIA) may provide a legal framework for AI (Mökander et al., 2021). However, given the need for ethical governance of AI, regulatory authorities like the Public Company Accounting Oversight Board (PCAOB) and the International Auditing and Assurance Standards Board (IAASB) should issue standards to provide regulatory advice and oversight (Munoko et al., 2020).

FUTURE RESEARCH DIRECTIONS

The main problems related to the adoption of AI technology in auditing are the ethical implications and the openness to different biases. More research should be conducted concerning possible solutions on frameworks for ethical AI systems and how each bias type may be addressed and prevented (Cho et al., 2020).

AI-enabled technologies are commonly used for decision-making during the audit processes. Therefore, future research can explore the eligibility of AI tools used by auditors for comparing human decisions with the decisions generated by AI. Moreover, the need for standards and the content of such standards to regulate AI technologies used by auditors may be discussed, considering the potential legal consequences of using such technologies in auditing decisions (Cho et al., 2020).

Further research can also explore the incorporation of current trends of AI use in auditing into the training of auditors regarding the professional examinations and the continuous professional development of auditors (Omoteso, 2012). Finally, more studies are needed on integrating AI and AI-related skills and competencies into the business and accounting curriculum.

CONCLUSION

Although emerging studies show that auditors tend to rely more on evidence collected by humans than on AI systems, audit companies continue making heavy investments in AI-based applications and tools (Brown et al., 2020).

The adoption of AI-based technologies has automated audit activities that may lead to fewer human auditors in the future. Therefore, to prevent non-accountants with data analysis skills from being employed in auditing companies, the auditors should focus on acquiring the necessary skills related to emerging technologies (Qasim & Kharbat, 2020). On the contrary, the user interface of AI applications should be user-friendly so that the auditors will not face so many problems even if they have lower soft skills.

Auditors should be skeptical about the results generated by AI-based applications, as there may be problems related to data and patterns identified. Therefore, data scientists and auditors need to work closely to understand how the algorithms work. In this regard, the auditors should verify the accuracy and completeness of input data, as the model's variables may change even according to the industry or business. For instance, user accounts of companies such as Facebook should be given the appropriate weight in algorithms as the user accounts might be an essential revenue predictor (Dickey et al., 2019). The auditors should be able to assess processes and controls around the AI audit tools and prepare the appropriate documentation that includes explanations of why AI identified certain transactions as unusual or anomalous. Otherwise, it may not be possible to conclude that the auditors used the AI tools to obtain relevant and sufficient audit evidence for forming an accurate opinion (Qayyum et al., 2020).

Current auditing standards based on labor-intensive procedures should be updated, considering the impact and role of AI on audit tasks (Bizarro & Dorian, 2017). And like other new technologies, AI should be tailored, tested, and monitored over the years to ensure that the risks and costs are not higher than the potential benefits (Bizarro & Dorian, 2017).

AI technology has brought compelling benefits and still offers future opportunities to the auditing profession. Therefore, the changing role of auditors and the potential for more intelligent and more effective auditing should be examined (Issa et al., 2016). The profession will not disappear, but as more tasks are automated, auditors will need to adapt their skills (Kaplan & Haenlein, 2020).

REFERENCES

Acar, D., Gal, G., Öztürk, M. S., & Usul, H. (2021). A Case Study in the Implementation of a Continuous Monitoring System. *Journal of Emerging Technologies in Accounting*, *18*(1), 17–25. doi:10.2308/JETA-17-04-29-9

ACFE. (2022). *Occupational Fraud 2022: A Report to the Nations*. Retrieved from https://acfepublic.s3.us-west-2.amazonaws.com/2022+Report+to+the+Nations.pdf

Aksoy, T., & Gurol, B. (2021). Artificial Intelligence in Computer-Aided Auditing Techniques and Technologies (CAATTs) and an Application Proposal for Auditors. In T. Aksoy & U. Hacioglu (Eds.), *Auditing Ecosystem and Strategic Accounting in the Digital Era* (pp. 361–384). Springer Nature Switzerland. doi:10.1007/978-3-030-72628-7_17

Alarcon, J. L., Fine, T., & Ng, C. (2019). Accounting AI and Machine Learning: Applications and Challenges. *Pennsylvania CPA Journal*, (Special Issue), 1–5.

Albawwat, I., & Frijat, Y. A. (2021). An analysis of auditors' perceptions towards artificial intelligence and its contribution to audit quality. *Accounting*, 7(4), 755–762. doi:10.5267/j.ac.2021.2.009

Alrashidi, M., Almutairi, A., & Zraqat, O. (2022). The Impact of Big Data Analytics on Audit Procedures: Evidence from the Middle East. *Journal of Asian Finance, Economics and Business*, 9(2), 93–102. doi:10.13106/jafeb.2022.vol9.no2.0093

Applegate, D., & Koenig, M. (2019, December). Framing AI audits. *Internal Auditor*, 76(6), 29–34.

Bizarro, P. A. & Dorian, M. (2017). Artificial intelligence: The future of auditing. *Internal Auditing*, 21-26.

Bolander, T. (2019). What do we loose when machines take the decisions? *The Journal of Management and Governance*, 23(4), 849–867. doi:10.100710997-019-09493-x

Brown, V. L., Dickins, D., Hermanson, D. R., Higgs, J. L., Jenkins, J. G., Nolder, C., Schaefer, T. J., & Smith, K. W. (2020). Comments of the Auditing Standards Committee of the Auditing Section of the American Accounting Association on Proposed Statement on Auditing Standards (SAS), Audit Evidence [Commentary]. *Current Issues in Auditing*, 14(1), C1–C9. doi:10.2308/ciia-52603

Bumgarner, N., & Vasarhelyi, M. A. (2015). Essay 1 – Continuous Auditing - A New View. In *Audit Analytics and Continuous Audit - Looking Toward the Future* (pp. 3-52). AICPA. https://us.aicpa.org/content/dam/aicpa/interestareas/frc/assuranceadvisoryservices/downloadabledocuments/auditanalytics_lookingtowardfuture.pdf

Cho, S., Vasarhelyi, M. A., Sun, T. S., & Zhang, K. (2020). Learning from Machine Learning in Accounting and Assurance. *Journal of Emerging Technologies in Accounting*, 17(1), 1–10. doi:10.2308/jeta-10718

Chukwudi, O. L., Echefu, S. C., Boniface, U. U., & Chukwuani, N. V. (2018). Effect of Artificial Intelligence on the Performance of Accounting Operations among Accounting Firms in South East Nigeria. *Asian Journal of Economics, Business and Accounting, 7*(2), 1–11.

Davenport, T. H. (2016). *The power of advanced audit analytics - Everywhere Analytics.* Retrieved from https://www2.deloitte.com/content/dam/Deloitte/us/Documents/deloitte-analytics/us-da-advanced-audit-analytics.pdf

Deloitte. (2017a). *Audit Evolved - The next generation of life sciences audit.* Retrieved from https://www2.deloitte.com/content/dam/Deloitte/us/Documents/audit/us-audit-lshc-brochure.pdf

Deloitte. (2017b). *Delivering smarter audits - Insights through innovation.* Retrieved from https://www2.deloitte.com/content/dam/Deloitte/us/Documents/audit/us-audit-smarter-audits-dynamic-insights-through-innovation.pdf

Deloitte. (2018a). *16 Artificial Intelligence projects from Deloitte - Practical cases of applied AI.* Retrieved from https://www2.deloitte.com/content/dam/Deloitte/nl/Documents/innovatie/deloitte-nl-innovatie-artificial-intelligence-16-practical-cases.pdf

Deloitte. (2018b). *Advanced Early Warning Systems for Financial Distress.* Retrieved from https://www2.deloitte.com/ce/en/pages/deloitte-analytics/solutions/eagle-eye-searching-the-web-for-early-warning-signals.html

Deloitte. (2020a). *Press Releases - Deloitte Launches CortexAI Platform to Help Organizations Accelerate Applied AI in the 'Age of With'.* Retrieved from https://www2.deloitte.com/us/en/pages/about-deloitte/articles/press-releases/deloitte-launches-cortex-ai-platform.html

Deloitte. (2020b). *Press Releases - Deloitte Wins 2020 'Audit Innovation of the Year' at the Digital Accountancy Forum & Awards.* Retrieved from https://www2.deloitte.com/us/en/pages/about-deloitte/articles/press-releases/deloitte-wins-2020-audit-innovation-of-the-year-at-digital-accountancy-forum-awards.html

Deloitte. (n.d.a). *Differentiate with quality - Explore audit innovation with Deloitte AI Robot #4.* Retrieved from https://www2.deloitte.com/cn/en/pages/audit/articles/explore-audit-innovation-with-deloitte-ai-robot-vol-4.html

Deloitte. (n.d.b). *Welcome to Icount.* Retrieved from https://inventory.deloitte.com/login/

Deloitte. (n.d.c). *Explore audit innovation with Deloitte AI Robot #8 - Lead in the future of audit*. Retrieved from https://www2.deloitte.com/cn/en/pages/audit/articles/explore-audit-innovation-with-deloitte-ai-robot-vol-8.html

Dickey, G., Blanke, S., & Seaton, L. (2019). Machine Learning in Auditing: Current and Future Applications. *The CPA Journal*, *89*(6), 16–21.

Dickins, D., & Urtel, K. (2021). Current Issues in Auditing: How We Are Advancing the Dialogue Between Academics and Practitioners. *Current Issues in Auditing*, *15*(2), E1–E2. doi:10.2308/ciia-10775

Ding, K., Lev, B., Peng, X., Sun, T., & Vasarhelyi, M. A. (2020). Machine learning improves accounting estimates: Evidence from insurance payments. *Review of Accounting Studies*, *25*(3), 1098–1134. doi:10.100711142-020-09546-9

Ding, K., Peng, X., & Wang, Y. (2019). A Machine Learning-Based Peer Selection Method with Financial Ratios. *Accounting Horizons*, *33*(3), 75–87. doi:10.2308/acch-52454

Dolev, N., & Itzkovich, Y. (2020). In the AI Era, Soft Skills are the New Hard Skills. In W. Amann & A. Stachowicz-Stanusch (Eds.), *Artificial Intelligence and Its Impact on Business* (pp. 55–77). Information Age Publishing.

Drydakis, N. (2022). Artificial Intelligence and Reduced SMEs' Business Risks. A Dynamic Capabilities Analysis During the COVID-19 Pandemic. *Information Systems Frontiers*, 1–25. doi:10.100710796-022-10249-6 PMID:35261558

Eulerich, M., & Kalinichenko, A. (2018). The Current State and Future Directions of Continuous Auditing Research: An Analysis of the Existing Literature. *Journal of Information Systems*, *32*(3), 31–51. doi:10.2308/isys-51813

EY. (n.d.a). *Audit innovation*. Retrieved from https://www.ey.com/en_gl/audit/innovation

EY. (n.d.b). *EY Atlas*. Retrieved from https://www.ey.com/en_gl/audit/technology/atlas

EY. (n.d.c). *EY Canvas*. Retrieved from https://www.ey.com/en_gl/audit/technology/canvas

EY. (n.d.d). *EY Helix*. Retrieved from https://www.ey.com/en_gl/audit/technology/helix

Fotoh, L. E., & Lorentzon, J. I. (2021). The Impact of Digitalization on Future Audits. *Journal of Emerging Technologies in Accounting, 18*(2), 77–97. doi:10.2308/JETA-2020-063

Gao, Y., & Han, L. (2021). Implications of artificial intelligence on the objectives of auditing financial statements and ways to achieve them. *Microprocessors and Microsystems*, 1–9. doi:10.1016/j.micpro.2021.104036

Haenlein, M., & Kaplan, A. (2019). A Brief History of Artificial Intelligence: On the Past, Present, and Future of Artificial Intelligence. *California Management Review, 61*(4), 1–10. doi:10.1177/0008125619864925

HCL Technologies. (n.d.). *Technology Q&A - Advantages of AI.* Retrieved from https://www.hcltech.com/technology-qa/what-are-the-advantages-of-artificial-intelligence

Hu, K, Chen, F., Hsu, M., & Tzeng, G. (2021). Identifying Key Factors for Adopting Artificial Intelligence-Enabled Auditing Techniques by Joint Utilization of Fuzzy-Rough Set Theory and MRDM Technique. *Technological and Economic Development of Economy, 27*(2), 459–492. doi:10.3846/tede.2020.13181

Hung, L., & Sun, K. (2020). How Will AI Change/Impact Management and Business World. In W. Amann & A. Stachowicz-Stanusch (Eds.), *Artificial Intelligence and Its Impact on Business* (pp. 17–37). Information Age Publishing.

IIA. (2017). *Global Perspectives and Insights: Artificial Intelligence – Considerations for the Profession of Internal Auditing.* Retrieved from https://www.iia.nl/SiteFiles/GPI-Artificial-Intelligence.pdf

Issa, H., Sun, T., & Vasarhelyi, M. A. (2016). Research ideas for artificial intelligence in auditing: The formalization of audit and workforce supplementation. *Journal of Emerging Technologies in Accounting, 13*(2), 1–20. doi:10.2308/jeta-10511

Kaplan, A., & Haenlein, M. (2020). Rulers of the world, unite! The challenges and opportunities of artificial intelligence. *Business Horizons, 63*(1), 37–50. doi:10.1016/j.bushor.2019.09.003

Kokina, J., & Davenport, T. H. (2017). The emergence of artificial intelligence: How automation is changing auditing. *Journal of Emerging Technologies in Accounting, 14*(1), 115–122. doi:10.2308/jeta-51730

KPMG. (n.d.a). *Artificial intelligence - Empowering a smarter, faster, more agile enterprise.* Retrieved from https://advisory.kpmg.us/services/artificial-intelligence.html

KPMG. (n.d.b). *KPMG Clara*. Retrieved from https://home.kpmg/xx/en/home/services/audit/kpmg-clara.html

Manyika, J., Silberg, J., & Presten, B. (2019). AI and Machine Learning: What Do We Do About the Biases in AI? *Harvard Business Review*. Retrieved from https://hbr.org/2019/10/what-do-we-do-about-the-biases-in-ai

Meskovic, E., Garrison, M., Ghezal, S., & Chen, Y. (2018). Artificial intelligence: Trends in business and implications for the accounting profession. *Internal Auditing*, 5-11.

Mökander, J., Axente, M., Casolari, F., & Floridi, L. (2021). Conformity Assessments and Post-market Monitoring: A Guide to the Role of Auditing in the Proposed European AI Regulation. *Minds and Machines*, 1–28. doi:10.100711023-021-09577-4 PMID:34754142

Mökander, J., & Floridi, L. (2021). Ethics-Based Auditing to Develop Trustworthy AI. *Minds and Machines*, *31*(2), 323–327. doi:10.100711023-021-09557-8

Munoko, I., Brown-Liburd, H. L., & Vasarhelyi, M. (2020). The ethical implications of using artificial intelligence in auditing. *Journal of Business Ethics*, *167*(2), 209–234. doi:10.100710551-019-04407-1

Nickerson, M. A. (2019). AI: New risks and rewards – Will reliance on AI increase accounting and financial fraud? *Strategic Finance*, 26-31.

O'Leary, D. E. (2009). Introduction. Value Creation from Expert Systems: An Economic Approach with Applications in Accounting, Auditing and Finance. In M. A. Vasarhelyi & D. O'Leary (Eds.), *Artificial Intelligence in Accounting and Auditing: Creating Value with AI* (Vol. 5, pp. 2–17). Markus Wiener Publisher.

Omoteso, K. (2012). The application of artificial intelligence in auditing: Looking back to the future. *Expert Systems with Applications*, *39*(9), 8490–8495. doi:10.1016/j.eswa.2012.01.098

Pash, C. (2016). *KPMG will soon be using artificial intelligence for audits in Australia*. Retrieved from https://www.businessinsider.com.au/kpmg-will-soon-be-using-artificial-intelligence-for-audits-in-australia-2016-6

Pereira, L. F., Resio, M., Costa, R. L., Dias, A., & Gonçalves, R. (2021). Artificial Intelligence in Strategic Business Management: The Case of Auditing. *International Journal of Business Information Systems*, *1*(1), 1–47. doi:10.1504/IJBIS.2021.10039269

Perols, J. (2011). Financial Statement Fraud Detection: An Analysis of Statistical and Machine Learning Algorithms. *Auditing, 30*(2), 19–50. doi:10.2308/ajpt-50009

PwC. (2017). *Sizing the prize: What's the real value of AI for your business and how can you capitalise?* Retrieved from https://www.pwc.com/gx/en/issues/analytics/assets/pwc-ai-analysis-sizing-the-prize-report.pdf

PwC. (n.d.a). *AI and the Audit.* Retrieved from https://www.pwc.com/gx/en/about/stories-from-across-the-world/harnessing-ai-to-pioneer-new-approaches-to-the-audit.html

PwC. (n.d.b). *Audit of General Ledger with Halo.* Retrieved from https://www.pwc.com/mu/en/services/assurance/risk-assurance/tech-assurance/general-ledger-audit.html

PwC. (n.d.c) *Harnessing the power of AI to transform the detection of fraud and error.* Retrieved from https://www.pwc.com/gx/en/about/stories-from-across-the-world/harnessing-the-power-of-ai-to-transform-the-detection-of-fraud-and-error.html

Qasim, A., & Kharbat, F. F. (2020). Blockchain Technology, Business Data Analytics, and Artificial Intelligence: Use in the Accounting Profession and Ideas for Inclusion into the Accounting Curriculum. *Journal of Emerging Technologies in Accounting, 17*(1), 107–117. doi:10.2308/jeta-52649

Qayyum, A., Watson, A., Buchanan, A., Paterson, M., & Hakimpour, Y. (2020). *CPA Canada & AICPA. The Data-Driven Audit: How Automation and AI are Changing the Audit and the Role of the Auditor.* Retrieved from https://us.aicpa.org/content/dam/aicpa/interestareas/frc/assuranceadvisoryservices/downloadabledocuments/the-data-driven-audit.pdf

Qureshi, A. A., Shim, J. K., & Siegel, J. G. (1998). Artificial intelligence in accounting & business. *The National Public Accountant, 43*(7), 13–18.

Raschke, R. L., Saiewitz, A., Kachroo, P., & Lennard, J. B. (2018). AI-Enhanced audit inquiry: A research note. *Journal of Emerging Technologies in Accounting, 15*(2), 111–116. doi:10.2308/jeta-52310

Ryan, M., & Stahl, B. C. (2021). Artificial intelligence ethics guidelines for developers and users: Clarifying their content and normative implications. *Journal of Information, Communication and Ethics in Society, 19*(1), 61–86. doi:10.1108/JICES-12-2019-0138

Shimamoto, D. C. (2018/2019, Winter). Is Artificial Intelligence a Threat to Government Accountants and Auditors? *Journal of Government Financial Management*, *67*(4), 12–16.

Song, X., Hu, Z., Du, J., & Sheng, Z. (2014). Application of Machine Learning Methods to Risk Assessment of Financial Statement Fraud: Evidence from China. *Journal of Forecasting*, *33*(8), 611–626. doi:10.1002/for.2294

Summers, S. L., & Sweeney, J. T. (1998). Fraudulently Misstated Financial Statements and Insider Trading: An Empirical Analysis. *The Accounting Review*, *73*(1), 131–146.

Sun, T., & Vasarhelyi, M. A. (2017). Deep Learning and the Future of Auditing: How an Evolving Technology Could Transform Analysis and Improve Judgment. *The CPA Journal*, *87*(6), 24–29.

Taniguchi, H., Sato, H., & Shirakawa, T. (2018). A machine learning model with human cognitive biases capable of learning from small and biased datasets. *Scientific Reports*, *8*(1), 1–13. doi:10.103841598-018-25679-z PMID:29743630

Ucoglu, D. (2020). Current machine learning applications in accounting and auditing. *PressAcademia Procedia*, *12*(1), 1–7. doi:10.17261/Pressacademia.2020.1337

Wang, K., Zipperle, M., Becherer, M., Gottwalt, F., & Zhang, Y. (2020). An AI-Based Automated Continuous Compliance Awareness Framework (CoCAF) for Procurement Auditing. *Big Data and Cognitive Computing*, *4*(23), 1–14. doi:10.3390/bdcc4030023

Whitehouse, T. (2015). *The technology transforming your annual audit*. Retrieved from https://www.complianceweek.com/the-technology-transforming-your-annual-audit/3166.article

Zemankova, A. (2019). Artificial Intelligence in Audit and Accounting: Development, Current Trends, Opportunities and Threats – Literature Review. *2019 International Conference on Control, Artificial Intelligence, Robotics & Optimization (ICCAIRO)*, 148-154. 10.1109/ICCAIRO47923.2019.00031

ADDITIONAL READING

Anandarajan, M., & Anandarajan, A. (1999). A comparison of machine learning techniques with a qualitative response model for auditor's going concern reporting. *Expert Systems with Applications*, *16*(4), 385–392. doi:10.1016/S0957-4174(99)00014-7

Bao, Y., Ke, B., Li, B., Yu, Y. J., & Zhang, A. J. (2020). Detecting Accounting Fraud in Publicly Traded U.S. Firms Using a Machine Learning Approach. *Journal of Accounting Research*, 58(1), 199–235. doi:10.1111/1475-679X.12292

Greenman, C. (2017). Exploring the Impact of Artificial Intelligence on the Accounting Profession. *Journal of Research in Business, Economics and Management*, 8(3), 1451–1454.

Lokanan, M., Tran, V., & Vuong, N. H. (2019). Detecting anomalies in financial statements using machine learning algorithm: The case of Vietnamese listed firms. *Asian Journal of Accounting Research*, 4(2), 181–201. doi:10.1108/AJAR-09-2018-0032

Pedrosa, I., Costa, C. J., & Aparicio, M. (2020). Determinants adoption of computer-assisted auditing tools (CAATs). *Cognition Technology and Work*, 22(3), 565–583. doi:10.1007/0111-019-00581 4

KEY TERMS AND DEFINITIONS

Audit Inquiry: In addition to other audit procedures, audit inquiry is the process of gathering complementary information from the management, accountants, and knowledgeable persons inside or outside the company about the transactions, events, or anything that could assist auditors in evidence evaluation.

Control Risk: Control risk is the probability of any material misstatement due to the lack or malfunctioning of internal controls to detect or prevent errors and fraud.

Detection Risk: Detection risk is the likelihood that an auditor would not be able to identify material misstatements in the financial statements due to factors such as incorrect audit procedure application, incorrect audit testing methods, misinterpretation, or wrong assessment of audit results.

Inherent Risk: Inherent risk can be defined as the probability of any material misstatement, independent of internal controls. So, inherent risk arises from the nature of business transactions or operations without any internal control implementation for mitigating risks.

Materiality: Materiality is a term related to the significance of an amount or item based on its size or nature. Auditors determine a materiality threshold at the planning stage of the audit as a benchmark so that reasonable assurance will be obtained regarding financial statements being free from material misstatements that can affect financial statement users' decisions.

Natural Language Processing (NLP): NLP is an artificial intelligence field where computers read, analyze, understand, and interpret human language.

Chapter 10

AI and Over-the-Top (OTT):
Industry Potential and Difficulties

Madhu Rani
Sharda University, India

Shagun
Sharda University, India

Manisha Gupta
Sharda University, India

ABSTRACT

Artificial intelligence (AI) is a field of study that focuses on the development and theory of computer systems that are capable of doing tasks that would normally need the intelligence of humans. Language translation, decision-making, and speech recognition are only a few of the tasks that, in general, need the use of a human brain to be performed properly. In the context of content delivery, an OTT platform (also known as over the top) is a platform that does not provide video via traditional cable or receivers. Video and audio distribution via the internet without the involvement of a multiple system operator (MSO) is referred to as online video and audio distribution. When it comes to the administration and transmission of information, there are several options. Viewers are able to access it from any place at any time and save it for later viewing convenience.

DOI: 10.4018/978-1-6684-4950-9.ch010

INTRODUCTION

The phrase "artificial intelligence" (AI) refers to computer systems or other technologies that are capable of learning and adapting as a consequence of repeated contact with their respective contexts. Examples of AI include IBM's Watson and Google's DeepMind. To put it simply, this is how artificial intelligence (AI) is described at its most fundamental level. Within the field of artificial intelligence, one may find a bewildering variety of different options. Several examples, like the ones that follow, serve to demonstrate this point:

- Chatbots use artificial intelligence (AI) to swiftly evaluate user inquiries and provide relevant responses. Chatbots are able to provide an improved experience all around as a result of this.
- Intelligent assistants make use of artificial intelligence in order to collect pertinent details from a large array of unstructured sources in order to build schedules that are more efficient.
- Recommendation engines are able to analyse the viewing habits of consumers and then provide recommendations to those customers based on the information obtained from the analysis. The purpose of this method is to assist consumers in discovering new programs that they would like viewing depending on the preferences that the customers have already established.

To a far larger degree than any particular form or function, what makes artificial intelligence is the process that is followed, as well as the potential for extremely powerful thinking and the processing of data. This is in addition to the fact that artificial intelligence can learn. In spite of the widespread perception that this is the case, the end objective of artificial intelligence (AI) is not to eliminate the need for human participation in whatever it is that is being done. The ultimate objective is to see a significant growth, not only in the skills of individuals, but also in the results produced by such individuals. Any business that acquires it will quickly realize that it is a very valuable asset due to the reasons stated above.

OTT platforms need to strengthen their data management methods and widen the breadth of their capabilities in order to provide customers with a more satisfactory experience. This will allow the companies to provide customers with a better overall product. AI and ML may be able to bridge these gaps and give audiences with a better and more engaging experience by using techniques to personalize content and services based on a variety of data. This would allow AI and ML to create a better and more interactive experience for audiences. This would make it possible for AI and ML to offer a viewing experience that is superior and more participatory for the audience. It is possible that as a direct result of this, artificial intelligence will be able to assist in the collection of deep content insights, the discovery of high intensity moments, and the acceleration of editorial processes at a much quicker rate, which may result in a significant shift in the user experience that is provided by OTT platforms. As a result of this, it is essential to educate oneself on artificial intelligence (AI) as well as over-the-top (OTT) platforms, both of which are now helpful and commonly used (Archit Shah, 2022).

When you make use of a service that is known as an over-the-top platform, often abbreviated as OTT for short, you give yourself the ability to acquire video and live stream feeds on any device that is linked to the internet. OTT services are also known as over-the-top platforms. When you use the service, you will have access to this capability for the first time. You will be able to directly distribute video content to viewers as well as monetise that material without making any use of a third-party platform in any manner, shape, or form. This will be possible for you. With the assistance of this, you will be able to do both of these tasks successfully.

The many live streaming and video-on-demand alternatives of a high quality that are made accessible to consumers are likely a significant contributing factor to the general attractiveness of these platforms. Live events often are presented in their most fundamental form, which is the broadcasting of them (VoD). In addition to this, they provide a large variety of other services, such as instant messaging, audio streaming, VoIP, and a great many more services that are comparable to these (Adam Enfroy, 2022).

You not only have the capacity to view movies as they are being streamed over the internet when you use an over-the-top (OTT) platform, but you also have the power to carry out the activities that are described below:

- • Manage videos.
- It is recommended that you record live broadcasts in a high-quality format so that you may play them back at a later time.
- • To disseminate the information, make advantage of content delivery networks (CDNs) that are situated in a variety of places all over the globe.
- • If you want to increase your earnings, you should be imaginative about the ways in which you may generate money off of your movies.
- • Give your customers the opportunity to combine all of their video subscriptions together into one monthly payment.
- • Make efficient use of the measurements that have been supplied by the people who will be using the product in question.
- • Modify the way the visual presentation is shown on your web player by making some adjustments to the settings.

ARTIFICIAL INTELLIGENCE

In its most fundamental form, artificial intelligence (AI) is a discipline that facilitates problem-solving via the combination of computer science and extensive datasets. In addition to that, it incorporates the sub-fields of machine learning and deep learning, both of which are often mentioned in conjunction with artificial intelligence. These subfields are comprised of AI algorithms that work toward the development of expert systems that can make predictions or classifications depending on the data that they are given. Applications of artificial intelligence have enormous potential advantages and have the potential to revolutionize any professional field. (Sunil Kumar, 2019).

Some of them are:

1. The most basic definition of artificial intelligence (AI) describes it as a field of study that, when combined with computer science and large amounts of data, makes it easier to find solutions to complex problems. In addition to that, it encompasses the subfields of machine learning and deep learning, both of which are often cited in association with artificial intelligence. Moreover, it is a subfield of artificial intelligence. These subfields are composed of AI algorithms that work toward the creation of expert systems that are able to make predictions or classifications depending on the data that they are provided. These expert systems may make these determinations based on the data that they are given. The applications of artificial intelligence have the potential to bring about huge benefits and to change any professional sector they are implemented in.

2. Is fallible and is willing to take chances: If we program a robot with artificial intelligence to act in our place, we circumvent many of the restrictions that come with being human. It can, among other things, be used to go to Mars, set off a nuclear bomb, investigate the depths of the ocean, harvest coal and oil, and respond to both natural and man-made calamities. Have you heard about the catastrophe that occurred at the Chernobyl nuclear power plant? Everyone who came within a few minutes of the fire's epicentre was killed since we did not have any robots powered by AI to assist us in putting out the fire when it first broke out. Sand and boron were dropped on the area from helicopters by the military. Robots with artificial intelligence might replace humans in circumstances where it would be risky for them to interact with one another.

3. 24X7 approachable: 24 hours a day, seven days a week They also get weekly time off so that they may keep a good balance between their personal and professional lives. On the other side, the development of artificial intelligence has made it possible for us to build robots that can work nonstop for extended periods of time without requiring any breaks; in addition, unlike us, these

robots do not experience boredom. For instance, educational institutions and helplines field a significant number of inquiries and concerns on a daily basis that may be resolved with greater degree of success with the assistance of artificial intelligence.

4. Dealing with Repetitive Tasks: When we go to a bank to apply for a loan, for instance, we often have to go through several document verifications. This is a method that is laborious for the owner of the bank since it takes a lot of time. The deployment of artificial intelligence cognitive automation will also be beneficial to the owner since it will speed up the process of certifying the papers, which will be to the advantage of both the owner and the clients.

5. Digital Assistants:

Some smart businesses use digital assistants to interact with customers, therefore saving both money and time. A large number of websites make use of digital assistants to fulfil user requests. They may be willing to talk with us about our requirements. Some chatbots are designed to make it difficult to distinguish between a conversation with a bot and a conversation with a human. For example, we are all aware that firms employ customer service representatives who respond to consumer inquiries. Businesses may use artificial intelligence to develop a Voice bot or a Chatbot to serve customers. Many businesses are presently using them on their websites and mobile applications.

Some forward-thinking companies replace human customer service representatives with digital assistants, which results in cost and time savings. The majority of websites nowadays make use of digital assistants in order to respond to the inquiries of site visitors. They could be open to discussing our needs in a conversation with us. Some chatbots are programmed to make it hard to tell the difference between having a discussion with a bot and having a communication with a real person. For instance, we are all aware that companies hire customer service personnel who are responsible for responding to questions posed by customers. A Voice bot or a Chatbot might be developed for customer service purposes by businesses with the use of artificial intelligence. They are now being used by a large number of companies across a variety of platforms, including websites and mobile apps.

Like every good thing has a bad side. AI has various drawbacks (Oleg Gubin 2021). Here are a few.

1) Exorbitant Costs of Creation Due to the ever-changing nature of artificial intelligence, both the hardware and software used to create it must be constantly updated in order to meet the requirements of the most recent applications. Repairs and maintenance on machines are expensive and must be performed

regularly in order to function properly. Due to the high level of complexity inherent in these tools, the cost to construct one will be substantial.

2) Making People Lazier The applications of artificial intelligence are automating the great majority of people's work, which is causing people to become lazier. In many cases, people wind up becoming reliant on these technologies, which, in the long run, might provide a problem for future generations.

3) Unemployment:

Human involvement in repetitive tasks and other occupations is reducing as AI takes their place, leading in a major drop in wage expectations. Many companies are looking for ways to reduce their workforce by using artificial intelligence robots that can do the same duties more quickly and more accurately. Because AI is increasingly taking over jobs that need humans to do repetitive activities and other vocations, the average income that can be expected to be earned will significantly decrease. A great number of businesses are looking at methods to minimize the size of their personnel by using intelligent robots that can do the same tasks in a shorter amount of time and with more precision.

4) Even if machines may be more efficient, they cannot replace the human connection that is crucial to forming a cohesive team. 'No Emotions' Controlling teams and collaborating effectively requires the ability to connect with humans, which is impossible for machines. Because AI is gradually taking over professions that need people to perform repetitive activities and other vocations, the average salary that can be anticipated to be earned will drastically fall. This is because the number of jobs that require humans to do repetitive activities is rising. A significant number of companies are investigating ways to reduce the size of their workforce by using intelligent robots that are able to do the same activities in a shorter period of time and with more accuracy than humans are capable of.

5) A lack of "out of the box" thinking:

Machines can only accomplish the tasks for which they have been developed or programmed; if they are asked to perform anything else, they tend to crash or provide irrelevant results, which might be a significant hindrance. A failure to think "beyond the box": Machines can only do the tasks for which they were designed or programmed; if they are requested to perform anything else, they have a tendency to crash or deliver irrelevant results, which might be a big obstacle.

OTT

Extremely Excessive (OTT) As a result, it is possible due to "over-the-top" distribution, which is a term that refers to the new technique of distributing film and television programmes over the internet without the requirement for traditional broadcast, cable, or satellite pay-tv providers. In layman's terms, customers pay an internet service provider such as Xfinity to stream Netflix without having to pay for cable TV. To a ridiculous degree Excessive (OTT) Because of this, it is feasible because of "over-the-top" distribution, which is a term that refers to the new method of distributing film and television programs over the internet without the need for conventional broadcast, cable, or satellite pay-tv providers. As a consequence, it is possible because of "over-the-top" distribution. Customers pay a fee to an internet service provider (ISP) such as Xfinity in order to watch content from Netflix without incurring additional fees for cable television.

One of the reasons OTT entertainments is so popular is its accessibility.

- Unlike TV, which needs a cable subscription, OTT material is paid for directly by customers. OTT material may be streamed anywhere, at any time, unlike conventional TV.
- OTT services may be accessed through computer, phone, tablet, smart TV, or game console. You don't require a pay-tv membership, but depending on the OTT service, you may need one. Services like Netflix and Disney+ allow subscribers to view handpicked material at any time.
- An internet connection and a device that can run applications or browsers are all consumers need to broadcast OTT (Meghna Krishna 2021 July 27).

Smartphones and tablets: Smartphones and tablets may be programmed to download OTT applications, allowing users to stream content while on the move.

Personal computers: People may access over-the-top (OTT) material using desktop applications or web browsers.

Smart TVs: Smart TVs are becoming more popular. Roku, Apple TV, Firestick, and other similar devices are among the most popular. Game consoles, such as the PlayStation, may also run applications that are not directly related to the game itself.

AI and OTT

In this day and age of digital disruption and internet access, developing nations have a responsibility to make use of new technology in order to promote digital entrepreneurship via the development of innovative solutions to meet the needs and address the issues of society (Wang et al., 2021)

In recent years, over-the-top (OTT) services such as Netflix, Hulu, Disney+, and Amazon Video have grown more popular. This has resulted in a new method of streaming and disseminating information.

Because of what consumers needed and what each platform sought to do better, innovation was accelerated during the lockdown. (Source: Leon Lawrence) 2021)

In particular, we are interested in artificial intelligence (AI) and machine learning (ML), as well as how inventors may effectively patent discoveries in this field or collaborate with media production services to bridge the gap between creation and dissemination.

Not only have connection speeds improved over the past several years, but the video quality on over-the-top (OTT) platforms has also improved as a result of this improvement.

More competition in the market makes it difficult for companies to remain relevant in the marketplace. As long as they are unable to distinguish themselves from their rivals, even the most well-known OTT brands cannot be certain of maintaining their market share.

It is critical to differentiate the user experience from the competition in order to succeed in the market.

OTT platforms may maintain their competitive edge and remain relevant to their clients by using artificial intelligence and machine learning technologies in the proper manner.

OTT Opportunity and Challenges

Challenges

1. Misinterpretation of your audience:

What are they going to watch? Who do you think they will be? This is particularly true for specialized channels, which may either target a specialty that is too restricted or attempt to infiltrate a niche that is too crowded. There are only a limited number of viewers and only a limited number of hours in the day.

2. Misuse of technology:

In today's world, there are proper and incorrect ways to achieve almost everything digitally. The most effective technique is to make advantage of the cloud's capabilities. Netflix expanded its global service by 130 new countries with a single click of a button at a CES presentation, a feat that would have taken five years in the traditional television company to accomplish.

3.   Misleading Content:

First and foremost, giving your viewers what they want and exploiting TV business data are important components of meeting these two requirements. It is possible to discover which areas of your content collection are working and which are not by analysing large amounts of data (the word "analytics" is popular right now). These statistics assist you in determining what to eliminate from your collection in order to save money on server expenditures and what to keep around in order to attract visitors for years to come. GIANNI ROSA (2019) is a fictional character created by the author.

4.   Unsatisfactory user experience:

One of the most difficult difficulties for operators is competing with the giant global SVOD businesses such as Netflix, Disney+, and Amazon Prime Video, which all have millions of subscribers. These companies have carefully built their user experience to connect customers with information as rapidly as possible. They do this via the use of personalised recommendations, good user interface design, and cross-platform compatibility.

5.   Establishing objectives:

Although this is an internal problem, it is still a problem. Just because some companies have had success with over-the-top (OTT), does not imply that others will. In addition, a company will not be as successful or return as quickly as investors want. Netflix's stock price remains very susceptible to swings in subscriber growth, and the market punishes the company for each quarter in which it performs poorly.

The long and the short of it is that companies may get subscribers and even revenues, yet they may still collapse inside as a result of unreasonable internal expectations.

Opportunities (AI Enhancing OTT)

1.   Consumer Insights: A Step-by-Step Guide: Predictive analysis is a critical foundation of artificial intelligence. It focuses on the viewing habits of a person, such as the kind of content they are watching, the time of day they are watching, and when they switch to another piece of content. Based on its findings, the AI makes adjustments to the viewer's ideas. Netflix has been enthralling its audience by using Dynamic Optimizer (an artificial intelligence technology)

for content recommendation. A good artificial intelligence-powered platform enhances the user experience and lowers bounce rates.

2. Improve Content Pricing: OTT owners may be able to depend on AI forecasts in order to correctly price content and determine its profitability in the future. How? It may be useful to a platform owner in determining the popularity of a movie, song, record, or television series. It may also aid them in determining when to distribute the show, what time slot to broadcast it in, or the attitudes of viewers toward the programme, among other things. Furthermore, when used in conjunction with social media, artificial intelligence can predict the probability of a new title's success as well as the efficacy of a certain pricing strategy (Naveen Joshi2019).

3. A straightforward conceptualization: Artificial intelligence (AI) may, in some contexts, be able to contribute to the elimination of the need for human labor. The process of creating a movie trailer is one that is both time-consuming and labour-intensive. In 2016, a trailer for the upcoming horror film Morgan was produced by using a system that was powered by artificial intelligence (IBM Watson). The artificial intelligence algorithm performed a minute-by-minute analysis of the movie, during which it identified several previews that had been removed by a human editor.

4. Optimization of the Over-the-Top (OTT) Delivery Network: AI will also optimise OTT delivery. That's quite interesting! Is that correct? Many packed lines, poor connection, and connectivity outages have developed as a consequence of the introduction of the Internet Protocol (IP). The AI platform can both see and track the flow of information. It can also keep track of how material is being distributed. Improvements in streaming and scalability of the broadcasting network may also be recommended by the committee.

CONCLUSION

We take a look at the shifting landscape of over-the-top (OTT) content development and delivery, as well as the patenting options available to innovators working in this space. To investigate the most recent developments in OTT that are being driven by AI and ML, our primary emphasis is on artificial intelligence (AI) and machine learning (ML). It is necessary to have rich content metadata available in order to make the information searchable. The appropriate collection of information enables AI to zero down on those feelings and construct individualized highlights. Because AI engines have a far higher throughput, OTT platforms are able to generate more content while spending significantly less time at the editing tables. IBM and 20th

Century Fox collaborated to produce the world's first "cognitive movie trailer" for the horror film "Morgan." This trailer was developed by IBM.

This feat was done in under twenty-four hours (with some help from human editors at the end), while the creation of a movie trailer typically takes anything from ten to thirty days when AI is not involved. Netflix has patented AI-based recommendation systems that take into account user preferences and are based on such systems. OTT platforms are increasingly competing for technical skills just as much as they are competing for content. The important thing is to not claim the invention in a way that is too broad and to clarify how the innovation that is being claimed is implemented. A business that specializes in digital transformation, Kilowott, makes the claim that it can provide "an exceptional Direct-to-Consumer fan experience at scale."

The goal of Kilowott is to garner interest from a diverse group of broadcasters and content owners. The reach, size, and reliability of the streaming of video content are all improved thanks to the use of OTT technology. Kilowott has been responsible for the drafting and prosecution of a significant number of software patents (with a focus on cutting-edge technologies such as, blockchain, cybersecurity, and extended reality) Because our team is comprised of professionals with expertise in both technology and marketing, we are in a unique position to have a comprehensive understanding of the technology that lies underneath AI-related patents.

Even though over-the-top (OTT) services have a lot of potential, they are operating in a market that is becoming more and more competitive, which means that companies need to make sure that the fundamentals of their operations are in order before they introduce new services. There is at least one solution that is of a technological character, such as cloud computing and data analytics. Other replies are simply sound business practices that may be applied to any aspect of their company's operations. In OTT, there is not going to be a gold rush in the traditional meaning of the term. It is possible to increase

both profits and audiences, but in order to do so, you will need to put in more effort than just presenting a product and crossing your fingers that people would begin purchasing it and watching it right away. You, on your end, are going to need to put in some work as well. In addition to having a sensible strategy, it will be essential to have the ability to provide material that is both fascinating and inexpensive. After that, you'll need to wait some time before using the product so that it can fully develop. For individuals who have already achieved some measure of success, making the shift to a phase in which there will be consistent and ongoing advancement may be an anxious time for everyone involved.

REFERENCES

Enfroy, A. (2022, June 22). *7 Best OTT Platforms of 2022 (Ranked and Reviewed)*. Retrieved from https://www.adamenfroy.com/ott-platform

Gubin, O. (2021, August 31). *Clutch Firms that deliver, development, thought leaders, 4 OTT (over-the-top) service challenges solved with AI*. Retrieved from, https://clutch.co/developers/resources/4-ott-service-challenges-solved-ai

Joshi. (2019, November 16). *AI and chill: How OTT platforms can benefit from AI*. Retrieved from, https://www.allerin.com/blog/ai-and-chill-how-ott-platforms-can-benefit-from-ai

Krishna, M. (2021, July 27). *How is AI benefitting the OTT industry*. Retrieved from, https://brandequity.economictimes.indiatimes.com/news/digital/how-is-ai-benefitting-the-ott-industry/84781042

Kumar, S. (2019, November 25). *Towards Data Science, Advantages and Disadvantages of Artificial Intelligence*. Retrieved from https://towardsdatascience.com/advantages-and-disadvantages-of-artificial-intelligence-182a5ef6588c

Lawrence, L. (2021, December 20). *Top AI-based OTT Trends That Will Impact The Media Industry*. Retrieved from, https://kilowott.com/blog/top-ott-trends-media-industry/

Rosa. (2019, March 29). *4 ways AI can improve user engagement in OTT video service*. Retrieved from, https://www.deltatre.com/insights/4-ways-ai-can-improve-user-engagement-ott-video-services

Shah, A. (2022, April 28). *AI and OTT media: How artificial intelligence is shaping the future of OTT markets*. Retrieved from https://www.ltts.com/blog/AI-shaping-future-of-OTT-markets

Wang, C., Teo, T. S., Dwivedi, Y., & Janssen, M. (2021). Mobile services use and citizen satisfaction in government: Integrating social benefits and uses and gratifications theory. *Information Technology & People, 34*(4), 1313–1337. Advance online publication. doi:10.1108/ITP-02-2020-0097

Chapter 11
Reinventing HR Practices Through Artificial Intelligence

Purnima Sharma
IIS (Deemed), India

ABSTRACT

Artificial intelligence, which is one of the most advanced and growing technologies in today's era, has helped a lot in improving the HR activities like recruitment, staffing, training and development, career planning, and so on. With the changing digitalized scenario, there are many technological advancements that take place in the area of human resources, which helps HR professionals to perform their tasks in a better way within a minimum timeframe. In this chapter, the author focuses on the revolution of AI in the field of human resources. The importance of AI in HR is also an area of concern in this chapter. With the fast-moving scenario, the author also focuses in the developmental areas of AI technology-based programs and applications in the organizations. Ethics in AI also needs to be followed by the organizations, which is also an area which is taken into consideration by the author. Among the applications, AI can shortlist the best possible fits in just the wink of eye and hence reduce human effort.

INTRODUCTION

In today's era many new approaches to Human Resource Management evolved as a need of time. Human Resource department referred as a personnel department having a key responsibility of staffing, recruiting, career planning and development of the employees in the organization. With a view, Human resources has evolved considerably in last 30 years. Last researches show the management of employees'

DOI: 10.4018/978-1-6684-4950-9.ch011

working reflects through how well organizations perform. In the present era AI comes with more advance version and implied to different sectors, a leading firm Microsoft showed in one of their research that AI-based application i.e. speech based recognition performance system was matching with the human outcomes (Resse, 2016). In past covid-19 scenario, there was a push in the development of AI technology-based programs and applications in the organizations. Every organisation adopted the technology to continue their businesses in a smooth way. Nowadays businesses renovating their organisational policies and practices with the help of many recent updated technologies, and among all AI is one of the foremost technologies that helps organization for greater productivity.

This figure shows Traditional Programming and Artificial Learning. Now AI in Human Resources transform jobs in many industries, this change takes place everywhere and with an increasingly faster pace. AI helps in task innovation and efficiency of work in HR. Automation in industries take over many jobs and processes. This is a great change in industries where new technologies such as AI capable software are utilized.

Artificial intelligence (AI) is as efficient as the humans and can process fruitful outcomes in the organisations. Data science can be able to deal with bulky data or information at a time as compared to Human. As in Organisations right and more updated practices are in need, similarly is applicable to Human resources area and AI systems is the trendy way. With the changing scenario, We've seen the modifications to the existing job that now jobs are shifted from labour-based jobs to skills oriented jobs and now a days requirements of skills for employees are changing into the KSA's that can handle todays automated technologies. These technologies are the easiest way to handle and process work and gives more efficient results by the proper utilization of resources and innovation.

Knowledge and skills of employees plays a major role in the organizational success and they are treated as the most important asset of an organization. The automated AI is a tool that provides effective outcomes with the combination of advanced technology and Human intelligence. This AI tool also helps in time utilization and energy efficient for which affects the working earlier style of HR. Presently Human Resource specialists understood about the need to do their work as well as set up the most appropriate organisational procedures with the automated AI instruments for HR functions like recruiting, staffing, performance appraisal process and its management and so on (Ruby Merlin,2018).

In this study, author included various literature related to Artificial Intelligence in Human Resource Management. Focus of this study is on relevance of AI, It's application in the organizations, benefits and challenges in Human Resource Management. Artificial Intelligence is a popular among all the organizations and there is a need of proper understanding of this new technology to all the employees regarding this so that they can also maintain every aspect of organization on ethical grounds like; transparency, fairness and justice.

LITERATURE REVIEW

AI is a tremendous force that will have an impact on customers, businesses, and governments all around the world. According to experts, machines will be able to execute around a third of present vocations in the next decade (Christoffer O. Hernces, 2015) According to the article "Get Intelligent in AI," certain businesses may try to attract clients by overselling their use of AI (Zielinski, 2017). According to a survey, 73% of respondents claimed they have not employed this technology in their enterprises. Sixty-six percent of individuals who use AI technology think it is fair, and 34 percent think it is effective (Leinonen, 2018). This gives a sense of how many businesses are still figuring out how to make the most of technology, and how many are still afraid to include it into their operations at all. Until now, the most time-consuming task in HR has been candidate screening. (2018, R & D) Recruitment with artificial intelligence: A Conceptual Study is the title of the research study. The importance of AI in recruitment has been described by the researchers, with artificial intelligence playing an important role in the recruitment process. Artificial intelligence aids in candidate screening, auto-generated messaging to candidates, employee relations, interview scheduling, and so on. (Merlin, P., and Jayam, R., 2018) The researcher has insight into the role of AI in human resource management in the research title, Artificial Intelligence in Human Resource Management. According to one author, AI is useful in a variety of situations. Workplace and HR professional assistance in understanding their work and identifying problems and trends ahead of time

AI-powered computers can find suitable candidates based on data fed to them describing the ideal candidate for a specific job. According to a post on Ideal's own website, 52 percent of recruiters say the most difficult part of the job is finding the appropriate individual from all of the candidates (Ideal, 2019). According to Ethan Lee's article "Impact of AI on Recruitment," applicant tracking systems (ATS) are considered modest technology by today's standards. He refers to ATS as technology that can scan CVs and search for keywords (Lee, 2019). Chatbots, he says, are a more advanced approach to leverage AI technology in recruitment. Gloat is a startup that connects job seekers with job openings by using natural language when engaging preferred platforms, converse with them, and assist them in locating available job possibilities that may have been difficult to find or otherwise overlooked by the job seeker (Schroer, 2018).

Importance of this Study

This review's contributions link artificial intelligence to human resource management and workplace results. The author gives instructions by referring to several HR functions. This is significant because it elucidates how various HRM functions are likely to employ AI, its application in organisations, ethical issues, and the outcomes that can be achieved as a result of its use. This area of research has received little attention in HRM literature, yet it is critical in assisting various HR functions in understanding how to best utilise smart technologies to improve their performance. Relevant drivers that initiate AI use at work, relevant phenomena that underpin AI implementation at work, and relevant results that highlight the benefits and challenges in AI implementation can all help to better understand AI influences.

Research Gaps Identified

Artificial Intelligence (AI) is becoming a new industrial revolution as a business technology. AI is being used in a variety of businesses to estimate demand, hire personnel, and provide customer service. The way we do business will alter when the next wave of cognitive, automated, and immersive technologies emerges. As a result, there was a rising need to assess Human Resource (HR) practises in light of technology, which has the potential to shift the Human Resource (HR) role from one of strategic advantage to one of operational benefit. The researcher has identified and focused mainly on revolution of AI in HRM area & HRS' Ethical Role in the organisations which will give brief understanding of the future aspiration of artificial intelligence.

REVOLUTION OF AI IN HUMAN RESOURCE MANAGEMENT

Human Resource management is advancing each day as is the Artificial Intelligence (AI). While HR is moving past its conventional jobs of recruiting, terminating, and payroll, AI is changing its gears from being simply a searching tool to enabling technology, machines and robotics. Computer based intelligence develops the AI system having knowledge created in a framework with the assistance of coding and programming, all set to replace the people from repetitive jobs as well as tasks.

By incorporating Artificial Intelligence with Human Resource (HR), it helps Human Resource (HR) to stress more towards the essential work when contrasted with the low value-added tasks. It has given another aspect to the Human Resource (HR) to smooth out and reshaped its unique capacities so it can accomplish the better effectiveness, readiness and aided in the decrease of cost via automation in repetitive task.

The usage of technology in Human Resource (HR) has passed through several phases:

First Phase: Human Resource (HR) was utilizing frameworks to keep up with records either physically or with less utilization of machines. The stage crossed from 1900 to 2000

Second Phase: Human Resource (HR) was utilizing mechanized framework for the projects like data set and dominate. The stage traversed from 2000 to 2012.

Third Phase: Human Resource (HR) are utilizing smart computerized frameworks like cloud, artificial intelligence.

Revolution of Artificial intelligence in Human Resource (HR) has demonstrated more comfort in the space of screening and obtaining. The important element of involving artificial intelligence in Human Resource (HR) is that it has decreased the time for searching the applicants continue in this manner bringing the effectiveness, it has also reduced the rate of errors that are caused by human beings and it becomes free from the biasness of the humans. Artificial Intelligence has also a helping hand to the organizations Human Resource (HR) team to resolve all the human related critical matters, increased the performance outcome which ultimately helps the organizations to make great profits.

AI is an automated system for making on the spot decisions. The HRD department of an organization will adapt this Automated AI systems in their organizations. Now advanced AI systems in Human Resource also promises for achieving efficient and faster outcomes on time. Imitation of Human Resource and creation of machines and devices is possible only through Artificial intelligence. This capability permits machines and devices to hold, change and modify spontaneously with the data analytical technique and later gives results which are more authentic.

Nowadays, many AI employing programming applications help with the different recruiting functions, enlisting, onboarding, retention, and everything in between. These instruments should have assorted applications and recruiting choices to gain from to combat this bias. After the recruiting of appropriate applicants, the AI frameworks will acquaint the recently recruited workers with the organization data and guidelines right from the beginning. New workers will get all the fundamental data like job details to the organization's guidelines, working, data of colleagues, and so forth by a versatile organised data in their PC. This interaction alludes to onboarding process of organization. Onboarding is a cycle to upgrade the ability to recall and recover the efficiency level of Human Resources department. The applicants who understands an efficient and onboarding process will generally in long relationship with the organization. The AI program will likewise help the employees of the organization to study and prepare self about the upper positions and future requirements. It helps them with acquiring facts related to continuous innovations in the marketplace to keep organizations ready for tomorrow. The automated AI system will understand and give appropriate learning sessions to the workers/ employees' by analysing and verifying the papers and tests.

Importance of Artificial Intelligence (AI) in Human Resource Management

With the AI based applications Human Resource department can easily be able to analyse today's workforce trends which helps the employees in working with new patterns. By using AI enabled software's business houses now easily be able to save their employees time and efforts. As a result of which HR department are able to invest most of their time, energy and effort towards the repetitive task in more strategic and creative way, as follows, to Artificial intelligence:

Better automated employee communication: HR teams can ensure that internal communication flows faster and more efficiently handled through AI enabled chatbots. These chatbots transfer every single information to employees that are needed to process their work or task in the organizations such as, changes in plans and policy, Routine announcements, specified instructions, SOP modifications, approval or rejection of messages. This not only helps in saving the time of HR Professionals but also to minimizes communication errors.

Measuring employee participation: Employee participation is very important in organizational Performance and Productivity. To increase level of participation of employees in the organization it is necessary for managers to measure the level of participation of existing employees till now which is time consuming process. To do this in more easiest way AI enabled tools are used by organizations to gauge the level of participation of individual employees. By using such automated tools mangers can assess the employees who are on verge of leaving the organization and they can minimize employee turnover.

Generating Hiring reports: Hiring in the organization is very time-consuming process, number of candidates who attracted to apply for a job and quality of candidates who hired for the organization together determines the effectiveness of HR Professionals. This task is more tedious for the large-scale organizations as they have to analyse more data for the same. The information related to data needs to be communicated to the senior HR Professionals so they can improve hiring decisions. Now through AI enabled HR Analytics and natural language generation technology organizations can generate insightful recruitment performance reports.

Data driven decision making: Mostly organisations still rely on manual method to draw conclusions regarding decision making from the data. Now AI enables HR teams extract insights from the data and give conclusions regarding decision making in real time. AI also gives information without human biases and inconsistencies that is very crucial and sensitive as Human Capital Management. Thus, decisions based on Artificial Intelligence is potentially much faster, consistent and unbiased.

Promote Personalised and collaborative learning: Learning for employees matters more when it is relevant for their working in the respective departments as well as they often need to learn together and with each other.AI can help to make employees learn as per their skills, responsibilities and work style and also help to pair up with each other. It helps in improving individual and team performances and also create learning culture in the organization.

Application of AI in Organizations

There are numerous applications of AI in the organizations which benefited the organization in its success through fast, consistent and error free outcomes.

Hiring and Onboarding: in this competitive environment everyone hunt for a best job every day for a single vacant position. It becomes very tedious task for HR professionals to go through every single resume and shortlist best among all applicants. To make it easier, companies use Artificial Intelligence and Natural language processing to shortlist the resumes of all those applicants who fit better to the vacant positions in the organizations. For this different attribute like region, education, skills and experience are analysed.

Proposal Review and Analysis: Proposals are very often exchanged in business world its not analysed properly sometimes which led towards wrong client. Through machine learning company's proposals can easily be analysed. AI can help the company to get a hold of the price and can also track history of source of proposals.

Cybersecurity: Data inventory and its management is very convenient in business through internet facility but there is always a risk of data leakage in it. Every business needs to be secure for their financial data, organisational strategies and professional information etc. which stored online. That is why Cybersecurity is very important application of AI required in organizations. It helps an organisation to be aware of unwanted, abnormal or malware and also prepare themselves for any attack. For reducing cyber threats, it also helps in analysing big data and develops the system accordingly.

Market Forecasting: Stock markets are always unpredictable markets due to changing market conditions. For making more profits many people invest in it but AI made it easier as well. Some machine learning technologies like Artificial Neural networks and Support Vector machines one can learned and predict the stock market patterns easily. This kind of technological analysis is now important to predict financial markets and helps in generating successful outcomes. Now -a-days many algorithms are used to predict data with 99% accuracy.

Customer Analysis: Success of any business depends of its customers. Customers can easily make or break image of brand or product. So, it is very important to analyse the preferences of the customers and strategize for more engagement and improvement in that field. It becomes more complex situation for the organizations to predict sales and emotional aspect manually. Today, AI enables to get the customer feedback, accurate data and also helps to create better strategies for better customer experience. This Artificial Intelligence benefits the organization through customer-centric approach.

Billing and Invoice: Organizations also have financial responsibilities of bills, check payments and invoice which is needed to be exchanged with others. If financial processes handled manually, it could turn out to be very burden for the management and also sometimes mistake in calculation could lead to terrible losses. Automated AI processes made financial management very easy and accurate. Many software has features like data extraction and segregation which can easily extract data from invoices.

Conversational Interface: Every business organization have their own products and services in which they are dealing also they have to make aware of it to the mass public in order to expand customer base and to increase their sales. It is not at all possible to meet individually for the owners to explain and clear the doubts. Now with the AI technology business organizations are inculcating chatbots and virtual assistants in their own applications and websites, as if anyone needs 27*7 customer services that can be answered.

Social Media Insights: In today's era social media becomes the strongest platform for the promotion of brands on a large scale through which business organisations can showcase their products and services. Companies can approach massive number of customers if they use social media platform accurately. It is not easy for business organizations to take their customer's feedback manually but with the AI companies can know their positions in the market and also get to know about their customer base.

Benefits of Artificial Intelligence (AI) In HR

Artificial Intelligence is more capable of developing increase productivity and effective workflow in the organizations. Now -a-days technology is rapidly impacting the Human Resources as to look on employees' behavioural patterns and organizations are adapting the technology to cope up with the complex business situations.

There are some benefits of artificial intelligence in Human Resource and know why it is necessary to implement technology in business growth:

Automation of routine task makes HR more productive like onboarding of new employees, employee attendance record, payroll process so that employee can focus more strategic working in the organization.

Recruitment process becomes more easier as candidates screening of resume and selecting right candidate is more complex process when it done manually but with the AI technology in recruitment process helps the HR Professional to gain insights about the candidates. For this, AI Chatbots helps the candidates to interact with it before recruiters and gets the details regarding updates and feedback.

Employee engagement to new high for the success of an organization. With the help of AI organizations can enhance engagement level of employees so that they can deliver high volume and quality outcome. Engaged employees are always treated as valuable assets to the company which ultimately lead organization to impressive growth. AI powered chatbots is the right way to engage employees in better way.

AI based interactive sessions makes learning more interesting as compared to traditional learning methods.

HR ETHICAL ROLE IN ORGANIZATIONS

HR Department is more anxious with an organizations labour planning and its growth. Organizations are more inclined towards efficient outcomes with cost minimization for which the artificial intelligence in HR department is in much trend but there is a need to focus on Ethical issues as well. human resource professionals have to encourage and foster transparency and justice to every worker and their managers. To promote an ethical environment is a productive step towards growth.

Ethical Implications of AI In HR

Use of Artificial intelligence (AI) and Machine Learning (ML) technologies in HR department including recruitment is targeted towards increasing efficiency and reducing cost of Human resource management practices. Along with that, globalisation of world has paved ways for international work force and global talent pool where artificial intelligence becomes very important to get right match of skills and expertise for the job profile. Artificial intelligence has proved its utility right from aggregating job vacancies to connect them with aggregating job vacancies. It also increases screening of candidates.

Not only recruitment, many other HR practices can be done quickly with correct application of AI. As the new employee joins at his workplace, AI can be used for his training, supervision and performance analysis. It helps to save quality time of human resource managers for more important works. Along with time saving, usage of AI is also important from financial point of view. engaging manpower is far costlier for organisation than engaging AI for implementation of certain project.

- **AI's blind spot**

Recruitment is complicated process as it initiates search of right match between job and suitable candidate. No particular process is standard for recruitment. It completely depends on type of job. It is necessary to understand the technology of AI that gets used for recruitment process. Outcome of AI should be measurable in the short and long-term.

Although usage of AI is believed to save time and money, we should not overlook its blind spots as well. There is equal probability of AI to set a pattern between the background of candidates and their recruitment. If this happens, AI may result completely biased towards candidates from certain background eliminating other probably capable candidates. This could cause unintentional discrimination in hiring process.

This directly means that many of the people coming from various different backgrounds will not be able to get the equal chance as others matching with the algorithm created by AI. This will affect the talent pool of organisation in every way.

There have been some incidents reported where people have found devising tact to match their applications with set algorithm of AI. Human manager of work force management can identify such fudge whereas artificial intelligence relies on final result only. So, experts doubt complete dependency on artificial intelligence in HR domain as it may be manipulated in absence of logical thinking capacity.

Researches reveal that a Complex AI system can reach to a certain decision with the help of composite data analysis. By getting the idea about the data type under consideration of AI, biasness can be eliminated. HR professionals, by having such knowledge about AI will be able to apply their own instinct to the data and take an informed decision on the AI's assessment. Here we can understand that AI works for reducing workload of human but it cannot replace them. Keeping its usability in mind, proper and balanced collaboration between human intelligence and artificial intelligence can reach to the desired goal.

Fairness, Transparency, and Justice in Socio-Technical HR Organizational Practices Involving AI

A huge number of job application can be scrutinised at just one click with the help of artificial intelligence. This kind of systems are usually acclaimed to be unbiased, rather better than manual approach in identifying the expertise and capabilities of applicants. Moreover, there are certain estimations that artificial intelligence logically calculates performance graph of applicant and match with it with current job profile requirement. This calculation generates such algorithm on which suitability of applicant can be judged for the offered job. Artificial intelligence can judge the applicant better than what experienced human resource managers have been doing so far.

Apart from all these acclamations, many practitioners, researchers, academicians and even the ethicists do not agree with this concept. At one side, in the domain of HR, the ethical challenges of AI showcase those who have received noteworthy consideration in other domains of AI application domains, including criminal justice, policing particularly covering discriminatory profiling problem which strengthens historical discrimination. Whereas On the flipside, another evolving ethical problem which has not been inspected much is the way of AI usage in HR domain. AI is overstepping candidates'/employees' independence over self-representation.

For many years organisations and specially the human resource management department is setting high hopes with the application of artificial intelligence. AI is expected to do many complicated calculations easily in almost all domains to make life of human being easier. But no certain claims have been put by the experts on ethical approach of artificial intelligence.

Robots are one of the most appropriate examples of using artificial intelligence to reduce human efforts and increase the accuracy of performance making it free from human errors. But even after development of highly advanced robot, we get sceptical on its decision-making ability where the current situation may not match with its set programs of instructions. Selection of integrity over accomplishment of task, having empathy with customer more than concentrating on target achievement has always been point of discussion in field of artificial intelligence. However, EQ of machines are going to be very much dependent on their developers. So now responsibility of making machines ethically correct is the responsibility of their creators. In this situation organisation's HR department plays crucial role in positively influencing the engineers so that they can further influence their machines having artificial intelligence.

HR practitioners, so far have identified for crucial areas where they can play significant role in influencing application of artificial intelligence in their organisations.

i)   Defining & reinforcing Organization Values in context of AI

AI is being predicted to raise as next competitive advantage for organisations. Professionals are expecting its valuable application in multiple domains as production, promotion, customer relationship management, supply chain management and many more which will eventually increase sustainability of company in market. Companies like IBM, Microsoft have already successfully implemented AI in their functioning. In such situation determining principles and values for AI is a crucial yest essential move by management. Both the leaders and HR professional have to come together for determining company's ethics and values and explaining it to the creators of machines functioning on artificial intelligence. These values should be imbibed in AI enabled machines as well. Few organizations such as MindTree are known to leverage outbound activities for reinforcing the Organization Values among employees.

ii) Identifying & developing the "right" talent

Most of today's AI systems are developed on the basis of machine learning. It is the technique which needs any one of hundreds of possible algorithms in order to "learn" patterns from huge database. This algorithm should be able to predict the future possibilities but biasness of AI reduces accuracy of such model. In today's global business market scenario, Companies are not only looking for high IQ of employees. Rather they are looking for proper balance between IQ and EQ of candidate which puts significant impact on person's overall productivity. Today when quantitative work is being taken care by machines, companies are looking for employees with correct level of emotional quotient.

In order to increase self-awareness among employees, HR managers have been using tools such as Johari Window, MBTI, Hogan Assessments, Strengths Finder and Emotional Quotient 2.0 Nevertheless, integrating these tools or probably newer and more predictive tools in the selection process would be essential to determine EQ level of candidate.

Contribution of HR managers are required in order to Developing employees at all levels on increasing self – awareness, enhancing emotional quotient and aligning Individual Values with Organisation Values.

iii) Establishing the right culture

Organisation's culture gets drafted by the actual practices of values by Leaders. If leaders have strong personal values aligned with organisation's values and it reflects in their behaviour and action, correct set of culture gets build in company.

However, in order to build an organization that is sustainable towards the impact of artificial intelligence, organizations will have to introduce additional checks and balances in the system. Many big sized corporates are making open processes for their employees to give comment on the decisions taken or biases reflected organizations. Such moves are not only going to enhance the self – awareness of the organization but also reinforcing the values at the micro level.

Establishing procedure for rewards and discipline may also be helpful in building the right culture in the context of AI.

Challenges in AI Ethics in HR

Vitality of AI application in HR domain cannot be underestimated as it is very much helpful in predictive analysis for recruiting. Among the thousand applications, AI can shortlist the best possible fit in just wink of eye and hence reduce human efforts manifolds. But it has its own set of challenges as well. Let's have a look on major hurdles in AI application -

i) **AI won't understand your company like you or a recruiter can:**

Although AI may support HR managers to scan various resumes very quickly but it can be expected to have understanding about the dynamics of global market and company's position in international perspective. It can only be understood by HR manager. While making s selection decision, HR manager evaluated the candidate on the basis of his current performance and position, his potential, company's future goals and company's culture. AI technology falls short in having this wider and deeper perspective while selection of employee.

HR manager develops expertise is reading between the lines and listening to the unsaid things with keen observation of body language, facial expressions, tone of communication and attitude while AI works on presented database only.

Taking an example an applicant may have work experience with a start - up which was not big in size but this reveals his flexibility and ability of multitasking. AI is not able to interpret the given facts in such way.

ii) **Possibility to miss out on hiring outliers:**

Sometimes a candidate which do not fir in selection criteria can have learning aptitude and positive attitude. Such outlier may prove to become a very productive human resource for company. But in case of AI application there is no scope for such outliers who do not clear the strict selection criteria. This lack of human touch may result in missing out selection of most creative and innovative candidates for the team. Although AI may be implemented in keeping an eye out for certain characteristics that we look in a new hire but there is always requirement of human intuition during selection process of candidate.

iii) **AI can't account for human emotion:**

Selection process do not only depend on degrees and work experience one has. It also considers the passion and zeal one possesses. Candidate's emotional traits, his attitude, presence of mind, motivation, ambition is also examined. AI cannot examine such human emotions. Neither it can calculate the relationship between state of mind and productivity.

AI do not understand human emotions so it does not understand the required personality traits required for being member of certain existing team. Here comes the role of Human resource manager itself who can evaluate the link between personalities and team dynamics

iv) **AI can't 'read' people:**

HR manager, with his constant growing experience gets able to evaluate talent of applicants. They can identify the difference between genuine and false claim people make with the help of their intuitions. AI lack this sense and hence often make wrong decisions regarding work force. HR manager assign work on the basis of employees' interest and expertise. In this process, manager also takes care about the personal problems of employees and give them support to sort it out whereas AI do not have ability to consider such aspects.

v) **AI lacks ethical responsibility:**

As the business is going global, keeping its ethical values and principles at highest priority is the foremost responsibility of organisation's management. Companies are opening their door for male and female candidates. Business is functioning round the clock. Talent is being acquired from around the world. with this versatile work force, giving equal growth opportunity to everyone, managing fair performance appraisal, ensuring employees' safety, keeping their motivation level high and making them engaged with their assignment and workplace is the ethical responsibility of HR team today. AI works on data and develops algorithm. It lacks ability to find unique solution for every individual. Hence, managing diversified workforce gets next to impossible with implementation of AI only. Input of Human is also required to handle the unpredictable challenges in Human resource management.

However, even after the above-mentioned shortcomings, Accuracy and impartiality can be ensured in AI and also the following steps.

vi) **Instruct candidates and get their permission** - Candidates should be aware that data being given by them to the company is going to be analysed by artificial intelligence. It should be informed to one and all that HR related decisions will be made on the scrutiny done by AI. Such AI should not be based completely on Black Box model. Rather, scope of explanation should also be provided to understand cause of any response. Personal information fille by candidate should always be kept safe.

vii) **Develop open-source systems and third-party audits** - Companies should allow external parties to check their AI tools in order to examine their accuracy and efficiency. Third party audits over AI applications can give 360-degree view to understand where is the possibility of going wrong and how it can be sorted.

viii) **Follow the same laws of traditional hiring for data collection and usage practices** No data should be included in AI system which cannot be included in traditional hiring system due to some legal or ethical reasons. Any sensitive data regarding mental condition, related to genetic data, should not ever be pass in.

IMPLICATIONS OF THE STUDY

The number of organisations now a days moving towards robotics and AI in their daily working affect the greater number of jobs, it's not true. Every company ensures about the system which will benefit both employees as well as company in long term. Artificial Intelligence (AI) in the workplace can help to enhance working conditions. In the employment and compensation of employees, AI will aid in the removal of unconscious and conscious prejudices. It also mentions how AI in the workplace will benefit employees in other ways, such as ensuring that the proper safety equipment, transparency, fairness is worn through the use of AI Ethically.

According to the findings of the study, the implications for AI in Human Resource Management are relevant to investigate. Chatbots are also being utilised by HR to assist with training operations. This is based on the success of many chatbots as in-house advisors to call centre employees in instances where excessive turnover of staff can affect the consistency of replies and the ability to respond to enquiries swiftly.

FUTURE DIRECTIONS

India is making progress in implementing artificial intelligence. It is still in its early stages, though. While some sectors, such IT, manufacturing, automobiles, etc., are making use of AI's abilities, there are still many others where its potential is untapped. In this chapter author focused more on specific content i.e importance of AI, its, benefits, application, challenges and ethical implications. There are many things which are untouched in this chapter like role of AI in human resource system in the organization, pre and post AI revolution, AI and organizational productivity.

The several additional technologies that fall under the purview of AI help to explain the enormous potential that it possesses. Self-improving algorithms, Machine

Learning, Pattern Recognition, Big Data, and many more technologies are instances of this type. It is anticipated that very few industries would be unaffected by this potent weapon during the next few years. This explains why India has such great potential for AI development.

CONCLUSION

There is no doubt that, over time, the impact of AI on HR will be real and long-lasting. AI framework must be adaptable enough to upgrade itself and modify as necessary because this technology is constantly evolving. AI can be used to automate the majority of repetitive HR tasks, analyse massive amounts of data to make actionable decisions, and have a positive overall influence on the business, its ethical implications on business and on its workforce. There are numerous applications of AI in the organizations which benefited the organization in its success through fast, consistent and error free outcomes. AI can be used for his training, supervision and performance analysis, etc. which helps to save quality time of human resource managers for more important works. AI systems need to be carefully managed by locating trustworthy learning data sets, choosing the best implementation strategy, looking for clarity, removing bias, and taking unintended consequences into account. Sooner AI will change the scenario of companies with greater and most efficient outcomes.

REFERENCES

Antoniou, J., & Andreou, A. (2019). Case study: The Internet of Things and Ethics. *The Orbit Journal, 2*(2), 67.

Bankins, S. (2021). The ethical use of artificial intelligence in human resource management: A decision-making framework. *Ethics and Information Technology, 23*. Advance online publication. doi:10.100710676-021-09619-6

Daugherty, P. R., & Wilson, H. J. (2018). *Human+Machine: Reimagining work in the age of AI.* Harvard Business Press.

Greenwood, M. (2002). Ethics and HRM: A Review and Conceptual Analysis. *Journal of Business Ethics, 36*(3), 261–279. doi:10.1023/A:1014090411946

Guenole, N., & Feinzig, S. (2018a). *The business case for AI in HR: With insights and tips on getting started.* IBM Smarter Workforce Institute. https://public.dhe. ibm.com/common/ssi/ecm/81/en/81019981usen/81019981-usen-

Gulliford, F., & Parker Dixon, A. (2019). AI: The HR revolution. *Strategic HR Review*, *18*(2), 52–55. doi:10.1108/SHR-12-2018-0104

Mathew, S. M., Oswal, N., & Ateeq, D. (2021). *Artificial Intelligence (AI): Bringing a New Revolution in Human Resource Management*. HRM.

Miller, P. (1996). Strategy and Ethical Management of Human Resources. *Human Resource Management Journal*, *6*(1), 5–18. doi:10.1111/j.1748-8583.1996.tb00393.x

Park, W. (2018), *Artificial intelligence and human resource management: new perspectives and challenges*. Japan Institute for Labour Policy and Training. https://www.jil.go.jp/profile/documents/w.park.pdf

PeartA. (2021). https://www.artificial-solutions.com/blog/impact-of-ai-in-the-workforce

Richa & Srinivas. (2020). Challenges of artificial intelligence in human resource management in Indian IT sector. *XXI Annual International Conference Proceedings*, 380-387. http://www.internationalconference.in/XXI_AIC/INDEX.HTM

Tambe, P., Cappelli, P., & Yakubovich, V. (2019). Artificial Intelligence in Human Resources Management: C hallenges and a Path Forward. *California Management Review*, *61*. doi:10.1177/0008125619867910

Uenole, N., & Feinzig, S. (2018b). *Competencies in the AI era*. IBM Smarter Workforce Institute.

Chapter 12

Artificial Intelligence:
The Best Fit or a Misfit in the Job Fit Analysis

Jayti Mahajan
Panipat Institute of Engineering and Technology, India

Suman Dahiya
Panipat Institute of Engineering and Technology, India

Puja Narang
Panipat Institute of Engineering and Technology, India

ABSTRACT

Disruptive technology is now a tool adopted by the organizations to cater to the HRM practices. Intelligent automation can not only complete manual tasks but also make intelligent decisions, much like a human. Its capabilities could allow machines to comprehend procedures and anomalies. With the escalating demand of artificial intelligence (AI), this chapter offers the fundamentals of AI in job-fit analysis and also shows how AI can enable HR teams to extract insights from data and give appropriate recommendations for real-time job-fit processes. AI is looked upon to change the role of a recruiter and improve their relationships with hiring managers by using data to measure KPIs such as quality of hire. It also emphasizes the significance of artificial intelligence in various aspects of job-fit analysis. The conclusions drawn from the literature are discussed and presented. In the conclusion, some challenges and potential solutions and future research are also presented.

DOI: 10.4018/978-1-6684-4950-9.ch012

INTRODUCTION OF ARTIFICIAL INTELLIGENCE

The intelligence illustrated by machines is known as Artificial Intelligence. In layman terms, artificial intelligence can be defined as a perspective to replicate how smartly human beings think in line with the computer intelligence. In times of problem-solving and decision-making, artificial intelligence will focus on how humans think, interpret, plan and execute. AI has turned out to be a part of computer and science that targets to develop quick-witted machinery. At present, technology as an industry has turned out to be very significant.

AI is capable of programming and imitating the human action in the form of simulating the natural intelligence with the help of machines. Hence, these kinds of machines become highly capable of performing and replacing the tasks done by human beings with perfection and quality.

With the increasing intervention of science and technology in our day-to-day lives, artificial intelligence is actually and rapidly changing people's traditional lifestyle in a different manner. AI based accomplishments of people are the real outcome of human's creativity and innovation.

From the automated production lines in factories to the machine learning algorithms, artificial intelligence applications exists everywhere, that extricate meaning from mountains of data.

On the one hand, as an outcome of emerging technologies in computer sciences, the world economy is found and observed to be more automated at present. On the other hand, artificial intelligence applications are also expected to enhance employability, drastic increase in profits in the near future and radically change the economy from one that depends on paucity to one that relies on superabundance.

Applications of AI are expected to create 3 kinds of jobs in the near future: trainers, explainers and sustainers. The role of trainers will be played by humans in teaching how AI systems can be more human in the real life. For example, customer service based chatbots are made to understand how to actually interpret the tone of the customer i.e. is he angry, doubtful or happy.

The explainers will lead the role in analyzing the large quantum of data and designing of the complex AI algorithms for effective decision-making in the areas of advertising, education and various sectors of the government. At last, the sustainers will act as monitors for AI so as to ensure that systems operate as per the designed algorithms.

AI has become the nervous system of almost all the organizations at present. Most of the companies are ripening the benefits of AI on a large scale. It is forecasted that by the year 2035, industries like ICT, BFSI and manufacturing could see a massive change in terms of their working and quality of work. Besides this, even the companies in the field of education, construction, retail, healthcare and many more are expected to earn multi-fold profits if they adopt AI based systems along with augmented reality.

One another important dimension of extended AI is Human-Centered Artificial Intelligence (HCAI). It's defined as a group of procedures for creating such relevant applications that are secure and faithful. This approach will help in extending the various procedures of design at the users end like observation and interviews, discussion with the members, experimenting and assessment in using systems that can employ artificial intelligence and the related algorithms. It is expected to assure highest levels of human controlling and automatization.

The research at the HCAI level involves the governing of structures including a culture of security within the boundaries of the organizations and also an indirect observation by an expert group of people so as to review the plans of future projects, regular assessments, and time-bound failure analysis.

AI AND HRM- LITERATURE REVIEW

A very significant achievement among hiring experts in 2018 was the implication of AI in HRM, as per Upadhyay and Khandelwal (2018). Extracting of the information, as per Stuart and Norvig (2016), is a technique of collecting latest data. Scanning a message is one way to do this. Information can make use of AI, particularly in the hiring of fresh workers and also in finding ways for shortlisting CVs so as to make the process of scanning and extracting resumes easier (Kaczmarek, Kowalkiewicz & Piskorski, 2005).

Many a creative systems have been created which are taken care of by computers in order to reduce the hard work of the recruiters. With the usage of outcome-based techniques and algorithms there are some softwares which are developed and can be used for extracting resumes (Montuschi, Gatteschi, Lamberti, Sanna, & Demartini, 2014).

The capacity to fetch the data about the applicants' personality traits, that can be specifically vital for fulfilling the vacancies, is an extra-ordinary feature of Artificial Intelligence-based rating algorithms.

However, these qualities are more often recognised while organizing the job-based interview processes, but the primary and basic data can only be found out via website research. It is easy to fetch the data on applicants' personality trails, moods and sentiments by conducting linguistic examination of their blog entries and LinkedIn profiles (Faliagka et al. 2012).

Talking about the applicants that have been rejected for a job, the mechanism of artificial intelligence would provide review on their education and skills, providing them scope for improvement in the future. (Upadhyay & Khandelwal, 2018).

Hardships of Artificial Intelligence

Personal privacy and the way data is handled and examined are two of the many issues that AI-based recruitment brings. Both HR professionals and online HRM users are affected when it comes to analysing data or providing personal information (Brewster & Bondarouk 2016)

Organizations cannot function effectively without some level of technical innovation. Martincevic and Kozina (2018), Organizations' ability to adapt to new technologies determines in large part how competitive they are in the market. Previous research has demonstrated that adopting new technology has a number of advantages in form of improved performance.

INTRODUCTION TO JOB FIT

Job fit defines whether a candidate is suitable for a particular position or not. It is one of the greatest ways to choose and select employees in terms of right person for the right job resulting in reduced employee turnover and also to increase attrition rate of employees in the long-term. Generally, when job-fit is targeted on a priority basis the organization tends to have higher chances of employees being happy and highly productive. Its can have direct impact on the employee morale and consequently benefits the company's market image and reputation as well.

An endless number of factors can affect job fit like personality of the individual that can actually convey that how happy or satisfied you are talking about a specific designation. It is quite possible that employees who are non-assertive can be unhappy in a particular position while the employees who are extrovert by nature can be dissatisfied while working on a position that includes least human interaction. For this purpose, various employability personality tests can be used to evaluate a broad range of personality traits associated with job fit for the organizations to feel highly confident that most of their workers will be satisfied with their job profiles.

It's a victory of all, as and when employee-job fits persists in an organization.

Determining Company's Employee-Job Fit – A Framework

The one's whose initial task is to enhance the organization's turnover by strictly working on and focusing on the individual teams and the culture of the organization must put in best efforts to aim for the more number of workers in their organizations who target better job-fit for the employees.

In order to cross check employee job-fit at your organizational level, the management should be aware of the individuals' competency and whether the right people are placed on the right job. Simultaneously, it is also important to ensure that the recruitment managers are utilizing appropriate and latest screening tools like including adequate and job-oriented questions in the interview round specially in case of preparing an assessment report of the job applicants so as to fulfill the best job-fit. An evaluation of the fitness for the job provides many viewpoints to support the reality, to support the reduction in the unfairness of individual relationships, and it also allows for a well-targeted interaction.

Alongside, person-job fit is an inclusive part of the person-environment fit. Significantly, person-environment fit also involves subordinate-supervisor fit, individual-group fit, and employee-organization fit. It is basically the idea that individuals interact with their surroundings which directly affects their individual well-being. At times, when an individual employee merges well with their surroundings, employee well-being goes up automatically. Simultaneously, when the workers are immersed deeply and particularly with their job i.e. knowledge, skills, abilities, personality, and interests can also be aligned with it.

Employee-job fit is vital. For instance, employees might not like the organization they work for, but if they really love and admire their jobs; their everyday struggle will be negligible. Conversely, if employees dislike their job, but like their organization, they might be able to associate greater purpose in the work they dislike. Resultantly, their day-to-day activities will still be in a mishap. Ultimately, employee-job fit is very much significant for the overall well-being.

RECRUITMENT AND SELECTION

The process of hiring is divided in 2 categories. In general, hiring can be characterized as a procedure aimed at attracting candidates so as to obtain applications for the posted vacancies from those that fit the individual specifications necessary to successfully handle the work tasks outlined in the job description. Selection, on the other hand, refers to the process of assessing differences between candidates in order to identify and pick the candidate who best fulfils the job description's person specification.

The term "recruitment" refers to all of an organization's practices and activities with the core objective of getting the right potential employees. Employers must be able to attract the top candidates to the maximum extent possible, especially today, in order to get a decent candidate pool from which to choose and make final recruitment decisions, as the demand for highly skilled prospects is fierce. Recruitment is a vital aspect of HRM since it is used to acquire intellectual capital, which is one of the organization's most valuable assets. Recruitment and enrolling new personnel are expensive processes, thus we must pay close attention to them. Because workers are recognized as the company's most valuable asset, poor recruitment results in massive costs.

From the beginning, in the 1970s, when the sector originally emerged, recruitment has undergone a dramatic transformation. Recruitment has been more challenging in recent years, and competition for good staff has increased. Presently, the outsourcing of the hiring process is very much in trend. As social networking sites, IT and the structures all over have evolved over time, they are getting complex and interconnected, making the hiring procedure more complex.

Furthermore, new technologies have resulted in significant changes in recruiting, necessitating extensive research into the phenomena of new technology-based recruitment approaches in order to fully comprehend its promise and threats. The prospect for artificial intelligence (AI) to transform recruitment is extremely captivating, wherein the study targets the new things that hiring procedures are and will encounter fresh and emerging resolutions. The goal of AI technologies is to better comprehend and create intelligent things. As a result, it should come as no surprise that enterprises may draw significant benefit via the Big Data, including the hiring process. AI tried to make significant possibilities for HRM strategies such as recruitment. To fully comprehend the potential and risks of new technology-based recruitment strategies, extensive research is required.

In a typical hiring procedure, the interviewer also plays an important role. Furthermore, the candidate's information is frequently one-sided, if not out rightly wrong, resulting in skewed consequences.

RECRUITMENT AND SELECTION USING AI

Electronic recruiting has been a success in the world of HR management since its debut, but further research into the episode of the latest technology-based hiring techniques is required to fully comprehend its prospective and pitfalls. Alongwith the merits that technology gives in upgraded selection and the future prospects, online hiring has provided significant advantages like money, time, pool of individuals and response standard. Electronic hiring is way ahead than just receiving applications for the various jobs on the internet; it even helps to cover many other relevant areas of hiring candidates. Online hiring is actually explained as the posting of the vacancies on the Internet, the respective applications being acceptable accordingly and utilizing electronic recruitment techniques like resume and application banks, robots for hiring and portals designed to assist hiring employees. (Panayotopoulou, Vakola & Galanaki, 2005)

Employers might be attracted to a company through both direct and indirect techniques. From the viewpoint of the typical paper-based hiring brochures to the board of the hiring teams, there has been a shift. As a result, businesses' vacancies are more visible, and applicants have a greater range of options. There are a lot of job openings to pick from. The internet has made it possible for individuals to obtain data about each other businesses, including the simulations and questions based of job-fit, provide job previews that are logical and provide insight into actual job-fit. (Searle, 2006) New technology and methodologies, both of which have the potential for surveillance, have had a significant impact on established methods when it comes to applications and assessment.

The procedure of identifying candidates has been substantially altered thanks to online applications. Also, the function of skill and ability evaluation has altered because nowadays online screening of individuals is done to improve the rationality of tests, eliminating the need to purchase 25 personality tests from third parties. Applicants can now participate fully in the recruiting process thanks to the internet, increasing the chances for people from poorly challenged parts of the world over (Baron & Austin, 2000).

Methods of exploring the data which systematize the procedure of identifying the relevant CVs and selection of essential data can be used to apply AI approaches in staff recruitment skimming a text to obtain knowledge and information is referred to as information extraction. By studying text and interaction through linguistic cues, artificial intelligence is even competent of identifying the candidate's personality and obtaining the various models of the personality for the Big Five personality traits. A lot of dimensions of job-related employee conduct, like the day-to-day work done (Furnham, Jackson, & Miller, 1999), are influenced by personality traits in disadvantaged countries and locations (Baron & Austin, 2000). As a result, artificial intelligence has determined a candidate's persona and suitability for the vacancy by merely looking at the job application written by the candidate. It's normal to inquire regarding individual's personality characteristics in a straight forward manner, but Mairesse et al (2007) anticipate that self-assessed personality models will outshine witness personality via language and dialogue.

New technology and methodologies, both of which have the potential for surveillance, have had a significant impact on established methods when it comes to applications and assessment.

The procedure of identifying candidates has been substantially altered thanks to online applications. Also, the function of skill and ability evaluation has altered because with the help of internet now days it becomes easier to identify the suitable applicants. According to Baron and Austin 2000, it is now easy for everyone to actively engage in the recruitment process, even from fiscally weak zones.

Now a days, getting information is well automated which further helps in identifying the resumes and digging out the important information to apply AI techniques in the recruitment of the staff which would be ultimately the goal of the having the information system. According to Furnham, Jackson & Miller 1999, with the use of dialectal indicators AI can very easily detect the personality and the qualities required to develop the personality. As per Baron and Austin, 2000 in most of the underprivileged countries it is seen that task performance is influenced by the personality attributes.

Figure 1.
Source: 123RF

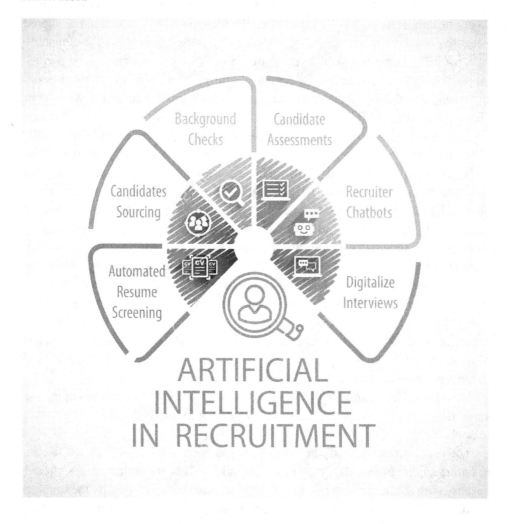

As a result, AI may be able to determine a candidate's personality and suitability for the job from an application letter. It's normal to inquire about one's personality characteristics directly, but Mairesse et al (2007) predict that self-assessed personality models will outshine witness personality via language and dialogue. These days it is at this point not adequate to create and prepare just individuals, since it additionally incorporates the turn of events and preparing of calculations. Creating and preparing calculations is fundamental since calculations can learn wrong things, very much like individuals, however as individuals can judge them, calculations are not. Today, calculations are likewise equipped for creating philosophies furthermore for making reality (Mager, 2012). HR's skills are clearly altering as a result of AI. According to a Deloitte analysis from 2017, 38% of survey respondents thought AI would be widely deployed in their firm within three to five years. In 2018, that figure had risen to 42%. It is still going up. In the next few years, 72 percent of CEOs believed AI will provide major business benefits, while 76 percent of recruiting managers felt AI will be at least somewhat essential in the future, according to a LinkedIn research. "AI is a wonderful approach to recruit the best personnel that will flourish at your firm, as it leverages vast volumes of data to anticipate outcomes better than any person can," said Eric Sydell, EVP of Innovation at Modern Hire. In contrast to the long-standing method of recruitment, AI based recruitment process is more elaborative and can be beneficial in number of ways. In the following figure the Recruitment process using AI is mentioned:

PROMOTE AI FOR JOB FIT

The effect of AI on human resource practices are out ranging which are helpful in mechanizing various HR processes and also in improving the decision making and developing the strong bond between employer and the employee. Companies like IKEA, L'Oreal, Unilever, and Amazon have used AI led recruitment systems like chatbot and Mya valuations to improve in locating the suitable candidate and moving from extensive and wide-ranging hires to eradicate unqualified candidates, estimating prospective workforces, and gathering data from facial expressions and gesture. Moreover, AI proponents argue that these levels of analysis can enhance staff selection by also utilizing strategies that are smart enough even to interpret 'micro-expressions' and to undertake 'spoken analysis', methods to take out qualities that make use of AI technologies are among the most commonly debated development of the World of Work 4.0.(AI). But what benefits can this innovation bring to the hiring process? It is undeniable that using AI to standardize all recruitment processes can promote a greater objectivity in candidate evaluation.

This assessment is made more unbiased by avoiding common assessor errors that can always be avoided despite decades work expertise and best efforts. This would include the so-called halo effect, in which you make the decisions without objective manner basing the choice on a dominant feature, but instead on other characteristics of the person. You can make assessments using artificial intelligence that thinks logically. Moreover, clear evaluation metrics can be defined at the start of the application procedure, leading to more objective assessment. For applicants, the objectivity as well as transparency provided by AI-driven decisions means a higher perception fairness, which has a positive impact on how the brand is perceived. Likewise convenient for candidates is AI's flexibility, which can completely meet the changing needs of the applicants, for example, by modifying the applicant's gender. Another advantage of using artificial intelligence is that the complete application method can be designed much more easily.

Candidates should ideally have only to create one pivotal profile. It is then used by company's artificial intelligence. The company's application is also facilitated by automatic pre-selection and judgment. Artificial intelligence also provides financial benefits to the company. Details can be obtained, merged, and evaluated in a couple of moments, resulting in a more comprehensive picture of the applicants than a recruiter could do in approximately the same amount of time. These factors imply that, in the upcoming years, even better assessments as to whether applicants would fit perfectly into the company could be made, implying that the application process will be more valid. Furthermore, AI is not tired or ill, and it can work at any moment and in any language. This gives the company and the recruiter more time to focus on a smaller number of participants.

With each implementation, the artificial intelligence tries to learn more and constantly improves itself. This knowledge is maintained by the company, whereas the anecdotal observation of a recruiter is difficult to transfer and may be lost entirely if they leave the company.

MAJOR BENEFITS OF AI IN RECRUITING

1. Time Savvy:

It saves a lot of time by utilizing AI tools to perform repetitive tasks. Recruiters must devote sufficient time to screening candidates' resumes. Screening is also a repetitive task. AI assists recruiters in saving time.

2. Capacity Sketching:

AI assists in understanding the requirements as well as the candidates' competency. This enables recruiters to strategize their career and put them in the appropriate position.

3. **Cost Savvy:**

As AI assists in qualitative hiring, the function of the third party in hiring is diminishing. This contributes to cost savings.

4. **Effective hiring:**

Because AI provides recruiters with massive amounts of data as well as non biased screening, it enhances the effectiveness of hires.

5. **Reduced turnover:**

Employees receive up-to date information and answers to their questions. The above satisfies the workers and leads to higher levels of employee engagement. It aids in lowering turnover because an employee engagement continues to serve the organization.

6. **Productive Workers:**

AI results in high-quality hiring. It also aids in employee training and development. This results in making the workforce more efficient and productive.

7. **Impartial in recruitment:**

Because the hiring is done by machine rather than by humans, there is no prejudice in screening or selection.

8. **Quality Applicants:**

AI provides not only a large number of candidates, but also candidates of high quality. The AI assists in understanding the candidates' attributes, competency, skills, and knowledge. The most qualified candidates are hired.

ROLE OF AI IN RECRUITMENT

1. **Initial candidate screening:**

For the first level screening, some mechanisms are used such as chatbots are used. Through these techniques HR managers use to ask different questions and after getting the responses the same were analyzed to understand the candidate.

2. **Candidate Engagement:**

With the help of AI now days, customized messages are being sent to the candidate and no need to of the intervention of seniors.

3. **Re-engagement of aspirants:**

When a vacancy's requirements are met, most candidates' records are lost. However, with AI, once the candidate's record is used, it is also modified concurrently. Also, it helps in adding the updated Education and expertise.

4. **Customized training & development:**

In order to improve performance and productivity trainees seek to get training. Each employee needs specialized skills in order to improvise specific skills which must be updated. AI helps in the making employees available with tailored professional learning to enhance their output and skills.

5. **After accepting an offer, a candidate must serve a notice period:**

With the help of AI organisation can maintain a continuous connection the employee and even at the time of the exit through AI based mechanisms they can openly interact and very easily can retain the required talent for increasing the productivity and saving ample time.

6. **New employee orientation:**

Orientation is essential for new employees because it make acquainted them with the culture of an organization. Also, IT helps in familiarizing workforce with the company's policies and procedures. However, employers dislike wasting time on orientation. Employee orientation is made easier with the assistance of artificial intelligence. Employees can also get any questions answered.

7. **Employee relations:**

The majority of employees have many questions, ranging from simple to complex. AI assists in providing answers to simple and repetitive questions. However, sometimes an HR manager must intervene to provide a human touch, particularly when the issues are exceptionally complex and logical.

CHALLENGES / ISSUES IN USING AI FOR JOB FIT

When decision makers attempt to apply machine learning predictions, they face three key issues. The first is about fairness as well as legal requirements, the second about the algorithm's lack of interpretability, and the final issue is about how professionals will respond to algorithmic decisions. All these are discussed as follows:

1.   Un-employability of existing skill set:

The foremost risk is to the employability opportunities created by the companies which are somewhere hampering not only the growth and employability of human resources but also the economic development. (Nadimpalli, 2017). Furthermore, Since 200 years prior, cautions and admonitions have been raised that machines and current innovations will supplant a significant number of occupations, primarily working class positions. The primary issue isn't just about having position vanishing, however likewise about the new posts won't be made in kind because of machines and computerization. Beforehand, new associations utilized a larger number of people than those they fire, which isn't viewed as the case these days. The fast development in innovation can bring monetary disarray, breakdown, and unrest rather than ecological since machines and processors are turning out to be strong and successful that organizations are depending on them to do the occupation as opposed to depending on the specialists and representatives. The speedy increase in innovation will influence and change occupations and what they pay. (Cavaliere, et al, 2021) According to some, AI-based enlistment stages could result in the replacement of 16% of occupations within the next ten years.

2.   Difficulty in maintaining the ethical standards:

Conventional staffing frameworks were developed to reimburse for our disappointment to pull together enough statistics on candidates' histories and behaviors in order to foretell their performance in the past. Without much past performance data, we were supposed to assume the person's potential capacity fit. But due to the maximum engagement in digital platforms, it has now become effortless to trace an enormous stalk of loaded data on their individual inclinations, morals, and knack. The only intricacy is in switching such records into pertinent talent signals, but scientific research show that it is possible.

3. **Personal Information Privacy:**

Algorithm of Machine-learning, for instance, can be applied to anticipate candidates' cerebral ability and special characteristics - together with their sordid underbelly - based on their Facebook pages. Similarly, Artificial Intelligence has already been utilized efficaciously to translate one's Twitter portfolio into such a fairly extensive personality characteristics, because the words we use mirror who we are, together with our talent as well as career potential. It should be noted that there are indeed free tools available to decipher someone's conduct from fair representation of text data set, along with IBM Watson's personality insights.

4. **Unreliable and unrealistic feedback:**

The feedbacks are unreliable as the automated process will only rely on the algorithm learnt by the machine without concerning any special skill thus, providing the unrealistic feedback too.

5. **Poor Data Science Techniques:**

Human resource records are typically quite little in context to data science standards. By comparing the quantity of purchases made by their clientele, the numeral of staff that even a major corporation may have is trivial. Additionally, countless attention-grabbing outcomes, like the count of employees being fired for poor performance, are rarely observed. When it comes to predicting relatively rare outcomes, data science system under performs.

6. **Biases in Decision-making:**

Employment decisions are indeed influenced by various intricate social and psychological concerns which subsist among populace employed, including such individual attraction and status, reward system, and relational expectations, which affect both organizational and personal result. As a matter of fact, being willing to clarify and justify one's practices is much more essential than in other fields. Because the results of HR decision making have had such severe implications for persons and society, concerns on the subject of fairness –distributive and procedural justice – precedes. Extensive lawful structure limits how owners must make those decisions. The apprehension with causation, which is usually transitory from algorithm-based investigation, is central to those frameworks.

7.   Biases in Gender:

Finally, employees have the ability to game or react negatively to the decisions which are based on algorithm. Their actions, in turn, have an impact on organizational outcomes. Consider the need for an algorithm to anticipate who to hire to illustrate these concerns. The use of AI &ML approaches generate an algorithm depending on the nature of workers and job performance in the present workforce. The social norms would direct to considerable issues for us if we act over. Amazon unveiled its framework for recruiting actually had this problem, and the company noted it down as a result (Meyer, 2018). At times when the gender of the applicants was not utilized as a criterion, the traits associated with women candidates, such as courses in "Women's Studies" caused them to be ruled out.

8.   Availability of Small Data:

The importance of small data in human resource analytics cannot be overstated. Because they do not have a large workforce and also they do not conduct enough performance evaluations or gather plenty other pieces of data for their working population so as to utilize machine learning techniques. According to the machine learning literature, having admittance to more data has significant advantages in terms of forecast validity (Fortuny, Martens, and Provost 2014).

9.   Biases in Sample Selection:

Because of the sampling procedure generated by using an algorithm or any optimization method in hiring, the "learning" component of machine learning is hampered. Once we govern out employing candidates who were not selected by the automated system, the potential to see whether numerous different features could perhaps contribute to stronger performers reduces and may end – for example, if we only use that algorithm can make employment decisions, the chance is for machine learning model to learn disappears.

PROPOSED SOLUTIONS

1.   For the security and Privacy reason each and every one should be aware of 'The General Data Protection Regulation (GDPR). Along with the awareness of the Act it should be a mandate in each organization to implement this Act.
2.   Ethical and impartial resource person to create the required algorithm taking in concern the human interface to provide the appropriate feedback.

3. Training to employees related to ethical code of conduct of employees.
4. Contact an AI vendor with experience and a relevant portfolio.
5. Find out the probable benefits from AI by functioning with a competent business analyst.
6. Due Consideration on how ethical concerns might forbid you from luring the most out of AI framework.
7. Creation of a trial product to exhibit the solution's feasibility
8. Create a blueprint of AI project implementation plan that is inclusive of solution development, integration, scaling, and employee on-boarding.
9. Begin constructing your system with your vendor while assuring continual information transfer.
10. Do not get your expectations up: developing AI solutions capable of enhancing or replacing vital functions takes time, patience, and a lot of data.
11. To fine-tune AI algorithms, appoint subject matter experts.
12. Up skilling the employees in context to the value of data-driven planning process and tracing the potential on how artificial intelligence can provide auotmotization.

Figure 2.

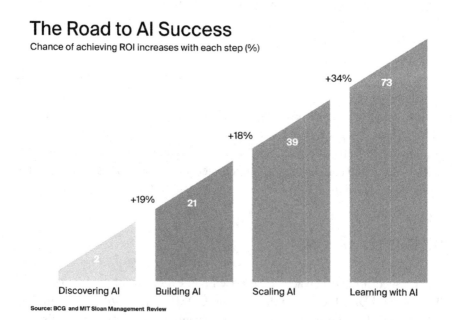

The Road to AI Success
Chance of achieving ROI increases with each step (%)

Source: BCG and MIT Sloan Management Review

Last but not least, keep exploring with AI, even if your pilot scheme falls short of expectations! 73 percent of organizations who revamp their processes based on failure lessons perceive a significant return on their artificially intelligent investments.

APPROACHES FOR INCREASING THE EFFICIENCY OF YOUR ARTIFICIAL INTELLIGENCE

As Artificial Intelligence is considered as an emergent technology that might supply some unanticipated hurdles, an escalating number of business ventures are geared up to take the opportunity and put into operation the latest technology. Their pivotal objective includes truncating the operational costs, increasing income, and immensely civilizing their customer service. Applications of this magical technology are used almost every day, every time and everywhere too for subjects like Web search, Each Day Commute, and keeping up with our social media feeds. Artificial intelligence applications whether we realize it or not, plays an important role in making our daily lives easier. It has a huge impact on our personal lives as well as our professional lives. Here are some major illustrations of AI in Business Management:

- Robotic responders
- Process automation Sales and business forecasts
- Automated insight outline and picture recognition
- Smart search with relevant features
- Purchase prediction and merchandise recommendation
- Speech recognition

FUTURE SCOPE OF STUDY

Like other studies, this chapter is also having some limitations. Though efforts have been made to highlight AI based recruitment through the importance of data, its benefits and challenges, but still there are some limitations. Firstly, this work was directed with a subjective exploration strategy, as it was critical to assemble enhanced comprehension around the peculiarity. To expand the unwavering excellence of this investigate, one must review and try to incorporate quantitative exploration strategy, to sum up the outcomes in more precise way. Secondly the point of view of candidates searching for jobs could be examined, to widen information about the peculiarity. It would be intriguing to see where further exploration on innovation based recruitment techniques will be in single framework.

MANAGERIAL IMPLICATIONS

1. Automation of the recruitment process.
2. Sustainability of the talented employees for AI based job-fit analysis.
3. Up gradation of the existing skill-sets of recruiters as per the latest technology trends.
4. Integration of data for the end-to-end recruitment process.
5. Rational model of decision-making.

CONCLUSION

After reviewing several journals of repute researchers found that in the parlance of AI numerous advantages have surpassed the disadvantages manifold. Enormous urgency of up-skilling and re-skilling of the Generation X will be required. The orientation of the applicants is now more vivid in comparison to the traditional recruitment. The way forward for this research will stand successful if more and more companies become akin to the AI enabled recruitment system which will lead to enhance employee performance, satisfaction with less conflict and attrition for collective organizational growth. A well-built AI structure will facilitate a deeper, brighter and a better understanding of people's behavior and pattern.

REFERENCES

Bara, A., Simonca, I., Belciu, A.& Nedelcu, B. (2016). Exploring Data in Human Resources Big Data. *Database Systems Journal Board, 3.*

Baron, H., & Austin, J. (2000). Measuring ability via the Internet: Opportunities and issues. In *Annual Conference of the Society for Industrial and Organizational Psychology*, New Orleans, LA.

Bondarouk, T., & Brewster, C. (2016). Conceptualizing the future of HRM and technology research. *International Journal of Human Resource Management*, 27(21), 2652–2671. doi:10.1080/09585192.2016.1232296

Carroll, M., Marchington, M., Earnshaw, J., & Taylor, S. (1999). Recruitment in small firms: Processes, methods and problems. *Employee Relations*, 21(3), 236–250. doi:10.1108/01425459910273080

Chien, C. F., & Chen, L. F. (2008). Data mining to improve personnel selection and enhance human capital: A case study in high-technology industry. *Expert Systems with Applications, 34*(1), 280–290.

Christozov, D., & Toleva-Stoimenova, S. (2015). Big data literacy: A new dimension of digital. *Strategic data-based wisdom in the big data era,* 156–171.

Faliagka, E., Ramantas, K., Tsakalidis, A., & Tzimas, G. (2012). Application of machine learning algorithms to an online recruitment system. *Proc. International Conference on Internet and Web Applications and Services.*

Furnham, A., Jackson, C. J., & Miller, T. (1999). Personality, learning style and work performance. *Personality and Individual Differences, 27*(6), 1113–1122. doi:10.1016/S0191-8869(99)00053-7

Galanaki, E. (2002). The decision to recruit online: A descriptive study. *Career Development International, 7*(4), 243–251. doi:10.1108/13620430210431325

Kaczmarek, T., Kowalkiewicz, M., & Piskorski, J. (2005). Information extraction from CV. *Proceedings of the 8th International Conference on Business Information Systems,* 3–7.

Knight, K., & Rich, E. (2010). *Artificial Intelligence* (3rd ed.). McGraw Hill India.

Koivisto, K. (2004). *Oikea valinta. Rekrytoinnin menetelmät.* Yrityskirjat.

Luger, G., & Stubblefield, W. (2004). *Artificial Intelligence: Structures and Strategies for Complex Problem Solving* (5th ed.). Benjamin/Cummings.

Mager, A. (2012). Algorithmic ideology: How capitalist society shapes search engines. *Information Communication and Society, 15*(5), 769–787. doi:10.1080/1369118X.2012.676056

Martincevic, I., & Kozina, G. (2018). The Impact Of New Technology Adaptation In Business. Varazdin: Varazdin Development and Entrepreneurship Agency (VADEA).

Mairesse, F., Walker, M. A., Mehl, M. R., & Moore, R. K. (2007). Using linguistic cues for the automatic recognition of personality in conversation and text. *Journal of Artificial Intelligence Research, 30,* 457–500. doi:10.1613/jair.2349

McLean, S., Stakim, C., Timner, H., & Lyon, C. (2016). Big data and human resources: Letting the computer decide? *Scitech Lawyer, 12*(2), 20.

Montuschi, P., Gatteschi, V., Lamberti, F., Sanna, A., & Demartini, C. (2014). Job recruitment and job seeking processes: How technology can help IT. *IT Professional, 16*(5), 41–49. doi:10.1109/MITP.2013.62

Nilsson, N. (1998). *Artificial Intelligence: A New Synthesis*. Morgan Kaufmann.

Panayotopoulou, L., Vakola, M., & Galanaki, E. (2007). E-HR adoption and the role of HRM: Evidence from Greece. *Personnel Review, 36*(2), 277–294. doi:10.1108/00483480710726145

Parry, E., & Olivas-Lujan, M. (2011) Drivers of the Adoption of Online Recruitment – An analysis using Innovation Attributes from Diffusion of Innovation Theory. *Electronic HRM in Theory and Practice*, 159–174.

Parry, E., & Wilson, H. (2009). Factors influencing the adoption of online recruitment. *Personnel Review, 38*(6), 655–673. doi:10.1108/00483480910992265

Poole, D., & Mackworth, A. (2017). *Artificial Intelligence: Foundations of Computational Agents* (2nd ed.). Cambridge University Press. doi:10.1017/9781108164085

Poole, D., Mackworth, A., & Goebel, R. (1998). *Computational Intelligence: A Logical Approach*. Oxford University Press.

Raviprolu, A. (2017). Role of Artificial Intelligence in Recruitment. *International Journal of Engineering Technology, Management and Applied Sciences, 5*(4).

Russell, S. J., & Norvig, P. (2003). *Artificial Intelligence: A Modern Approach* (2nd ed.). Prentice Hall.

Russell, S. J., & Norvig, P. (2009). *Artificial Intelligence: A Modern Approach* (3rd ed.). Prentice Hall.

Russell, S. J., & Norvig, P. (2021). *Artificial Intelligence: A Modern Approach* (4th ed.). Pearson.

Researchers design AI tool to combat human bias in hiring. (n.d.). HR Dive.

Searle, R. H. (2006). New technology: The potential impact of surveillance techniques in recruitment practices. *Personnel Review, 35*(3), 336–351. doi:10.1108/00483480610656720

Stuart, R., & Norvig, P. (2016). *Artificial Intelligence: A Modern Approach* (3rd ed.). Prentice Hall Press.

Upadhyay, A. K., & Khandelwal, K. (2018). Applying artificial intelligence: Implications for recruitment. *Strategic HR Review, 17*(5), 255–258. doi:10.1108/SHR-07-2018-0051

Chapter 13
Metamorphose Recruitment Process Through Artificial Intelligence

Aditi Vijaysingh Aljapurkar

 https://orcid.org/0000-0001-8766-3111
Dr. D. Y. Patil B-School Tathawade, Pune, India

Shraddha Prasad Purandare

 https://orcid.org/0000-0002-7914-2225
Dr. D. Y. Patil B-School Tathawade, Pune, India

Satyajit Dasharathrao Ingawale
Sanjay Ghodawat University, India

ABSTRACT

Business value creation rests in the hands of organizational resources, and no doubt, human resources are one of the prime contributors. HR practices have a high impact, and organizations should leverage human resource competencies. In today's situation, where technology forms the pillar of improving people, structures, and cultures, reviewing the technological impact on HR practices becomes imperative. One such technological intervention can and is seen through artificial intelligence. The chapter thus provides a journey to comprehend the traditional recruitment process which defines the employee life cycle and the limitations faced. A section describes the framework to deploy AI usage in the recruitment process to improve the recruitment metrics for the organization. The laborious task of reducing anchoring bias, confirmatory bias, and similarity bias amongst the recruiters using AI technology is explored. The chapter concludes with analytics power backed by AI to help the stakeholders of the recruitment process to revitalize strategies and improve decision making.

DOI: 10.4018/978-1-6684-4950-9.ch013

INTRODUCTION: EMPLOYEE LIFE CYCLE (ELC)

Huong (2021) describes human resource management as "the people and staff who administer an organization," as opposed to an organization's financial and material resources. The HR model tracks an employee's entire journey in an organization. The journey spans from the point of brand awareness to the last day of working of that individual in the company. It starts with talent attraction and offboarding forming the foundation of the cycle process. The ELC also considers recruitment and onboarding, retention at the early stages of the cycle, career development, and the overall employee experience.

The aftermath considered to be important of having a life cycle model is to better comprehend its impact of it. It helps improve the employee experience in the organization and encourages the recruiter/hiring managers/analysts to enhance these experience metrics. Given improving the yield ratio, the hiring managers take the help of technological software that enhances these experience metrics. However, if the decision-makers know every stage of the ELC, it would be more effective and efficient too.

The Stages in Employee Life Cycle

The life cycle involves attraction, recruitment, onboarding, retention, development, and separation. The stakeholders in the recruitment process are expected to enhance every stage to help improve the ELC.

1. **Attraction**

As a primary stage in ELC, employer branding is focused. This stage is completed only when the branding also reflects a company culture that also emphasizes employee development and innovation. Within this stage the companies can adopt myriad strategies through their official websites, social media platforms to attract external candidates. However, this attraction strategy is not confined to external but covers internal existing employees too. An organization that appreciates co-creation and employer-employee dialogue as strategic processes for supporting sustainable organizational development (*Aggerholm, Kryger 2011*). As a recruiter, the metrics that must be focused on is how your attraction strategy can increase the **'number of vacancies handled by the recruiter'** and **'number of CVs received** after the employer organization advertises for vacancies.

2. Recruitment

A stage wherein an applicant transits to an employee. The very first impression about the candidate happens at this stage. It's important the recruiter communicates the required skills and abilities, to portray as an attractive employer by offering competitive compensation and benefits packages, also to attract the best talent. As a recruiter, the metrics that must be focused on is how your attraction strategy can increase

- *the number of candidates called for interview,*
- *the number of CVs/profiles shortlisted,*
- *the number of candidates attending the interviews,*
- *the number of candidates shortlisted for the final interview round,*
- *the number of candidates approved after the final interview,*
- *the number of offers made to the candidates,*
- *the number of candidates accepting the offer.*

3. Onboarding

The objective is to help new employees understand and blend in with your corporate culture. Welcoming warmly, setting right expectations, training provisions, expanding for digital onboarding (pandemic and non-pandemic times too. This stage requires more conducting regular follow-ups. This is needed to better understand whether the new members are dwelling well in the system or not. As a recruiter, the metrics that must be focused on is how your attraction strategy can increase

1. **Retaining the new joinee rate up to max 85%**
2. **Ensuring that there is no turnover in the first 90 days of joining**
3. **Assuring for buddy/mentor allocations.**
4. **Discussion career progression periodically**

4. Retention

The stage is focused terms of keeping employees happy in terms of clarity of them being into the organizational and business systems, thus valuing their contribution. The best way to do this is through a rewards and awards program. You also need to make sure that you are building an effective and supportive culture to promote employee well-being and engagement.

Ensure that the ratio of (Number of employees who stayed with the company for the entire period/ Number of employees in the firm at the start of the period) is maximum (recruiters/hiring managers can compare the last retention rate of the company and design strategies accordingly.

5. Development

Skill acquisition to enhancement is one of the objectives at this stage. Most organizational managers want that the skill enhancement is progressive and that programs are designed in a way that there is better role execution and retention of talent/individuals in the organization.

6. Separation

The stage wherein the employee gets permanently separated from services on employment. Also called off-boarding, which eventually is either voluntary or involuntary due to resignations, retirements, or personal reasons. Many times, organizations conduct exit interviews to maintain a low turnover rate for the department or organization.

MAIN FOCUS OF THE CHAPTER

Limitations of Traditional Employee Life Cycle

Not every organization has analytical orientations for data-driven modelling to improve the recruitment process metrics. Many organizations do use analytics for enhancing the metrics. If it comes to the limitation in the traditional employee life cycle, data definition (variables affecting recruitment), data types, data sources, data gatherings, data structures, data analysis, and modelling may not be present. For such organizations, technological interventions through analytical modelling, artificial intelligence, and machine learning could prove to be a solution for metrics enhancement. However, the platforms used for modelling and decision-making shall be chosen keeping in mind the financial, operational, and training feasibility at the organizational level. The labour force available at the organization is also a crucial aspect. To use AI/ML, for better modelling structures technology intervention must be accepted to avoid resistance to change among the employee (especially those working in the recruitment process cycle).

RECOMMENDATIONS

Artificial Intelligence in Human Resources

The global AI market is predicted to snowball in the next few years, reaching a $190.61 billion market value in 2025. A lack of trained and experienced staff is an expected restriction in the AI market's growth. The top three most significant challenges companies face when considering the implementation of AI are staff skills (56%), the fear of the unknown (42%), and finding a starting point (26%). Google, IBM, Amazon, Tesla, Apple etc. are using AI in their HR procedures and solving problems of employees related to HR innovatively (Aspan, 2020).

Though many company decision-makers are on their way to finding solutions, it is to be comprehended that AI in HR is used for the automation of low-value HR functions. AI will not merely be integrated in the field of HR, but will show its dynamic aspect to human psychology, behaviour, etc. (Wilfred, 2018). In the employee life cycle stages, if AI is deployed it majorly enhances the employee experience at stages from recruitment to retention. In today's era, vendors of AI-based HR software are changing the way of process functionality due to speedy and accurate data processing thus improving upon the service delivery of HR functionalities. Artificial intelligence would have two categories-machine learning and deep learning

1. *The usage of machine learning involves algorithms that work upon recorded data to find out patterns. There is no need of programming the algorithm for an informed decision-making process.*

Automation as a basis forms the usage of machine learning. Being an integral part of AI its widely used in organisations automating processes, industries spanning different businesses and sectors too. Organisations that want to automate the recruitment process can make use of ML technology. This technology encompasses the humanistic capabilities within a machine enabling them to learn and design their programs. The learnings of the machine are automated, and it keeps on enhancing as the machine goes through different experiences. The vendors in the market provide varied solutions like data mining, robotic process automation, computer, and 3D vision, deep and reinforcement learning, natural language processing. The capabilities and solutions of ML technology can be leveraged into the recruitment process. Recently, the worlds attention w.r.t technology has shifted to machine learning. The reason being the wide range of possibilities it has opened in terms of automation, duly followed by recent advances in artificial intelligence

Recruitment is a business-oriented process that needs to be effective. Measuring the effectiveness requires determining and measuring the recruitment metrics of the organization. Within the recruitment process, many steps need to be catered for effectiveness. These include-recruitment marketing, passive candidate search, referrals, candidate search, hiring team collaboration, candidate evaluations, applicant tracking, reporting, compliance & security, onboarding, and support. What is significant in deciding to use machine learning technology is the benefits driven out for business e.g., cost. Let's take an example-how well is the company's website designed to have a cost-effective process to reach out to potential employees and how easy it is for an applicant to apply for the desired positions? If the website of the company/organization is AI prone to make use of Chatbot or Recruiter bot costs can be taken care of, and the reach factor too can be enhanced. Web-based e-recruitment platforms utilizing AI can be more effective in assuring objectivity and reducing costs for both applicant and employer (Konradt, Warszta, & Ellwart, 2013; Viswesvaran, 2003). To find the best talent for the organization it is needed to minimally provide job conditions, requirements, policies, benefits, and regulations. The applicant is to provide information that reflects the attitude, career standalone pointers, education, and skill inventory that matches with the job requirements. O'Donovan (2019) asserts that the inherent limitations of human abilities often pose challenges in recruitment exercises, among which include keeping up with the necessary procedures of accessing, screening, and analysing resumes, contacting applicants, sending feedback to both successful and unsuccessful candidates, and conducting face-to-face interviews with the various candidates. Unfortunately, most e-recruitment technologies do not validate the employment information (e.g., cover letter, resume, video) that prospective candidates submit, and often, there is little to no feedback from employers to candidates on job suitability based on the prerequisite selection criteria (Bogle & Sankaranarayanan, 2012). The major impact is seen in information dissemination done from the employer and information provided by the candidate/applicant. This is where AI in recruitment can help. This would involve the AI having rules in terms of search criteria, employee and employer ratings, past and present employer references, validation, and evaluation of applications, and submitted data, as well as a proper decision based on attitudinal and physical attributes in terms of ability to perform the job role (Lohani et al., 2017). Whilst the marketing and use of AI is new in e-recruitment, AI itself has been around for some time; yet there is still much controversy as to both its use and definition (Franklin & Graesser, 1996). Machine learning solutions capabilities span in providing assessment for the said aspects in the recruitment cycle. The hiring managers and recruiters can store the assessment metrics in the machine that is modelled to process them and evaluate the progress of the evaluated applicant. For example, the machine can comprehend the feelings carried during interview sessions, the candidate's test score assessment, etc. Figure 1 describes the contribution of ML towards recruitment cycle.

Along with assessment, the ML solutions are known for maintaining a high level of accuracy with the data handling as it works on objective data against subjective data used by recruiters alone. ML makes it a more data-driven decision making avoiding and/or eliminating the biases occurring due to human errors and perceptions held while in the recruitment process.

Machine learning technologies mitigate the challenges of reducing the time recruiters invested in screening a bunch of resumes to find the matched candidate. Advanced keyword analysis backed by the machine's capability to identify and map the talent, work experience, and other significant factors saving time and effort.

Machine learning also enhances the way you search for the right talent across portals, databases (current and historical data), or any platform that helps in the candidate search. The ML technology helps in standardization procedures to procure, recruit, and screen the matched profile.

The search process for employers/recruiters to find the best candidate across different sources limits their qualified candidate lists. This is where the machine learning technology would help to find and suggest better search options and suggest which candidate is best suited for the role.

Figure 1. Contribution of ML towards recruitment cycle

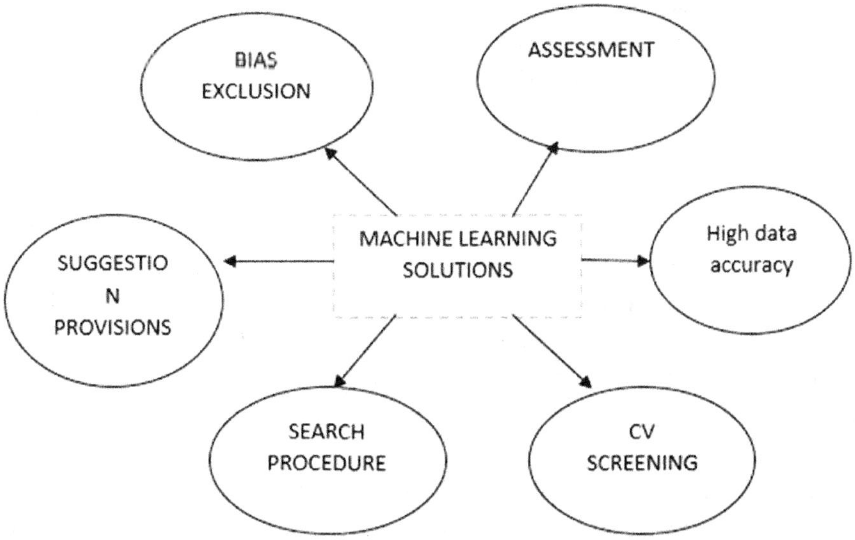

When it comes to human inclusion there are chances of bias affecting the decisions at various stages. Machine learning technology can help reduce the bias, wherein the algorithms that are running are skill-focused which helps in screening them for further stages.

2. *Deep learning as a part of the machine learning family is based on neural networks. This type reflects the representation of learning as an inherent part.*

The rationale why deep learning technology is popular today is its capability in dealing with complex big data. Deep learning had representation learning capability that involves discovering featured representations of the data in inquiry. It acts as a subset of machine learning but has a thin difference. Using neural networks, deep learning has become progressively usual in some data-rich contexts and has represented the competence of machines for mimicking adaptive human decision-making (Raub, 2018).

Framework For AI in Recruitment

Kulkarni and Che (2019) reported the great importance of AI implementation in talent recruitment, concluding in the extensive use of proper machine learning techniques to support HR managers. In order that the AI/ML platform can be used for the recruitment process, an understanding of business, and data, modeling of the data (AI/ML), determining which model fits the best, and then assessing how stakeholders assess the results is required. WEKA: The Waikato Environment for Knowledge Analysis can be used here. This is an exploratory approach that involves *a what-if...analysis approach.*

This model involves three main stages: processing (Input as data set), machine learning schemes, and output processing. As an input data set it involves information within the data set that would be further divided as test sets and training sets. These set are then forwarded as per the machine learning scheme to be used or in usage, filtering out features in the data not required by the user. With a specific rule set, the ML schemes are algorithms which are further converted into a data set to give output. Output processing modules are concerned with taking the output from a machine learning scheme and performing some tasks with it, and display of the output. For the recruitment process, it will involve selecting a recruitment dataset (input source) that needs to be trained through an algorithmic process, deciding the exclusion of data sets that do not match the features, choosing a machine learning scheme, run the scheme on the training data, and then looking over rules. Figure 2 shows the stages in the analysis process of the model.

Figure 2. Model of ML for HR recruitment process using WEKA: The Waikato Environment for Knowledge Analysis

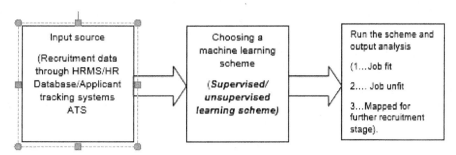

Data Set Format

Irrespective of the machine learnings scheme chosen/used there assess a common file format for where the HR data can be stored and further utilized. The Attribute-Relation File Format (ARFF) defines a data set in terms of a relation or table. This file is made up of attributes or columns of data. The recruitment data shall be presented in the tabular format or relations. e.g., demographic variables like age, gender; job profile data like-experience, sector, competencies). The tools available in the model has facilities that allow the data sets to split into two types of sets 1. Test sets and 2.Training sets, attribute filtration per say inquiry, missing value frequencies. Additionally, a tool range is available that helps in converting the file into the input format as required by the machine learning scheme used for processing further.

Machine Learning Schemes WEKA currently incorporates a variety of machine learning schemes from the areas of unsupervised and unsupervised learning. There are several schemes available as shown in the table below: Machine learning schemes supported by the workbench. Table 1 describes the different schemes.

Anyone scheme for the output required in 3 instances: job fit, job unfit, and up-gradation to the next stage of recruitment can be applied.

Output Processing

In the current version of WEKA any output that is created by a machine learning scheme is passed back to WEKA in text form that can display in a scrollable text viewer. This view allows text to be copied to other X applications, printed, or save to a file. If the user selected external evaluation in one of the schemes that allows it then the output will be passed back as per normal, but it will also be converted into the WEKA rule format and evaluated using the WEKA PROLOG rule evaluator, PREval. This output translation varies for the schemes.

Table 1. Describes the different schemes

Scheme	Description
Autoclass	Unsupervised Bayesian classification
OC1	Oblique decision tree construction for numeric data
Classweb	Incremental conceptual clustering
C4.5 and variants	Supervised decision tree induction
CNF & DNF	Conjunctive and disjunctive normal form decision trees
Prism	DNF rule generator
Induct	Improved Prism
FOIL	First-order inductive learner

Source: Author compiled

Software in AI

The AI market growth rate is positive, and the players are increasing in numbers. Organizations transitioning to AI platforms have multiple options to choose from. The trend followed by these vendors is to mix and match many technologies to satisfy users' needs be it organizations, homes, or the greater community. Machine learnings bags the number one position, but the vendors in the market are venturing into technologies like deep learning, data warehousing, predictive analytics, and business intelligence too.

Giant companies like Microsoft, Google are investing in these AI companies and acting as venture capitalists. The investment is seen in solutions for automotive and assembly processes, business processes, financial services, high tech, and healthcare. Fig 1.2 shows the distribution of investments as per McKinsey's report 2020. The company's interest in investment is keeping in mind the vendor capabilities to provide solutions to the corporates or for individual use. Consulting giant Accenture argues that AI has the potential to boost rates of profitability by an average of 38%. This contribution could lead to an economic boost of a whopping $14 trillion in additional gross value added (GVA) by 2035.

Guidelines to Choose the Vendors

1. Better and detailed product understanding. Product demo by the CEO/head of product is an added advantage. The demo is to be executed for understanding the UI, workflows, and other features
2. Designing a practice where users' feedback for the product is highly significant

Table 2. List of leading companies that are into cloud-based AI services

	Company name	AI-based services
1.	Amazon Web Services	Text to speech Recognition services-Lex (business version of Alexa)
2.	Google Cloud Platform	Tensor AI chip project-an an industry-led software project, also selling many AI and machine learning services.
3.	IBM Cloud	IBM Watson, SaaS, AI-based service that is available on a cloud platform.
4.	Microsoft Azure	Projects that are a mix of Business/ Information technology/consumer faced projects, bot services, machine learning, and cognitive services.
5.	Alibaba Cloud	ML Platform for AI-visual interface for ease of use, pre-built solutions

Source: Author compiled

Table 3. Notable vendors

Sr. No	Company name	What do they provide?
1.	Anduril Industries	Bought by Facebook in 2014, offers products like Sentry Tower (autonomous awareness), Ghost 4 sUAS (intelligent air support), and Anvil sUAS (precision kinetic intercept).
2.	Sift	multiple online fraud management services
3.	Nauto	behavior learning platform to improve the safety of fleet systems.
4.	Tempus	precision medicine to customized treatments
5.	Salesforce	It has machine learning to help employees to perform efficient tasks focusing on the simplification and speeding the process.

Source: Author compiled

3. Financial metrics of the product that talk about the product's retention rate, the growth, the product's contribution towards profit, scalability of the product.
4. Product diversification

An effective and best AI tool would be that supports and allows the recruitment team to complete their work intelligently, streamlining the process by automated workflow by eliminating tedious work. The tools' inherent capability allows the members to work and focus more on the strategic part of the process. AI is like an exoskeleton that allows humans to be smarter and more efficient. AI shall not replace humans but will automate the tasks. Table 4 shows how automation in processes are possible in companies.

Table 4. AI Software and Services

Company name	Recruitment task	What does it do?
Seekout	Talent sourcing	1. Used by recruiters to augment their capabilities. 2. It helps in preparing a customized shortlist of candidates that match the job description. 3. The software will seek out the list names from its own ATS or database 4. It provides services to companies like VMware, Twitter, 23and Me 5. Catering to 300 plus customers.
AmazingHiring	Talent sourcing	1. Sourcing through more than 70 different platforms 2. Aligning the data collected from different platforms and then matching it with the requirements 3. boolean search capabilities and manual scoring of candidates 4. Candidate filtration by demographic factors like age, experience 5. Folder arrangement, multi-stage emailing, and data enrichment feature to emails. 6. Few customers that EPAM, Akamai Technologies 7. Services to more than 400 plus companies. 8. Licensing feature, annual with $4800
eightfold	Talent intelligence platform	1. candidates profile reviewing 2. Instant pipeline for qualified employees 3. Guidance in career site for visitor's experience 4. Source data and predict the matched requirement 5. Customers like Air Asia, Capital One, Mercado Libre, 6. valued between $500M and $1B.

Source: Author compiled

AI Recruiting Tools can Help With:

1. Screening: The major time invested by a recruiter is in screening thousands of profiles to find the right talent matc.AI recruiting software/tools with its vendor design will screen the profile in no time. One component is the AI chatbot asking questions to the candidate.AI not only contributes here but is involved in the interpretation of the responses provided to systematically decide the employee potential and also answer back to any queries the applicant has concerning the job descriptions.

2. Video Interviews: Video interview stages are beginning to use AI to take the primary cut at getting the critical attributes of a job applicant. In the first place, these stages can comprehend the reactions provided for a given inquiry and determine how that fits with your job description components. The data processing can be used by the tool to comprehend personality analysis. E.g., the candidate to be extroverted, introverted, had high neuroticism.

3. Screening tech-talent: Automated technical assessment is an excellent method to screen engineers, be in any of the employment sector, especially those not having resumes. These platforms use AI to examine the quality of a particular candidate's answer and understand key still images such as setups in different languages, pair programming, and test-driven development.

4. Sourcing: Artificial intelligence is great for talent scouting and has been used for some time in this use case. Across a job portal, an AI tool can interpret the requests, run an algorithm to find relevant people/candidates in various databases (an applicant tracking system that is AI-powered). This is the automation of the initial steps of the procurement process and then initiate the multi-staged process to reach many via text and email

5. Schedule: Scheduling candidates for different stages of employment recruitment is always a challenge. This challenge escalates especially when there are many candidates on the internal calendars onsite Appropriate interview scheduling software provides a better experience for candidates (such as not losing the ball, female candidates do not interview all men, etc.) and significantly reduces the headaches of the hiring team.

6. ATS Re-engagement: Recruiter's major time is invested in going across many profiles and records. The ATS used many times lacks the capability in reviewing and rediscovering old records.AI tool can get into rehirng by finding the list of candidates suitable and matched with the job requirements.

7. Referrals: AI recruitment tools are also great for boosting referrals. This use case is like the ATS re-join use case, except that the database is a network of employees rather than ATS. AI will look at the requirements and then look at the employee's network to recommend people who need to see the hiring team.

8. Career Site Visitor Conversion: Most visitors to your career site do not apply for a job. Job seekers can use the career site chatbots to ask questions about benefits, job categories, and more. As a result, you can get more qualified candidates in the applicant tracking system

Challenges in using AI

Like any technology, AI also has pros and cons. Not being feared it is to be comprehended that AI will not take up jobs but would expect individuals to enhance their skills to use it in everyday tasks and jobs. Every organization venturing into the usage of AI should always remember that it's still the business of humans and human interaction.

Candidate Experience: There is huge stress in the hiring process. AI cannot be used to replace every candidate through the process of automation. Human touch stands significance and technology cannot be taking the face value of what humans can do. The recruiter must spend time with the candidate for the decisions in the entire hiring process.

Set Expectations: Every employee working in a culture and system of an organization becomes comfortable with the usage of machines. A peer or manager being human may be available for any concerns/queries. However, while working with machines it's important what level of expectation we keep for our concerns and issue in the way we expect it to go.

AI Training

The algorithms within AI are trained to provide outcomes, these are based on the data that is trained within the system. DATA holds an important place, its availability within the data stores of the organization. Or a vendor that has data sets created to help you out-train the AI.

Biases in AI

Artificial intelligence is not here to replace human strengths, but if you train them in the wrong manner. It shall create a bias. For e.g.: if the algorithm is trained to discriminate on gender, it may result out with it. One must be very cautious about knowing how your AI is trained to provide decisions without discrimination.

Return On Investment from AI Recruiting Platforms

It's imperative to calculate the ROI over any software used and AI is no exception. Organizations can decide the parameters that they would consider determining the return. For e.g., Leading to higher productivity, employee engagement rates, customer satisfaction, improved profits, new products, and services, etc. An organization's maturity to use Ai in its business process needs to be monitored.

Questions For Demos

The organizational decision-makers, viz. the hiring manager and recruiting team need to conduct the demos through the vendor. Significantly, the right questions are asked to the vendor about the product and the services. Here is a tentative list:

1. What company size can your tool cater to?
2. What unique aspects and business functional processes the tool can address for effectiveness?
3. What metrics mention your tool accuracy?
4. What way the recruiting team can interact with this tool?
5. What experience shall the tool provide to the candidates?
6. Where does the data source come from? how long is the fetch time from a mentioned source? How Is the data set trained for processes?

Challenges for Artificial Intelligence usage in Process Automation

1. **Amount of data**

Artificial intelligence reflects human intelligence. To do so and automate a part of the process or the entire process it needs to gather voluminous data.

For example, Screening through AI base tools/ software

If the AI tool must screen profiles as humans do, it will require more amount of profile/data to be screened to find a suitable match.

2. **Learning capability of the tool**

AI and its sub-parts-: machine learning and deep learning work on the patterns of data. Many think that AI can build the capability to understand human biases and act accordingly. For example, unconscious bias, anchoring bias as what humans carry while in the recruitment process can be adopted by the AI tool, which completely cannot stand true in most cases. While the vendor is chosen for its services, ensure the vendor's tool is developed and monitored continuously for any data pattens. These patterns may reveal the existence of potential bias if any.

3. **Scepticism of new technology**

The trends in HR are varied and there are many players in the market with their software. Many times, human resources are skeptical about the adoption of any technology that would be a part of their tasks and jobs. The skepticism is much seen amongst the members when the technology becomes a part of the entire HR ecosystem. Resistance to change is what is realized and should be overcome.

Innovations in AI for Recruiting

AI for recruiting has several potential applications for automating high-volume, repetitive tasks such as resume screening and pre-qualifying candidates

1. **Intelligent screening software**

Resume screening is conducted by using AI (machine learning platform allows extended service where the machine learns by experience). It helps in notifying which candidate failed and succeeded based on parameters like performance, tenure, experience, etc.

2. **Recruiter chatbots**

Chatbots are common AI-powered tools that are used at any service provisions be it the recruitment services rendered. These chatbots are now being tested and used for providing real-time interaction with the candidates, asking questions, providing feedback, keeping the updates informed to the candidates is what he chatbots take care of.

3. **Digitized interviews**

A job fit is to be achieved by every recruiter to enhance the selection ratio. There is online software that helps in doing so. But the market of Ai has opened forums wherein the AI tool is able to record facial expressions speech patterns and word choices to determine the job role fit.

Changing Recruiter's Role with AI Usage

Augmented intelligence in the future of AI. It is a belief system that the replacement of humans by technology doesn't completely stand true. Instead, augmented intelligence proposes how this technology will help create systems that would enhance human aptitude and efficiency. The usage of this technology to automate the repetitive tasks within the hiring processes is always valuable thus affecting the recruiter's role. The parameters are:

1. Strategic hiring: recruiters role becomes proactive in data gathering and processing
2. The recruiter's engagement would be more into the relationship building with the applicants thus ensuring the retention until the recruitment cycle.

3. Metrics improvement especially in Quality of hire. This is possible as AI will help in the visible data processing.

Biases in Recruitment: How Artificial intelligence Contributes?

The success depends on the metrics considered significant by the organization that is in the cycle process. The usage is based on the proposition that the technology can automate those tasks that are repetitive and monotonous. But can AI reduce human biases while in the recruitment process? Augmented or collaborative artificial intelligence that blends the power and strength of the humans and machines may in the future help in reducing the biases if the algorithms are written are not examined and validated carefully. This was found on account of Amazon, in which they found that their AI models were acquainting predispositions inclining toward men due to the way that it had been prepared on male-ruled sets of Cv. Since the information used to "train" the AI was vigorously one-sided towards men and was not customized to disregard segment data, the actual AI got the orientation predisposition of its makers. AI-based recruitment should be carefully planned, designed, and executed and should include frequent human foresight. The bias identification with AI-based tool/software is much easier by performing an audit of hired candidate demographic and an algorithm running helping to identify a pattern that indicates bias. The audit performance will help organizations to alter algorithms and make sure that baizes are minimal or not at all.

While a recruiter analyses a resume in the recruitment process if he analyses it by not focusing on the demographics of the candidate, the skill sets and experience, or parameters that the role requires, he is creating a bias. Many times, the recruiter has pre-conceived notions about the candidate and that clouds his opinion about him/her he is creating hiring bias. Table 5 enlists the types of biases and metrics affected.

Challenges to Recruiters: Reducing Recruitment Bias

Companies are already reducing hiring bias with AI. Companies from Fortune 500 use "psychometric games" to filter through their candidates with less bias. They are AI-powered and designed to test candidates' "personalities" to see if they match the job they applied for. Several other ways hiring with AI can reduce bias in recruitment, like automating the resume selection step. A resume aggregator will analyze a huge amount of data and give you specific resumes based on the job requirements, without the subjective human factor involved. An AI-powered ranking tool will further help you select objectively only the candidates with the desired skill set for the job. With a technical assessment tool, you will be able to schedule and review talent assessments with minimum biases in the process. Using AI to

Table 5. What are the different types of hiring bias?

Sr. No	Type of bias	Description	Probable recruitment Metrics affected
1	Bandwagon Effect	Panelists tend to favor a specific candidate by ignoring other worthy candidates	1. Cost of hire, 2. Source of hire, 3. Quality of hire, 4. Candidate experience, 5. Hiring managers satisfaction, 6. Selection ratio
2	Anchoring Bias	Only a certain piece of information such as age, and gender is focused on, and further filtration is based on this limited piece of information	1. Cost of hire, 2. Source of hire, 3. Quality of hire, 4. Candidate experience, 5. Hiring managers satisfaction, 6. Selection ratio, 7. Diversity ratio, 8. Yield ratio
3	Horn/Halo Effect	The decision is generalized keeping in mind some positive aspects (like gender/profile matching with the job) against the negative behavior like job-hopping. The final offer to such candidates is still made leading to the halo effect. If candidate pipeline has less desirable physical attributes but the assessment	1. Cost of-hire, 2. The source of hire, 3. quality of hire, 4. Candidate experience, 5. Hiring managers satisfaction, 6. Selection ratio, 7. Diversity ratio, 8. Yield ratio
4	Affinity bias	This refers to the hiring manager's tendency to select a person who is like him/her either culturally or socially. In this case, familiarity, relatability, and comfort with the candidate tend to override the fair assessment of a candidate's skill and abilities.	1. Cost of hire, 2. The source of hire, 3. quality of hire, 4. Candidate experience, 5. Hiring managers satisfaction, 6. Selection ratio, 7. Diversity ratio, 8. yield ratio
5	Confirmation Bias	This occurs when recruiters make an initial judgment about a candidate and then actively seek evidence to back up their judgment. For example, when a candidate projects confidence, recruiters may unconsciously focus on the candidate's positive attributes and dismiss all negative signs.	1. Cost of hire, 2. source of hire, 3. quality of hire, 4. Candidate experience, 5. Hiring managers satisfaction, 6. Selection ratio, 7. Diversity ratio, 8. yield ratio
6	Recall Bias	When a hiring manager recalls some ex-colleague of his/her with similar traits and unfairly match both despite different test scores it leads to recall bias	Cost of hire, source of hire, quality of hire, Candidate experience, Hiring managers satisfaction, Selection ratio, Diversity ratio, yield ratio
7	Exposure Bias	A sense of familiarity wherein the previous candidate's profile overrides the current.	1. Cost of hire, 2. Source of hire, 3. quality of hire, 4. Candidate experience, 5. Hiring managers satisfaction, 6. Selection ratio, 7. Diversity ratio, 8. yield ratio
8	Performance Bias	When the recruiters focus more only on the performance ignoring other specifications it leads to performance bias	1. Cost of hire, 2. source of hire, 3. quality of hire, 4. Candidate experience, 5. Hiring managers satisfaction, 6. Selection ratio, Diversity ratio, 7. yield ratio, 8. Time to Productivity, 9. Cost of Getting OPL

eliminate bias from hiring is an efficient tool. And it's only going to get better with time. As technology evolves moving into the future, so will the AI-powered tools, helping recruiters hire a more diverse workforce and tackle the hiring bias problem.

Hiring with AI helps reduce bias in recruiting, so companies can include a more diverse workforce and get innovative and profitable benefits as a result. Automating a part of the recruiting process will also help recruiters be more productive and save companies precious time and money.

Case Example of AI-Based Recruitment Strategies by Companies

"The life of an applicant can and has dramatically changed as of late, thanks to the ubiquity of smartphones and the increased comfort of chat as a communication standard," says Ankit Somani, co-founder of AllyO, an end-to-end AI recruiter.

Hilton

AllyO tool helps to navigate between thousands of applications to provide a top-quality candidate experience. Additionally, with its basic notion, it automates the recruiter's tasks, conducts follow-up interviews for call centre applicants, interview scheduling, and final offer calls.

Most of the candidates who undergo this tools experience have given positive feedback. E.g., a candidate who had applied for a catering assessment position talked about her interview experience's tool letting the recruiter conduct a video interview, automatically scheduled by the AI tool and then in-person interview (either the manager or the hierarchical manager)

ThredUp

The company was facing high turnovers and had got into slow email responses sent by the recruitment tea. They decided to go for the AI tool- TextRecruit. They decided to have on-board hourly workers to recruit. As the name suggests they had a service of mass texting by SMS, and many other message templates. This toll helped in recruiting 100-200 per month. The usage of this tool was so increased that they used it for scheduling a phone screen, newly hired directions provisions, etc. The improvement was seen in the metrics of TTH (Time to Hire) wherein the accessibility between recruiters and candidates in the interview process was enhanced.

Candidate's feedback: "After you apply, they contact you via text message to set up an interview. The interviews are group interviews, and they have specific days/times that they do them. You arrive and they have you sign in, once you have finished signing in and everyone is there, they will have you all introduce yourselves. After introductions, they take you on a tour of the facility. They take you up for the group interview, ask you four questions, and then ask if you have any questions. Following this, they will take around 24 hours to email you to let you know if you have been accepted."

Humana

The services offered by the AI tool/software include an on-demand video and voice interviewing. This service is used as a screening tool. Rather than schedule phone interviews with applicants who passed Humana's initial screening questionnaire, the candidate now automatically receives an invite to complete an on-demand video interview or voice interview.

It asks for questions like, "Have you ever worked for Humana or one of its affiliates?", "Why are you looking for part-time work?" and "What is the best part of customer service?" —Pharmacy Customer Care Specialist Candidate.

CONCLUSION

Usage of artificial intelligence is inevitable and then a precautionary step in its designing and implementation would help organizations to reap the benefits of technology interventions. The talent acquisition function of the organizations has variedly benefitted due to artificial intelligence by enhancing the metric as mentioned in the chapter. However, systems and cultural integration is required for all types and sizes of the organization to adopt this technology in the HR fraternity asks, jobs, and functional areas.

FUTURE RESEARCH DIRECTIONS

AI is here to stay, robotic process automation, IoT is the future. The chapter focused only usage of general intelligence usage in the talent acquisition function. All other functional areas in the employee cycle management can be enhanced through artificial, augmented artificial intelligence. The propositions made in this chapter would benefit students, and recruitment practitioners to be aware and use them in their roles.

REFERENCES

Albert, E. T. (2019). AI in talent acquisition: A review of AI-applications used in recruitment and selection. *Strategic HR Review*, *18*(5), 215–221. doi:10.1108/SHR-04-2019-0024

Aspan, H. (2020). Individual characteristics and job characteristics on work effectiveness in the state-owned company: The moderating effect of emotional intelligence. *Int J Innov Creat Chang*, *13*(6), 761–774.

Bogle, S., & Sankaranarayanan, S. (2012). Job search system in Android environment—Application of intelligent agents. *International Journal of Information Sciences and Techniques*, *2*(3), 1–17. doi:10.5121/ijist.2012.2301

Franklin, S., & Graesser, A. (1996). Is it an agent, or just a program? A taxonomy for autonomous agents? In *International workshop on agent theories, architectures, and languages* (pp. 21–35). Springer.

Huong, P. N. Q. (2021). The quality OF human resources IN small and medium enterprises: Current situation, reason, recommendations ON solutions. *Journal of Natural Remedies*, *21*, 73–81.

Kulkarni, S. B., & Che, X. (2019). Intelligent Software Tools for Recruiting. *Journal of International Technology and Information Management, 28*, Article 1. https://scholarworks.lib.csusb.edu/jitim/vol28/iss2/1

Konradt, U., Warszta, T., & Ellwart, T. (2013). Fairness perceptions in web-based selection: Impact on applicants' pursuit intentions, recommendation intentions, and intentions to reapply. *International Journal of Selection and Assessment*, *21*(2), 155–169. doi:10.1111/ijsa.12026

Lohani, M., Stokes, C., Dashan, N., McCoy, M., Bailey, C. A., & Rivers, S. E. (2017). A framework for human-agent social systems: The role of non-technical factors in operation success. In Advances in human factors in robots and unmanned systems (pp. 137–148). Springer International Publishing.

Nascimento, M. A., & Queiroz, M. C. A. (2017). Overview of research on Artificial Intelligence in Administration in Brazil. *ANPAD Meetings – Enanpad*, 1-4.

Raub, M. (2018). Bots, bias and big data: Artificial intelligence, algorithmic bias and disparate impact liability in hiring practices. *Arkansas Law Review*, *71*, 529.

Reddy, K. (2021). *AI in Recruitment: Benefits and Challenges You Need to Know.* https://content.wisestep.com/ai-recruitment/

Kryger Aggerholm, H., Esmann Andersen, S., & Thomsen, C. (2011). Conceptualizing employer branding in sustainable organizations. *Corporate Communications, 16*(2), 105–123. doi:10.1108/13563281111141642

Merin. (2021). *Benefits & Challenges of Using AI in Recruitment*. HR Shelf.

Neelie. (2020). *11 Innovative Uses of AI In Recruitment In 2020*. Harver.

Rainer. (2012). *From Capability to Profitability: Realizing the Value of People Management, Realising the value of people management*. Academic Press.

Tandon, L., Joshi, P., & Rastogi, R. (2017). Understanding the Scope of Artificial Intelligence in Human Resource Management Processes - A Theoretical Perspective. *International Journal of Business and Administration Research Review*. Available from: http://www.ijbarr.com/ downloads/0509201711.pdf

O'Donovan, D. (2019). HRM in the organization: An overview. *Management Science, Management and Industrial Engineering*, 75–110.

Okolie, U., & Irabor, I. (2017). E-Recruitment: Practices, Opportunities, and Challenges. *European Journal of Business and Management*.

Wilfred, D. (2018). AI in recruitment. *NHRD Netw J, 11*(2), 15–18. doi:10.1177/0974173920180204

Compilation of References

Zhang, X., & Chen, Y. (2017, September). An artificial intelligence application in portfolio management. In *International Conference on Transformations and Innovations in Management (ICTIM 2017)* (pp. 775-793). Atlantis Press. 10.2991/ictim 17.2017 60

Albuquerque, P. H. M., de Moraes Souza, J. G., & Kimura, H. (2021). Artificial intelligence in portfolio formation and forecast: Using different variance-covariance matrices *Communications in Statistics. Theory and Methods*, 1–18. doi:10.1080/03610926.2021.1987472

Dunis, C., Middleton, P., Karathanasopolous, A., & Theofilatos, K. (2016). *Artificial intelligence in financial markets*. Palgrave Macmillan. doi:10.1057/978-1-137-48880-0

Ghimire, A., Thapa, S., Jha, A. K., Adhikari, S., & Kumar, A. (2020, October). Accelerating business growth with big data and artificial intelligence. In *2020 Fourth International Conference on I-SMAC (IoT in Social, Mobile, Analytics and Cloud) (I-SMAC)* (pp. 441-448). IEEE. 10.1109/I-SMAC49090.2020.9243318

Ferreira, F. G., Gandomi, A. H., & Cardoso, R. T. (2021). Artificial intelligence applied to stock market trading: A review. *IEEE Access: Practical Innovations, Open Solutions, 9*, 30898–30917. doi:10.1109/ACCESS.2021.3058133

Yuan, M., Fang, Y., Lv, J., Zheng, S., & Zhou, Z. (2019, June). Research on power trading platform based on big data and artificial intelligence technology. *IOP Conference Series. Materials Science and Engineering, 486*(1), 012109. doi:10.1088/1757-899X/486/1/012109

16 Machine Learning in Healthcare Examples. (2022). Retrieved 16 July 2022, from https://builtin.com/artificial-intelligence/machine-learning-healthcare

Tan, C. N. (1999). A hybrid financial trading system incorporating chaos theory, statistical and artificial intelligence/soft computing methods. *Queensland Finance Conference.*

Vanstone, B., Coast, G., & Tan, C. (2003). A survey of the application of soft computing to investment and financial trading. *Pattern Recognition, 6*, 7.

Kaastra, I., & Boyd, M. S. (1995). Forecasting futures trading volume using neural networks. *The Journal of Futures Markets, 15*(18), 953.

Belanche, D., Casalo, L. V., & Flavi'an, C. (2019). Artificial Intelligence in FinTech: Understanding robo-advisors adoption among customers. *Industrial Management & Data Systems*, *119*(7), 1411–1430. doi:10.1108/IMDS-08-2018-0368

Paulson, F. L. (1991). What Makes a Portfolio a Portfolio? *Educational Leadership*, *48*(5), 60–63.

21 Examples of Big Data In Healthcare With Powerful Analytics. (2022). Retrieved 16 July 2022, from https://www.datapine.com/blog/big-data-examples-in-healthcare/

Russell, S. J. (2010). *Artificial intelligence a modern approach*. Pearson Education, Inc.

PK, F. A. (1984). *What is Artificial Intelligence?* Academic Press.

Zhang, C., & Lu, Y. (2021). Study on artificial intelligence: The state of the art and future prospects. *Journal of Industrial Information Integration*, *23*, 100224. doi:10.1016/j.jii.2021.100224

Holzinger, A., Langs, G., Denk, H., Zatloukal, K., & Mu¨ller, H. (2019). Causability and explainability of artificial intelligence in medicine. *Wiley Interdisciplinary Reviews. Data Mining and Knowledge Discovery*, *9*(4), e1312. doi:10.1002/widm.1312 PMID:32089788

Dick, S. (2019). *Artificial Intelligence*. Academic Press.

Singh, S. P. (2019). *Artificial narrow intelligence adaptive audio processing* [Doctoral dissertation]. Dublin Business School.

Goertzel, B. (2007). *Artificial general intelligence* (C. Pennachin, Ed., Vol. 2). Springer. doi:10.1007/978-3-540-68677-4

Gill, K. S. (2016). Artificial super intelligence: Beyond rhetoric. *AI & Society*, *31*(2), 137–143. doi:10.100700146-016-0651-x

Marr, D. (1977). Artificial intelligence—A personal view. *Artificial Intelligence*, *9*(1), 37–48. doi:10.1016/0004-3702(77)90013-3

Long, J. B. Jr. (1990). The numeraire portfolio. *Journal of Financial Economics*, *26*(1), 29–69. doi:10.1016/0304-405X(90)90012-O

Das, S., Dey, A., Pal, A., & Roy, N. (2015). Applications of artificial intelligence in machine learning: Review and prospect. International. *Jisuanji Yingyong*, *115*(9).

Greene, D., Hoffmann, A. L., & Stark, L. (2019). *Better, nicer, clearer, fairer: A critical assessment of the movement for ethical artificial intelligence and machine learning*. Academic Press.

Rashidi, H. H., Tran, N. K., Betts, E. V., Howell, L. P., & Green, R. (2019). Artificial intelligence and machine learning in pathology: The present landscape of supervised methods. *Academic Pathology*, *6*. doi:10.1177/2374289519873088 PMID:31523704

Berry, M. W., Mohamed, A., & Yap, B. W. (Eds.). (2019). *Supervised and unsupervised learning for data science*. Springer Nature.

Kamilaris, A., & Prenafeta-Boldú, F. X. (2018). Deep learning in agriculture. A survey. *Computers and Electronics in Agriculture, 147*, 70–90. doi:10.1016/j.compag.2018.02.016

Spronk, J., & Hallerbach, W. (1997). Financial modelling: Where to go? With an illustration for portfolio management. *European Journal of Operational Research, 99*(1), 113-125.

Baker, M., & Gompers, P. A. (2003). The determinants of board structure at the initial public offering. *The Journal of Law & Economics, 46*(2), 569–598. doi:10.1086/380409

Perold, A. F. (2004). The capital asset pricing model. *Journal of Economic Perspectives, 18*(3), 3-24.

Womack K. L. Zhang Y. (2003). *Understanding risk and return, the CAPM, and the Fama-French three-factor model.* Available at SSRN 481881.

Katsikis, V. N., & Mourtas, S. D. (2021). Binary beetle antennae search algorithm for tangency portfolio diversification. *Journal of Modeling and Optimization, 13*(1), 44–50. doi:10.32732/jmo.2021.13.1.44

Graves, D. H., & Sunstein, B. S. (1992). Portfolio portraits. Heinemann.

Mishra, S., Padhy, S., Mishra, S. N., & Misra, S. N. (2021). A novel LASSO–TLBO–SVR hybrid model for an efficient portfolio construction. *The North American Journal of Economics and Finance, 55*, 101350. doi:10.1016/j.najef.2020.101350

Riesener, M., Doelle, C., Schuh, G., Zhang, W., & Jank, M. H. (2019, August). Implementing Neural Networks within Portfolio Management to Support DecisionMaking Processes. In *2019 Portland International Conference on Management of Engineering and Technology (PICMET)* (pp. 1-7). IEEE. 10.23919/PICMET.2019.8893760

Sharma, B., Thulasiram, R. K., & Thulasiraman, P. (2012, July). Portfolio management using particle swarm optimization on GPU. In *2012 IEEE 10th International Symposium on Parallel and Distributed Processing with Applications* (pp. 103-110). IEEE.

Fabozzi, F. J., Kolm, P. N., Pachamanova, D. A., & Focardi, S. M. (2007). Robust portfolio optimization. *Journal of Portfolio Management, 33*(3), 40–48. doi:10.3905/jpm.2007.684751

Zhang, Y., Li, X., & Guo, S. (2018). Portfolio selection problems with Markowitz's mean–variance framework: A review of literature. *Fuzzy Optimization and Decision Making, 17*(2), 125–158. doi:10.100710700-017-9266-z

Briec, W., Kerstens, K., & Jokung, O. (2007). Mean-variance-skewness portfolio performance gauging: A general shortage function and dual approach. *Management Science, 53*(1), 135–149. doi:10.1287/mnsc.1060.0596

Khan, A. H., Cao, X., Katsikis, V. N., Stanimirovi'c, P., Brajevi'c, I., Li, S., Kadry, S., & Nam, Y. (2020). Optimal portfolio management for engineering problems using nonconvex cardinality constraint: A computing perspective. *IEEE Access: Practical Innovations, Open Solutions, 8*, 57437–57450. doi:10.1109/ACCESS.2020.2982195

Liang, Z., Chen, H., Zhu, J., Jiang, K., & Li, Y. (2018). *Adversarial deep reinforcement learning in portfolio management.* arXiv preprint arXiv:1808.09940.

Beraldi, P., Violi, A., Ferrara, M., Ciancio, C., & Pansera, B. A. (2021). Dealing with complex transaction costs in portfolio management. *Annals of Operations Research, 299*(1), 7–22. doi:10.100710479-019-03210-5

Brinson, G. P., Hood, L. R., & Beebower, G. L. (1986). Determinants of portfolio performance. *Financial Analysts Journal, 42*(4), 39–44. doi:10.2469/faj.v42.n4.39

Hansen, K. B. (2020). The virtue of simplicity: On machine learning models in algorithmic trading. *Big Data & Society, 7*(1). doi:10.1177/2053951720926558

Velu, R., Hardy, M., & Nehren, D. (2020). *Algorithmic Trading and Quantitative Strategies.* Chapman and Hall/CRC. doi:10.1201/9780429183942

Bartram, S. M., Branke, J., De Rossi, G., & Motahari, M. (2021). Machine Learning for Active Portfolio Management. *The Journal of Financial Data Science, 3*(3), 9–30. doi:10.3905/jfds.2021.1.071

Sunchalin, A. M., Kochkarov, R. A., Levchenko, K. G., Kochkarov, A. A., & Ivanyuk, V. A. (2019). *Methods of risk management in portfolio theory.* Academic Press.

Bartram, S. M., Branke, J., & Motahari, M. (2020). *Artificial intelligence in asset management.* CFA Institute Research Foundation. doi:10.2139srn.3692805

Zheng, X. L., Zhu, M. Y., Li, Q. B., Chen, C. C., & Tan, Y. C. (2019). FinBrain: when finance meets AI 2.0. *Frontiers of Information Technology & Electronic Engineering, 20*(7), 914-924.

Zhang, Y. J. (2021). *Forecasting the Artificial Intelligence index returns: a hybrid approach.* Department of Economics, University of Pretoria.

Lotfi, I., & El Bouhadi, A. (2022). Artificial Intelligence Methods: Toward a New Decision Making Tool. *Applied Artificial Intelligence, 36*(1), 1992141. doi:10.1080/08839514.2021.1992141

Bussmann, N., Giudici, P., Marinelli, D., & Papenbrock, J. (2021). Explainable machine learning in credit risk management. *Computational Economics, 57*(1), 203–216. doi:10.100710614-020-10042-0

Smith, M. R., Martinez, T., & Giraud-Carrier, C. (2014). An instance level analysis of data complexity. *Machine Learning, 95*(2), 225–256. doi:10.100710994-013-5422-z

Kalayci, C. B., Ertenlice, O., & Akbay, M. A. (2019). A comprehensive review of deterministic models and applications for mean-variance portfolio optimization. *Expert Systems with Applications, 125*, 345–368. doi:10.1016/j.eswa.2019.02.011

Li, L., & Abu-Mostafa, Y. S. (2006). *Data complexity in machine learning.* Academic Press.

Guo, L., Wu, J., & Li, J. (2019). Complexity at Mesoscales: A common challenge in developing artificial intelligence. *Engineering, 5*(5), 924–929. doi:10.1016/j.eng.2019.08.005

Batrouni, M., Bertaux, A., & Nicolle, C. (2018). Scenario analysis, from BigData to black swan. *Computer Science Review, 28,* 131–139. doi:10.1016/j.cosrev.2018.02.001

Bhanja, S., & Das, A. (2022). A Black Swan event-based hybrid model for Indian stock markets' trends prediction. *Innovations in Systems and Software Engineering,* 1–15. doi:10.100711334-021-00428-0 PMID:35018169

Bunz, M. (2019). The calculation of meaning: On the misunderstanding of new artificial intelligence as culture. *Culture, Theory & Critique, 60*(3-4), 264–278. doi:10.1080/14735784.2019.1667255

VanLehn, K. (1990). *Mind bugs: The origins of procedural misconceptions.* MIT Press.

Broussard, M. (2018). *Artificial unintelligence: How computers misunderstand the world.* MIT Press.

Hovorushchenko, T., Pavlova, O., & Medzatyi, D. (2019, May). Ontology-based intelligent agent for determination of sufficiency of metric information in the software requirements. In *International Scientific Conference "Intellectual Systems of Decision Making and Problem of Computational Intelligence"* (pp. 447-460). Springer.

Samtani, S., Kantarcioglu, M., & Chen, H. (2020). Trailblazing the artificial intelligence for cybersecurity discipline: A multi-disciplinary research roadmap. *ACM Transactions on Management Information Systems, 11*(4), 1–19. doi:10.1145/3430360

Zhao, S., Blaabjerg, F., & Wang, H. (2020). An overview of artificial intelligence applications for power electronics. *IEEE Transactions on Power Electronics, 36*(4), 4633–4658. doi:10.1109/TPEL.2020.3024914

Bullock, J., Luccioni, A., Pham, K. H., Lam, C. S. N., & Luengo-Oroz, M. (2020). Mapping the landscape of artificial intelligence applications against COVID-19. *Journal of Artificial Intelligence Research, 69,* 807–845. doi:10.1613/jair.1.12162

Zawacki-Richter, O., Marín, V. I., Bond, M., & Gouverneur, F. (2019). Systematic review of research on artificial intelligence applications in higher education–where are the educators? *International Journal of Educational Technology in Higher Education, 16*(1), 1-27.

Bahrammirzaee, A. (2010). A comparative survey of artificial intelligence appli-cations in finance: Artificial neural networks, expert system and hybrid intelligent systems. *Neural Computing & Applications, 19*(8), 1165–1195. doi:10.100700521-010-0362-z

Aaron Smith, H. N. (2020). Artificial Intelligence in Banking A Mini Review. SSRN *Electronic Journal.*

Abbott, J., Basham, J., Nordmark, S., Schneiderman, M., Umpstead, B., Walter, K., & Wolf, M. A. (2014). *Technology-enabled personalized learning: Findings & recommendations to accelerate implementation.* Friday Institute for Educational Innovation. https://www.fi.ncsu.edu/resources/technology-enabled-personalized-learning-findings-recommendations-to-accelerate-implementation

Abdel-Wahab, A. G. (2008). Modeling Students' Intention to Adopt E-learning: A Case from Egypt. *The Electronic Journal on Information Systems in Developing Countries, 34*(1), 1–1. doi:10.1002/j.1681-4835.2008.tb00232.x

Abduljabbar, R., Dia, H., Liyanage, S., & Bagloee, S. A. (2019). Applications of artificial intelligence in transport: An overview. *Sustainability, 11*(1), 189. doi:10.3390u11010189

Abou El-Seoud, M. S., Taj-Eddin, I. A., Seddiek, N., El-Khouly, M. M., & Nosseir, A. (2014). E-learning and students' motivation: A research study on the effect of e-learning on higher education. *International Journal of Emerging Technologies in Learning, 9*(4), 20-26.

Acar, D., Gal, G., Öztürk, M. S., & Usul, H. (2021). A Case Study in the Implementation of a Continuous Monitoring System. *Journal of Emerging Technologies in Accounting, 18*(1), 17–25. doi:10.2308/JETA-17-04-29-9

ACFE. (2022). *Occupational Fraud 2022: A Report to the Nations.* Retrieved from https://acfepublic.s3.us-west-2.amazonaws.com/2022+Report+to+the+Nations.pdf

Adopting A. I. in Drug Discovery. (2022). Retrieved 16 July 2022, from https://www.bcg.com/publications/2022/adopting-ai-in-pharmaceutical-discovery

Agarwal, A. (2019). Exploring the Impact of Artificial Intelligence: Prediction vs Judgement. *Information Economics and Policy, 47*, 1–6. doi:10.1016/j.infoecopol.2019.05.001

Agrawal, B. (2021). Use of Social media by small women entrepreneurs of India for growing their business. *SMS Journal of Entrepreneurship & Innovation, 8*(1), 72–79.

Ajzen, I. (1991). The Theory of Planned Behavior. In Organization Behavior and Human Decision Processes. Academic Press, Inc. doi:10.1016/0749-5978(91)90020-T

Akbulut, Y., Kuzu, A., Latchem, C., & Odabaşi, F. (2007). Change readiness among teaching staff at Anadolu University, Turkey. *Distance Education, 28*(3), 335–350. doi:10.1080/01587910701611351

Aksoy, T., & Gurol, B. (2021). Artificial Intelligence in Computer-Aided Auditing Techniques and Technologies (CAATTs) and an Application Proposal for Auditors. In T. Aksoy & U. Hacioglu (Eds.), *Auditing Ecosystem and Strategic Accounting in the Digital Era* (pp. 361–384). Springer Nature Switzerland. doi:10.1007/978-3-030-72628-7_17

Alalwan, N., Al-Rahmi, W. M., Alfarraj, O., Alzahrani, A., Yahaya, N., & Al-Rahmi, A. M. (2019). Integrated three theories to develop a model of factors affecting students' academic performance in higher education. *IEEE Access: Practical Innovations, Open Solutions, 7*, 98725–98742. doi:10.1109/ACCESS.2019.2928142

Alanazi, A. (2022). Using machine learning for healthcare challenges and opportunities. *Informatics In Medicine Unlocked, 30*, 100924. doi:10.1016/j.imu.2022.100924

Alarcon, J. L., Fine, T., & Ng, C. (2019). Accounting AI and Machine Learning: Applications and Challenges. *Pennsylvania CPA Journal*, (Special Issue), 1–5.

Albawwat, I., & Frijat, Y. A. (2021). An analysis of auditors' perceptions towards artificial intelligence and its contribution to audit quality. *Accounting*, *7*(4), 755–762. doi:10.5267/j.ac.2021.2.009

Albert, E. T. (2019). AI in talent acquisition: A review of AI-applications used in recruitment and selection. *Strategic HR Review*, *18*(5), 215–221. doi:10.1108/SHR-04-2019-0024

Aljawarneh, S. A. (2020). Reviewing and exploring innovative ubiquitous learning tools in higher education. *Journal of Computing in Higher Education*, *32*(1), 57–73. doi:10.100712528-019-09207-0

Alnajjar, F., Bartneck, C., Baxter, P., Belpaeme, T., Cappuccio, M. L., Di Dio, C., & Reich-Stiebert, N. (2021). *Robots in Education: An Introduction to High-tech Social Agents, Intelligent Tutors, and Curricular Tools*. Routledge. doi:10.4324/9781003142706

Al-Nuaimi, M. N., & Al-Emran, M. (2021). Learning management systems and technology acceptance models: A systematic review. *Education and Information Technologies*, *26*(5), 5499–5533. doi:10.100710639-021-10513-3

Al-Omar, K. (2018, February). Evaluating the Usability and Learnability of the" Blackboard" LMS Using SUS and Data Mining. In *2018 Second International Conference on Computing Methodologies and Communication (ICCMC)* (pp. 386-390). IEEE. 10.1109/ICCMC.2018.8488038

Al-Qaysi, N., Mohamad-Nordin, N., & Al-Emran, M. (2021). Factors affecting the adoption of social media in higher education: a systematic review of the technology acceptance model. *Recent advances in intelligent systems and smart applications*, 571-584.

Al-Rahmi, W.M., Yahaya, N., Aldraiweesh, A.A., Alamri, M.M., Aljarboa, N.A., Alturki, U., & Aljeraiwi, A.A. (2019). Integrating technology acceptance model with innovation diffusion theory: An empirical investigation on students' intention to use E-learning systems. *IEEE Access*, *7*, 26797–26809.

Alrashidi, M., Almutairi, A., & Zraqat, O. (2022). The Impact of Big Data Analytics on Audit Procedures: Evidence from the Middle East. *Journal of Asian Finance, Economics and Business*, *9*(2), 93–102. doi:10.13106/jafeb.2022.vol9.no2.0093

Alturki, U. T., Aldraiweesh, A., & Kinshuck, D. (2016). Evaluating the usability and accessibility of LMS "Blackboard" at King Saud University. *Contemporary Issues in Education Research*, *9*(1), 33–44. doi:10.19030/cier.v9i1.9548

Alzaidi, A. A. (2018, October). Impact of Artificial Intelligence on Performance of Banking Industry in Middle East. *International Journal of Computer Science and Network Security*, *18*(10), 140–148.

Ambrish Kumar Mishra, A. P. (2021). Impact of Covid19 Outbreak on performance of Indian banking sector. *International Semantic Intelligence conference*.

Amist, D. A. D., Tulpule, D. D., & Chawla, D. M. (2021). A Comparative Study of Online Food Delivery Start-ups in the Food Industry. *International Journal of Current Research, 13*(5), 17540-17549.

Andresen, S. L. (2002). John McCarthy: Father of AI. *IEEE Intelligent Systems, 17*(5), 84–85. doi:10.1109/MIS.2002.1039837

Andrews, J. E. (2003). An Author Co-Citation: A literature measure of the intellectual Structure. *Journal of the Medical Library Association: JMLA.*

Anita, S., & Lata, S. (2017). E-Learning for Employability Skills: Students Perspective. *Procedia Computer Science, 122*, 400-406.

Anju, P., & Sharma, H. L. (2016). Effectiveness of EDUCOMP smart classroom teaching on achievement in mathematics at elementary level. *IJAR, 2*(6), 683–687.

Antoniou, J., & Andreou, A. (2019). Case study: The Internet of Things and Ethics. *The Orbit Journal, 2*(2), 67.

Appana, S. (2008). A review of benefits and limitations of online learning in the context of the student, the instructor and the tenured faculty. *International Journal on E-Learning, 7*(1), 5–22.

Applegate, D., & Koenig, M. (2019, December). Framing AI audits. *Internal Auditor, 76*(6), 29–34.

Artificial Intelligence: Definition, Types, Examples, Technologies. (2022). Retrieved 16 July 2022, from https://chethankumargn.medium.com/artificial-intelligence-definition-types-examples-technologies-962ea75c7b9b

Asan O, C. A. (2020). Role of Artificial Intelligence in Patient Safety Outcomes: systematic literature review. *JMIR Medical Information, 8*(7).

Ashish Bagewadi, D. D. (2020). Analysis of Banking sector in India: Post Covid 19. *International Journal of Research and Analytical Reviews, 7*(3), 299-308.

Aspan, H. (2020). Individual characteristics and job characteristics on work effectiveness in the state-owned company: The moderating effect of emotional intelligence. *Int J Innov Creat Chang, 13*(6), 761–774.

Ayswarya, R., Sarala, D., Muralidharan, P., & Ilankadhir, M. (2019). Service Quality of Mobile Banking Services in ICICI Bank Limited. *Journal of Service Science and Management.*

B.R., P. L. (2019, June). Advent of Arificial Intelligence and its impact on Top leading Commecial Banks in India. *International Journal of Trend in Scientifc Research and Development, 3*(4), 614–616.

Babu, J., Xavier, J. D., & Sophia, J. (2020). *Consumer perception towards online food ordering and delivery services with special reference to zomato, swiggy and uber eats.* Academic Press.

Baig, H. G. (2017). A systemetic review of wearable patient monitoring system. *Journal of Medical Systems.* Advance online publication. doi:10.100710916-017-0760-1

Balakrishnan, N., & Teo, C. P. (2008). Mumbai Tiffin (Dabba) Express. In *Supply Chain Analysis* (pp. 271–278). Springer. doi:10.1007/978-0-387-75240-2_12

Balihara, A., & Venkatesh, G. (2011). *A study on rapid growth of educomp solutions limited.* Academic Press.

Ball, S. J. (2021). *The education debate.* Policy Press. doi:10.2307/j.ctv201xhz5

Bankins, S. (2021). The ethical use of artificial intelligence in human resource management: A decision-making framework. *Ethics and Information Technology, 23.* Advance online publication. doi:10.100710676-021-09619-6

Bara, A., Simonca, I., Belciu, A.& Nedelcu, B. (2016). Exploring Data in Human Resources Big Data. *Database Systems Journal Board, 3.*

Baron, H., & Austin, J. (2000). Measuring ability via the Internet: Opportunities and issues. In *Annual Conference of the Society for Industrial and Organizational Psychology*, New Orleans, LA.

Basilaia, G., Dgebuadze, M., Kantaria, M., & Chokhonelidze, G. (2020). Replacing the classic learning form at universities as an immediate response to the COVID-19 virus infection in Georgia. *International Journal for Research in Applied Science and Engineering Technology, 8*(3), 101–108. doi:10.22214/ijraset.2020.3021

Basu, K., Sinha, R., Ong, A., & Basu, T. (2020). Artificial Intelligence: How is It Changing Medical Sciences and Its Future? *Indian Journal of Dermatology, 65*(5), 365–370. doi:10.4103/ijd.IJD_421_20 PMID:33165420

Bates, T. (2019). *What's right and what's wrong about Coursera-style MOOCs.* EdTech in the Wild.

Belpaeme, T., Kennedy, J., Ramachandran, A., Scassellati, B., & Tanaka, F. (2018). Social robots for education: A review. *Science Robotics, 3*(21), eaat5954. doi:10.1126cirobotics.aat5954 PMID:33141719

Beniwal, T., & Mathur, D. (2021). Multi-Brand Cloud Kitchens: The Efficient Route. *IARJSET, 8.* Advance online publication. doi:10.17148/IARJSET.2021.8892

Bers, M. U. (2010). The TangibleK robotics program: Applied computational thinking for young children. *Early Childhood Research & Practice, 12*(2), n2.

Bertea, P. (2009). Measuring students' attitude towards e-learning: A case study. *Proceedings of 5th Inter-national Scientific Conference on e-Learning and Software for Education.*

Bhandge, K., Shinde, T., Ingale, D., Solanki, N., & Totare, R. (2015). A proposed system for touchpad based food ordering system using android application. *International Journal of Advanced Research in Computer.*

Bhargave, A., Jadhav, N., Joshi, A., Oke, P., & Lahane, S. R. (2013). Digital ordering system for restaurant using Android. *International Journal of Scientific and Research Publications, 3*(4), 1–7.

Bizarro, P. A. & Dorian, M. (2017). Artificial intelligence: The future of auditing. *Internal Auditing*, 21-26.

Bogle, S., & Sankaranarayanan, S. (2012). Job search system in Android environment—Application of intelligent agents. *International Journal of Information Sciences and Techniques*, 2(3), 1–17. doi:10.5121/ijist.2012.2301

Bolander, T. (2019). What do we loose when machines take the decisions? *The Journal of Management and Governance*, 23(4), 849–867. doi:10.100710997-019-09493-x

Bondarouk, T., & Brewster, C. (2016). Conceptualizing the future of HRM and technology research. *International Journal of Human Resource Management*, 27(21), 2652–2671. doi:10.1080/09585192.2016.1232296

Brown, V. L., Dickins, D., Hermanson, D. R., Higgs, J. L., Jenkins, J. G., Nolder, C., Schaefer, T. J., & Smith, K. W. (2020). Comments of the Auditing Standards Committee of the Auditing Section of the American Accounting Association on Proposed Statement on Auditing Standards (SAS), Audit Evidence [Commentary]. *Current Issues in Auditing*, 14(1), C1–C9. doi:10.2308/ciia-52603

Bumgarner, N., & Vasarhelyi, M. A. (2015). Essay 1 – Continuous Auditing - A New View. In *Audit Analytics and Continuous Audit - Looking Toward the Future* (pp. 3-52). AICPA. https://us.aicpa.org/content/dam/aicpa/interestareas/frc/assuranceadvisoryservices/downloadabledocuments/auditanalytics_lookingtowardfuture.pdf

Busteed, B. (2019). Why Goodwill (Not Udacity, EdX Or Coursera) May Be The World's Biggest MOOC. *Forbes*, 26, 2019.

Carroll, M., Marchington, M., Earnshaw, J., & Taylor, S. (1999). Recruitment in small firms: Processes, methods and problems. *Employee Relations*, 21(3), 236–250. doi:10.1108/01425459910273080

Cha, E., Sajid, Q., & Mataric, M. (2016, March). Enabling access to K-12 education with mobile remote presence. *2016 AAAI Spring Symposium Series*.

Chakraborty, D. (2019). Customer satisfaction towards food service apps in Indian metro cities. *FIIB Business Review*, 8(3), 245–255. doi:10.1177/2319714519844651

Charniak, E. (1985). *Introduction to artificial intelligence*. Pearson Education India.

Chassignol, M., Khoroshavin, A., Klimova, A., & Bilyatdinova, A. (2018). Artificial Intelligence trends in education: A narrative overview. *Procedia Computer Science*, 136, 16–24. doi:10.1016/j.procs.2018.08.233

Cheng, K., Xiang, L., Hirota, T., & Kazuo, U. (2005, July). A web-based classroom environment for enhanced residential college education. In *International Conference on Web-Based Learning* (pp. 56-65). Springer. 10.1007/11528043_6

Chen, L., Chen, P., & Lin, Z. (2020). Artificial intelligence in education. A review. *IEEE Access: Practical Innovations, Open Solutions*, 8, 75264–75278. doi:10.1109/ACCESS.2020.2988510

Chien, C. F., & Chen, L. F. (2008). Data mining to improve personnel selection and enhance human capital: A case study in high-technology industry. *Expert Systems with Applications*, *34*(1), 280–290.

Cho, S., Vasarhelyi, M. A., Sun, T. S., & Zhang, K. (2020). Learning from Machine Learning in Accounting and Assurance. *Journal of Emerging Technologies in Accounting*, *17*(1), 1–10. doi:10.2308/jeta-10718

Choudhury, A. E. R. (2020). Use of machine learning in geriatric clinic care. JAMIA Open, 459-71.

Christian Catalini, C. F. (2018, August). *Machine Intelligence vs. Human judgement in new venture finance.* Academic Press.

Christozov, D., & Toleva-Stoimenova, S. (2015). Big data literacy: A new dimension of digital. *Strategic data-based wisdom in the big data era*, 156–171.

Chukwudi, O. L., Echefu, S. C., Boniface, U. U., & Chukwuani, N. V. (2018). Effect of Artificial Intelligence on the Performance of Accounting Operations among Accounting Firms in South East Nigeria. *Asian Journal of Economics, Business and Accounting*, *7*(2), 1–11.

Cojocariu, V. M., Lazar, I., Nedeff, V., & Lazar, G. (2014). SWOT anlysis of e-learning educational services from the perspective of their beneficiaries. *Procedia: Social and Behavioral Sciences*, *116*, 1999–2003. doi:10.1016/j.sbspro.2014.01.510

Cole, J., & Foster, H. (2007). *Using Moodle: Teaching with the popular open source course management system.* O'Reilly Media, Inc.

Collins, G., & Moons, K. G. M. (2019). Reporting of Artificial Intelligence Predictions Models. *Lancet*, *393*(10181), 1577 1579. doi:10.1016/S0140-6736(19)30037-6 PMID:31007185

Connelly, T. M., Malik, Z., Sehgal, R., Byrnes, G., Coffey, J. C., & Peirce, C. (2020). The 100 most influential robotic surgery: A bibliometric analysis. *Journal of Robotic Surgery*, *14*(1), 155–165. doi:10.100711701-019-00956-9 PMID:30949890

Conti, D., Di Nuovo, S., Buono, S., & Di Nuovo, A. (2017). Robots in education and care of children with developmental disabilities: A study on acceptance by experienced and future professionals. *International Journal of Social Robotics*, *9*(1), 51–62. doi:10.100712369-016-0359-6

Coogle, C., Floyd, K., Cole, A. W., Timmerman, C. E., Holbeck, R., Greenberger, S., ... Becker-Lindenthal, H. (2015). Synchronous and asynchronous learning environments of rural graduate early childhood special educators utilizing Wimba© and Ecampus. *Journal of Online Learning and Teaching*, *11*(2).

Cook, D. A. (2007). Web-based learning: Pros, cons and controversies. *Clinical Medicine*, *7*(1), 37–42. doi:10.7861/clinmedicine.7-1-37 PMID:17348573

Corbeil, J. R., & Corbeil, M. E. (2015). E-learning: Past, present, and future. In International Handbook of E-Learning Volume 1 (pp. 79-92). Routledge.

Daley, S., & Pennington, J. (2020). Alexa the Teacher's Pet? A Review of Research on Virtual Assistants in Education. *EdMedia+ Innovate Learning*, 138-146.

Das, S. R. (2019). Future of Fintech. *Financial Management,* (48), 981-1007.

Das, J. (2018). Consumer perception towards "online food ordering and delivery services": An empirical study. *Journal of Management, 5*(5), 155–163.

Daugherty, P. R., & Wilson, H. J. (2018). *Human+Machine: Reimagining work in the age of AI.* Harvard Business Press.

Davenport, T. H. (2016). *The power of advanced audit analytics - Everywhere Analytics.* Retrieved from https://www2.deloitte.com/content/dam/Deloitte/us/Documents/deloitte-analytics/us-da-advanced-audit-analytics.pdf

Davenport, T., & Kalakota, R. (2019, June). The potential for artificial intelligence in healthcare. *Future Healthcare Journal, 6*(2), 94–98. doi:10.7861/futurehosp.6-2-94 PMID:31363513

Davis, F. D. (1986). *A technology acceptance model for empirically testing new end-user information systems: Theory and results.* Sloan School of Management, Massachusetts Institute of Technology.

Davis, F. D. (1989). Perceived usefulness, perceived ease of use, and user acceptance of information technology. *Management Information Systems Quarterly, 13*(3), 319–340. doi:10.2307/249008

Davis, F. D., Bagozzi, R. P., & Warshaw, P. R. (1992). Extrinsic and intrinsic motivation to use computers in the workplace 1. *Journal of Applied Social Psychology, 22*(14), 1111–1132. doi:10.1111/j.1559-1816.1992.tb00945.x

Davis, F. D., & Venkatesh, V. (1996). A critical assessment of potential measurement biases in the technology acceptance model: Three experiments Internet. *J. Human-Comput. Stud., 45*, 19–45.

Deepa, T., & Selvamani, P. (2018). Online Food Ordering System. *International Journal of Emerging Technologies and Innovative Research.*

Defining Basic Health Care. (2022). Retrieved 16 July 2022, from https://www.ama-assn.org/delivering-care/ethics/defining-basic-health-care

Deloitte. (2017a). *Audit Evolved - The next generation of life sciences audit.* Retrieved from https://www2.deloitte.com/content/dam/Deloitte/us/Documents/audit/us-audit-lshc-brochure.pdf

Deloitte. (2017b). *Delivering smarter audits - Insights through innovation.* Retrieved from https://www2.deloitte.com/content/dam/Deloitte/us/Documents/audit/us-audit-smarter-audits-dynamic-insights-through-innovation.pdf

Deloitte. (2018a). *16 Artificial Intelligence projects from Deloitte - Practical cases of applied AI*. Retrieved from https://www2.deloitte.com/content/dam/Deloitte/nl/Documents/innovatie/deloitte-nl-innovatie-artificial-intelligence-16-practical-cases.pdf

Deloitte. (2018b). *Advanced Early Warning Systems for Financial Distress*. Retrieved from https://www2.deloitte.com/ce/en/pages/deloitte-analytics/solutions/eagle-eye-searching-the-web-for-early-warning-signals.html

Deloitte. (2020a). *Press Releases - Deloitte Launches CortexAI Platform to Help Organizations Accelerate Applied AI in the 'Age of With'*. Retrieved from https://www2.deloitte.com/us/en/pages/about-deloitte/articles/press-releases/deloitte-launches-cortex-ai-platform.html

Deloitte. (2020b). *Press Releases - Deloitte Wins 2020 'Audit Innovation of the Year' at the Digital Accountancy Forum & Awards*. Retrieved from https://www2.deloitte.com/us/en/pages/about-deloitte/articles/press-releases/deloitte-wins-2020-audit-innovation-of-the-year-at-digital-accountancy-forum-awards.html

Deloitte. (n.d.a). *Differentiate with quality - Explore audit innovation with Deloitte AI Robot #4*. Retrieved from https://www2.deloitte.com/cn/en/pages/audit/articles/explore-audit-innovation-with-deloitte-ai-robot-vol-4.html

Deloitte. (n.d.b). *Welcome to Icount*. Retrieved from https://inventory.deloitte.com/login/

Deloitte. (n.d.c). *Explore audit innovation with Deloitte AI Robot #8 - Lead in the future of audit*. Retrieved from https://www2.deloitte.com/cn/en/pages/audit/articles/explore-audit-innovation-with-deloitte-ai-robot-vol-8.html

Devedžić, V. (2004). Web intelligence and artificial intelligence in education. *Journal of Educational Technology & Society, 7*(4), 29–39.

Dewey, J. (1986), September. Experience and education. In *iñe. The Educational Forum, 50*(3), 241–252. doi:10.1080/00131728609335764

Dhingra, A. B. (2020). Analysis of Banking sector in India. *International Journal of Research and Analytical Reviews, 7*(3), 299-308.

Dickey, G., Blanke, S., & Seaton, L. (2019). Machine Learning in Auditing: Current and Future Applications. *The CPA Journal, 89*(6), 16–21.

Dickins, D., & Urtel, K. (2021). Current Issues in Auditing: How We Are Advancing the Dialogue Between Academics and Practitioners. *Current Issues in Auditing, 15*(2), E1–E2. doi:10.2308/ciia-10775

Dilek, S., Çakır, H., & Aydın, M. (2015). *Applications of artificial intelligence techniques to combating cyber crimes: A review*. arXiv preprint arXiv:1502.03552.

Ding, K., Lev, B., Peng, X., Sun, T., & Vasarhelyi, M. A. (2020). Machine learning improves accounting estimates: Evidence from insurance payments. *Review of Accounting Studies, 25*(3), 1098–1134. doi:10.100711142-020-09546-9

Ding, K., Peng, X., & Wang, Y. (2019). A Machine Learning-Based Peer Selection Method with Financial Ratios. *Accounting Horizons*, *33*(3), 75–87. doi:10.2308/acch-52454

Director, I. (2020). *AI in Banking*. Reserve Bank of India.

Dirsehan, T., & Cankat, E. (2021). Role of mobile food-ordering applications in developing restaurants' brand satisfaction and loyalty in the pandemic period. *Journal of Retailing and Consumer Services*, *62*, 102608. doi:10.1016/j.jretconser.2021.102608

Dolev, N., & Itzkovich, Y. (2020). In the AI Era, Soft Skills are the New Hard Skills. In W. Amann & A. Stachowicz-Stanusch (Eds.), *Artificial Intelligence and Its Impact on Business* (pp. 55–77). Information Age Publishing.

Doll, J., & Ajzen, I. (1992). Accessibility and stability of predictors in the theory of planned behavior. *Journal of Personality and Social Psychology*, *63*(5), 754–765. doi:10.1037/0022-3514.63.5.754

dos Santos, S. M. (2019). data Mininig and machine learning techniquesapplied to public health problems: a bibliometric analysis from 2009 to 2018. *Comput Ind Eng*.

Dr Navleen Kaur, M. S. (2020, June). Banking 4.0: The Influence of Artificial Intelligence on the banking industry and how AI is changing the face of modern day banks. *International Journal of Management*, *11*(6), 577–585.

Drydakis, N. (2022). Artificial Intelligence and Reduced SMEs' Business Risks. A Dynamic Capabilities Analysis During the COVID-19 Pandemic. *Information Systems Frontiers*, 1–25. doi:10.100710796-022-10249-6 PMID:35261558

Dubey, V. (2019). Fintech innvovations in Digital Banking. *International Journal of Engineering Research and Technology*, 597-601.

Dumay, M. M. (2016). On the shoulders of giants: Undertaking a Structured literarture Review in Accounting. *Account Auditing Account*, 767-801.

Dwivedi, S., & Roshni, V. K. (2017, August). Recommender system for big data in education. In *2017 5th National Conference on E-Learning & E-Learning Technologies (ELELTECH)* (pp. 1-4). IEEE. 10.1109/ELELTECH.2017.8074993

Edelman, F. (1981). Managers, computer systems, and productivity. *Management Information Systems Quarterly*, *5*(3), 1–19. doi:10.2307/249287

Elena Carletti, S. C. (2020). *The Bank business model in the Post Covid 19 world*. IESE Banking Initiative.

Enfroy, A. (2022, June 22). *7 Best OTT Platforms of 2022 (Ranked and Reviewed)*. Retrieved from https://www.adamenfroy.com/ott-platform

Eulerich, M., & Kalinichenko, A. (2018). The Current State and Future Directions of Continuous Auditing Research: An Analysis of the Existing Literature. *Journal of Information Systems, 32*(3), 31–51. doi:10.2308/isys-51813

EY. (n.d.a). *Audit innovation*. Retrieved from https://www.ey.com/en_gl/audit/innovation

EY. (n.d.b). *EY Atlas*. Retrieved from https://www.ey.com/en_gl/audit/technology/atlas

EY. (n.d.c). *EY Canvas*. Retrieved from https://www.ey.com/en_gl/audit/technology/canvas

EY. (n.d.d). *EY Helix*. Retrieved from https://www.ey.com/en_gl/audit/technology/helix

Faliagka, E., Ramantas, K., Tsakalidis, A., & Tzimas, G. (2012). Application of machine learning algorithms to an online recruitment system. *Proc. International Conference on Internet and Web Applications and Services.*

Fang, Y., Chen, P., Cai, G., Lau, F. C., Liew, S. C., & Han, G. (2019). Outage-limit approaching channel coding for future wireless communications: Root-protograph low-density parity-check codes. *IEEE Vehicular Technology Magazine, 14*(2), 85–93. doi:10.1109/MVT.2019.2903343

Ferdous, M., Debnath, J., & Chakraborty, N. R. (2020). Machine Learning Algorithms in Healthcare: A Literature Survey. *2020 11th International Conference on Computing, Communication and Networking Technologies (ICCCNT)*, 1-6, 10.1109/ICCCNT49239.2020.9225642

Fintech Innovations in Digital Banking. (2019). *International Journal of Engineering Research and Technology, 8*(10), 597-601.

Fishbein, M., & Ajzen, I. (1975). *Belief, attitude, intention, and behavior: An introduction to theory and research.* Addison-Wesley Pub. Co.

Fitter, N. T., Chowdhury, Y., Cha, E., Takayama, L., & Matarić, M. J. (2018, March). Evaluating the effects of personalized appearance on telepresence robots for education. In Companion of the 2018 ACM/IEEE international conference on human-robot interaction (pp. 109-110). doi:10.1145/3173386.3177030

Fotoh, L. E., & Lorentzon, J. I. (2021). The Impact of Digitalization on Future Audits. *Journal of Emerging Technologies in Accounting, 18*(2), 77–97. doi:10.2308/JETA-2020-063

Franklin, S., & Graesser, A. (1996). Is it an agent, or just a program? A taxonomy for autonomous agents? In *International workshop on agent theories, architectures, and languages* (pp. 21–35). Springer.

Frazer, C., Sullivan, D. H., Weatherspoon, D., & Hussey, L. (2017). Faculty perceptions of online teaching effectiveness and indicators of quality. *Nursing Research and Practice, 2017*, 2017. doi:10.1155/2017/9374189 PMID:28326195

Fredericksen, E., Pickett, A., Shea, P., Pelz, W., & Swan, K. (2000). *Factors influencing faculty satisfaction with asynchronous teaching and learning in the SUNY learning network.* Academic Press.

Friedel, J. M., Cortina, K. S., Turner, J. C., & Midgley, C. (2010). Changes in efficacy beliefs in mathematics across the transition to middle school: Examining the effects of perceived teacher and parent goal emphases. *Journal of Educational Psychology*, *102*(1), 102–114. doi:10.1037/a0017590

From enhancing patient care to driving down costs, AI has enormous potential. (2022). Retrieved 16 July 2022, from https://stefanini.com/en/trends/news/7-ways-healthcare-benefits-from-artificial-intelligence

Furnham, A., Jackson, C. J., & Miller, T. (1999). Personality, learning style and work performance. *Personality and Individual Differences*, *27*(6), 1113–1122. doi:10.1016/S0191-8869(99)00053-7

Gaebel, M., Kupriyanova, V., Morais, R., & Colucci, E. (2014). *E-Learning in European Higher Education Institutions: Results of a Mapping Survey Conducted in October-December 2013*. European University Association.

Galanaki, E. (2002). The decision to recruit online: A descriptive study. *Career Development International*, *7*(4), 243–251. doi:10.1108/13620430210431325

Ganapathy, V., Mahadevan, P., & Ravikeerthi, J. V. (2016). An Empirical Study of the Feasibility of Introducing the Mumbai Dabbawala Food Delivery System in Bangalore. *SAMVAD*, *12*, 9–22.

Gao, Y., & Han, L. (2021). Implications of artificial intelligence on the objectives of auditing financial statements and ways to achieve them. *Microprocessors and Microsystems*, 1–9. doi:10.1016/j.micpro.2021.104036

Gautam, P. (2020). *Advantages and Disadvantages of Online Learning*. https://elearningindustry.com/advantages-and-disadvantages-online-learning

Ghodasara, R. (2022). *Smart Healthcare Solutions To Streamline Patient Experience*. Retrieved 16 July 2022, from https://www.zealousweb.com/smart-healthcare-solutions-to-streamline-patient-experience/#:~:text=Ease%20of%20appointments%20and%20check,the%20time%20of%20check%2Din

Goodhue, D. L., & Thompson, R. L. (1995). Task technology fit and individual performance. *Management Information Systems Quarterly*, *19*(2), 213–236. doi:10.2307/249689

Goudzwaard, M., Smakman, M., & Konijn, E. A. (2019, August). Robots are good for profit: A business perspective on robots in education. In *2019 Joint IEEE 9th International Conference on Development and Learning and Epigenetic Robotics (ICDL-EpiRob)* (pp. 54-60). IEEE. 10.1109/DEVLRN.2019.8850726

Govindasamy, T. (2001). Successful implementation of e-learning: Pedagogical considerations. *The Internet and Higher Education*, *4*(3-4), 287–299. doi:10.1016/S1096-7516(01)00071-9

Goyal, S. (2012). E-Learning: Future of education. *Journal of Education and Learning, 6*(2), 239-242.

Greenwood, M. (2002). Ethics and HRM: A Review and Conceptual Analysis. *Journal of Business Ethics, 36*(3), 261–279. doi:10.1023/A:1014090411946

Gubenko, A., Kirsch, C., Smilek, J. N., Lubart, T., & Houssemand, C. (2021). Educational Robotics and Robot Creativity: An Interdisciplinary Dialogue. *Frontiers in Robotics and AI, 8,* 178. doi:10.3389/frobt.2021.662030 PMID:34222352

Gubin, O. (2021, August 31). *Clutch Firms that deliver, development, thought leaders, 4 OTT (over-the-top) service challenges solved with AI.* Retrieved from, https://clutch.co/developers/resources/4-ott-service-challenges-solved-ai

Guenole, N., & Feinzig, S. (2018a). *The business case for AI in HR: With insights and tips on getting started.* IBM Smarter Workforce Institute. https://public.dhe.ibm.com/common/ssi/ecm/81/en/81019981usen/81019981-usen-

Gulliford, F., & Parker Dixon, A. (2019). AI: The HR revolution. *Strategic HR Review, 18*(2), 52–55. doi:10.1108/SHR-12-2018-0104

Guo, J., & Li, B. (2018). the application of medical Artificial Intelligence technology in rural areas of developing countries. *Health Equity, 2*(1), 174–181. doi:10.1089/heq.2018.0037 PMID:30283865

Guo, Y. H. Z., Hao, Z., Zhao, S., Gong, J., & Yang, F. (2020). Artificial Intelligence in Health Care: A Bibliometric Analysis. *Journal of Medical Internet Research, 22*(7), e18228. doi:10.2196/18228 PMID:32723713

Gupta, M. (2019). A Study on Impact of Online Food delivery app on Restaurant Business special reference to zomato and swiggy. *International Journal of Research and Analytical Reviews, 6*(1), 889–893.

Gurer, M., Tekinarslan, E., & Yavuzalp, N. (2016). Opinions of instructors who give lectures online about distance education. *Turkish Online Journal of Qualitative Inquiry, 7*(1), 47–78.

Haenlein, M., & Kaplan, A. (2019). A Brief History of Artificial Intelligence: On the Past, Present, and Future of Artificial Intelligence. *California Management Review, 61*(4), 1–10. doi:10.1177/0008125619864925

Haleem, A., Javaid, M., & Khan, I. H. (2019). Current status and applications of artificial intelligence (AI) in medical field: An overview. *Current Medicine Research and Practice, 9*(6), 231–237. doi:10.1016/j.cmrp.2019.11.005

Hamid, S. (2017). *The opportunities and risks of artificial Intelligence in medicine and Healthcare.* Retrieved from www.cuspe.org

Hao, T. C. X. (2018). A bibilometric analysis of text mining in medical research. *Soft Computing, 22.*

HCL Technologies. (n.d.). *Technology Q&A - Advantages of AI.* Retrieved from https://www.hcltech.com/technology-qa/what-are-the-advantages-of-artificial-intelligence

Health Care - Healthy People 2030. (2022). Retrieved 16 July 2022, from https://health.gov/healthypeople/objectives-and-data/browse-objectives/health-care

Hong, J. C., Yu, K. C., & Chen, M. Y. (2011). Collaborative learning in technological project design. *International Journal of Technology and Design Education, 21*(3), 335–347. doi:10.100710798-010-9123-7

How Healthcare Industry Helps in Contributing to the Economy. (2022). Retrieved 16 July 2022, from https://www.trivitron.com/blog/how-healthcare-industry-helps-in-contributing-to-the-economy/

Howarth, R., Ndlovu, T., Ndlovu, S., Molthan-Hill, P., & Puntha, H. (2019). Integrating education for sustainable development into a higher education institution: Beginning the journey. *Emerald Open Research, 1*, 9. doi:10.12688/emeraldopenres.13011.1

Hu, K., Chen, F., Hsu, M., & Tzeng, G. (2021). Identifying Key Factors for Adopting Artificial Intelligence-Enabled Auditing Techniques by Joint Utilization of Fuzzy-Rough Set Theory and MRDM Technique. *Technological and Economic Development of Economy, 27*(2), 459–492. doi:10.3846/tede.2020.13181

Hung, L., & Sun, K. (2020). How Will AI Change/Impact Management and Business World. In W. Amann & A. Stachowicz-Stanusch (Eds.), *Artificial Intelligence and Its Impact on Business* (pp. 17–37). Information Age Publishing.

Huong, P. N. Q. (2021). The quality OF human resources IN small and medium enterprises: Current situation, reason, recommendations ON solutions. *Journal of Natural Remedies, 21*, 73–81.

Hussain, A. (2020). *AI techbiques for COVID 19*. IEEE Acess.

Huynh, E., Hosny, A., Guthier, C., Bitterman, D. S., Petit, S. F., Haas-Kogan, D. A., Kann, B., Aerts, H. J. W. L., & Mak, R. H. (2020). Artificial intelligence in radiation oncology. *Nature Reviews. Clinical Oncology, 17*(12), 771–781. doi:10.103841571-020-0417-8 PMID:32843739

IIA. (2017). *Global Perspectives and Insights: Artificial Intelligence – Considerations for the Profession of Internal Auditing*. Retrieved from https://www.iia.nl/SiteFiles/GPI-Artificial-Intelligence.pdf

Inaki Aldasoro, I. F. (2020, May). Effect of Covid 19 on the Banking sector. *BIS Bulletin*.

Issa, H., Sun, T., & Vasarhelyi, M. A. (2016). Research ideas for artificial intelligence in auditing: The formalization of audit and workforce supplementation. *Journal of Emerging Technologies in Accounting, 13*(2), 1–20. doi:10.2308/jeta-10511

Izzati, B. M. (2020). Analysis of customer behavior in mobile food ordering application using UTAUT model (case study: GoFood application). *International Journal of Innovation in Enterprise System, 4*(01), 23–34. doi:10.25124/ijies.v4i01.45

Jain, V., Ambika, A., & Sheth, J. N. (2022). Customer-Centric Service Ecosystem for Emerging Markets. In The Palgrave Handbook of Service Management (pp. 393-410). Palgrave Macmillan. doi:10.1007/978-3-030-91828-6_21

Jain, S., Lall, M., & Singh, A. (2021). Teachers' voices on the impact of COVID-19 on school education: Are ed-tech companies really the panacea? *Contemporary Education Dialogue, 18*(1), 58–89. doi:10.1177/0973184920976433

Jeevan, P. (2015). A Conceptual Study on Customers Adoption of IMobile App Technology In *National conference on Recent trends in Management*. K S School of Engineering and Management.

Jewandah, D. S. (2018, July). How Artificial Intelligence is changing the banking sector. *International Journal of Management. Technology and Engineering, 8*(7), 525–531.

Jiang, F., Jiang, Y., Zhi, H., Dong, Y., Li, H., Ma, S., Wang, Y., Dong, Q., Shen, H., & Wang, Y. (2017). Artificial intelligence in healthcare: Past, present and future. *Stroke and Vascular Neurology, 2*(4), 230–243. doi:10.1136vn-2017-000101 PMID:29507784

Johal, W., Castellano, G., Tanaka, F., & Okita, S. (2018). Robots for learning. *International Journal of Social Robotics, 10*(3), 293–294. doi:10.100712369-018-0481-8

Jonathan Donner, A. T. (2008, December). Mobile banking and economic development:Linking adoption, impact and use. *Asian Journal of Communication, 18*(4).

Joshi. (2019, November 16). *AI and chill: How OTT platforms can benefit from AI*. Retrieved from, https://www.allerin.com/blog/ai-and-chill-how-ott-platforms-can-benefit-from-ai

Joshi, S. (2021). Impact of Covid 19 Induced Conditions on the Consumer Behavior on A Short, Mid and Long Term, for Consumption of Services. *Turkish Journal of Computer and Mathematics Education, 12*(2), 1906–1923.

Jurubescu, T. (2008) Learning content management system. *Revista Informatica Economica, 4*(48), 91–94.

Jurubescu, T. (2008). Learning Content Management Systems. *Informações Econômicas, 12*(4), 91–94.

Kaczmarek, T., Kowalkiewicz, M., & Piskorski, J. (2005). Information extraction from CV. *Proceedings of the 8th International Conference on Business Information Systems*, 3–7.

Kahraman, H. T., Sagiroglu, S., & Colak, I. (2010, October). Development of adaptive and intelligent web-based educational systems. In *2010 4th international conference on application of information and communication technologies* (pp. 1-5). IEEE. 10.1109/ICAICT.2010.5612054

Kallis, B. (2018). Promising AI applications in Healthcare. *Journal of Medical Systems*.

Kanteti, V. (2018). Innovative strategies of startup firms in India-A study on online food delivery companies in India. *International Research Journal of Management Science & Technology, 9*(3), 17–23.

Kapale, G., Naikwadi, R., Devkar, R., Pardeshi, O., & Gorde, S. (n.d.). *Online tiffin service.* Academic Press.

Kaplan, A., & Haenlein, M. (2020). Rulers of the world, unite! The challenges and opportunities of artificial intelligence. *Business Horizons, 63*(1), 37–50. doi:10.1016/j.bushor.2019.09.003

Kasim, N. N. M., & Khalid, F. (2016). Choosing the right learning management system (LMS) for the higher education institution context: A systematic review. *International Journal of Emerging Technologies in Learning, 11*(6).

Keenam, J. M. (2020). Covid, Resilience and the built environment. *Springer. Environment Systems & Decisions, 40*(2), 216–221. doi:10.100710669-020-09773-0 PMID:32412522

Keeton, M. T. (2004). Best online instructional practices: Report of phase I of an ongoing study. *Journal of Asynchronous Learning Networks, 8*(2), 75–100.

Kepuska, V., & Bohouta, G. (2018, January). Next-generation of virtual personal assistants (microsoft cortana, apple siri, amazon alexa and google home). In *2018 IEEE 8th annual computing and communication workshop and conference (CCWC)* (pp. 99-103). IEEE.

Khan, G. (2019). Information technology management Domain: Emerging Themes and keyword analysis. *Scientometrics.*

Kim, K.-J., & Bonk, C. J. (2006). The future of online teaching and learning in higher education: The survey says. *EDUCAUSE Quarterly, 4*, 22–30.

Knight, K., & Rich, E. (2010). *Artificial Intelligence* (3rd ed.). McGraw Hill India.

Koivisto, K. (2004). *Oikea valinta. Rekrytoinnin menetelmät.* Yrityskirjat.

Kokina, J., & Davenport, T. H. (2017). The emergence of artificial intelligence: How automation is changing auditing. *Journal of Emerging Technologies in Accounting, 14*(1), 115–122. doi:10.2308/jeta-51730

Kolowich, S. (2013). How EdX plans to earn, and share, revenue from its free online courses. *The Chronicle of Higher Education, 21*, 1–5.

Konradt, U., Warszta, T., & Ellwart, T. (2013). Fairness perceptions in web-based selection: Impact on applicants' pursuit intentions, recommendation intentions, and intentions to reapply. *International Journal of Selection and Assessment, 21*(2), 155–169. doi:10.1111/ijsa.12026

Kovalenko, O. (2022). *12 Real-World Applications of Machine Learning in Healthcare - SPD Group Blog.* Retrieved 16 July 2022, from https://spd.group/machine-learning/machine-learning-in-healthcare

Kozelka, E. E., Jenkins, J. H., & Carpenter-Song, E. (2021). Advancing Health Equity in Digital Mental Health: Lessons From Medical Anthropology for Global Mental Health. *JMIR Mental Health, 8*(8), e28555. doi:10.2196/28555 PMID:34398788

KPMG. (n.d.a). *Artificial intelligence – Empowering a smarter, faster, more agile enterprise.* Retrieved from https://advisory.kpmg.us/services/artificial-intelligence.html

KPMG. (n.d.b). *KPMG Clara.* Retrieved from https://home.kpmg/xx/en/home/services/audit/kpmg-clara.html

Krishna, M. (2021, July 27). *How is AI benefitting the OTT industry.* Retrieved from, https://brandequity.economictimes.indiatimes.com/news/digital/how-is-ai-benefitting-the-ott-industry/84781042

Kryger Aggerholm, H., Esmann Andersen, S., & Thomsen, C. (2011). Conceptualizing employer branding in sustainable organizations. *Corporate Communications, 16*(2), 105–123. doi:10.1108/13563281111141642

Kulkarni, S. B., & Che, X. (2019). Intelligent Software Tools for Recruiting. *Journal of International Technology and Information Management, 28,* Article 1. https://scholarworks.lib.csusb.edu/jitim/vol28/iss2/1

Kulkarni, P. V., Rai, S., & Kale, R. (2020). Recommender system in elearning: a survey. In *Proceeding of International Conference on Computational Science and Applications* (pp. 119-126). Springer. 10.1007/978-981-15-0790-8_13

Kumar, A., Agrawal, A., & Agrawal, P. (2015). *Massive open online courses: EdX. org, Coursera. com and NPTEL, a comparative study based on usage statistics and features with special reference to India.* Academic Press.

Kumar, S. (2019, November 25). *Towards Data Science, Advantages and Disadvantages of Artificial Intelligence.* Retrieved from https://towardsdatascience.com/advantages-and-disadvantages-of-artificial-intelligence-182a5ef6588c

Kumari, R. (2022). *What is the Role of Big Data in the Healthcare Industry?* Analytics Steps. Retrieved 16 July 2022, from https://www.analyticssteps.com/blogs/what-role-big-data-healthcare-industry

Kunwar, M. (2019, Aug). Understanding how Automation and Machine learning is transforming the financial industry. *Artificial Intelligence in Finance,* 36.

Kurode, T. (2018, January). Review of applicability of Artificial Intelligence in various financial services. *Journal of Advance Management Research, 6*(1), 2019–2214.

Lara, J. A., Aljawarneh, S., & Pamplona, S. (2020). Special issue on the current trends in E-learning Assessment. *Journal of Computing in Higher Education, 32*(1), 1–8. doi:10.100712528-019-09235-w

Large, A. (2010). *Mobile technology for children: Designing for Interaction and Learning.* Academic Press.

Lawrence, L. (2021, December 20). *Top AI-based OTT Trends That Will Impact The Media Industry.* Retrieved from, https://kilowott.com/blog/top-ott-trends-media-industry/

Lee, M. K., Cheung, C. M., & Chen, Z. (2005). Acceptance of Internet-based learning medium: The role of extrinsic and intrinsic motivation. *Information & Management, 42*(8), 1095–1104. doi:10.1016/j.im.2003.10.007

Leung, X. Y., & Cai, R. (2021). How pandemic severity moderates digital food ordering risks during COVID-19: An application of prospect theory and risk perception framework. *Journal of Hospitality and Tourism Management, 47*, 497–505. doi:10.1016/j.jhtm.2021.05.002

Li, B. H., Hou, B. C., Yu, W. T., Lu, X. B., & Yang, C. W. (2017). Applications of artificial intelligence in intelligent manufacturing: A review. *Frontiers of Information Technology & Electronic Engineering, 18*(1), 86–96. doi:10.1631/FITEE.1601885

Lin, W. S., & Wang, C. H. (2012). Antecedences to continued intentions of adopting e-learning system in blended learning instruction: A contingency framework based on models of information system success and task technology fit. *Computers and Education, 58*(1), 88–99. doi:.compe du.2011.07.008 doi:10.1016/j

Lin, C. H., Liu, E. Z. F., & Huang, Y. Y. (2012). Exploring parents' perceptions towards educational robots: Gender and socio-economic differences. *British Journal of Educational Technology, 43*(1), E31–E34. doi:10.1111/j.1467-8535.2011.01258.x

Lingle, J. C., Tiffin, L. O., & Brown, J. C. (1963). Iron uptake-transport of soybeans as influenced by other cations. *Plant Physiology, 38*(1), 71–76. doi:10.1104/pp.38.1.71 PMID:16655756

Liz, K. (2022). *Top 10 Use Cases for AI in Healthcare.* Retrieved 16 July 2022, from https://www.mobihealthnews.com/news/contributed-top-10-use-cases-ai-healthcare

Lizcano, D., Lara, J. A., White, B., & Aljawarneh, S. (2020). Blockchain-based approach to create a model of trust in open and ubiquitous higher education. *Journal of Computing in Higher Education, 32*(1), 109–134. doi:10.100712528-019-09209-y

Lohani, M., Stokes, C., Dashan, N., McCoy, M., Bailey, C. A., & Rivers, S. E. (2017). A framework for human-agent social systems: The role of non-technical factors in operation success. In Advances in human factors in robots and unmanned systems (pp. 137–148). Springer International Publishing.

Luger, G., & Stubblefield, W. (2004). *Artificial Intelligence: Structures and Strategies for Complex Problem Solving* (5th ed.). Benjamin/Cummings.

Maatuk, A. M., Elberkawi, E. K., Aljawarneh, S., Rashaideh, H., & Alharbi, H. (2021). The COVID-19 pandemic and E-learning: Challenges and opportunities from the perspective of students and instructors. *Journal of Computing in Higher Education*, 1–18. PMID:33967563

Machine Learning in Healthcare. (2022). *12 Real-World Use Cases – NIX United.* Retrieved 16 July 2022, from https://nix-united.com/blog/machine-learning-in-healthcare-12-real-world-use-cases-to-know/

Mager, A. (2012). Algorithmic ideology: How capitalist society shapes search engines. *Information Communication and Society, 15*(5), 769–787. doi:10.1080/1369118X.2012.676056

Mahajan, K., & Deore, A. (2020). On line Food Ordering Tiffin Service using Reusable Containers. *IJETT, 3*(3).

Mairesse, F., Walker, M. A., Mehl, M. R., & Moore, R. K. (2007). Using linguistic cues for the automatic recognition of personality in conversation and text. *Journal of Artificial Intelligence Research, 30*, 457–500. doi:10.1613/jair.2349

Malik, P. (2020). *Expat Life Under Quarantine: Reflections of a Reluctant Cook.* Academic Press.

Manyika, J., Silberg, J., & Presten, B. (2019). AI and Machine Learning: What Do We Do About the Biases in AI? *Harvard Business Review.* Retrieved from https://hbr.org/2019/10/what-do-we-do-about-the-biases-in-ai

Marie Paule, O. P. (2020, May). *Banking model after Covid 19: Taking model risk management to the next level.* McKinsley and Company.

Marr, B. (2022). *How Is AI Used In Healthcare - 5 Powerful Real-World Examples That Show The Latest Advances.* Retrieved 16 July 2022, from https://www.forbes.com/sites/bernardmarr/2018/07/27/how-is-ai-used-in-healthcare-5-powerful-real-world-examples-that-show-the-latest-advances/?sh=6c5c0e985dfb

Martincevic, I., & Kozina, G. (2018). The Impact Of New Technology Adaptation In Business. Varazdin: Varazdin Development and Entrepreneurship Agency (VADEA).

Martin, F., Sun, T., & Westine, C. D. (2020). A systematic review of research on online teaching and learning from 2009 to 2018. *Computers & Education, 159*, 104009. doi:10.1016/j.compedu.2020.104009 PMID:32921895

Mas, F., & Dal, A. P.-G. (2020). Knowledge Translation in the Healthcare Sector. *Electronic Journal of Knowledge Management.*

Mashamba-Thompson, T. P., & Crayton, E. D. (2020). Blockchain and artificial intelligence technology for novel coronavirus disease 2019 self-testing. *Diagnostics (Basel), 10*(4), 198. doi:10.3390/diagnostics10040198 PMID:32244841

Mathew, S. M., Oswal, N., & Ateeq, D. (2021). *Artificial Intelligence (AI): Bringing a New Revolution in Human Resource Management.* HRM.

Mathur, M., Mehta, R., & Swami, S. (2020). Developing a marketing framework for the bottom of the pyramid consumers. *Journal of Advances in Management Research, 17*(3), 455–471. doi:10.1108/JAMR-01-2020-0015

Maurya, A., Subramaniam, G., & Dixit, S. (2021, January). Laying the table from the cloud during Lockdown: Impact of Covid crisis on Cloud Kitchens in India. In *2021 2nd International Conference on Computation, Automation and Knowledge Management (ICCAKM)* (pp. 299-302). IEEE.

McBrien, J. L., Cheng, R., & Jones, P. (2009). Virtual spaces: Employing a synchronous online classroom to facilitate student engagement in online learning. *International Review of Research in Open and Distributed Learning, 10*(3).

McCoy, L., Brenna, C., Chen, S., Vold, K., & Das, S. (2022). Believing in black boxes: Machine learning for healthcare does not need explainability to be evidence-based. *Journal of Clinical Epidemiology, 142*, 252–257. doi:10.1016/j.jclinepi.2021.11.001 PMID:34748907

Mckenzie, W. (2019). *Experiences of graduate-level Faculty regarding interaction in online courses* (Doctoral dissertation). Sam Houston State University.

McLean, S., Stakim, C., Timner, H., & Lyon, C. (2016). Big data and human resources: Letting the computer decide? *Scitech Lawyer, 12*(2), 20.

Mehta, A. P. (2019). Transforming Healthcare with Big data analytics and artificial intelligence: a systematic mapping study. *Decision Support System.*

Mehta, M., & Sinha, R. (2022). Women Entrepreneurs and Information Communication Technology: The Journey from Intention to Usage. *Journal of Entrepreneurship and Innovation in Emerging Economies.*

Merin. (2021). *Benefits & Challenges of Using AI in Recruitment.* HR Shelf.

Meskovic, E., Garrison, M., Ghezal, S., & Chen, Y. (2018). Artificial intelligence: Trends in business and implications for the accounting profession. *Internal Auditing,* 5-11.

Michael, G. (2022). Retrieved 16 July 2022, from https://imaginovation.net/blog/5-real-world-applications-ai-in-medicine-examples/

Miller, P. (1996). Strategy and Ethical Management of Human Resources. *Human Resource Management Journal, 6*(1), 5–18. doi:10.1111/j.1748-8583.1996.tb00393.x

Mishra, L., Gupta, T., & Shree, A. (2020). Online teaching-learning in higher education during lockdown period of COVID-19 pandemic. *International Journal of Educational Research Open, 1*, 100012. doi:10.1016/j.ijedro.2020.100012 PMID:35059663

Mishra, S., & Anand, S. (2020). Migration and Dietary Diversity Changes among the Students: Case Study of the University of Delhi in India. *Space and Culture, India, 8*(3), 58–70. doi:10.20896aci.vi0.906

Mohaimemul Islam, Md., T. N. (2021). Application of Artificial Intelligence in COVID-19 pandemic: Bibliometric Analysis. *Health Care.* PMID:33918686

Mohamad, A. H., Hamzah, A. A., Ramli, R., & Fathullah, M. (2020, May). E-commerce beyond the pandemic coronavirus: Click and collect food ordering. *IOP Conference Series. Materials Science and Engineering, 864*(1), 012049. doi:10.1088/1757-899X/864/1/012049

Mohammed, M., Khan, M., & Bashier, E. (2016). *Machine Learning: Algorithms and Applications.* . doi:10.1201/9781315371658

Mohan, D., Bashingwa, J. J. H., Dane, P., Chamberlain, S., Tiffin, N., & Lefevre, A. (2019) Use of big data and machine learning methods in the monitoring and evaluation of digital health programs in India: An exploratory protocol. *JMIR Research Protocols*, *8*(5), e11456. doi:10.2196/11456 PMID:31127716

Mökander, J., Axente, M., Casolari, F., & Floridi, L. (2021). Conformity Assessments and Post-market Monitoring: A Guide to the Role of Auditing in the Proposed European AI Regulation. *Minds and Machines*, 1–28. doi:10.100711023-021-09577-4 PMID:34754142

Mökander, J., & Floridi, L. (2021). Ethics-Based Auditing to Develop Trustworthy AI. *Minds and Machines*, *31*(2), 323–327. doi:10.100711023-021-09557-8

Montuschi, P., Gatteschi, V., Lamberti, F., Sanna, A., & Demartini, C. (2014). Job recruitment and job seeking processes: How technology can help IT. *IT Professional*, *16*(5), 41–49. doi:10.1109/MITP.2013.62

Moore, J. C. (2002). *Elements of Quality: The Sloan-C Tm Framework*. Olin College-Sloan-C.

Ms Bhavna Aggarwal, D. H. (2019). Application of Artificial Intelligence for successful strategy implementation in India's Banking Sector. *International Journal of Advanced Research*, *7*(11), 157–166. doi:10.21474/IJAR01/9988

Ms, P., & Toro, U. (2013). A review of literature on knowledge management using ICT. *Higher Education*, *4*(1), 62–67.

Muangmee, C., Kot, S., Meekaewkunchorn, N., Kassakorn, N., & Khalid, B. (2021). Factors determining the behavioral intention of using food delivery apps during COVID-19 pandemics. *Journal of Theoretical and Applied Electronic Commerce Research*, *16*(5), 1297–1310. doi:10.3390/jtaer16050073

Munoko, I., Brown-Liburd, H. L., & Vasarhelyi, M. (2020). The ethical implications of using artificial intelligence in auditing. *Journal of Business Ethics*, *167*(2), 209–234. doi:10.100710551-019-04407-1

Murdoch, J. (1998). The spaces of actor-network theory. *Geoforum*, *29*(4), 357–374. doi:10.1016/S0016-7185(98)00011-6

Naim, A., & Alahmari, F. (2020). Reference Model of E-learning and Quality to Establish Interoperability in Higher Education Systems. *International Journal of Emerging Technologies in Learning (iJET)*, *15*(2), 15-28. https://www.learntechlib.org/p/217170/

Namratha, S. J. (2019). *Impact of Artificial Intelligence in chosen Indian Commercial Bank- A Cost Benefit Analysis*. Academic Press.

Nascimento, M. A., & Queiroz, M. C. A. (2017). Overview of research on Artificial Intelligence in Administration in Brazil. *ANPAD Meetings – Enanpad*, 1-4.

Naveh, G., Tubin, D., & Pliskin, N. (2010). Student LMS use and satisfaction in academic institutions:The organizational perspective. *The Internet and Higher Education*, *13*(3), 127–133. doi:10.1016/j.iheduc.2010.02.004

NDTV Food. (2022). *4 Tiffin Service Apps For Ghar Ka Khana Delivered To Your Office*. NDTV Food. Available at: https://food.ndtv.com/food-drinks/4-best-tiffin-service-apps-for-home-cooked-meals-delivered-to-your-office-2833488

Neelie. (2020). *11 Innovative Uses of AI In Recruitment In 2020*. Harver.

Ngiam, K., & Khor, I. (2019). Big data and machine learning algorithms for health-care delivery. *The Lancet. Oncology*, *20*(5), e262–e273. doi:10.1016/S1470-2045(19)30149-4 PMID:31044724

Nickerson, M. A. (2019). AI: New risks and rewards – Will reliance on AI increase accounting and financial fraud? *Strategic Finance*, 26-31.

Nilsson, N. (1998). *Artificial Intelligence: A New Synthesis*. Morgan Kaufmann.

Nirupam Bajpai, M. W. (2020). *Artificial Intelligence and Healthcare in India*. Center for Sustainable Development, Earth Institute, Columbia University.

Nizam Verda, A. A. (2021). Challenges of Applying Health care in India. *Journal of Pharmaceutical Research International*.

O'Donovan, D. (2019). HRM in the organization: An overview. *Management Science, Management and Industrial Engineering*, 75–110.

O'Leary, D. E. (2009). Introduction. Value Creation from Expert Systems: An Economic Approach with Applications in Accounting, Auditing and Finance. In M. A. Vasarhelyi & D. O'Leary (Eds.), *Artificial Intelligence in Accounting and Auditing: Creating Value with AI* (Vol. 5, pp. 2–17). Markus Wiener Publisher.

Obeid, C., Lahoud, I., El Khoury, H., & Champin, P. A. (2018, April). Ontology-based recommender system in higher education. In *Companion Proceedings of the The Web Conference 2018* (pp. 1031-1034). 10.1145/3184558.3191533

Okolie, U., & Irabor, I. (2017). E-Recruitment: Practices, Opportunities, and Challenges. *European Journal of Business and Management*.

Oktavia, T., Prabowo, H., & Supangkat, S. H. (2018, September). The comparison of MOOC (massive open online course) platforms of edx and coursera (study case: Student of programming courses). In *2018 International Conference on Information Management and Technology (ICIMTech)* (pp. 339-344). IEEE. 10.1109/ICIMTech.2018.8528178

Omoteso, K. (2012). The application of artificial intelligence in auditing: Looking back to the future. *Expert Systems with Applications*, *39*(9), 8490–8495. doi:10.1016/j.eswa.2012.01.098

Oren, O., Gersh, B., & Bhatt, D. (2020). Artificial Intelligence in medical imaging: Switching from radiographic pathological data to clinically meaningful endpoints. *The Lancet. Digital Health*, 2(9), e486–e488. doi:10.1016/S2589-7500(20)30160-6 PMID:33328116

Ornstein, A. C., Levine, D. U., Gutek, G., & Vocke, D. E. (2016). *Foundations of education.* Cengage Learning.

Ozaydin, B., Berner, E. S., & Cimino, J. J. (2021). Appropriate use of machine learning in healthcare. *Intelligence-Based Medicine, 5.* doi:10.1016/j.ibmed.2021.100041

Packard, R. (2013). *Education transformation: How K-12 online learning is bringing the greatest change to education in 100 years.* Beyond Words Publishing.

Panayotopoulou, L., Vakola, M., & Galanaki, E. (2007). E-HR adoption and the role of HRM: Evidence from Greece. *Personnel Review*, 36(2), 277–294. doi:10.1108/00483480710726145

Parasuraman, A., & Colby, L. C. (2001). *Techno-Ready Marketing.* The Free Press.

Park, W. (2018), *Artificial intelligence and human resource management: new perspectives and challenges.* Japan Institute for Labour Policy and Training. https://www.jil.go.jp/profile/documents/w.park.pdf

Parkes, M., Stein, S., & Reading, C. (2015). Student preparedness for university e-learning environments. *The Internet and Higher Education*, 25, 1–10. doi:10.1016/j.iheduc.2014.10.002

Park, S. Y. (2009). An Analysis of the Technology Acceptance Model in Understanding University Students' Behavioral Intention to Use e-Learning. *Journal of Educational Technology & Society*, 12(3), 150–162.

Parry, E., & Olivas-Lujan, M. (2011) Drivers of the Adoption of Online Recruitment – An analysis using Innovation Attributes from Diffusion of Innovation Theory. *Electronic HRM in Theory and Practice*, 159–174.

Parry, E., & Wilson, H. (2009). Factors influencing the adoption of online recruitment. *Personnel Review*, 38(6), 655–673. doi:10.1108/00483480910992265

Partlow, K. M., & Gibbs, W. J. (2003). Indicators of constructivist principles in internet-based courses. *Journal of Computing in Higher Education*, 14(2), 68–97. doi:10.1007/BF02940939

Pash, C. (2016). *KPMG will soon be using artificial intelligence for audits in Australia.* Retrieved from https://www.businessinsider.com.au/kpmg-will-soon-be-using-artificial-intelligence-for-audits-in-australia-2016-6

PeartA. (2021). https://www.artificial-solutions.com/blog/impact-of-ai-in-the-workforce

Peredo, R., Canales, A., Menchaca, A., & Peredo, I. (2011). Intelligent Web-based education system for adaptive learning. *Expert Systems with Applications*, 38(12), 14690–14702. doi:10.1016/j.eswa.2011.05.013

Pereira, L. F., Resio, M., Costa, R. L., Dias, A., & Gonçalves, R. (2021). Artificial Intelligence in Strategic Business Management: The Case of Auditing. *International Journal of Business Information Systems*, *1*(1), 1–47. doi:10.1504/IJBIS.2021.10039269

Perols, J. (2011). Financial Statement Fraud Detection: An Analysis of Statistical and Machine Learning Algorithms. *Auditing*, *30*(2), 19–50. doi:10.2308/ajpt-50009

Phillipe Dintrans, B. H. (2019). *Artificial Intelligence in Financial Services: From nice to must have*. Cognizant.

Pokrivčáková, S. (2019). Preparing teachers for the application of AI-powered technologies in foreign language education. *Journal of Language and Cultural Education*.

Poole, D., Mackworth, A., & Goebel, R. (1998). *Computational Intelligence: A Logical Approach*. Oxford University Press.

Poole, D., & Mackworth, A. (2017). *Artificial Intelligence: Foundations of Computational Agents* (2nd ed.). Cambridge University Press. doi:10.1017/9781108164085

Popenici, S. A., & Kerr, S. (2017). Exploring the impact of artificial intelligence on teaching and learning in higher education. *Research and Practice in Technology Enhanced Learning*, *12*(1), 1–13. doi:10.118641039-017-0062-8 PMID:30595727

Price, J. K. (2015). Transforming learning for the smart learning environment: Lessons learned from the Intel education initiatives. *Smart Learning Environments*, *2*(1), 1–16. doi:10.118640561-015-0022-y

PwC. (2017). *Sizing the prize: What's the real value of AI for your business and how can you capitalise?* Retrieved from https://www.pwc.com/gx/en/issues/analytics/assets/pwc-ai-analysis-sizing-the-prize-report.pdf

PwC. (n.d.a). *AI and the Audit*. Retrieved from https://www.pwc.com/gx/en/about/stories-from-across-the-world/harnessing-ai-to-pioneer-new-approaches-to-the-audit.html

PwC. (n.d.b). *Audit of General Ledger with Halo*. Retrieved from https://www.pwc.com/mu/en/services/assurance/risk-assurance/tech-assurance/general-ledger-audit.html

PwC. (n.d.c). *Harnessing the power of AI to transform the detection of fraud and error*. Retrieved from https://www.pwc.com/gx/en/about/stories-from-across-the-world/harnessing-the-power-of-ai-to-transform-the-detection-of-fraud-and-error.html

Qasim, A., & Kharbat, F. F. (2020). Blockchain Technology, Business Data Analytics, and Artificial Intelligence: Use in the Accounting Profession and Ideas for Inclusion into the Accounting Curriculum. *Journal of Emerging Technologies in Accounting*, *17*(1), 107–117. doi:10.2308/jeta-52649

Qayyum, A., Watson, A., Buchanan, A., Paterson, M., & Hakimpour, Y. (2020). *CPA Canada & AICPA. The Data-Driven Audit: How Automation and AI are Changing the Audit and the Role of the Auditor*. Retrieved from https://us.aicpa.org/content/dam/aicpa/interestareas/frc/assuranceadvisoryservices/downloadabledocuments/the-data-driven-audit.pdf

Qureshi, A. A., Shim, J. K., & Siegel, J. G. (1998). Artificial intelligence in accounting & business. *The National Public Accountant, 43*(7), 13–18.

Rahamat, R., Shah, P. M., Din, R., Puteh, S. N., Aziz, J. A., Norman, H., & Embi, M. A. (2012). Measuring learners' perceived satisfaction towards e-learning material and environment. *WSEAS Transactions on Advances in Engineering Education, 3*(9), 72–83.

Rainer. (2012). *From Capability to Profitability: Realizing the Value of People Management, Realising the value of people management*. Academic Press.

Rajesh Bansal, A. B. (2020, Sep). *Recovery, Resilience and Adaptation: India from 2020 to 2030*. Carnegie India.

Raschke, R. L., Saiewitz, A., Kachroo, P., & Lennard, J. B. (2018). AI-Enhanced audit inquiry: A research note. *Journal of Emerging Technologies in Accounting, 15*(2), 111–116. doi:10.2308/jeta-52310

Raub, M. (2018). Bots, bias and big data: Artificial intelligence, algorithmic bias and disparate impact liability in hiring practices. *Arkansas Law Review, 71*, 529.

Raviprolu, A. (2017). Role of Artificial Intelligence in Recruitment. *International Journal of Engineering Technology, Management and Applied Sciences, 5*(4).

Reddy, K. (2021). *AI in Recruitment: Benefits and Challenges You Need to Know*. https://content.wisestep.com/ai-recruitment/

Reich-Stiebert, N., & Eyssel, F. (2016, November). Robots in the classroom: What teachers think about teaching and learning with education robots. In *International conference on social robotics* (pp. 671-680). Springer. 10.1007/978-3-319-47437-3_66

Researchers design AI tool to combat human bias in hiring. (n.d.). HR Dive.

Richa & Srinivas. (2020). Challenges of artificial intelligence in human resource management in Indian IT sector. *XXI Annual International Conference Proceedings*, 380-387. http://www.internationalconference.in/XXI_AIC/INDEX.HTM

Ricky, M. Y. (2014). Mobile food ordering application using android os platform. In *EPJ Web of Conferences* (*Vol. 68*, p. 00041). EDP Sciences. 10.1051/epjconf/20146800041

Rockwell, S. K., Schauer, J., Fritz, S., & Marx, D. B. (1999). Incentives and obstacles influencing higher education faculty and administrators to teach via distance. Faculty Publications: Agricultural Leadership, Education & Communication Department, 53.

Rogers Everett, M. (1995). *Diffusion of innovations*.

Rogers, D. L. (2016). *The digital transformation playbook: Rethink your business for the digital age*. Columbia University Press. doi:10.7312/roge17544

Rong, G., Mendez, A., Bou Assi, E., Zhao, B., & Sawan, M. (2020). Artificial Intelligence in Healthcare: Review and Prediction Case Studies. *Engineering*, *6*(3), 291–301. doi:10.1016/j.eng.2019.08.015

Rosa. (2019, March 29). *4 ways AI can improve user engagement in OTT video service*. Retrieved from, https://www.deltatre.com/insights/4-ways-ai-can-improve-user-engagement-ott-video-services

Russell, S. J., & Norvig, P. (2003). *Artificial Intelligence: A Modern Approach* (2nd ed.). Prentice Hall.

Ryan, M., & Stahl, B. C. (2021). Artificial intelligence ethics guidelines for developers and users: Clarifying their content and normative implications. *Journal of Information, Communication and Ethics in Society*, *19*(1), 61–86. doi:10.1108/JICES-12-2019-0138

Ryan, R. M., & Deci, E. L. (2000). Intrinsic and extrinsic motivations: Classic definitions and new directions. *Contemporary Educational Psychology*, *25*(1), 54–67. doi:10.1006/ceps.1999.1020 PMID:10620381

Saadé, R. G., Tan, W., & Nebebe, F. (2008). Impact of motivation on intentions in online learning: Canada vs China. *Issues in Informing Science & Information Technology*, *5*, 137–147. doi:10.28945/1001

Sahin, I. (2006). Detailed review of Rogers' diffusion of innovations theory and educational technology-related studies based on Rogers' theory. *Turkish Online Journal of Educational Technology-TOJET*, *5*(2), 14–23.

Saleh, A., & Mrayan, S. A. (2016). Faculty Perceptions of Online Teacher Education Programs in Jordan: A Case Study. *Asian Journal of Education and e-Learning*, *4*(6).

Salunkhe, R. T. (2019, November). Role of Artificial Intelligence in providing customer service with Special reference to SBI and HDFC Bank. *International Journal of Recent Technology and Engineering*, *8*(4), 12251–12260. doi:10.35940/ijrte.C6065.118419

Samarawickrema, G., & Stacey, E. (2007). Adopting Web-Based Learning and Teaching: A case study in higher education. *Distance Education*, *28*(3), 313–333. doi:10.1080/01587910701611344

Samin, H., & Azim, T. (2019). Knowledge based recommender system for academia using machine learning: A case study on higher education landscape of Pakistan. *IEEE Access: Practical Innovations, Open Solutions*, *7*, 67081–67093. doi:10.1109/ACCESS.2019.2912012

Samsudin, N. A., Khalid, S. K. A., Kohar, M. F. A. M., Senin, Z., & Ihkasan, M. N. (2011, September). A customizable wireless food ordering system with realtime customer feedback. In *2011 IEEE Symposium on Wireless Technology and Applications (ISWTA)* (pp. 186-191). IEEE. 10.1109/ISWTA.2011.6089405

Samuel, A. (2016). *Faculty perceptions and experiences of" presence" in the online learning environment* (Doctoral dissertation). The University of Wisconsin-Milwaukee.

Santosh, K. (2020). AI driven tools for Corona Virus outbreak: Need of active learning and cross population. *Journal of Medical Systems*. Advance online publication. doi:10.100710916-020-01562-1

Sarvamangala, D. R., & Kulkarni, R. V. (2022). Convolutional neural networks in medical image understanding: A survey. *Evolutionary Intelligence*, *15*(1), 1–22. doi:10.100712065-020-00540-3 PMID:33425040

Saxena, A. (2019). An analysis of online food ordering applications in India: Zomato and Swiggy. *International Journal of Research in Engineering, IT and Social Sciences*, *9*, 13–21.

SC, B., S. A. S., & Andrew, S. A. (2021). *Emerging Trends Towards Online Food Delivery Apps in India.* Available at *SSRN* 3837117.

Schoegler, P., Ebner, M., & Ebner, M. (2020, June). The Use of Alexa for Mass Education. In EdMedia+ Innovate Learning (pp. 721-730). Association for the Advancement of Computing in Education (AACE).

Searle, R. H. (2006). New technology: The potential impact of surveillance techniques in recruitment practices. *Personnel Review*, *35*(3), 336–351. doi:10.1108/00483480610656720

Secinaro, S., & Calandra, D. (2020). Halal Food: Structured Literature review and Research Agenda. *British Food Journal*, *123*(1), 225–243. doi:10.1108/BFJ-03-2020-0234

See-Kwong, G., Soo-Ryue, N. G., Shiun-Yi, W., & Lily, C. (2017). Outsourcing to online food delivery services: Perspective of F&B business owners. *Journal of Internet Banking and Commerce*, *22*(2), 1–18.

Sengupta, S. M. (2020). *Impact of Covid19 on Indian economy.* Mumbai: Indira Gandhi Institute of Development Research.

Şerban, C., & Todericiu, I. A. (2020). Alexa, What classes do I have today? The use of Artificial Intelligence via Smart Speakers in Education. *Procedia Computer Science*, *176*, 2849–2857. doi:10.1016/j.procs.2020.09.269 PMID:33042313

Shah, A. (2022, April 28). *AI and OTT media: How artificial intelligence is shaping the future of OTT markets.* Retrieved from https://www.ltts.com/blog/AI-shaping-future-of-OTT-markets

ShahN.ShahH.ShethS.ChauhanR.DesaiC. (2021). *Local Food Delivery System.* Available at SSRN 3867478.

Sheeja, N. (2018). Open Educational Resources in India: A Study of NPTEL and its Usage. *Library Herald*, *56*(1), 122–129. doi:10.5958/0976-2469.2018.00012.X

Shimamoto, D. C. (2018/2019, Winter). Is Artificial Intelligence a Threat to Government Accountants and Auditors? *Journal of Government Financial Management*, *67*(4), 12–16.

Shreaves, D. (2019). *Faculty Perceptions of Online Teaching at a Mid-Sized Liberal Arts University in the Pacific Northwest: A Mixed Methods Study.* Academic Press.

Silvana Secinaro, D. C. (2021). *The role of Artificial intelligence in helathcare: a structured literature Review.* BMC Medical Informatics and Decission Making.

Singh, R.P., Hom, G.L., Abramoff, M.D., Campbell, J.P., & Chiang, M.F. (2020). AAO Task Force on Artificial Intelligence. Current Challenges and Barriers to Real-World Artificial Intelligence Adoption for the Healthcare System, Provider, and the Patient. *Transl Vis Sci Technol., 9*(2), 45. doi:10.1167/tvst.9.2.45

Singh, V., & Thurman, A. (2019). How many ways can we define online learning? A systematic literature review of definitions of online learning (1988-2018). *American Journal of Distance Education, 33*(4), 289–306. doi:10.1080/08923647.2019.1663082

Singh, Y., & Suri, P. K. (2022). An empirical analysis of mobile learning app usage experience. *Technology in Society, 68*, 101929. doi:10.1016/j.techsoc.2022.101929

Smakman, M. H., Konijn, E. A., Vogt, P., & Pankowska, P. (2021). Attitudes towards social robots in education: Enthusiast, practical, troubled, sceptic, and mindfully positive. *Robotics, 10*(1), 24. doi:10.3390/robotics10010024

Smakman, M., Jansen, B., Leunen, J., & Konijn, E. A. (2020, March). Acceptable social robots in education: A value sensitive parent perspective. In *Proceedings of the INTED2020 Conference* (pp. 7946-7953). 10.21125/inted.2020.2161

Snyder, H. (2019). Literature review as a research methodology: An overview and guidelines. *Journal of Business Research, 104*, 333–339. doi:10.1016/j.jbusres.2019.07.039

Somayeh, M., Dehghani, M., Mozaffari, F., Ghasemnegad, S. M., Hakimi, H., & Samaneh, B. (2016). The effectiveness of E-learning in learning: A review of the literature. *International Journal of Medical Research & Health Sciences, 5*(2), 86-91.

Song, L., Singleton, E. S., Hill, J. R., & Koh, M. H. (2004). Improving online learning: Student perceptions of useful and challenging characteristics. *The Internet and Higher Education, 7*(1), 59–70. doi:10.1016/j.iheduc.2003.11.003

Song, X., Hu, Z., Du, J., & Sheng, Z. (2014). Application of Machine Learning Methods to Risk Assessment of Financial Statement Fraud: Evidence from China. *Journal of Forecasting, 33*(8), 611–626. doi:10.1002/for.2294

Struszczyk, S., Galdas, P. M., & Tiffin, P. A. (2019). Men and suicide prevention: A scoping review. *Journal of Mental Health, 28*(1), 80–88. doi:10.1080/09638237.2017.1370638 PMID:28871841

Summers, S. L., & Sweeney, J. T. (1998). Fraudulently Misstated Financial Statements and Insider Trading: An Empirical Analysis. *The Accounting Review, 73*(1), 131–146.

Sun, T., & Vasarhelyi, M. A. (2017). Deep Learning and the Future of Auditing: How an Evolving Technology Could Transform Analysis and Improve Judgment. *The CPA Journal, 87*(6), 24–29.

Super, W. 1. (2022). *Artificial Intelligence (AI): Definition, Threats, and Trends*. Retrieved 16 July 2022, from https://www.spiceworks.com/tech/artificial-intelligence/articles/super-artificial-intelligence/

Syamala Rao, G., & Nagaraj, K. V. (2018). A conceptual study on opportunities and challenges of online food services market in India. International Journal of Business. *Management and Allied Sciences, 5*, 48–50.

Tagliaferri, A. M. (2020). Artificial Intelligence to improve back pain outcomes and lessons learnt from clinical classificatio approaches: three systematic reviews. *NPJ Digi Med, 3*(1), 1-16.

Tambe, P., Cappelli, P., & Yakubovich, V. (2019). Artificial Intelligence in Human Resources Management: C hallenges and a Path Forward. *California Management Review, 61.* doi:10.1177/0008125619867910

Tandon, L., Joshi, P., & Rastogi, R. (2017). Understanding the Scope of Artificial Intelligence in Human Resource Management Processes - A Theoretical Perspective. *International Journal of Business and Administration Research Review.* Available from: http://www.ijbarr.com/downloads/0509201711.pdf

Taniguchi, H., Sato, H., & Shirakawa, T. (2018). A machine learning model with human cognitive biases capable of learning from small and biased datasets. *Scientific Reports, 8*(1), 1–13. doi:10.103841598-018-25679-z PMID:29743630

Tanpure, S. S., Shidankar, P. R., & Joshi, M. M. (2013). Automated food ordering system with real-time customer feedback. *International Journal of Advanced Research in Computer Science and Software Engineering, 3*(2).

Taylor, S., & Todd, P. A. (1995). Understanding information technology usage: A test of competing models. *Information Systems Research, 2*(6), 144–178. doi:10.1287/isre.6.2.144

Terzopoulos, G., & Satratzemi, M. (2019, September). Voice assistants and artificial intelligence in education. In *Proceedings of the 9th Balkan Conference on Informatics* (pp. 1-6). 10.1145/3351556.3351588

Thamaraiselvan, N., Jayadevan, G. R., & Chandrasekar, K. S. (2019). Digital food delivery apps revolutionizing food products marketing in India. *International Journal of Recent Technology and Engineering, 8*(2), 662–665.

Thomas, A., Prajapati, R. T., & Kaur, A. (2022). Technology-Powered Education Post Pandemic: Importance of Knowledge Management in Education. In S. Iyer, A. Jain, & J. Wang (Eds.), *Handbook of Research on Lifestyle Sustainability and Management Solutions Using AI, Big Data Analytics, and Visualization* (pp. 185-196). IGI Global. . doi:10.4018/978-1-7998-8786-7.ch011

Timms, M. J. (2016). Letting artificial intelligence in education out of the box: Educational cobots and smart classrooms. *International Journal of Artificial Intelligence in Education, 26*(2), 701–712. doi:10.100740593-016-0095-y

Toh, C., & Brody, J. (2021). *Applications of Machine Learning in Healthcare.* . doi:10.5772/intechopen.92297

Toh, L. P. E., Causo, A., Tzuo, P. W., Chen, I. M., & Yeo, S. H. (2016). A review on the use of robots in education and young children. *Journal of Educational Technology & Society, 19*(2), 148–163.

Tomlinson, C. A. (2004). Sharing responsibility for differentiating instruction. *Roeper Review, 26*(4), 188. doi:10.1080/02783190409554268

Tran, B. X., Vu, G., Ha, G., Vuong, Q.-H., Ho, M.-T., Vuong, T.-T., La, V.-P., Ho, M.-T., Nghiem, K.-C., Nguyen, H., Latkin, C., Tam, W., Cheung, N.-M., Nguyen, H.-K., Ho, C., & Ho, R. (2019). Global evolution of Research in Artificial Intelligence in Health and medicine: A bibliometric study. *Journal of Clinical Medicine, 8*(3), 360. doi:10.3390/jcm8030360 PMID:30875745

Tripathy, S., & Devarapalli, S. (2021). Emerging trend set by a start-ups on Indian online education system: A case of Byju's. *Journal of Public Affairs, 21*(1), e2128. doi:10.1002/pa.2128

Trupthi, B., Rakshitha Raj, R., Akshaya, J. B., & Srilaxmi, C. P. (2019). Online food ordering system. *International Journal of Recent Technology and Engineering, 8*(2), 834–836.

Ucoglu, D. (2020). Current machine learning applications in accounting and auditing. *PressAcademia Procedia, 12*(1), 1–7. doi:10.17261/Pressacademia.2020.1337

Uenole, N., & Feinzig, S. (2018b). *Competencies in the AI era.* IBM Smarter Workforce Institute.

UNESCO. (2018). *Guidebook on Education for Sustainable Development for Teachers. Effective teaching and learning in teacher education institutions in Africa.* UNESCO.

Upadhyay, A. K., & Khandelwal, K. (2018). Applying artificial intelligence: Implications for recruitment. *Strategic HR Review, 17*(5), 255–258. doi:10.1108/SHR-07-2018-0051

ur Rehman, I., Bano, S., & Mehraj, M. (2019). MOOCS: A case study of ALISON platform. *Library Philosophy and Practice*, 1-8.

van Twillert, A., Kreijns, K., Vermeulen, M., & Evers, A. (2020). Teachers' beliefs to integrate Web 2.0 technology in their pedagogy and their influence on attitude, perceived norms, and perceived behavior control. *International Journal of Educational Research Open, 1*.

Varney, M. W., Janoudi, A., Aslam, D. M., & Graham, D. (2011). Building young engineers: TASEM for third graders in Woodcreek Magnet Elementary School. *IEEE Transactions on Education, 55*(1), 78–82.

Vedapradha, H. R. (2018). Application of Artificial Intelligence in Investment Banks. *Review of Economic and Business Studies, 11*(2), 131-136.

Veerla, V. (2021). To study the impact of Artificial Intelligence as Predictive model in banking sector: Novel approach. *International Journal of Innovative Research in Technology, 7*(8), 94-105.

Venkatesh, V., Speier, C., & Morris, M. G. (2002). User acceptance enablers in individual decision-making about technology: Toward an integrated model. *Decision Sciences, 33*(2), 297–316. doi:10.1111/j.1540-5915.2002.tb01646.x

Vijai, D. C. (2019). Artificial Intelligence in Indian Banking Sector. *International Journal of Advanced Research, 7*(5), 1581-1587.

von Blottnitz, H., Case, J. M., & Fraser, D. M. (2015). Sustainable development at the core of undergraduate engineering curriculum reform: A new introductory course in chemical engineering. *Journal of Cleaner Production, 106*, 300–307. doi:10.1016/j.jclepro.2015.01.063

Wadhwa, O. (2022). Social Media: An Upswing For The Marketing Business. *DME Journal of Management, 2*(01), 72–80.

Waks, L. J. (2016). MOOCs and career qualifications. In *The evolution and evaluation of massive open online courses* (pp. 83–101). Palgrave Pivot.

Wakunuma, K., & Jiya, T. (2019). Stakeholder Engagement and Responsible Research & Innovation in promoting Sustainable Development and Empowerment through ICT. *European Journal of Sustainable Development, 8*(3), 275–275. doi:10.14207/ejsd.2019.v8n3p275

Wang, C., Teo, T. S., Dwivedi, Y., & Janssen, M. (2021). Mobile services use and citizen satisfaction in government: Integrating social benefits and uses and gratifications theory. *Information Technology & People, 34*(4), 1313–1337. Advance online publication. doi:10.1108/ITP-02-2020-0097

Wang, K., Zipperle, M., Becherer, M., Gottwalt, F., & Zhang, Y. (2020). An AI-Based Automated Continuous Compliance Awareness Framework (CoCAF) for Procurement Auditing. *Big Data and Cognitive Computing, 4*(23), 1–14. doi:10.3390/bdcc4030023

Wang, Y. S., Lin, H. H., & Liao, Y. W. (2010). Investigating the individual difference antecedents of perceived enjoyment in the acceptance of blogging. *World Academy of Science, Engineering and Technology, 67*.

Wan, Z., Wang, Y., & Haggerty, N. (2008). Why people benefit from e-learning differently: The effects of psychological processes on e-learning outcomes. *Information & Management, 45*(8), 513–521. doi:10.1016/j.im.2008.08.003

Wasnik, P. B., Bhandarkar, A. S., Memon, N. A., Urkude, L. R., & Awathare, P. (2018). *Android Application for LUNCHEON Services. Academic Press.*

Whitehouse, T. (2015). *The technology transforming your annual audit.* Retrieved from https://www.complianceweek.com/the-technology-transforming-your-annual-audit/3166.article

Wilfred, D. (2018). AI in recruitment. *NHRD Netw J, 11*(2), 15–18. doi:10.1177/0974173920180204

Wingo, N. P., Ivankova, N. V., & Moss, J. A. (2017). Faculty perceptions about teaching online: Exploring the literature using the technology acceptance model as an organizing framework. *Online Learning, 21*(1), 15–35. doi:10.24059/olj.v21i1.761

Winston, P. H. (1992). *Artificial intelligence.* Addison-Wesley Longman Publishing Co., Inc.

Wu, W. S., & Hua, C. (2008). The application of Moodle on an EFL collegiate writing environment. *Journal of Education and Foreign Languages and Literature, 7*(1), 45–56.

Xie, G., Chen, T., Li, Y., Chen, T., Li, X., & Liu, Z. (2019). Artificial Intelligence in Nephrology: How Can Artificial Intelligence Augment Nephrologists' Intelligence? *Kidney Diseases, 6*(1), 1–6. doi:10.1159/000504600 PMID:32021868

Yang, F. (2014). *Mobile food ordering application.* Academic Press.

Yengin, I., Karahoca, A., & Karahoca, D. (2011). E-learning success model for instructors' satisfactions in perspective of interaction and usability outcomes. *Procedia Computer Science, 3,* 1396–1403. doi:10.1016/j.procs.2011.01.021

Yeo, V. C. S., Goh, S. K., & Rezaei, S. (2017). Consumer experiences, attitude and behavioral intention toward online food delivery (OFD) services. *Journal of Retailing and Consumer Services, 35,* 150–162. doi:10.1016/j.jretconser.2016.12.013

Young, J. R. (2012). Inside the Coursera contract: How an upstart company might profit from free courses. *The Chronicle of Higher Education, 19*(7).

Yüksel, T., Aydin, Ö., & Dalkiliç, G. (2022). Performing DoS Attacks on Bluetooth Devices Paired with Google Home Mini. *Celal Bayar University Journal of Science, 18*(1), 53–58.

Yusoff, M., McLeay, F., & Woodruffe-Burton, H. (2015). Dimensions driving business student satisfaction in higher education. *Quality Assurance in Education, 23*(1), 86–104. doi:10.1108/QAE-08-2013-0035

Yusoff, R. M. M. (2015). Tahap Kesediaan Pelajar Dalam Penggunaan Teknologi, Pedagogi, Dan Kandungan (TPACK) Dalam Pembelajaran Kurikulum Di IPT. *Proceeding of the 3rd International Conference on Artifical Intelligence and Computer Science (AICS2015),* 307–315.

Zarra, A., Simonelli, F., Lenaerts, K., Luo, M., Baiocco, S., Shenglin, B., ... Kilhoffer, Z. (2019). *Sustainability in the Age of Platforms.* EMSD Challenge Fund-Final Report.

Zemankova, A. (2019). Artificial Intelligence in Audit and Accounting: Development, Current Trends, Opportunities and Threats – Literature Review. *2019 International Conference on Control, Artificial Intelligence, Robotics & Optimization (ICCAIRO),* 148-154. 10.1109/ICCAIRO47923.2019.00031

About the Contributors

Madhu Agnihotri is currently engaged as an Assistant Professor in the Faculty of Information Technology, Department of Commerce St. Xavier's College (Autonomous), Kolkata. She currently teaches both in the Post Graduate and Under Graduate level. Apart from being an erudite Scholar, Dr. Agnihotri is the Author of Text Books, Book Chapters as well as Several Research Papers published in Web of Science indexed and Peer Reviewed Journals. Alongside being a Doctorate she has to her credit the rare event of having two Post Graduate Degrees; one in Commerce and the other in Computer Application. Her Research interests span across multiple disciplines focusing on Information Technology and Finance.

Bikram Pratim Bhuyan completed his M.Tech. in information technology at Tezpur University in 2016. He is currently working as an Assistant Professor in the School of Computer Science and Engineering, University of Petroleum and Energy Studies, Dehradun, India. His areas of interest are knowledge representation and reasoning, graph theory, game theory, complexity analysis and algorithms. Mr. Bhuyan is a professional member of the ACM (Association for Computing Machinery) and ICSES (International Computer Science and Engineering Society). His work on formal concept analysis was awarded as the best paper in an IEEE sponsored International conference (CSCITA 2017). He has worked as a peer review panel member in various international conferences and journals including IEEE CINE 2017, ICCISN 2017, IEEE ICCSCE 2017 AJFAM, IJSTR, etc.

Neha Garg is working as Assistant Professor in Bhagwan Parshuram Institute of Technology, Delhi and pursuing PhD from Bharati Vidyapeeth Deemed University, Pune. MBA from IBS, Hyderabad, B Com Hons from Ramjas College. Successfully worked as Bank manager in nationalised bank, Bank of Maharashtra for almost 12 years.

Satyajit Ingawale is Assistant Professor at Sanjay Ghodawat University, Kolhapur. He has 11 years of teaching experience. He has experience working with the MBA

Unit Department of Commerce and Management, Shivaji University, Kolhapur where he initiated writing and teaching. He has a keen interest in research of Supply chain management, general management, and Human resources management. His other interest is in the administration field and social services. To his credit are more than 20 research papers at the National and International levels. She is actively engaged in student developmental activities and initiates them passionately.

Neetu Jain has been working in economics field since 2005. Presently working as Assistant professor in BVIMR Delhi.

Arkajyoti Pandit set out on his journey of academics with the esteemed St. Xavier's College (Autonomous), Kolkata in 2021. He is presently an Assistant Professor of Accounting and Finance in the Department of Commerce (Morning) of this very institution. Prof. Pandit credits his entire academic life to St. Xavier's College, Kolkata where he studied under full scholarship in the B.Com (Morning) department. After that he completed his Post-Graduation in Finance from the University of Calcutta and simultaneously qualified UGC-NET & JRF as well as WB-SET in 2019. Prof. Arkajyoti believes in applying the intricacies of Commerce to solve societal problems, and that's why pursued a course in Applied Sociology from University Grants Commission (UGC). He started off with his Ph.D from Burdwan University in 2021. Apart from his research papers finding place in a host of National and International Journals, Prof. Pandit is a published poet with a dozen of his poetry featuring in reputed International Anthologies. He is also an artist by passion and has been awarded the title of 'Chitra Visharad' by Pracheen Kala Kendra, Chandigarh.

Shraddha Purandare has over a decade of experience in Academics, Corporate Training, and Consulting activities. She brings insightful hands-on expertise in areas of Business Strategy, HR, and Organizational Development to implement pragmatic & high-impact solutions to business challenges. Her Key competencies include HR policy drafting, Employee relations & engagement, Performance management system, HR Process improvisation, HR Matrix, Audit, and compliances, HR operations, Designing Reward & Recognition structures, and Conduction of HR Audits. She is a Result-oriented, decisive mentor Provided consultancy to corporates across different sectors to improve business results. Extensively work in Management Education to facilitate employability skills in students. Her areas of research includes employee relations, talent management, organizational justice, etc.

Richa Sharma is Assistant Professor of International Business and Finance at Sharda University. She has 8 years of academic teaching experience. As part of teaching portfolio she specializes in the area of International Business and Finance. She has qualified UGC NET in the field of Management. She has published papers and presented papers at various national and international journals and conferences.

Anita Singh has more than 25 years of experience in academics, research and training. She has published 2 books and more than 80 publications in refereed International/National Journals and Conference proceedings. She has been awarded with best paper awards, 'Most Fabulous Professor in India Award by WHRD Congress and 'Indo Pacific Distinguished Professor Award 2021 by IMRF.

T. P. Singh is currently serving as Professor and Head at School of Computer Science, University of Petroleum and Energy Studies, Dehradun, UK. He holds Doctorate in Computer Science from Jamia Millia Islamia University, New Delhi. He carries more than 26 years of rich experience with him drawn both from industry and academia. He has earlier been associated with Tata Group and Sharda University, Greater Noida. He has been a member of the curriculum draft committee for B.Tech. (CSE) program of IGNOU. Dr. Singh is serving as expert member of his field in Board of Studies of different universities. His research interests include machine intelligence, pattern recognition and development of hybrid intelligent systems. He has guided 15 Masters Theses. Currently 06 research scholars are working towards their Doctoral degree under him. There are more than three dozens of publications to his credit in various national and international journals. He is also having 05 edited books to his credit which cut across the recent technical topics of computer science. Dr. Singh is a Fellow of IETA, senior member of IEEE, member IEI and various other professional bodies including ISTE, IAENG etc. and also on the editorial/reviewer panel of different reputed journals.

Risha Thakur holds a position in academic field that would entrust her with creating students-oriented, high-performance research-based learning sessions to help students achieve new heights in the academics. Currently, Ms. Thakur is associated with Sharda University as an Assistant Professor. Ms. Thakur is pursuing her PhD in the area of Green Marketing & Consumer Behavior, she has completed her schooling from Kendriya Vidyalaya, UG degree B.com (hons) from Manav Rachna International University & PG MBA (Marketing & Finance) from Guru Gobind Singh Indraprastha University New Delhi. She did her Industrial Training in Finance from Indian Government Enterprise - "Telecommunications Consultants India LTD, New Delhi". She has also completed a Live Project in company "Edumentor Educational Services Pvt Ltd" in the area of Marketing.

Derya Üçoğlu received her MSc in Financial Economics (Accounting and Finance Path) from İstanbul Bilgi University in 2006 and her Ph.D. in Accounting and Finance from Marmara University in 2012. After working in different financial institutions, she has been an Assistant Professor of Accounting at Istanbul Bilgi University since 2014. She has published articles mainly on financial reporting. She currently focuses on the changes in the recognition and presentation of financial statement items due to the pandemic and disclosures regarding COVID-19, environmental reporting, and the impact of technological innovations on accounting and auditing.

Seema Wadhawan is Doctorate in Management from Amity University, Noida, Master of Business Administration from Mahatma Gandhi University, Meghalaya, Post Graduate Diploma in Management from AIMA and graduation in B.Com (H) from Delhi University. She carries a Satiating 20+ year experience comprising of substantial stints in corporate and the academia. After foraying into academia, she has continuously worked as a member of core committee for seminars, workshops & conferences and she has been an editor of Journal affiliated with GGSIPU for past 3 years. She has contributed immensely to quality research through paper publications in national, international conferences and journals, having indexing in SCOPUS, ABDC & UGC Care. She has been conferred with 4 best research paper awards in national and international conferences of repute. Her interest is in Organization Behavior, Human Resource management, Performance management and Research.

Index

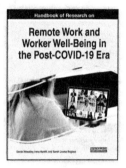
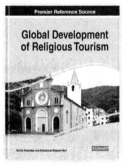

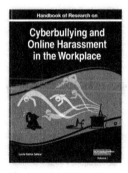

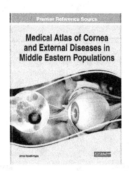

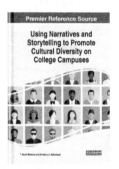

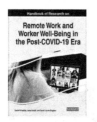

Are You Ready to
Publish Your Research ?

IGI Global
PUBLISHER of TIMELY KNOWLEDGE

IGI Global offers book authorship and editorship opportunities across 11 subject areas, including business, computer science, education, science and engineering, social sciences, and more!

Benefits of Publishing with IGI Global:

- Free one-on-one editorial and promotional support.
- Expedited publishing timelines that can take your book from start to finish in less than one (1) year.
- Choose from a variety of formats, including Edited and Authored References, Handbooks of Research, Encyclopedias, and Research Insights.
- Utilize IGI Global's eEditorial Discovery® submission system in support of conducting the submission and double-blind peer review process.
- IGI Global maintains a strict adherence to ethical practices due in part to our full membership with the Committee on Publication Ethics (COPE).
- Indexing potential in prestigious indices such as Scopus®, Web of Science™, PsycINFO®, and ERIC – Education Resources Information Center.
- Ability to connect your ORCID iD to your IGI Global publications.
- Earn honorariums and royalties on your full book publications as well as complimentary copies and exclusive discounts.

Join Your Colleagues from Prestigious Institutions, Including:

Australian National University

Massachusetts Institute of Technology

JOHNS HOPKINS UNIVERSITY

HARVARD UNIVERSITY

COLUMBIA UNIVERSITY IN THE CITY OF NEW YORK

Learn More at: www.igi-global.com/publish
or by Contacting the Acquisitions Department at: acquisition@igi-global.com